Palgrave Studies in the History of Finance

The study of the history of financial institutions, markets, instruments and concepts is vital if we are to understand the role played by finance today. At the same time, the methodologies developed by finance academics can provide a new perspective for historical studies. Palgrave Studies in the History of Finance is a multi-disciplinary effort to emphasise the role played by finance in the past, and what lessons historical experiences have for us. It presents original research, in both authored monographs and edited collections, from historians, finance academics and economists, as well as financial practitioners.

More information about this series at
http://www.palgrave.com/gp/series/14583

Count Ludwig Zinzendorf, founder and first president of the *Hofrechenkammer* 1762–1773. (Source: Rechnungshof Vienna)

Simon Adler

Political Economy in the Habsburg Monarchy 1750–1774

The Contribution of Ludwig Zinzendorf

palgrave
macmillan

Simon Adler
Visiting Research Fellow
Austrian Academy of Sciences
Vienna, Austria

ISSN 2662-5164 ISSN 2662-5172 (electronic)
Palgrave Studies in the History of Finance
ISBN 978-3-030-31006-6 ISBN 978-3-030-31007-3 (eBook)
https://doi.org/10.1007/978-3-030-31007-3

Cover illustration: Ludwig Zinzendorf's repayment plan of a bond issued by the Estates of Lower Austria, Sept. 1757, HHStA Nachlass Zinzendorf, vol.33, fol.259r © Haus-, Hof- und Staatsarchiv Vienna

This Palgrave Macmillan imprint is published by the registered company Springer Nature Switzerland AG.
The registered company address is: Gewerbestrasse 11, 6330 Cham, Switzerland

To Josef and Giselle

Acknowledgements

This book in most parts is the result of my doctorate at the University of Cambridge. In researching and writing this study, I incurred many debts. My greatest single debt is to my doctoral supervisor, John Robertson. From the very beginning, he appreciated my research ideas. He was most caring, encouraging and efficient, and showed me how to think straight and stay the course. My debt to Grete Klingenstein is second only to this. She introduced me to Ludwig Zinzendorf and encouraged me to look at his ideas in the context of eighteenth-century European political economy. Over the years, she generously shared her discoveries of sources and provided helpful criticism which resulted in considerable improvement. Derek Beales, Joachim Whaley, Hamish Scott and William Godsey not only read and commented on my doctoral thesis, but also gave me invaluable advice and stimulated my thinking. I am grateful to the two anonymous readers at Palgrave Macmillan for their valuable suggestions. Rudolf Muhs offered me constant support. Keith Tribe made time to discuss the subject with me and guided me with materials and sources. I am greatly indebted to Markus Gneiss who generously offered help with reading mid-eighteenth-century manuscripts and making sense of their technicalities. Several scholars have supported me and have given me copies of their books and articles. I owe thanks to Moritz Baumstark, Ivo Cerman, Loïc Charles, Peter Dickson, Tim Hochstrasser, Julian Hoppit, Christine Lebeau, Simone Meyssonnier, Antoin Murphy, David Raynor, William Roberds and François Velde. I am also grateful for the award of a Visiting Research Fellowship at the Institute for Habsburg and Balkan Studies of the Austrian Academy of Sciences in Vienna.

Librarians and archivists have been helpful with my requests at the following institutions: in Britain, the British Library and the University of Cambridge Library; in Austria, the Haus-, Hof- und Staatsarchiv, the Austrian National Library, the Landesarchiv of Lower Austria and the Deutschordenszentralarchiv; and in France, the Municipal Library in Saint-Brieuc. At the Haus-, Hof- und Staatsarchiv, Gerhard Gonsa gave advice and friendship and took much trouble on my behalf. Nancy E.M. Bailey copy-edited the typescript with skill and great attention to detail, and has saved me from many errors and inconsistencies. At the Press, I owe thanks to the editors of the series headed by D'Maris Coffman and to Tula Weis, who have been most supportive and accommodating.

I owe most of all to my family who has been my biggest support throughout. From the beginning, my wife, Kate, as well as my mother and sister encouraged me to pursue a doctorate even though I had been away from academia for a long time. I could not have done it if Kate had not shouldered the pressures of parenthood, leaving me mostly with the pleasurable episodes. She is the wind beneath my wings. Our children make sure that life is fun and varied. This book is dedicated to them with my greatest love.

London Simon Adler
July 2019

Contents

Abbreviations and Conventions

Abbreviations

AÖG	*Archiv für österreichische Geschichte*
DOZA	Deutschordenszentralarchiv, Vienna
fl.	Austrian florins, or gulden
fr.	French franc
HHStA	Haus-, Hof- und Staatsarchiv, Vienna
£	English pounds sterling
liv.	French livres
m.	million
MIÖG	*Mitteilungen des Instituts für österreichische Geschichtsforschung*
MÖStA	*Mitteilungen des österreichischen Staatsarchivs*
NÖLA	Niederösterreichisches Landesarchiv, St. Pölten
ÖNB	Österreichische Nationalbibliothek, Vienna
ÖZV	T. Fellner, H. Kretschmayer et al. (eds), *Die österreichische Zentralverwaltung* (1909–1971). Volumes are cited by their year of publication.

Conventions

Names of cities are given in standard English-language equivalents, so Vienna rather than Wien.

Ludwig Zinzendorf did not differentiate between 'England' and the post-1707 settlement in his writings, even when he was obviously referring to the new British state. His usage has been preserved to avoid introducing confusion.

Many currencies were in circulation in the eighteenth century. *Livres*, *francs*, *florins*, *écus* and *guilders* as well as other denominations mentioned by Ludwig Zinzendorf in his writings have been set out in full in the text, although abbreviated in the notes if they are mentioned.

Several of the source manuscripts exist as unpaginated folios. In the notes, notional page numbers are given in square brackets.

List of Figures

CHAPTER 1

Introduction

Scholars have used the concept of fiscal–military state to study the importance of finance in the development of the states in Europe between the sixteenth and eighteenth centuries. The term was first used in the late 1980s by John Brewer in a study on eighteenth-century Britain.[1] It has since been employed widely, notably in a comparative context.[2] The term was apposite to describe the evolution of states and their fiscal systems to meet the demands of larger armies and more expensive equipment. A central question was the effectiveness with which economic resources could be mobilised. For Brewer, to cover the increasing costs of warfare, a fiscal–military state had to be able to raise funds through both credit and taxation. Further, a good administrative structure was necessary to support

[1] John Brewer, *The Sinews of Power: War, Money and the English State, 1688–1783* (London, 1989).

[2] Richard Bonney (ed.), *The Rise of the Fiscal State in Europe, c.1200–1815* (Oxford, 1999); Jan Glete, *War and the State in Early Modern Europe: Spain, the Dutch Republic and Sweden as Fiscal Military States, 1500–1660* (London, 2002); Christopher Storrs (ed.), *The Fiscal-Military State in Eighteenth-Century Europe: Essays in Honour of P.G.M. Dickson* (Farnham: Ashgate, 2009); Rafael Torres Sanchez, *Constructing a Fiscal-Military State in Eighteenth-Century Spain* (Basingstoke: Palgrave Macmillan, 2015); Aaron Graham and Patrick Walsh (eds.), *The British Fiscal Military States, 1660–c.1783* (London, 2016). This collection of articles extends Brewer's analysis by studying the importance of interested parties for the operation of the fiscal-military states.

S. Adler, *Political Economy in the Habsburg Monarchy 1750–1774*,
Palgrave Studies in the History of Finance,
https://doi.org/10.1007/978-3-030-31007-3_1

its fiscal and military activities.[3] This became particularly relevant in the eighteenth century when the costs of warfare in Europe increased significantly. Recently, the relevance of a fiscal–military state has also been examined for the Habsburg monarchy in the eighteenth century.[4]

For the monarchy, funding was of utmost importance. It had fought several wars and at the beginning of the eighteenth century had dramatically extended its power. In addition to the Nine Years Wars (1689–1697) and the War of the Spanish Succession (1701–1714), the monarchy had fought two expensive military campaigns (1683–1699 and 1716–1718) against the Ottoman Empire. In the late 1730s, it had been involved in the War of the Polish Succession (1733–1738) and in renewed fighting with the Turks (1737–1739).[5] To finance the rapidly rising military commitments, the government was dependent on tax revenues (contribution) paid by the Estates.[6] In addition, with military expenditure well exceeding the income from taxes, the government needed to borrow heavily. Between 1700 and 1740, the monarchy's debt had quadrupled. At the beginning of Maria Theresa's reign, borrowings had surpassed 100 million *florins*. At the same time, however, the income side had deteriorated. Total state revenues had fallen to approximately 20 million *florins*, and the cash available had dwindled to 87,000 *florins*.[7] At the time of her father's sudden death on 20 October 1740, the empress had quickly recognised the desperate situation. In her memorial of 1750, Maria Theresa lamented that she had been left 'without money, without credit and without [an] army'

[3] Brewer, *Sinews of Power*, p. xvii.

[4] William D. Godsey, Petr Mat'a and Thomas Winkelbauer (eds.), *The Habsburg Monarchy as a Fiscal-Military State c.1648–1815* (Proceedings of the British Academy/Oxford University Press, forthcoming). For conceptual issues in relation to the term 'fiscal–military state', see Hamish M. Scott, 'The Habsburg "Fiscal Military State" in International Perspective', in ibid. I am very grateful to Hamish Scott for having sent me a typescript of his paper. On the role of the Lower Austrian Estates in the Austrian fiscal-military state, see William D. Godsey, *The Sinews of Habsburg Power: Lower Austria in a Fiscal-Military State, 1650–1820* (Oxford, 2018); on the fiscal–military state in the European context, see Hamish Scott, 'The Fiscal Military State and International Rivalry During the Long Eighteenth Century', in Christopher Storrs (ed.), *The Fiscal Military State in Eighteenth Century Europe*, pp. 23–53.

[5] See Michael Hochedlinger, *Austria's Wars of Emergence. War, State and Society in the Habsburg Monarchy 1683–1797* (London: Pearson, 2003).

[6] Ibid., pp. 31–8.

[7] Gustav Otruba, 'Staatshaushalt und Staatsschuld unter Maria Theresia und Joseph II.' in Richard Georg Plaschka and Grete Klingenstein (eds.), *Österreich im Europa der Aufklärung* (2 vols, Vienna, 1985), vol. 1, pp. 200–1.

and had been lacking in political experience and competent advice. In her second memorial of 1755/1756, she complained anew about the poor financial state of the monarchy when she became empress. She deplored the difficulties of inheriting a country that had had only a few thousand *gulden* left as reserves and almost no domestic and foreign credit.[8] Early in her reign, the combined pressures of keeping a standing army and servicing government debt, to which was added the armed hostility of Prussia, forced Maria Theresa to decide on significant reforms. The military expenditure of the Seven Years War (1756–1763) demanded financial commitments on a new scale.[9]

Throughout Maria Theresa's reign, public finances and administrative changes to central government in order to gain more fiscal and military control were key concerns. It was in these important areas in the 1750s, 1760s and early 1770s that, with the strong support of the influential Austrian state chancellor and creator of the *Staatsrat* Count Wenzel Anton Kaunitz, Count Ludwig Zinzendorf became the monarchy's leading expert. Zinzendorf's unusual ideas attracted attention and had a significant impact on the economic discussions in government. The only biography of Ludwig Zinzendorf was published in German in 1879.[10] In two sections, the editor Eduard Gaston Pettenegg presented the biographies of Ludwig Zinzendorf and of his half-brother Karl Zinzendorf. Both sections were, in fact, written by Karl.[11] Pettenegg was a local Austrian priest whose main interest in compiling the 'autobiographies of Karl and Ludwig Zinzendorf' was genealogy. His edition was not primarily intended as a historical account and may have omitted relevant biographical elements on the Zinzendorfs.

As part of their analyses of financial policies under Maria Theresa, scholars have primarily concentrated on Zinzendorf's proposals on state credit. Adolf Beer, writing his monographs on financial administration and public finance at the end of the nineteenth century, gave significant room

[8] Josef Kallbrunner (ed.), *Kaiserin Maria Theresias politisches Testament* (Vienna, 1952), pp. 29, 76. The two memorials are not dated. Kallbrunner gave 1750 and 1755/1756: ibid., p. 23. The memorials are also printed in *Maria Theresia. Briefe und Aktenstücke in Auswahl*, ed. Friedrich Walter (Darmstadt, 1968), pp. 63–97, 108–30.

[9] On the significant influence and the strains of the Seven Years War on belligerents in Europe, see Hamish M. Scott, 'The Seven Years War and Europe's *Ancien Régime*', *War in History*, 18:4 (2011), pp. 419–55.

[10] Eduard Gaston von Pettenegg (ed.), *Ludwig und Karl Grafen und Herren von Zinzendorf. Ihre Selbstbiographien nebst einer kurzen Geschichte des Hauses Zinzendorf* (Vienna, 1879).

[11] For Karl's authorship, see ibid., footnote, p. 8.

Fig. 1.1 The Habsburg monarchy from the 1740s to 1780

Generally accepted boundary of the Holy Roman Empire
Principal ecclesiastical states
Prussian gains by partition of Poland in 1772
Prussia from the 1740s
The Habsburg monarchy from the 1740s
The Habsburg monarchy's gains in the 1770s
Military frontier regions
0 100 200 miles
0 100 200 300 km
Danzig
EAST PRUSSIA
Vistula
Warsaw
POLAND
SILESIA
Breslau
Neisse
SILESIA
Teschen
Olmütz
MORAVIA
Brunn
Wieliczka
GALICIA (1772)
Lemberg
Sereth
Sbrutz
Dniester
ZIPS (1770)
Pruth
LOWER
Melk
Vienna
AUSTRIA
Pressburg
Danube
Vac
Buda
Pest
BUKOVINA (1775)
MOLDAVIA
HUNGARY
TRANSSYLVANIA
Hermannstadt
Temesvar
BANAT
Carlstadt
SLAVONIA
CROATIA
WALLACHIA
Belgrade
Old Orsova
Save
Passarowitz
LITTLE WALLACHIA
BOSNIA
OTTOMAN
Danube
SERBIA
EMPIRE
DALMATIA (to Venice)
MONTENEGRO
N

to Zinzendorf's financial plans.[12] Zinzendorf's theoretical knowledge, Beer pointed out, was unrivalled in the monarchy.[13] Karl Hock and Ignaz Bidermann's study on the *Staatsrat* was based on documents which are now lost and showed Zinzendorf's forceful presence during the discussions in central government in the 1760s, including his rivalry with Count Karl Friedrich Hatzfeld (1718–1793).[14] The only study specifically dedicated to Ludwig Zinzendorf was published in German more than 60 years ago. The slim monograph *Staatsbildung und Finanzentwicklung* by Johann Schasching was based on primary material and gave a good exposition of Zinzendorf's ideas on public finances.[15] As the subtitle of the book indicated, Schasching's focus was Austrian state credit in the 1760s and his starting point was Zinzendorf's contribution to war finance. He also set out Zinzendorf's proposals to unify state credit, to create new financial institutions for the monarchy, and gave an account of the resistance which Zinzendorf faced against his plans. In Schasching's view, even though Zinzendorf eventually lost the power struggle against other ministers and could not translate some of his important proposals into policies, his new approach and his radical ideas were important for the development of the monarchy's public finances.[16] Similarly, P.G.M. Dickson's monumental study on the monarchy threw considerable light on Zinzendorf's financial proposals and his involvement in policy discussions.[17] For the most part, Dickson was interested in those of Zinzendorf's plans which impacted financial policy formulation and so he also explained the operations of the monarchy's audit office (*Hofrechenkammer*) which was Zinzendorf's political brainchild.[18] Franz A.J. Szabo showed the decisive influence of Zinzendorf's ideas on the financial policies of

[12] Adolf Beer, 'Die Finanzverwaltung Österreichs 1749–1816', *MIÖG* 15 (1894), pp. 237–366; Adolf Beer, 'Die Staatsschulden und die Ordnung des Staatshaushaltes unter Maria Theresia', *AÖG* 82 (1895), pp. 1–135.

[13] Beer, 'Die Staatsschulden', p. 33.

[14] Karl Freiherrn von Hock and Ignaz Bidermann, *Der österreichische Staatsrath (1760–1848). Eine geschichtliche Studie* (Vienna, 1879; reprint, 1972).

[15] Johann Schasching, *Staatsbildung und Finanzentwicklung. Ein Beitrag zur Geschichte des österreichischen Staatskredites in der 2. Hälfte des 18. Jahrhunderts* (Innsbruck, 1954).

[16] Ibid., p. 86.

[17] P.G.M. Dickson, *Finance and Government under Maria Theresia 1740–1780* (2 vols, Oxford, 1987).

[18] Ibid., vol. 1, pp. 82–113.

Kaunitz.[19] On the grounds that Zinzendorf's plans entailed a significant development of the monarchy's war efforts, Szabo reported them at some length in his monograph on the Seven Years War in Europe.[20] By contrast, in the most recent major publication on the eighteenth-century monarchy, the biography of Maria Theresa by Barbara Stollberg-Rilinger, Zinzendorf is only briefly mentioned in relation to financial reform.[21]

This book, the first in English dedicated to Ludwig Zinzendorf's writings, builds on these contributions and those of other scholars. However, it offers a different perspective and examines aspects of Zinzendorf's work which have only partially been dealt with or have been neglected in the literature. A significant part of the study will be devoted to Zinzendorf's earlier works, written before he was nominated to a senior government post. As such, Zinzendorf's plans on state credit, which have been the clear emphasis for most scholars, represent only one part of the analysis. The book offers a more a systematic examination of Zinzendorf's thinking based on the most relevant primary sources. Also, rather than focussing on policies and their impact on policy-making in the monarchy, it is primarily concerned with ideas.

The first objective is to show the development of Zinzendorf's ideas on political economy and his role as a sophisticated and well-informed expert in introducing advanced economic ideas to the monarchy. As in other European countries, the 1750s were a key period for the debates of such ideas among the ruling elite in Vienna, and the discussion continued into the 1760s. The second objective is the identification of the intellectual influences on Zinzendorf's thinking. Zinzendorf, I contend, drew inspiration from thinkers in Europe and from financial institutions abroad and attempted to provide a different kind of economic advice. The third objective is to show how Zinzendorf operated in government as a sophisticated promoter of political economy. He sought to emulate on a more moderate scale the model of the French writers and administrators around Vincent de Gournay. Thus, I wish to argue, Zinzendorf was very firmly rooted in the European Enlightenment discourse on political economy.

[19] Franz A.J. Szabo, *Kaunitz and enlightened absolutism 1753–1780* (Cambridge, 1994). The book is the first of two volumes. The second, as yet unpublished, is intended to take the study up to 1790.

[20] Franz A.J. Szabo, *The Seven Years War in Europe, 1756–1763* (Harlow and New York: Pearson/Longman, 2008).

[21] Barbara Stollberg-Rilinger, *Maria Theresia: Die Kaiserin in Ihrer Zeit. Eine Biographie* (Munich: C.H. Beck, 2017).

Grete Klingenstein first recognised the significant influence of European ideas in general, and non-German ideas in particular, on the monarchy's governing elite. In her perceptive review of Harm Klueting's study of relative power in eighteenth-century Central Europe, she criticised the author for failing to show the intellectual presence of Montesquieu's *De L'Esprit des Lois* in the cameralist works of Heinrich Gottlob von Justi (1717–1771) and Jakob Friedrich Bielfeld (1717–1770).[22] These writers, Klueting argued, influenced the views of leading figures and practitioners of political arithmetic at that time, including Kaunitz, to whom he devoted his longest treatment. But as Klingenstein made clear in her review, Kaunitz was not bound by cameralist thinking. He was clearly drawing on the practices in other European countries in order to appraise the monarchy's strength relative to its allies and competitors. She developed this argument in her excellent overview of the dissemination of economic theory in the monarchy in the second half of the eighteenth century.[23] A group of administrators around Kaunitz, which included Ludwig and Karl Zinzendorf, were actively involved in the reception of ideas from Europe. The Zinzendorf brothers were part of the inner circle of government and could shape economic debates. Klingenstein's article provides a useful context for this study of Ludwig Zinzendorf.

In general, Zinzendorf scholarship has been mostly driven by an interest in Karl Zinzendorf and his 63 volumes of daily diaries. Christine Lebeau's monograph on Karl and Ludwig Zinzendorf, which was based on her two-volume doctoral thesis, gave greater weight to Karl.[24] Analysing

[22] Harm Klueting, *Die Lehre von der Macht der Staaten: Das aussenpolitische Machtproblem in der 'politischen Wissenschaft' und in der praktischen Politik im 18. Jahrhundert* (Berlin, 1986) and Grete Klingenstein's review can be found in *English Historical Review*, 103:406 (1988), pp. 134–38. For a discussion of Montesquieu's influence on J.H.G. von Justi, see Ulrich Adam, *The Political Economy of J.H.G. Justi* (Berne, 2006) and Ulrich Adam 'Justi and the Post-Montesquieu French debate on Commercial Nobility in 1756' in Jürgen Georg Backhaus (ed.), *The Beginnings of Political Economy: Johann Heinrich Gottlob von Justi* (New York: Springer, 2009), pp. 75–99.

[23] Grete Klingenstein, 'Between Mercantilism and Physiocracy. Stages, Modes and Functions of Economic Theory in the Habsburg Monarchy, 1748–63' in Charles W. Ingrao (ed.), *State and Society in Early Modern Austria* (West Lafayette, IN: Purdue University Press, 1994), pp. 181–214.

[24] Christine Lebeau, 'Ludwig et Karl von Zinzendorf, administrateurs des finances. Aristocratie et pouvoir dans la Monarchie des Habsbourg, 1748–1791' (PhD dissertation, 2 vols, Université de Paris IV—Sorbonne, 1991); Christine Lebeau, *Aristocrates et grands commis à la Cour de Vienne (1748–1791). Le modèle français* (Paris, 1996).

Karl's readings, Lebeau attempted to show the presence of European ideas in Karl's thought. The strongest influence, she thought, came from France, and she reflected this in the subtitle '*le modèle français*'. In the final section of the book, Lebeau offered some discussion of Ludwig Zinzendorf's ideas.[25] Using the Zinzendorf brothers as a case study, Lebeau's work is more a characterisation of the position and influence of the nobility in the monarchy than a study of ideas. Other contributions have likewise concentrated on Karl's role as an economic and financial administrator.[26]

However, the largest number of works by far have dealt with his diaries. Publications included an edition of the diaries covering Karl Zinzendorf's early years as well as his travel notes on Tuscany, the Austrian Netherlands, Spain and England.[27] The most ambitious and extensive work to date on the diaries was the four-volume edition by Grete Klingenstein, Eva Faber and Antonio Trampus on Zinzendorf's

[25] Lebeau, *Aristocrates*, pp. 163–92.

[26] P.G.M Dickson, 'Count Karl von Zinzendorf on Joseph II's New Taxation', *English Historical Review*, 133:561 (2018), pp. 323–50; P.G.M Dickson, 'Count Karl von Zinzendorf's "New Accountancy": The Structure of Austrian Government Finance in Peace and War, 1781–1791', *International History Review*, 19 (2007), pp. 22–56.

[27] Maria Breunlich and Marieluise Mader (eds.), *Karl Graf von Zinzendorf, Aus den Jugendtagebüchern 1747, 1752–1763. Nach Vorarbeiten von Hans Wagner*, Veröffentlichung der Kommission für Neuere Geschichte Österreichs 84 (Vienna, 1997); Elisabeth Reiner, 'Karl von Zinzendorf und das Eisenwesen in Innerösterreich. Ein Beitrag zur mariatheresianischen Wirtschaftspolitik', *Mitteilungen des österreichischen Staatsarchivs*, 13 (1960), pp. 258–330; Adam Wandruszka, 'Pietro Leopoldo e le sue riforme in Toscana (dal diario edito del conte Carlo Zinzendorf)', *Archivio storico italiano*, 117 (1960), pp. 286–87; Georges Englebert (ed.) 'Deux voyages du Comte Charles de Zinzendorf, 1769–1770', *Bulletin de la Société des Bibliophiles Liegois*, 22 (1976), pp. 125–27; *J.K.C.H. Comte de Zinzendorf. Journal. Chronique belgo-bruxelloise 1766–1770*, ed. Georges Englebert (Brussels, 1991); Grete Klingenstein, 'Spanien im Horizont der österreichischen Aufklärung. Zinzendorfs Kommerzialreise nach Spanien im Jahre 1767' in Herwig Ebner, Horst Haselsteiner and Ingeborg Wiesflecker-Friedhuber (eds.), *Geschichtsforschung in Graz. Festschrift zum 125-Jahr-Jubiläum des Instituts für Geschichte der Karl-Franzens-Universität Graz* (Graz, 1990), pp. 115–26; Elisabeth Fattinger, 'Gestaltung und Gewinn eines Auftragsreise: Karl Graf Zinzendorf in Großbritannien (1768)' in Joachim Rees, Winfried Siebers and Hilmar Tilgner (eds.), *Europareisen politisch-sozialer Eliten im 18. Jahrhundert. Theoretische Neuorientierung-kommunikative Praxis- Kultur- und Wissenschaftstransfer* (Berlin, 2002), pp. 112–29; Robert Rill, 'Die Reise des Grafen Karl von Zinzendorf und Pottendorf über die britischen Inseln im Jahre 1768 an Hand seiner Tagebuchaufzeichnungen-Kommentare und Auswahledition' (unpublished PhD dissertation, University of Vienna, 1983).

time in Trieste as the city's governor.[28] As part of the comprehensive introduction in the first volume, Klingenstein included an overview of the scholarship on Karl Zinzendorf, together with an extensive bibliography and a history of the Zinzendorf estate from Karl's death in early 1813 to today.[29]

Ludwig Zinzendorf pursued political economy as an independent and defining science which had its place alongside a country's strategy for power and military conquest. He closely followed the expansion of new ideas on political economy in England and France. The aim of political economy was to generate sufficient revenue for the people and for the services of the state. A growing volume of scholarship has been dedicated to this rise of political economy to intellectual prominence in the eighteenth century.[30] In seven essays and a book-length introduction of more than 150 pages, Istvan Hont offered a revision of political thought between Thomas Hobbes and the French Revolution and drew out the intellectual foundations of political economy and international market rivalry.[31] Following Hont's death in 2013, two recently published collections of essays evaluate the influence of his ideas and methods.[32] John Robertson used political economy as a central element of the Enlightenment to show the shared aspirations of thinkers in the kingdoms of Naples and Scotland for people to have better lives.[33] A number of monographs have examined the ideas about commerce and state finances in France and England. Michael Sonenscher analysed the relationship between political economy and political life in France in the eighteenth century and the

[28] Grete Klingenstein, Eva Faber and Antonio Trampus (eds.), *Europäische Aufklärung zwischen Wien und Triest: die Tagebücher des Gouverneurs Karl Graf von Zinzendorf, 1776–1782*, Veröffentlichung der Kommission für Neuere Geschichte Österreichs 103 (4 vols, Vienna, 2009).

[29] Ibid., vol. 1, pp. 22–61. For the bibliography, see ibid., pp. 219–300.

[30] For a review of the historiography on commercial humanism with an emphasis on France, see Arnault Skornicki, 'La France des Lumières et l'humanisme commercial. Bilan et perspectives historiographiques', *Histoire, Économie et Société*, 32:4 (2013), pp. 75–89.

[31] Istvan Hont, *Jealousy of Trade. International Competition and the Nation-State in Historical Perspective* (Cambridge, MA, 2005).

[32] Béla Kapossy, Isaac Nakhimovsky, Sophus A. Reinert and Richard Whatmore (eds.), *Markets, Morals, Politics: Jealousy of Trade and the History of Political Thought* (Cambridge, MA and London: Harvard University Press, 2018); Béla Kapossy, Isaac Nakhimovsky and Richard Whatmore (eds.), *Commerce and Peace in the Enlightenment* (Cambridge, 2017).

[33] John Robertson, *The Case for the Enlightenment: Scotland and Naples, 1680–1760* (Cambridge, 2005).

arguments over the effects of state borrowing on the monarchy.[34] John Shovlin presented a different viewpoint, that of writers in the eighteenth century preoccupied with the social issues of wealth, including the corrupting effects of money, and with the restoration of French economic leadership through economic development.[35] Henry Clark offered a broader perspective. He gave a synthetic analysis of French economic thought covering the time from Louis XIII to the French Revolution during which intellectuals struggled to establish commerce as a model of civil society.[36] Paul Cheney's approach emphasised the challenges which the rise of commerce presented to eighteenth-century France and the struggle of contemporary philosophers and economic thinkers to find a harmonious relationship between commerce, politics and society.[37] A recently published collection of essays has examined the connection between commerce and the political order in Enlightenment Europe through the writings of a variety of thinkers, including Montesquieu, David Hume, Jean-Jacques Rousseau, Adam Smith and Johann Gottlieb Fichte.[38] Others have studied the development of concepts of credit in England and the early use of credit instruments by the rural nobility in Austria.[39]

In the eighteenth century, as growing international market rivalry became a major concern for European states, intellectuals began to examine more thoroughly the connection between politics and the economy. The theories of economic competition recognised emulation to be a vehicle for economic growth.[40] Unlike envy, which flatly resented the achievement of others, emulation was a positive disposition. It was based on the

[34] Michael Sonenscher, *Before the Deluge: Public Debt, Inequality and the Intellectual Origins of the French Revolution* (Oxford, 2007).

[35] John Shovlin, *The Political Economy of Virtue: Luxury, Patriotism, and the Origins of the French Revolution* (Ithaca, NY, and London: Cornell University Press, 2006).

[36] Henry C. Clark, *Compass of Society: Commerce and Absolutism in Old-Regime France* (Lanham, MD: Rowman & Littlefield/Lexington Books, 2007).

[37] Paul Cheney, *Revolutionary Commerce: Globalization and the French Monarchy* (Cambridge, MA: Harvard University Press, 2010).

[38] Olaf Asbach (ed.), *Der moderne Staat und 'le doux commerce': Politik, Ökonomie und internationale Beziehungen im politischen Denken der Aufklärung* (Baden-Baden: Nomos, 2014).

[39] Carl Wennerlind, *Casualties of Credit: The English Financial Revolution, 1620–1720* (Cambridge, MA: Harvard University Press, 2011); Martin Khull-Kholwald, *Der Adel auf dem Lande und sein Kredit. Der Schuldschein als zentrales Finanzinstrument in der Steiermark (1515–1635)*, Forschungen zur geschichtlichen Landeskunde der Steiermark, Band 57 (Vienna and Berlin: LIT, 2013).

[40] See Hont, *Jealousy of Trade*, pp. 115–23.

admiration of other nations and hence offered a very different perspective to envy. Emulation was a worthwhile attitude which could trigger progress for a nation and the adoption of new economic methods.[41] Its impact also went beyond economic factors. It embodied a drive to further the interests of countries and to increase national dominance. Like fighting in wars, emulation should be perceived as a patriotic duty, and writers, including Adam Smith, supported government and private initiatives which encouraged it.[42] The translation of foreign economic texts was a medium of emulation and also the subject of Sophus Reinert's study of the adaptations of John Cary's *Essay on the State of England in Relation to Its Trade, Its Poor and Its Taxes, for Carrying Out the Present War Against France* (1695).[43] Translations played an important role in the dissemination of economic argument, and Reinert showed how in the eighteenth century, the cumulative French, Italian and German translations of Cary's book shared the same aspirations for economic development, but did not follow the same paths. The translations both altered the original text and added to it as each one was shaped by and assimilated into the different political and economic environments for which it was written. In the 1750s in France, the writers associated with Gournay played a decisive role in promoting interest in emulation. Their initiative involved the publication in French of a wide range of foreign economic writings which were intended for government ministers and for the wider public. Their important enterprise has been the subject of much scholarly interest.[44]

[41] Ibid., p. 118.

[42] Ibid., p. 120.

[43] Sophus A. Reinert, *Translating Empire: Emulation and the Origins of Political Economy* (Cambridge, MA: Harvard University Press, 2011).

[44] See most recently the contributions on Forbonnais and physiocracy: Loïc Charles and Arnaud Orain, 'François Véron de Forbonnais and the invention of Antiphysiocracy' in Steven L. Kaplan and Sophus A. Reinert (eds.), *The Economic Turn. Recasting Political Economy in Enlightenment Europe* (London and New York: Anthem Press, 2019), pp. 139–68; Antonella Alimento, 'Between Mercantilism and Physiocracy: Forbonnais' "Est Modus in Rebus" Vision' in ibid., pp. 169–92; the articles on 'Translation, Reception and Enlightened Reform: The Case of Forbonnais in Eighteenth-Century Political Economy', *History of European Ideas*, 40:8 (2014); Antonella Alimento, 'La Concurrence comme Politique Moderne. La Contribution de L'école de Gournay à la naissance d'une sphère publique dans la France des années 1750–1760' in Jesús Astigarraga and Javier Usoz (eds.), *L'économie politique et la sphère publique dans le débat des Lumières* (Madrid: Collection de la Casa de Velázquez, 2013), pp. 213–27. For the most rigorous account on Gournay's circle and its activities, see Loïc Charles, Frédéric Lefebvre and Christine Théré (eds.), *Le Cercle de Vincent Gournay. Savoirs économiques et pratiques administratives en France au milieu du XVIIIe siècle* (Paris: Institut National D'Études Démographiques, 2011); Arnault Skornicki,

Finally, Zinzendorf's ideas should be considered in relation to the tradition of economic thought known as cameralism. The latter was largely confined to the German language and derived from the term *Kammer* which denoted the place of administration of the prince's territorial state.[45] So at the outset, cameralism was characterised as a practical science of administrative and economic management.[46] In 1988, Keith Tribe shifted the emphasis towards academia and underlined the didactic character of cameralism.[47] It was, he has argued, 'a form of academic pedagogy aimed at future administrators of the eighteenth-century German territorial states'.[48] In 2017, scholars sought not only to reconcile the two approaches—practical and academic—but also to extend the geographic impact of cameralism beyond the German states and the Habsburg monarchy. Marten Seppel and Keith Tribe shifted the pendulum back to the practical relevance of cameralism in managing the economy and presented the influence of cameralist teaching in Northern Europe, including Sweden, Denmark, the Baltics.[49] The chapter by Alexandre Mendes Cunha

L'économiste, la cour et la patrie. L'économie politique dans la France des Lumières (Paris, 2011), pp. 75–112; John Shovlin, 'Rethinking Enlightened Reform in a French Context' in Gabriel Paquette (ed.), *Enlightened Reform in Southern Europe and its Atlantic Colonies c.1750–1830* (Farnham: Ashgate, 2009), pp. 47–62; Antonella Alimento, 'Entre animosité nationale et rivalité d'émulation: la position der Véron de Forbonnais face à la compétition anglaise' in Manuela Albertone (ed.), *Governare il mondo. L'economia come linguaggio della politica nell'Europa del Settecento* (Milan: Fondazione Giangiacomo Feltrinelli, 2009), pp. 125–48; Simone Meyssonnier (ed.), *Traités sur le commerce de Josiah Child suivis des Remarques de Jacques Vincent de Gournay* (Paris, 2008); Clark, *Compass of Society*, pp. 129–44; John Shovlin, 'Emulation in Eighteenth-Century French Economic Thought', *Eighteenth Century Studies*, 36 (2003), pp. 224–30; Simone Meyssonnier, *La Balance et l'Horloge: La Genèse de la pensée libérale en France au XVIIIe siècle* (Paris, 1989).

45 Keith Tribe, *Governing Economy. The Reformation of German Economic Discourse 1750–1840* (Cambridge, 1988), p. 6.

46 Albion W. Small, *The Cameralists: The Pioneers of German Social Polity* (Chicago: University of Chicago Press, 1909).

47 Tribe, *Governing Economy.*

48 Keith Tribe, 'Cameralism and the sciences of the state' in Mark Goldie and Robert Wokler (eds.), *The Cambridge History of Eighteenth-Century Political Thought* (Cambridge, 2006), pp. 525–46, at p. 525. For a summary of the practical versus academic cameralism, see Andre Wakefield, *The Disordered Police State. German Cameralism as Science and Practice* (Chicago, 2009), pp. 3–5.

49 Marten Seppel, 'Introduction. Cameralism in practice' in Marten Seppel and Keith Tribe (eds.), *Cameralism in Practice: State Administration and Economy in Early Modern Europe* (Suffolk: Boydell and Brewer, 2017), pp. 1–16, especially pp. 3, 12.

on dissemination of cameralist ideas from Austria to Portugal is notable for covering a geographic outlier.[50]

Cameralist thought began to develop in the sixteenth century and reached its heyday in the mid-eighteenth century. Justi and Joseph von Sonnenfels (1733–1817) were among the most sophisticated cameralist writers and produced comprehensive textbooks which set out the conceptual framework of cameralism. Both taught in Vienna and were contemporaries of Zinzendorf. Cameralism was the orthodoxy in certain parts of the Austrian administration. Count Friedrich Wilhelm von Haugwitz, who planned and, in 1749, implemented a new central administrative structure for the monarchy, recruited Justi to develop the study of the economy. Justi travelled to Vienna in 1750. He became the tutor of Haugwitz's son and a professor at the *Theresianum*, a new school created to educate nobility for careers in government administration. Haugwitz assigned Justi to teach German eloquence and to develop lectures on cameralism, commerce and mining.[51] In 1752, he approved Justi's curriculum.[52] While Haugwitz and Justi sought to develop cameralist thinking, Zinzendorf, supported by Kaunitz, adopted French and, to a lesser extent, English economic thought. As I will argue in this book, his ideas on political economy were more developed than those of Justi and Sonnenfels. For Zinzendorf, it seems, cameralism offered little that was useful in addressing the economic and financial challenges of a large economy such as the Habsburg monarchy.

Cunha's contribution in *Cameralism in Practice* highlights the similarities between the administrative reforms initiated by the Marquis of Pombal in mid-eighteenth-century Portugal to consolidate power, and those of the *Directorium in publicis et camerabilus* in the monarchy. From 1745 to 1749, Pombal was living in Vienna as a Portuguese diplomat and witnessed first-hand the reforms of Haugwitz. Through his marriage in 1745 to Countess Eleonore Ernestine Daun, who came from a respected noble family of Austrian military leaders, Pombal gained good access to officials and to the court in Vienna.[53] Subsequently, Cunha argues, after becoming

[50] Alexandre Mendes Cunha, 'Administrative Centralisation, Police Regulations and Mining Sciences as Channels for the Dissemination of Cameralist Ideas in the Iberian World' in Marten Seppel and Keith Tribe (eds.), *Cameralism in Practice: State Administration and Economy in Early Modern Europe* (Suffolk: Boydell and Brewer, 2017), pp. 155–78.

[51] Klingenstein, 'Between Mercantilism and Physiocracy', pp. 203–4; Tribe, *Governing Economy*, p. 57.

[52] Adam, *Justi*, p. 34.

[53] Cunha, 'Administrative Centralisation', pp. 164–65.

State Secretary in Portugal, Pombal used cameralist ideas for his policies. Notably, Pombal's decrees and new regulations which he issued between 1755 and 1757 to alleviate the situation of the indigenous population of Brazil display the intellectual influence of the cameralists, in particular the ideas of the mid-seventeenth-century writer Johann Joachim Becher and of Justi.[54] According to Culha's narrative, Pombal followed Haugwitz's reformist agenda and also assimilated cameralist ideas, which were then taught to administrators in the monarchy. Pombal seems, however, to have overlooked the existence of a very different type of economic discourse. This new debate, more international, sophisticated and bolder than the ideas Pombal adopted, was led by Zinzendorf and only conducted among Vienna's ruling elite.[55]

The chapters of this book follow a chronological approach. Chapter 2 explores the important relationship between Kaunitz and Zinzendorf. It then examines Zinzendorf's output during his formative years in France with Kaunitz. Chapter 3 shifts to a comparative approach and sets out the important intellectual influences on Zinzendorf. Jean-François Melon and Gournay in particular, it will be argued, provided intellectual inspiration. The subject of Chap. 4 is Zinzendorf's German translation of John Law's *Money and Trade* (1705). It showed Zinzendorf's interpretation of Law's ideas and why he thought that they were still important and relevant to German readers. Heavily footnoted with textual additions, Zinzendorf's book throws light on the nature of translation in the eighteenth century. Chapter 5 is devoted to Zinzendorf's thinking on state credit and the reference points he took from other European countries. Chapter 6 is an analysis of his work as a sophisticated promoter of political economy and draws on the arguments developed in the previous chapters. It shows how Zinzendorf operated as a sophisticated financial expert and examines his role in government from a variety of perspectives. The discussion centres on the type of economic thinker Zinzendorf became, on Zinzendorf's circle of like-minded individuals, his contribution to debates within government, his engagement with the public sphere in the monarchy and the distinctiveness of his ideas.

[54] Ibid., pp. 167–71. Becher (1635–1682) was from the Rhineland. His main work was *Politischer Diskurs von den eigentlichen Ursachen des Auf- und Abnehmens der Städte, Länder und Republicken* (Frankfurt, 1688). For Justi, see Chap. 6.

[55] For the two levels of economic discourse in the mid-eighteenth-century monarchy, see also Klingenstein, 'Between Mercantilism and Physiocracy'.

Most of the relevant primary sources are in manuscript form, and four archives in Austria contain many of the papers. The main archival source is the Zinzendorf *Nachlaß* located at the Austrian State Archives in Vienna.[56] It is an extensive collection which also includes the documents and writings of both Ludwig and his brother Karl. Karl left an enormous and rich collection of diaries, travel accounts, maps and letters. However, it has suffered significant losses. During World War II, the *Nachlaß* was moved for 'safekeeping' from Vienna to *Schloß Guntersdorf* in Lower Austria. There, 72 out of 204 volumes of manuscripts were thrown away, partially destroyed or looted. Loose collections of mixed papers from volumes which had disintegrated were collected in haste and returned to Vienna in October 1945. Important manuscripts from Ludwig Zinzendorf were also lost.[57] Two other important archives are the National Library and the Teutonic Order, both in Vienna. The latter has the correspondence between Ludwig Zinzendorf and Karl Zinzendorf which is a collection of 11 volumes of letters from the late 1750s to the 1770s. The fourth significant source for primary material is the Zinzendorf *Nachlaß* in the archives of Lower Austria. It encompasses 40 boxes with a variety of papers and 2 boxes with official documents. This is the first book to systematically consult the archive of the *Nachlaß* in relation to Ludwig Zinzendorf.[58]

At the outset, it will help the reader to set out short biographies of the Zinzendorf brothers. Ludwig (1721–1780) and Karl (1739–1813) were half-brothers, and both were remarkable figures in Austrian political life for over half a century from the early 1750s until the early 1800s. The Zinzendorf family had a long aristocratic history reaching back to twelfth-century Lower Austria. In the seventeenth century, because of their Lutheran beliefs, they were exiles, emigrating to Nürnberg. Their common father, Count Friedrich Christian (1697–1756), was in Saxon service, and their uncle, Count Nikolaus Ludwig (1700–1760), their father's half-brother, was the founder of the Moravian Brethren.[59] The family was relatively poor. It had very limited financial means and was in debt.

[56] *Nachlaß* refers to Karl Zinzendorf's collection of papers.

[57] Klingenstein et al. (eds.), *Europäische Aufklärung*, vol. 1, pp. 34–6. For lists of missing volumes and the content of the *Nachlaß* in the Austrian State Archives, see footnotes 87, 89, 92 and 93 in ibid. For the general deficiencies in archival sources for the eighteenth-century monarchy, see Dickson, *Finance and Government*, vol. 1, pp. 11–12.

[58] I am very grateful to Grete Klingenstein for having brought the archive to my attention.

[59] For the Zinzendorf family history, and in particular for biographical details on Karl, see Breunlich and Mader (eds.) *Karl Graf von Zinzendorf*, pp. 3–44 and Klingenstein et al.

Details of the early life and education of Count Ludwig Friedrich Julius von Zinzendorf und Pottendorf, known also as 'Louis', are scarce, and the only source for them is Karl's biography. Ludwig was born in Nürnberg. In 1739, at the age of 18, he joined the Saxon army and took part in campaigns in Bohemia. The same year, he converted to Catholicism in anticipation of inheriting the Zinzendorf family estate in Enzesfeld in Lower Austria. Becoming Roman Catholic was a prerequisite for the inheritance and in 1742, when the last member of the branch of the Austrian Catholic family died, Ludwig decided to cut short his military career.[60] He moved to Vienna and in 1745 assumed the inheritance. Zinzendorf started with debts of 4000 *florins* and immediately struggled financially as the income from the estate was minimal.[61] Financial worries were present throughout his life, and he was never able to give enough attention to his personal finances. One year later, Zinzendorf decided to read law at the University of Leipzig and upon his return the following year joined the provincial government of Lower Austria. There, he was able to improve his understanding of provincial law. In 1748, Zinzendorf was elected assessor (*Landrechtsbeisitzer*) which was a post for young nobles and usually a stepping stone to service in central government.[62] The position gave him an invaluable insight into the workings of the Estates and would prove important for Zinzendorf's subsequent proposals on financial reform. The seminal moment of his professional career occurred in 1749 when he was introduced to Kaunitz. He joined Kaunitz's ambassadorial mission to France in 1750, the subject of Chap. 2 of this book. In November 1752, he left France for England and on his way back to Vienna, he briefly visited Brussels, Hannover, Leipzig and Berlin.[63]

Zinzendorf's career progression was not straightforward. In the summer of 1753, Kaunitz organised a government post for Zinzendorf as privy councillor (*Hofrat*) in the *Commerzien-Directorium* which was headed by Count Rudolf Chotek.[64] The assignment turned out to be brief. Chotek

(eds.), *Europäische Aufklärung*, vol. 1, pp. 13–19. For a detailed chronology on Karl Zinzendorf, see Klingenstein et al. (eds.), *Europäische Aufklärung*, vol. 1, pp. 301–9; Lebeau, *Aristocrates*, pp. 21–9.

[60] Pettenegg (ed.), *Selbstbiographien*, pp. 47–51; Klingenstein et al. (eds.), *Europäische Aufklärung*, vol. 1, p. 15.

[61] Pettenegg (ed.), *Selbstbiographien*, p. 51.

[62] Ibid., pp. 51–4.

[63] Ibid., p. 60.

[64] See Chap. 6, particularly the section 'The Institutions for Commercial Affairs'.

became jealous of Zinzendorf's economic expertise, which was highly valued by the emperor, and dismissed him the following year.[65] Again, Kaunitz intervened and arranged for Zinzendorf to be sent on a new diplomatic mission to Russia, Sweden and Denmark. There, Zinzendorf was intended to extend his international knowledge on economic affairs and where his expertise would be more useful in a permanent government post.[66] However, Zinzendorf complained that poverty prevented him from pursuing a diplomatic career.[67] In 1757, after further brief stints in government as a censor for the official court circular and vice president in the department of mines and minerals, he left public office.[68] Nevertheless, through his close friendship and advisory role to Kaunitz, Zinzendorf remained actively involved in government business.

On 15 April 1761, Zinzendorf returned to an administrative position as the first president of the Estate Credit Deputation.[69] One year later, he achieved his professional breakthrough when he was made a government minister: on 1 January 1762, Zinzendorf became president of the newly created audit office.[70] At the Deputation, he was replaced by Hatzfeld.[71] Subsequently, on 2 August 1767, Zinzendorf was appointed president of a new political bank within the monarchy. It was to be the high point in his political career, but it was only to last for three months before Maria Theresa cancelled the project.[72] From then on, his influence in the administration declined, and he lost the struggle for power with Hatzfeld. One

[65] Pettenegg (ed.), *Selbstbiographien*, p. 61.

[66] Ibid., pp. 62–5. On Zinzendorf's memoir on the Russian court in St Petersburg, 'Mémoire sur la Russie, sur L'impératrice Elisabeth, sa cour et son gouvernement', Staatenabteilung, Russland II, Karton 209, HHStA, see Lothar Schilling, *Kaunitz und das Renversement des alliances. Studien zur außenpolitischen Konzeption Wenzel Antons von Kaunitz* (Berlin, 1994), pp. 118–19. On the goals for Zinzendorf's mission to Stockholm and Copenhagen, see Kaunitz's memorandum to Zinzendorf, undated, pp. 516–21, vol. 3, 1752–1755, in Rudolf Graf Khevenhüller-Metsch and Hans Schlitter (eds.), *Aus der Zeit Maria Theresias. Tagebuch des Fürsten Johann Josef Khevenhüller-Metsch, Kaiserlichen Obersthofmeisters, 1742–1746* (8 vols, Vienna, 1910).

[67] Letter of Ludwig Zinzendorf to Wenzel Kaunitz, 21 October 1756, in Pettenegg (ed.), *Selbstbiographien*, p. 70.

[68] Pettenegg (ed.), *Selbstbiographien*, p. 72.

[69] Dickson, *Finance and Government*, vol. 2, p. 135.

[70] Pettenegg (ed.), *Selbstbiographien*, p. 83.

[71] Dickson, *Finance and Government*, vol. 2, p. 136.

[72] Pettenegg (ed.), *Selbstbiographien*, p. 112. Zinzendorf's presidency of the bank would have started on 1 January 1768: Dickson, *Finance and Government*, vol. 2, p. 66. On Maria Theresa's change of mind, see ibid., p. 68. On Zinzendorf's ideas for the political bank, see Chap. 5.

of Zinzendorf's political ambitions was to use the audit office as a powerful instrument of control ex ante on all financial business.[73] This very clearly did not make him a popular figure with other departments and created many enemies in government. Zinzendorf bitterly deplored the tactics used to undermine the work of the audit office as well as Hatzfeld's claims that there was an insurmountable clash of personalities.[74] In January 1773, following proposals by Hatzfeld and Joseph II, the empress demoted the audit office to a subsidiary of the rival *Hofkammer*.[75] Ludwig retired with a pension and a pay-off to cover his personal debts. As a gesture of goodwill, he was also made a minister in the *Staatsrat*.[76] Joseph II had never favoured him much, and Zinzendorf's political career was over. Very soon thereafter, he fell ill. After battling with poor health for six years, Zinzendorf died in Vienna on 4 October 1780.[77] Two weeks before his death, the empress made her last visit to him. She wrote about the painful symptoms of his illness, and his wish to have a Catholic funeral, but also noted the low value of his estate.[78] Zinzendorf was already over 40 years old when in October 1764, he married Maria Anna, the daughter of Count Josef Adam von Schwarzenberg.[79] His marriage into a well-established noble family was probably a further attempt to anchor himself among the elite in the monarchy. The couple had only one daughter whom they named Maria Theresa and who was baptised in the presence of the empress.[80] The lack of a male offspring and his concern for a continuation of the family probably spurred Ludwig's strong interest and involvement in his brother's career.

Count Johann Karl Christian Heinrich von Zinzendorf und Pottendorf was 'shy, awkward, fiercely ambitious, emotionally deprived by his rigor-

[73] Pettenegg (ed.), *Selbstbiographien*, p. 89.

[74] Ludwig Zinzendorf, 'Sur l'utilité de la Chambre des Comptes et la nécessité de la conserver', October 1771, fol. 611r and fol. 614r, vol. 4, Nachlaß Zinzendorf, HHStA.

[75] Letter from Joseph II to Maria Theresa, 27 November 1771 in *Maria Theresia und Joseph II. Ihre Correspondenz sammt Briefen Josephs an seinen Bruder Leopold*, ed. Alfred Ritter von Arneth (3 vols, Vienna, 1887), vol. 1, pp. 352–56 at p. 356; Dickson, *Finance and Government*, vol. 1, p. 250.

[76] Pettenegg (ed.), *Selbstbiographien*, pp. 140–41.

[77] Ibid., pp. 151–62.

[78] Letter from Maria Theresa to Erzherzog Ferdinand, 5 October 1780 in *Briefe der Kaiserin Maria Theresia an Ihre Kinder und Freunde*, ed. Alfred Ritter von Arneth (4 vols, Vienna, 1881), vol. 3, pp. 297–98.

[79] Pettenegg (ed.), *Selbstbiographien*, p. 98.

[80] Ibid., pp. 101–2.

Fig. 1.2 Count Karl Zinzendorf, governor of Trieste 1776–1782 and president of the *Hofrechenkammer* 1782–1792. (Source: Rechnungshof Vienna)

ous spartan Protestant upbringing' and 'by his own admission, unversed in the ways of the world, better at paper than people'.[81] In 1752, at the age of 13, he began to keep a diary and continued with meticulous regularity until his death. Written in French, it recorded his days in considerable detail, describing what he did, with whom he met and conversed and what was discussed. It is a very insightful account of a man with enlightened and

[81] Dickson, 'Count Karl von Zinzendorf's "New Accountancy"', p. 26.

liberal views who travelled to see, learn and understand. As I will argue in Chap. 6, Karl made it a point throughout his travels, on the advice of Ludwig, to meet leading European thinkers of his time. In his Viennese notes he records the discussions with his brother, his evenings as a guest of Kaunitz and his audiences with Joseph II. Together with Karl's other documents, 'his diary forms probably the most complete picture of a minister's relationship with an absolute ruler which survives for any country or period.'[82]

Karl was educated at the University of Jena from 1757 to 1761, where he read law and history as well as cameral and natural sciences.[83] While in Jena, Karl corresponded regularly with Ludwig who guided him with these studies. In 1761, with neither good career prospects in war-torn Saxony nor financial support from the family, Karl took up Ludwig's invitation to move to Vienna. Ludwig wanted to groom his brother as his political *confident* and eventual successor.[84] Ludwig was Karl's financial back-up and was thus eager to find economic security for his brother. He introduced Karl to Kaunitz with whom he developed a close relationship. To increase his prospects for a career in the Austrian government, Karl followed Ludwig's advice which required two significant changes to his personal life. In 1764, at the age of 24, Karl converted to Catholicism.[85] Six years later he also took a vow of celibacy by becoming a Knight of the Teutonic Order.[86] In 1766, he had become a Freemason and remained an active member until the end of his life.[87]

Following the intervention of Ludwig and Friedrich Binder von Krieglstein (1708–1782), Kaunitz's closest adviser, Karl was sent by the

[82] Derek Beales, *Joseph II.* Vol. 2: *Against the World, 1780–1790* (Cambridge, 2009), p. 7.

[83] Klingenstein et al. (eds.), *Europäische Aufklärung*, vol. 1, p. 14.

[84] Letter from Ludwig Zinzendorf to Karl Zinzendorf, Vienna, 19 April 1768, vol. 65, DOZA; Christine Lebeau, 'Die Tagebücher des Grafen Karl von Zinzendorf' in Josef Pauser, Martin Scheutz and Thomas Winkelbauer (eds.), *Quellenkunde der Habsburgermonarchie (16.–18. Jahrhundert): Ein exemplarisches Handbuch* (*MIÖG*, Ergänzungsband, Vienna, 2004), pp. 796–800, at p. 797.

[85] See Christine Lebeau, 'La conversion de Karl von Zinzendorf: Affaire d'état ou affaire de famille?' in *Revue de synthèse*, *114* (1993), pp. 473–95.

[86] Klingenstein et al. (eds.), *Europäische Aufklärung*, vol. 1, pp. 16–17. In 1776, having not had any male offspring, Ludwig seemingly regretted this advice. Within two years of his death, Ludwig wrote in his will, he wanted Karl to leave the Order and marry. If these conditions were met, Karl could assume some of Ludwig's inheritance: Pettenegg (ed.), *Selbstbiographien*, p. 151.

[87] Klingenstein et al. (eds.), *Europäische Aufklärung*, vol. 1, p. 18.

empress on extended commercial travels.[88] It was the continuation of a tradition which had begun in the mid-1750s. Sponsored by the emperor, his travels were fuelled by the competition with Prussia and the growing opportunities for commerce with Italy and the Ottoman Empire.[89] From 1763 to 1775, Karl was mostly on the move. As a commercial councillor, he visited Europe, including England, Scotland and Ireland, as well as Russia, and compiled detailed travel accounts on politics, geography and economics which were sent to the rulers and Kaunitz. He also travelled throughout the monarchy and submitted detailed reports.[90] From 1776 to 1782, Karl was governor of Trieste, where he pursued liberal commercial and religious agendas.[91] In 1782, he was recalled by Joseph II to Vienna and appointed president of the court of audit. But Karl was cautious, fearing a resurgence of the old animosities against his brother. He also thought that the post was given to him to keep him from more interesting work, including his plans to align the economic interests of the monarchy's provinces.[92] Despite these things, until 1792, Karl was head of the same government department that his brother had directed ten years earlier.[93] Thereafter, he remained close to government policies and was part of the group of ministers to whom Francis II proclaimed the creation of the hereditary title Emperor of Austria on 11 August 1804.[94] Karl died in Vienna on 4 January 1813, the last male member of his house.

[88] On Binder, see Chap. 6, particularly the section 'The Circle Around Zinzendorf'.

[89] Grete Klingenstein, 'Kommerz und Aussenpolitik. Habsburgische Kommerzialreisen im Vorfeld der diplomatischen Revolution, 1756' in Othmar Pickl (ed.), *Wirtschaftsbeziehungen zwischen den österreichischen Niederlanden und den österreichischen Erblanden im 18. Jahrhundert* (Graz, 1991), pp. 55–70.

[90] Klingenstein et al. (eds.), *Europäische Aufklärung*, vol. 1, p. 17.

[91] Ibid., pp. 107–58.

[92] Ibid., p. 217.

[93] On Karl's work at the audit office, see Dickson, 'Count Karl von Zinzendorf's "New Accountancy"'.

[94] Klingenstein et al. (eds.), *Europäische Aufklärung*, vol. 1, p. 18.

CHAPTER 2

Zinzendorf with Kaunitz in France, 1750–1752

As a steadfast Protestant, Ludwig Zinzendorf's great-grandfather Maximilian Erasmus (1633–1672) emigrated from Austria to Nürnberg where many of his co-religionists had sought refuge. He was not allowed to keep his estates and thus sold them to his brother Otto Sigismund Ernst (1638–1701) who was a Catholic. Over the next two generations, Maximilian's offspring became established at the court of Dresden and integrated into the Saxon aristocracy. Friedrich Christian, Ludwig's father, had a difficult childhood, losing both parents at a very young age. He was raised by private tutors and received a military upbringing. In 1720, Friedrich Christian married his cousin Countess Dorothea Juliana Polheim who died seven years later, when Ludwig was six years old. Ludwig had two younger siblings: Maximilian Erasmus (1722–1780) and Susanna Magdalena (1723–1785). Unlike Friedrich Christian, who was quick tempered, and more drawn to the fine arts and philosophy than to business, Dorothea was calm, practical and crafty in managing the family's finances. Recognising her husband's inability to produce sufficient income from their estate, she suggested, shortly before her own death, that he marry Countess Christiana Sophia Callenberg, who came from a well-established and powerful family in Saxony. In 1728, following his first wife's death, Friedrich Christian duly married Christiana Sophia. Their marriage produced ten children, three of whom died in infancy, and Christiana Sophia also helped to raise Ludwig and his two siblings. However, the relationship between Friedrich Christian and his second wife deteriorated as the

S. Adler, *Political Economy in the Habsburg Monarchy 1750–1774*,
Palgrave Studies in the History of Finance,
https://doi.org/10.1007/978-3-030-31007-3_2

financial situation worsened and she realised that he showed little initiative in providing financially for the large family. Also, Christiana Sophia was disappointed that her husband failed to use her strong family connections in Dresden to build a political career for himself.[1]

Ludwig Zinzendorf had a hard and rigid pietistic education the impetus for which came from his stepmother.[2] She probably was instrumental in placing Ludwig and his brother Maximilian in the Saxon army under the tutelage of a *Hofmeister*.[3] Like his mother, Zinzendorf was a practical and clear-thinking individual and viewed the move from Saxony to Lower Austria as a good stepping stone for a career in the Austrian government, with more freedom and better prospects for income. Soon after arriving in Vienna, Zinzendorf began to build up a network of contacts. Early on, he joined the Freemasons. On 17 September 1742, he became a member of Vienna's first Masonic lodge *Aux Trois Canons*. Other members included the industrialist Count Johann Anton Waldstein, the medical doctor Gilgen zu Gilgenburg, the Catholic bishop and theologian Sigismund Conte Gondola, the Russian diplomat Czernichew and Giovanni Marchese Doria, the son of the Genoese envoy in Vienna. The name of the lodge was probably chosen in reference to the three grades of seniority of members. *Aux Trois Canons* was founded in 1741 by Count Albrecht Joseph Hoditz, a friend of Frederick the Great. Hoditz may have been purposely sent from Breslau to Vienna to extend the influence of the *Aux Trois Globes* lodge in Berlin.[4] Through his career in the military, Zinzendorf knew senior officers, including Count Paul Anton Eszterhāzy, who was a successful general in the Austrian army.[5] Also, the Zinzendorfs' long-established aristocratic status in the Habsburg monarchy and Ludwig's conversion to Catholicism served him well in making connections with other noble and high-placed families. In July 1745, he was part of the entourage of Count Johann Josef Khevenhüller-Metsch, one of the chief officers of the imperial household, who followed emperor Francis Stephen

[1] Maria Breunlich and Marieluise Mader (eds.), *Karl Graf von Zinzendorf, Aus den Jugendtagebüchern 1747, 1752–1763. Nach Vorarbeiten von Hans Wagner*, Veröffentlichung der Kommission für Neuere Geschichte Österreichs 84 (Vienna, 1997), pp. 5–6, 9–14.

[2] Ibid., p. 15.

[3] Eduard Gaston von Pettenegg (ed.), *Ludwig und Karl Grafen und Herren von Zinzendorf. Ihre Selbstbiographien nebst einer kurzen Geschichte des Hauses Zinzendorf* (Vienna, 1879), p. 47.

[4] Museumsverein Schloß Rosenau, *Österreichische Freimaurerlogen. Humanität und Toleranz im 18. Jahrhundert* (Vienna, 1976), illus. 13 and pp. 66–7, 71–2.

[5] Pettenegg (ed.), *Selbstbiographien*, p. 51.

to Frankfurt for the coronation. It was also Khevenhüller who advised Zinzendorf to pursue university studies in Leipzig in order to prepare for a role in the provincial government of Lower Austria.[6]

On 2 May 1746, Zinzendorf left Vienna for the University of Leipzig and matriculated in June. Little is known about his formal education, and the only details available are from Karl's biography. Ludwig Zinzendorf followed a rigorous study routine, working 14 hours a day.[7] He attended lectures on law, history and German language by leading university academics: Professors Friedrich August Hommel, Gottfried Mascov and Johann Gottfried Bauer taught Roman law, natural law and German history; Christian Gottlieb Jöcher was the university's librarian and a professor of history, and Johann Christoph Gottsched gave lectures in poetry, logic and German grammar. As early as December, Zinzendorf was quick to apply for the position of *Landrechtsbeisitzer* in Lower Austria. Despite his diligence and hard work, he was fearful that he would forget what he had learnt should there be a long delay between finishing his studies and taking up his position. He had hoped to join the provincial government by Easter 1747, but instead found himself back in Vienna where he took classes with a lawyer for two hours a day to acquire practical legal skills.[8] It wasn't until March of the following year that Zinzendorf took up his position at the government of Lower Austria, where he soon received praise for his work.[9]

The precise origins of Zinzendorf's ideas about political economy are difficult to pinpoint. He did not receive any formal education in political economy.[10] During his short stay in Leipzig, the university did not have a chair in cameral sciences.[11] It was during his time in Leipzig, however, that Zinzendorf developed an appreciation for translations, particularly economic texts.[12] He never directly engaged with cameralist thought; rather, for his intellectual formation, he chose the wider, more European

[6] Ibid., pp. 51–2.

[7] Ibid., p. 52. For a record of Zinzendorf's entry in the student registry of the university on 18 June 1746, see ibid., and also *Die Jüngeren Matrikel der Universität Leipzig 1559–1809*, ed. Georg Erler (3 vols, Leipzig: Giesecke and Devrient, 1909), vol. 3, p. 474.

[8] Pettenegg (ed.), *Selbstbiographien*, p. 53.

[9] Ibid., pp. 53–4.

[10] See also Chap. 6, particularly the section 'Zinzendorf's Formation'.

[11] From 1740 to 1745, Georg Heinrich Zincke lectured on cameralism at the University of Leipzig. At the end of 1745, he moved to the Collegium Carolinum in Brunswick.

[12] See Chap. 4.

perspective of the latest economic thinking. By the time he met Kaunitz, Zinzendorf had read works in both English and French on finance and state credit and had written short essays on these subjects.[13]

Zinzendorf and Kaunitz

In 1749, Countess Maria Anna Eszterhāzy, wife of Count Paul Anton Eszterhāzy, introduced Ludwig Zinzendorf to Wenzel Anton Kaunitz.[14] For Zinzendorf, this encounter was of major significance and shaped his personal and professional development. Eszterhāzy had an important salon in Vienna where liberal-minded individuals came together regularly to exchange ideas. Members of the monarchy's ruling elite also visited her assembly.[15] It was probably at one of these gatherings that Kaunitz and Zinzendorf met for the first time. In the late 1740s, Kaunitz was already an important figure at the court in Vienna. He was an experienced diplomat in the European arena, having held diplomatic positions in Turin and the Austrian Netherlands, and he had been the Austrian representative at the peace negotiations in Aachen in 1748. He was a trusted adviser of Maria Theresa and her main sounding board for matters of foreign policy.[16] These international postings gave Kaunitz a wider European perspective on economic questions and, like Zinzendorf, a lack of interest in cameralism. Early on, Kaunitz encouraged Zinzendorf to study French and English economic texts.

By the time Kaunitz first met Zinzendorf, he had been appointed ambassador to France and was eager to recruit competent and promising youngsters to his ambassadorial staff.[17] The monarchy's government suf-

[13] Pettenegg (ed.), *Selbstbiographien*, p. 59.

[14] Ibid., p. 58.

[15] Letter of Joseph II to Maria Theresa, 22 July 1775 in *Maria Theresia und Joseph II. Ihre Correspondenz sammt Briefen Josephs an seinen Bruder Leopold*, ed. Alfred Ritter von Arneth (3 vols, Vienna, 1887) vol. 2, pp. 72–6; Grete Klingenstein, Eva Faber and Antonio Trampus (eds.), *Europäische Aufklärung zwischen Wien und Triest: die Tagebücher des Gouverneurs Karl Graf von Zinzendorf, 1776–1782*, Veröffentlichung der Kommission für Neuere Geschichte Österreichs, 103 (4 vols, Vienna, 2009), vol. 1, p. 172.

[16] Grete Klingenstein, *Der Aufstieg des Hauses Kaunitz, Studien zur Herkunft und Bildung des Staatskanzlers Wenzel Anton* (Göttingen, 1975), p. 288; Franz A.J. Szabo, *Kaunitz and enlightened absolutism 1753–1780* (Cambridge, 1994), p. 19.

[17] Due to diplomatic etiquette, Kaunitz's departure to France had to be delayed to the autumn of 1750: Schilling, *Kaunitz und das Renversement des alliances. Studien zur außenpolitischen Konzeption Wenzel Antons von Kaunitz* (Berlin: Duncker and Humblot Gmbh, 1994), p. 159.

Fig. 2.1 Count, later prince, Wenzel Anton Kaunitz, *Hof- und Staatskanzler* 1753–1792. (Source: Federal Chancellery of Austria/Christopher Dunker)

fered from ministerial rivalries and was lacking a pool of skilled diplomats with international experience.[18] Kaunitz considered the development of talent as an important part of his work. He recruited young men to work for him in Paris so as to form and mould them for government service. Zinzendorf, Kaunitz wrote to the emperor, will be trained to become an

[18] Klingenstein, *Der Aufstieg des Hauses Kaunitz*, p. 289. On rivalries in the administration, see Chap. 6, particularly the section 'Debates Within Government'.

effective government official.[19] Alongside Zinzendorf, other members of aristocratic families such as Georg Adam Starhemberg, Florimond-Claude de Mercy-Argenteau and Emmanuel-Philibert Wallenstein worked in France, and Kaunitz reported regularly to the empress on their abilities and progress.[20] Sponsorship of talent, he argued, was in the interest of the state.[21] Kaunitz's young recruits were ambitious, with elements of rivalry among them. During their ceremonial entry to Paris, for example, Zinzendorf complained that Mercy, who was of lower diplomatic rank, was given preferential treatment to sit in the same carriage as the ambassador. It must have been a matter of importance to Zinzendorf since he complained formally in writing to Kaunitz. Sensitive to such jealousies, Kaunitz promised Zinzendorf to seat him in his carriage on a subsequent *cortège* which would take place a few days later.[22]

Zinzendorf was a preferred member of Kaunitz's entourage, and they had a very close relationship.[23] Also, they shared similarities. Both Kaunitz and Zinzendorf had had a rigorous and demanding education. They were workaholics, had inquisitive minds, logical thought processes and the ability to understand and present complex issues.[24] Both were proficient in several languages and received their academic training at the University of Leipzig.[25]

[19] Letter of Wenzel Anton Kaunitz to Francis Stephen, 10 January 1752, Staatsakte Frankreich Berichte 1750–1754, Karton 84, HHStA.

[20] On Starhemberg, see Chap. 6, particularly the section 'The Circle Around Zinzendorf'.

[21] Letter of Kaunitz to Ignaz Koch, Paris, 12 February 1752 in *Correspondance Secrète entre le Comte A.W. Kaunitz-Rietberg, ambassadeur imperial à Paris, et le Baron Ignaz de Koch, secrétaire de l'Impératrice Marie-Thérèse, 1750–1752*, ed. Hans Schlitter (Paris, 1899), pp. 166–67.

[22] Pettenegg (ed.), *Selbstbiographien*, p. 60. For the list and rankings of officials who took part in Kaunitz's *cortèges*, see letters of Kaunitz to Count Rudolf Colloredo, Paris, 17 and 19 September 1752, Staatsakte Frankreich Berichte 1750–1754, Karton 84, HHStA.

[23] Kaunitz used cordial expressions: 'mais il m'importe de Vous faire ressouvenir que je vous aime': letter of Kaunitz to Zinzendorf, Vienna, 16 September 1755, in Pettenegg (ed.), *Selbstbiographien*, p. 65.

[24] Ibid., *Selbstbiographien*, p. 47; Alexander Novotny, *Staatskanzler Kaunitz als geistige Persönlichkeit. Ein österreichisches Kulturbild aus der Zeit der Aufklärung und des Josephinismus* (Vienna, 1947), p. 78.

[25] From 1731 to 1732, Kaunitz had been studying law and history in Leipzig. One of his lecturers was Johann Jakov Maskov, the brother of Gottfried Maskov, whose lectures Zinzendorf attended: Klingenstein, *Der Aufstieg des Hauses Kaunitz*, pp. 192–94, 198.

Their first government postings were in Lower Austria.[26] But there were also differences in character. Whereas Kaunitz was patient and aloof towards peers and superiors and rarely lost his temper, Zinzendorf had, like his father, an exuberant, expressive and choleric personality.[27] This trait emerged in Zinzendorf's writings which were often long and sometimes repetitive.

Kaunitz referred to Zinzendorf as his '*élève*' and maintained that he knew Zinzendorf's 'strengths and weaknesses'.[28] Kaunitz also argued on Zinzendorf's behalf for more pay. He implored the empress to grant Zinzendorf a good salary knowing that his pupil struggled financially.[29] In late 1750, when Kaunitz suffered from one of his recurrent bouts of illness, it was Zinzendorf who provided timely updates to Vienna on the pace of Kaunitz's recovery. In a series of letters to Count Corifz Anton Ulfeld, Kaunitz's predecessor as State Chancellor, he described the development of Kaunitz's illness, gave details of treatments and reported on the vast improvement in his medical condition and eventual cure.[30]

Zinzendorf came to France as Kaunitz's expert on economic affairs. It was an important portfolio. Knowledge of political economy and of ways to improve the commerce of the monarchy was high on the agenda of the ambassadorial mission.[31] Kaunitz, too, sought direct contact with professionals in commerce and finance as they, rather than court officials or high aristocracy, could provide an accurate account of the state of the French economy.[32] The Marquis d'Argenson, French minister of foreign affairs until 1747 and a representative of the anti-Habsburg faction at the court, noted sarcastically on 23 January 1752 that Kaunitz was living a reclusive lifestyle in France: he was not interested in the company of the French

[26] For Kaunitz's appointment in Lower Austria in June 1734, see ibid., pp. 257–58.

[27] Pettenegg (ed.), *Selbstbiographien*, p. 47; Novotny, *Staatskanzler Kaunitz*, p. 78.

[28] Letter of Kaunitz to Koch, Brussels, 16 October 1750, in *Correspondance Secrète*, ed. Schlitter, p. 18; 'Je connois son fort et son faible', letter of Kaunitz to Koch, Paris, 12 February 1752, in ibid., p. 166.

[29] Letter of Kaunitz to Koch, Paris, 24 October 1751, in ibid., p. 140. Kaunitz was generally sympathetic to Zinzendorf's money problems. At the beginning of his career, Kaunitz had also faced financial worries: Klingenstein, *Der Aufstieg des Hauses Kaunitz*, pp. 271–72.

[30] Letters of Ludwig Zinzendorf to Anton Ulfeld, 31 December 1750, 3 January 1751, 7 January 1751 and 8 January 1751, Frankreich Varia 1750–1752, Karton 22, HHStA.

[31] Letter of Kaunitz to Koch, Paris, 27 September 1752, ibid.

[32] Schilling, *Kaunitz*, pp. 165–66.

aristocracy or ministers, and chose to only 'live with French financiers'. They were easy prey for Kaunitz as they divulged all the information they had. But Kaunitz, d'Argenson argued, went even further. By seeking good relationships with financers, he sought to obtain the true picture of the country's poor financial situation. Accurate knowledge of French finance must be the 'first article of his mission'.[33]

As Zinzendorf's mentor, Kaunitz was mindful of the need to chart an appropriate career path for his pupil. When asked by Vienna whether Zinzendorf was a suitable candidate for his replacement as ambassador in France, Kaunitz replied that Zinzendorf was not yet experienced enough for such a mission. He proposed instead an easier posting in Turin which would be a more suitable preparation for a future ministerial appointment in the monarchy. On Zinzendorf's abilities, Kaunitz was very explicit. He characterised Zinzendorf as someone who had '*du monde, de l'esprit et des talents*'.[34] He praised Zinzendorf's intellectual abilities and 'high potential'.[35] Zinzendorf also made a very positive impression on his rulers. The empress commented: 'how very pleased she was with Zinzendorf's way of thinking.'[36] The emperor asked him to write a memorandum with anecdotes on the French court.[37]

Zinzendorf wrote the document in late 1751.[38] Notes which he made for the text are in the archives.[39] They are in the form of short statements under various subject headings of key officials, institutions and practices followed at the French court. In the same year, Zinzendorf travelled to Brittany. On his return at the end of 1751, he wrote 'über die französische Marine und die ostindische Compagnie'.[40] Completed on Christmas Eve,

[33] E.J.B. Rathery (ed.), *Journal et Mémoires du Marquis D'Argenson* (9 vols, Paris, 1859), vol. 7, p. 79. Following the French alliance with the monarchy in 1756, d'Argenson repeated his claims that Kaunitz, while ambassador to France, extracted with great skill information on the economy and the country's military capability from French financiers. See diary of 25 June 1756, in ibid., vol. 9, p. 289.

[34] Letter of Kaunitz to Koch, 24 October 1751, in *Correspondance Secrète*, ed. Schlitter, p. 140.

[35] Letter of Kaunitz to Francis Stephen, 10 January 1752.

[36] Letter of Count of Johann Joseph Khevenhüller-Metsch to Ludwig Zinzendorf, 10 September 1753, Archiv Zinzendorf, Karton 9, NÖLA.

[37] Letter of Kaunitz to Francis Stephen, 10 January 1752, in Pettenegg (ed.), *Selbstbiographien*, p. 60.

[38] I could not trace the document in the archives.

[39] Ludwig Zinzendorf, no title [notes on the French court and government officials], undated, fols 1–6, Archiv Zinzendorf, Karton 39, NÖLA.

[40] Ludwig Zinzendorf, Paris, 24 December 1751, 'über die französische Marine und die ostindische Compagnie', written in French, HS Suppl. 961–W923, fols 200r–221v, HHStA.

it was a well-informed account, written in French, which described in two sections the state of the French navy and the trading company. For Kaunitz, it was an important document, and he swiftly sent a copy to Baron Ignaz Koch, the Cabinet Secretary to Maria Theresa.[41] The main product of Zinzendorf's stay in France was the 'Mémoire sur les richesses, le commerce et les finances de la France'.[42] Completed at the end of Kaunitz's ambassadorial mission, it was a remarkable and perceptive assessment of the French economy and state finances.

Travels in Brittany

The commercial company was a key instrument for national trade. Zinzendorf wanted to see for himself how the Compagnie des Indes, which was based in the port of Lorient, operated. In October 1751, he sought permission from Kaunitz to visit Lorient as well other ports in Brittany.[43] Zinzendorf did not choose his timing at random. He set out to travel in the autumn when the Compagnie traditionally conducted its sale of produce. In addition, Kaunitz, who was preoccupied with isolating Prussia politically, had requested permission to gather information from locals on Prussia's commercial forays in France through its recently created trading company in the port of Emden.[44] Zinzendorf's travel party included the young Count Wallenstein and was led by Emmanuel Armand de Richelieu, the Comte d'Aiguillon, then a French army officer who rapidly rose to become an important French official.[45] In 1753, d'Aiguillon was appointed governor of Brittany and subsequently minister of foreign affairs.

Zinzendorf and Kaunitz received a detailed travel itinerary.[46] It was probably written by d'Aiguillon or by an influential French contact in Paris who had arranged the meetings with local officials in Brittany and

[41] Letter of Kaunitz to Francis Stephen, 10 January 1752. The text, Kaunitz argued, was too long and thus not suitable to be sent directly to the emperor.

[42] Ludwig Zinzendorf, 'Mémoire sur les richesses, le commerce et les finances de la France', undated, fols 1–151, Cod. 14302, ÖNB.

[43] Pettenegg (ed.), *Selbstbiographien*, p. 59.

[44] Letter of Kaunitz to Koch, Paris, 14 October 1751, Karton 22, Frankreich Varia 1750–1752, HHStA. On Prussia's trade company, see Florian Schui, 'Prussia's "Trans-Oceanic" Moment: The Creation of the Prussian Asiatic Trade Company in 1750', *The Historical Journal*, 49:1 (2006), pp. 143–60.

[45] Letter from Kaunitz to Koch, Paris, 14 October 1751, Frankreich Varia 1750–1752, Karton 22, HHStA.

[46] Ludwig Zinzendorf, no title [fragment of the travel itinerary in Brittany], undated, fols 1r–2, Archiv Zinzendorf, Karton 40, NÖLA.

provided Zinzendorf with letters of introduction. The document, which is a fragment, is important. It gives some of the places Zinzendorf visited and government officials he met, and sets out the travel plan to the ports of Lorient, Brest and St Malo. Rather than a simple itinerary, it was more of an instruction for Zinzendorf on how to travel, what to see and, importantly, what cities and sites to disregard. It included distances between cities and villages, duration and condition of travel, and the points of interest along the route. The document begins with the description of the route to take to arrive to Lorient and ends with the visit to Saint-Malo. Zinzendorf and his party travelled via Chambord, Richelieu, Tours, Saumur, Angers, Nantes and Auray. From Auray, the group went to the harbour of Port Louis where they met with officials of the port and the navy. The travellers were forewarned of the long journey, the poor road conditions and the bad food. From Port Louis they would make a short transfer by boat to Lorient. This, the author thought, was more convenient and direct than travelling by road. In the city, the Commandant de Lorient and the director of the Compagnie des Indes, Charles Godeheu, would show Zinzendorf and his party the places of interest. The city itself, the author argued, did not offer anything of interest except the strategic positions the English had attacked in 1746. The Compagnie's infrastructure on the other hand, its buildings and storage facilities, were worthwhile visiting and ought to be studied carefully.[47]

The group would leave Lorient overland to continue to Brest via Rennes and Guingamp. The journey by road was longer, but due to strong winds and treacherous rocks, the more direct route by boat was inadvisable. In Brest, the *Intendant de la marine*, Gilles Hocquart, a first rank naval officer, the Comte de Quélen, as well as other naval officials who were friends of the Duc d'Aiguillon were put on notice to receive the travellers well and show them interesting and unusual sites of the harbour. Due to its unique geographic position, Saint-Malo, which was close by, was also worthwhile to see. The commandant of Saint-Malo, Monsieur de Tavignon, would organise a tour of the city. The Fort de la Conchée, a fortification on a small island northwest of the city, was noteworthy. The journey to St Malo by boat, the author warned, could be time-consuming: in case of an arrival during high tide, disembarkation would have to be delayed by several hours. Moreover, as dangerous dogs guarded the city from the beaches, an arrival during nightfall was not advisable.[48]

[47] Ibid., fols 1–1v.
[48] Ibid., fols 2r–2v.

The French Navy and the French Trade Company

Zinzendorf's travel account is a revealing text which has not been studied before by scholars.[49] The draft of the document is also very instructive and shows how Zinzendorf's thinking evolved.[50] He used tight writing with a wide blank column to have room for corrections and insertions. Originally, he had planned to add a third section with general remarks on French commerce, but by the end of the second part, Zinzendorf chose to write a separate piece on trade and on the development of the province.[51] Presumably, he then decided to incorporate the arguments on commerce into the detailed 'Mémoire sur les richesses, le commerce et les finances de la France'.

Zinzendorf began with an assessment of the French navy.[52] People in Paris and in Europe knew about France's efforts to rebuild its navy and talked about 80 ships of the line which would be ready to sail. However, as Zinzendorf pointed out, this represented the total number of ships of the line, galleys and barques in French ports. In support of the argument, he provided a full list of French ships and included the name, the year of construction and the port where each vessel was anchored.[53] The English had taken away most of France's older ships including armament, ammunition and other essential items of equipment. Approximately a quarter of the ships anchored in Brest, Zinzendorf reported, could not be used and had a shortage of ammunition and equipment. Also, a significant number of the city's warehouses were empty.[54]

[49] The document has been noted in the historiography. See Grete Klingenstein et al. (eds.), *Europäische Aufklärung*, vol. 1, pp. 15 and 35, footnote 92.

[50] Ludwig Zinzendorf, no title [draft of the 'Mémoire sur l'Etat present de la Marine de France, du Commerce de la Compagnie des Indes et quelques réflexions detachées sur le Commerce général du Royaume'], undated, fols 1–15, Archiv Zinzendorf, Kartons 38, 9 and 39, NÖLA. For the intended content of Zinzendorf's final version of the *Mémoire*, see Archiv Zinzendorf, in part 1, Karton 38, fol. 1 and in part 3, Karton 39, fol. 4.

[51] I could not find this text in the archives. For Zinzendorf's intention to have three sections in the text, see Archiv Zinzendorf, Karton 38, fol. 1 and Karton 39, fol. 4, and 'über die französische Marine', fol. 221r.

[52] Zinzendorf, 'über die französische Marine', fol. 200v. In the introduction, Zinzendorf showed his admiration for the buildings and fortifications of Brest. If, Zinzendorf argued, he would have written the account for his own benefit and not for Kaunitz, he would have added more detailed information on the port.

[53] The list is not part of the document in the archive.

[54] Zinzendorf, 'über die französische Marine', fols 200v–202r.

Zinzendorf was surprised about the willingness of naval personnel to share information. It was, he thought, a cultural issue, reflecting the 'weak state of mind' of the French, their natural tendency for affability and their propensity to talk. Nonetheless, Zinzendorf was vigilant when trying to obtain information. To Hocquart, he hid his background when d'Aiguillon introduced him as traveller who was curious and eager to learn. Zinzendorf actively played upon the vanity of the French and used flattery to extract confidential information. He encouraged locals to be open about matters of state interest and made out that the secrecy of other countries in these issues was a sign of weakness. Zinzendorf succeeded in obtaining sensitive facts from a lieutenant of the navy who complained about the lack of professional recognition from his superiors. It was information which Hocquart had previously refused to divulge.[55]

The French court, Zinzendorf argued, was weak and ridden with ministerial intrigues. The navy did not receive sufficient financial support because as much as a quarter of its budget was earmarked for the French colonies, and the balance was not sufficient to build new ships and buy the necessary equipment. The minister for naval affairs was afraid to speak up in government, and the French chancellor, the *Gardes des Sceaux*, with the support of the king, refused to commit more money. Instead of purchasing equipment, the minister used the finances available to him to build ships. He was driven by vanity. For each new vessel ready to sail, he received immediate recognition from the ruler. Seven new ships were built in Brest, but new equipment was not made available for them. No one, to Zinzendorf's surprise, expressed concern.[56] Payment delays of five months were a striking proof of administrative inefficiencies.[57] Also, the government gave priority to pieces of work which could be undertaken on credit. Important projects which required immediate payment were not initiated

[55] Ibid., fols 201v–202v.

[56] Ibid., fols 202v–203r.

[57] Zinzendorf set out the administrative steps before payment was eventually made to navy personnel. It took at least four months: the minister only received the payment claims of the navy one month after the actual payments were due. He then forwarded the claims to the audit office for review. There, after a further month of delay, they were once more returned to him. The minister subsequently raised an *état de fond* and instructed one of the *Trésoriers Généraux de la Marine* to settle the claims. The *Trésorier*, who was assigned payment, passed the claims to one of its wealthier provinces which had sufficient funds. As the provinces operated fixed payment runs, a further two months passed before money was eventually paid out to the navy: ibid., fols 203r–203v.

or were postponed. So, on the one hand, shipbuilding was a government priority because wages could be paid six months late. On the other hand, the purchase of new equipment, which was a time-intensive undertaking, was not high on the agenda since payment had to be made promptly and the material was imported from Russia, Spain and Sweden. The shortage of equipment, Zinzendorf argued, was so severe that in case of military conflict, France would be unable to use even its old navy ships from the late seventeenth century.

Without liquidity, the French government could only make purchases on credit. Therefore, it had to pay significantly more than cash buyers. For the same type of wood as used by the Compagnie des Indes, the state paid a premium of 30 per cent. Also, because it was unable to make prompt payments, it had to use ropes and cables from Brittany which were of poorer quality than the Russian equivalent used by the trade company. In general, the state was six months in arrears with wages, and navy personnel as well as sailors lived in great poverty. The *Intendant*, Zinzendorf reported, was surrounded by destitute sailors. He had to borrow to make the most pressing payments and received money by special courier from Versailles.[58]

Given the good geographic location of Brest and its importance for the operations of the navy, the chaos there was surprising. It was even more acute than in the smaller ports of Rochefort and Toulon. The officials in charge of the navy, Zinzendorf maintained, were incompetent and overpaid. The Grand Amiral de France was a political appointment which attracted a large salary, but was without any real authority. Important decisions were made by the minister for naval affairs who was a lawyer by training. He had no naval experience and prior to his government appointment had never seen a ship.[59]

Zinzendorf, however, also recognised positive aspects of the French navy. Three of which in particular he thought ought to be highlighted. First, the navy corps had a distinguished heritage with its origins in old nobility. It was the only group where the state made an effort to provide a systematic level of education. A naval instructor had to be trained for eight

[58] Ibid., fols 203v–204v. Kaunitz, Zinzendorf claimed, had received independently information which corroborated these observations. He knew that pension payments and new government appointments were 15 months in arrears, and that the French court had to finance itself on future revenues: ibid., fol. 205r.

[59] Ibid., fols 204v–205v.

years. Career progression followed a set path, and for the captaincy of a ship, the minimum age was 40. Also, naval officers were dedicated. They never left the port except for duty on board ship.[60] Second, the division of the population of the maritime provinces into *classes* was an asset, and was admired by the English. The system was orderly and balanced, and made it possible to enter the population living in proximity to the sea into a central register. The entries were divided into four classes, each to take its turn to serve the state. Classes not involved in government duties were free to engage in private commercial activities. Each *classe* was made up of good, mediocre and bad sailors, and the ships' crews had to be a mix of sailors of each class. The different pay among the classes was an incentive for the less able sailors to improve and earn more. The system of *classes*, however, had greatly suffered during the War of the Austrian Succession. Since England had refused to return captured sailors, the lack of experienced navy personnel in France was very noticeable.[61] The third remarkable aspect of the navy's operations was the *gardes côtes*. They represented a large *milice* force of more than 200,000 men on foot and horseback which provided important support services. The system was successful because its administration was well structured and clear: coastal areas were separated into 12 maritime zones and subdivided into 112 *captaineries gardes côtes*. Following a strict hierarchy, each of these was governed by a captain, a major and a lieutenant.[62] These strong naval institutions were the results of Colbert's good works. What normally took more than 100 years to build, Colbert achieved in merely 15. Subsequently, however, under the ministry of Cardinal de Fleury, the navy received little new financial support and its operations had been scaled back.[63]

In the second part of the account, Zinzendorf examined the Compagnie des Indes. In its current form, he maintained, the Compagnie was merely a remnant of John Law's ambitious economic system.[64] However, its operations were now stable. The Compagnie's commerce was based on exclusive trading rights with India, Africa and Senegal and a monopoly on

[60] Ibid., fols 205v.

[61] Ibid., fols 206r–206v.

[62] Ibid., fol. 206v.

[63] Ibid., fols 206v–207r. This also was the case subsequently in the Seven Years War: Jonathan Dull, *The French Navy and the Seven Years War* (Lincoln, NB: University of Nebraska Press, 2005).

[64] On Law's system, see Chap. 4.

commerce in beaver pelts and coffee. The operations were located at the port of Lorient where the Compagnie had undertaken substantial real estate developments.[65] It had a capital base of 180 million *livres*. The number of shares issued by the late 1740s had decreased dramatically by over 90 per cent to just over 50,000 shares. Of those, after a significant share purchase by the state, only 38,000 were available to the public. Now, the shares were supported by public confidence and traded easily.[66] The war with England had inflicted heavy losses on its operations, and the Compagnie had to fall back on debt financing. It used three types of financial instruments. First, in return for a cash contribution of 200 *livres* per share, it offered shareholders a *billet d'emprunt*. The latter had a face value of 500 *livres* and a rate of interest of 5 per cent. It was not convertible into shares. Second, the Compagnie issued *billet de caissiers* with a limited term of one year and a rate of interest of 5 per cent. At the end of the year, the *billets* had to be re-issued if repayment was to be avoided. The third type, *rentes viagères*, had been issued twice in 1724 and 1748. The total amount raised was small and was gradually repaid in full.[67] Zinzendorf provided a summary of the financial position in a balance sheet where he set out the debt and the revenues. The debts outstanding, he concluded, were covered by revenues, and there was a good profit in the year.[68]

The Compagnie's debt, Zinzendorf thought, was beneficial for French finances. Their market value, excluding the *rentes viagères*, well exceeded 100 million *livres*. The debt instruments were traded directly by investors, and their liquidity gave them a cash-equivalent character. Thus, they contributed to an increase of the supply of money in the economy. The shares and the *billets* could be traded without administrative formalities. Liquidity was supported by a clearing house, or '*bureau*',[69] where papers could be left for safekeeping or traded with other investors without incurring costs.[70]

[65] In India, the Compagnie owned the city of Pondicherry which was the gateway for the trade with the coasts of Coromandel and Bengal. It also held trading posts in Chandannagar (West Bengal), Karikal and Mahé: Zinzendorf, 'über die französische Marine', fols 207r–207v.

[66] Ibid., fol. 207v. In his draft text only, Zinzendorf made explicit references to public confidence and the attributes of the shares. See Archiv Zinzendorf, part 2, p. 1, Karton 9, NÖLA.

[67] Zinzendorf, 'über die französische Marine', fols 208r–208v.

[68] Zinzendorf referred to the excess of revenue over debt as '*excédent de fond*'. He classified the shares as financial debt where the dividend payment was equivalent to an interest payment: ibid., fol. 208v.

[69] In the draft, Zinzendorf called it a '*Bureau de Depot*'.

[70] Zinzendorf, 'über die französische Marine', fols 212v–213r.

However, the Compagnie's finances were not transparent. Financial disclosure was incomplete, and the corporate accounts were not accessible. Instead of a discussion of financial results, the shareholders' meeting was limited to a presentation of events which were generally meaningless and which nobody could verify.[71] Bad management was particularly damaging since the trading company was a complex organisation with its own navy and a considerable military presence in India. Directors were locked in protracted internal debates, and they depleted the company's reserves with expenditure on buildings and sundry items. They did not own shares in the Compagnie. This, Zinzendorf pointed out, reflected the fact that they had very little confidence in their own abilities. The shareholders also criticised the absence of capable independent advisers to help guide the decision-making.[72]

The Compagnie was an important employer of almost 5000 people. It provided work to people in Brittany who otherwise would have remained unemployed. During peacetime, it offered training to officers and sailors who served in the military.[73] The purchase of luxury produce in India was the object of criticism. However, Zinzendorf argued that such produce had become items of necessity in Europe. Before, France was reliant on other trading nations for the supply of luxury produce and, in addition, had to pay for transport. Now, the Compagnie could supply such produce directly and provided subsidy payments for regions in Northern France in addition. Zinzendorf warned of the emerging commercial threat to France of the Prussian trading company. In due course, he thought, the Compagnie would lose its German and Polish customers who, due to the geographic proximity of Emden, would choose to trade with the Prussians.[74]

For Zinzendorf, observing the auction process in Lorient was a significant highlight of his travels. It represented a remarkable '*spectacle*' which,

[71] Ibid., fol. 209r.

[72] Ibid., fols 209v–210r. Zinzendorf gave details of corrupt behaviour by administrators. He also criticised the reckless decision-making of the governor of Pondicherry in India, who decided to get involved in Indian civil wars. Even though the military engagements so far had been favourable, the Compagnie's remit was to conduct commerce: see ibid., fols 210r–211r.

[73] Ibid., fol. 213r.

[74] Ibid., fols 213r–213v. The exclusive trade of produce and slaves with the coasts of Africa, formerly undertaken by the Compagnie du Senegal et de la Guinée, was also part of the Compagnie's activities As it had recognised that the vast African trade was incompatible with its commitments in India, it had surrendered part of its trading privileges to merchants in Nantes: see ibid., fol. 214r.

if followed closely, could give ideas about how to conduct the '*commerce en grand*'.[75] The Compagnie, he argued, had implemented a transparent sales process which was based on fair pricing. In advance of the auction, to guide expectations of merchants, it printed a book which listed the sale prices of produce from its previous ten auctions, gave a description of the items now for sale and specified the payment terms. For the auction, the Compagnie printed books referred to as *dispositions*. It assigned each lot a unique reference number, specified weight, type and quality and disclosed the name of the successful bidder and the purchase price. The *dispositions* were useful reference books for both seller and merchants, and Zinzendorf admired the practicalities of the process. To potential purchasers, it gave a true picture of the quality of produce.[76]

Generally, produce had protective cover. It was impractical to display it without wrapping. Tea, coffee and other produce sold by weight could easily be weighed at designated areas. For other produce, including silk and fabric, it was a more delicate undertaking. The seller had to find a sample which was as accurate a representation as possible of the produce's quality to guide the decision-making of the interested parties. If this process was not managed carefully, it could damage the reputation of the seller. Produce not sold by weight was divided, based on quality, into five groups. Groups two and four were displayed in the show area prior to the sale so that potential buyers would be reassured of the variety of quality on offer. To underline the credibility of this process, Zinzendorf related an incident which he witnessed. A group of potential purchasers from Montpellier demanded that 160 containers of produce be opened. Reassured of the quality, the buyers stopped already after the twentieth container. Other purchasers took comfort, and the sale of all containers was successfully completed.[77]

The auction process was conducted in the Hôtel des Ventes. It was a large room which was specifically arranged for this purpose. Bidding was done in the morning after the information on the produce was distributed to the merchants. The directors of the Compagnie, flanked by *commissaires* of the ruler, sat on armchairs. They faced the potential purchasers who sat in an amphitheatre-type semicircle. When frenzied bidding activities pushed prices up, the directors intervened to stop the process and

[75] Ibid., fol. 215v. A separate memoir, Zinzendorf thought, was required to record the whole variety of interesting and useful details of the auction.

[76] Ibid., fols 215v–216v.

[77] Ibid., fols 216v–217r.

appealed to the prudence of market participants. In fact, in advance of the bidding, the directors had already decided on the sale price. Once the target price was reached, they indicated, by banging a stick, that higher bids would not be accepted. This peculiar process, Zinzendorf explained, was a necessary practice and reflected the rivalry with the Dutch and English trading companies. If the Compagnie were to sell dearer than its competitors, foreign merchants would stop buying and domestic traders would begin to offer smuggled produce.[78]

In 1751, the Compagnie recorded a turnover of almost 30 million *livres*.[79] It traded three types of produce. First, it sold, non-exclusively, produce which was required by French industry. The second type of produce was essential for the French economy, and the Compagnie was the exclusive supplier. It included tea, pepper and *mousseline* and, for the authorities not to confiscate it, had to carry the seal of the Compagnie. The third category was 'prohibited produce' which was considered to be in direct competition to domestic manufacturing. It included canvasses and embroideries from India. These items had to be registered on arrival, and the trading company was required to produce written proof that the produce would only be sold abroad.[80]

The facilities in Lorient, Zinzendorf marvelled, were remarkable. The Compagnie's navy, dockyards and storage facilities as well as the Hôtel des Ventes were impressive. The port of Lorient was smaller than Brest, but its buildings were sumptuous and kept in good condition. They testified to the Compagnie's 'enormous' wealth.[81] The organisation and the layout of the port were also noteworthy. At nightfall, the keys used for storage, individually labelled for each unit, were deposited at the designated office situated in a self-contained building in the port and guarded by soldiers. The port's layout was well planned. It was purposely designed so that all cargo could be discharged from the ships in proximity to the storage facilities.[82] Detailed knowledge of the set-up in Lorient,

[78] Ibid., fols 217r–217v.

[79] Sales, Zinzendorf maintained, could vary significantly. In the previous year, turnover was 16m. to 18m. liv. because the Compagnie's ships did not arrive back to France in time. So, it had to purchase an additional 8m. liv. worth of produce from English and Dutch merchants to cover the domestic requirements: ibid., fol. 218r.

[80] Ibid., fols 217v–218r.

[81] Ibid., fol. 218v.

[82] The port's good set-up was not only the result of clever planning. It was also borne out of luck following the English military blunder in 1746 when they attempted to raid Lorient. This episode, Zinzendorf argued, forced the French to build solid walls and good roads: ibid., fols 219v–221r.

Zinzendorf noted, might prove useful for the monarchy's own naval projects.[83] He probably had in mind Austria's efforts to develop its Adriatic seaports of Trieste and Fiume.[84]

The Compagnie owned a fleet of small and large ships, and employed approximately 2000 professional soldiers. At any one time, 60 per cent of its fleet, with large tonnage, was being used for the commerce with India. But only half of these ships carried produce. The other vessels transported money, soldiers and ammunition. Frigates were used for intra-Asian commerce and for transporting black slaves to France.[85] The naval ministry, Zinzendorf thought, should be given credit for the Compagnie's impressive operations. Contrary to the disorder and the neglect which were widespread in the navy, the Compagnie's affairs were conducted with foresight, intelligence and order. Its storage facilities were well stocked, and each ship was well equipped. Even though, Zinzendorf argued, its operations were still a long way from the level of perfection required for an '*économie marchande*', the Compagnie was certainly a model for the French navy.[86]

The 'Mémoire' on the French Economy

Shortly after writing the Brittany travel account, Zinzendorf presented his findings on the French economy in the 'Mémoire sur les richesses, le commerce et les finances de la France'. Again, the document was intended for Kaunitz and completed in November 1752 when Zinzendorf left Paris for a two-month visit to England.[87] It extends to 150 folios and is a remark-

[83] Ibid., fols 219r–219v.

[84] For a comprehensive account of Trieste, including Karl Zinzendorf's policies as governor of the city, see Klingenstein et al. (eds.), *Europäische Aufklärung*, vol. 1, pp. 83–145. On Trieste's commerce, see Wilhelm Kaltenstadler, 'Der österreichische Seehandel über Triest im 18. Jahrhundert', *Vierteljahresschrift für Sozial- und Wirtschaftsgeschichte*, 55 (1968), pp. 481–500, and 56 (1969), pp. 1–104. On trade in Fiume, see Ivan Erag, 'Übersicht der wirtschaftlichen Entwicklungen der Stadt Rijeka/Fiume' in Jürgen Schneider (ed.), *Wirtschaftskräfte und Wirtschaftswege: auf dem Weg zur Industrialisierung. Festschrift für Hermann Kellenbenz* (5 vols, Stuttgart, 1978), vol. 3, pp. 135–54.

[85] Zinzendorf, 'über die französische Marine', fol. 218v.

[86] Ibid., fol. 219r.

[87] In June 1752, in a letter to Kaunitz, Koch sent a table of economic data on the population, revenue and wealth of France. In his reply, Kaunitz offered to give more detail on the figures and explained that he had asked Zinzendorf to draft a comprehensive account of the French economy: letter of Kaunitz to Koch, 26 June 1752, Frankreich Varia 1750–1752, Karton 22, HHStA. For the dates of Zinzendorf's visit to England, see letters of Anton von

ably well-informed account of the state of the French economy and its state finances in the early 1750s. Fragments of the draft, which contain Zinzendorf's outline of the text's structure and notes with calculations, are in the archives of Lower Austria.[88]

The 'Mémoire sur les richesses, le commerce et les finances de la France' provided a critical analysis of France's population, wealth and resources, and was Zinzendorf's attempt to assess the economic potential of 'this rival nation'.[89] It was based on theoretical studies of political economy, confidential memoranda written for government officials and private conversations between Zinzendorf and local experts. The wealth of a nation together with state credit, Zinzendorf argued, determined the economic strength of a state. Accordingly, Zinzendorf divided his 'Mémoire sur les richesses' into two parts. First, he provided an analysis of France's national wealth: its population, agriculture and commerce. In the second part, he gave an assessment of its finances. With this structure for national wealth, he followed the argument of Jean-François Melon's book *Essai politique sur le commerce* which was first published in 1734.[90] In the draft of the 'Mémoire sur les richesses', Zinzendorf characterised the book as an '*ouvrage excellent*', but then crossed it out.[91] Often, Zinzendorf noted, there were large gaps between actual and potential economic output. Good economic performance was influenced by intelligent and moderate administrative practices, good conduct of financial affairs and public confidence in government policies.[92]

France, Zinzendorf estimated, had a population of 17.4 million people. Zinzendorf's calculation was the mean of 19.4 million, as per the *dime royale* of 1707, and 15.4 million which was the figure given in the *Dictionnaire de la France*. Over the first 50 years of the century, therefore, France had experienced a depopulation and lost two million people. Five

Zöhrern to Count Rudolf Colloredo, London, 24 November 1752 and 23 January 1753, England Berichte, Karton 102 and 103 respectively, HHStA. At the end of January 1753, Zinzendorf left England for Brussels: letter of Zöhrern to Colloredo, 23 January 1753, England Berichte, Karton, 103, HHStA.

[88] Ludwig Zinzendorf, fragments of the draft of 'Mémoire sur les richesses, le commerce et les finances de la France', undated, Archiv Zinzendorf, Karton 9, Karton 38 and Karton 39, NÖLA.

[89] Zinzendorf, 'Mémoire sur les richesses', fol. 1v.

[90] Ibid., fol. 3v. On the influence of Melon on Zinzendorf's thinking, see Chap. 3.

[91] Zinzendorf, draft of 'Mémoire sur les richesses', fol.1v, Archiv Zinzendorf, Karton 39, NÖLA.

[92] Zinzendorf, 'Mémoire sur les richesses', fols 2v–3r.

factors, Zinzendorf thought, contributed to this significant decrease. First, war had a destructive influence on population growth. The increase of the large standing armies, even in peacetimes, led to a refusal of a sizeable proportion of the population to get married and have children.[93] Two further aspects were the high death toll during long travels by citizens and the outbreak of famines.[94] Fourth, Zinzendorf identified a range of moral reasons. The most important, he thought, was the intransigence of the French government in failing to address adequately the poverty in rural areas. Villagers did not consider land to be a source of economic stability. They were afraid to marry and have offspring, and the country experienced a migration away from the rural areas towards the cities.[95] Finally, Zinzendorf thought, the political arrangements in France played an important role. The *droit d'aubaine*, an ancient right of the state which allowed it to confiscate assets of foreigners who died on French soil, was '*un reste de barbarie*'.[96] In French border regions, the high tariff system on tobacco consumption, the *ferme de tabac*, had triggered a population exodus from Béarn in the Pyrenees, Flanders and Alsace-Lorraine. Also, the government had not intervened to stop entrepreneurial Calvinist families from relocating to Prussia.[97]

Agriculture was the basic and most important economic activity of a country. To examine the state of French agriculture, Zinzendorf argued, it was necessary first to determine the level of output, then to assess production and finally to evaluate government policies.[98] The French state, he noted, had no data on agricultural output. However, by good fortune, Zinzendorf had seen relevant information on production. He had reviewed an extract of a *mémoire* on French agriculture compiled for Orry de Fulvy who, as *Intendant de Commerce* in charge of agriculture, had collected information on prices and harvest yields to decide on export permissions for produce. The *mémoire*, Zinzendorf pointed out, had been forgotten after Fulvy's death in 1751, but one of Fulvy's secretaries had produced an

[93] Ibid., fols 6v–10r.

[94] Ibid., fols 10v–11r.

[95] Ibid., fols 11v–14.

[96] Ibid., fol. 14v.

[97] Ibid., fols 14r–15v.

[98] Ibid., fols 21r–21v. On agriculture and the French economy, see Steven L. Kaplan, *The Stakes of Regulation. Perspectives on Bread, Politics and Political Economy Forty Years later* (London: Anthem Press, 2015).

extract of it.[99] According to the document, French agricultural output in 1732 reached a maximum of 52 million *septiers* a year.[100] With a population of 17.4 million and an estimated per capita consumption of 2.5 *septiers* annually, the total consumption of agricultural produce in France was 43 million *septiers* a year. After allowing for several deductions, including grain consumption in the colonies, feedstock supply to animals and storage of grain, the country was left with a small surplus of 3.6 million *septiers*. This, Zinzendorf argued, was certainly not enough to support the popular belief that the country benefitted from an almost inexhaustible fertility of land. The frequent famines over the last century were good evidence that output, unevenly spread across provinces, was mediocre.[101]

In terms of the surface of arable land, Zinzendorf conceded, France might well be self-sufficient. However, physical barriers between provinces made domestic agricultural trade difficult. Demand for grain was uneven. Major cities consumed large amounts of produce, and overseas colonies required continuous supplies. Grain shortage and degradation made harvests unprofitable. There was a threat of domestic famine; instead of importing produce, the state did not react. With depressed domestic prices, landowners could not cover their production costs, so they sought to make sales abroad where they could take advantage of higher grain prices. However, the government failed to track outflows of produce. Under the current ruler, Zinzendorf argued, agricultural self-sufficiency was an impossible undertaking. Officials had no records on the consumption in the provinces. Unlike Italy, the United Provinces and England, the French failed to move produce between domestic provinces and did not built granaries to cover future demand.[102] Moreover, the

[99] Zinzendorf did not give the author or the date of the text on which the extract was based. It might have been a private and anonymous document on agriculture presented in 1749 by the controlleur général Machault D'Arnouville: see Dupont de Nemours, *Analyse historique de la législation des grains depuis 1692* (Paris, 1789), pp. 90–3 and Marcel Marion, *Machault d'Arnouville, Étude sur l'histoire du contrôle général des finances de 1749 à 1754* (Paris, 1891), pp. 429–31.

[100] Zinzendorf, 'Mémoire sur les richesses', fols 25–26. A *septier* was a measurement unit for grain and liquid.

[101] Ibid., fols 26v–29r.

[102] Ibid., fols 29v–30v. Both the Italian states and the United Provinces made use of granaries and moved agricultural produce to areas where it was needed. In England, the government used an active trade policy. In times of surplus production and falling prices, it encouraged exports and, in case of production shortages, offered incentives for merchants to import foreign produce: ibid., fols 31r–32v.

'*esprit de désunion*' among the country's *Intendants de Commerce* aggravated the situation. The *Intendants* pursued parochial policies and managed their provinces like closed and independent entities. They refused to share agricultural surpluses to the point of choosing a degradation of produce over distributing excess production to other provinces. In 1751, Zinzendorf maintained, in horrendous examples of '*guerre civile dans la famine*', some provinces were guarding their surplus whereas others suffered from famine. The grain from the surplus provinces became idle and because the French refused to help each other, produce had to be imported from abroad.[103]

The absence of intelligent government planning, Zinzendorf argued, contributed decisively to the shortages. First, the state refused the export of grain. Due to the lack of domestic demand, produce began to degrade and created an earnings loss for peasants. It led to social unrest which eventually forced the state to reverse the export ban. Subsequently, Zinzendorf observed, due to a lack of data on agricultural productivity, the government pursued an uncontrolled and open-ended export policy. Merchants would quickly sell down their surpluses, and after a bad harvest in France, foreigners would resell the produce back at inflated prices. Bad government policies, therefore, turned agricultural self-sufficiency into insufficiency. Zinzendorf pointed out that French experts, who included Melon, Charles-Henri Dutot and Charles Dupin, could not have arrived at the same conclusions. They did not have the facts and figures on harvest yields, consumption and surplus production from Fulvy's document and thus could only reason from conjectures.[104]

Agricultural supply was difficult enough during times of peace. War, which required large-scale provisioning, would make the shortfalls in France more acute. French officials had confirmed to Zinzendorf that during the War of the Austrian Succession, Guyenne and the province of Languedoc had been struck by famine. During the War of the Spanish Succession, when France had suffered from food shortage, Dutch merchants had smuggled produce to France, and England had supplied the city of Lyon with grain. An efficient way to fight against France, Zinzendorf suggested, would be for its enemies to withhold agricultural imports to the country.[105]

[103] Ibid., fols 34r–35v.
[104] Ibid., fols 36–36v; fols 37r–39r.
[105] Ibid., fols 40r–42v.

Agriculture was certainly not a preferential activity for the state. Not only did the government fail to support its development, it also implemented measures which actively contributed to the poor state of agriculture. The army, the militia and industry were all draining peasant resource, resulting in lower agricultural output. Rural villages had a surplus of females, but the harsh conditions of labour threatened women's fertility at an early stage. Agricultural depopulation was an important challenge for France. Financial considerations and taxation, Zinzendorf thought, were additional impediments to productivity. The legacy of Louis XIV had created high levels of debt and expenses which made tax decreases unacceptable to the state. Farmers were crushed by the burden of taxes and randomness of tax levels and did not have sufficient capital to reinvest in the land. Their output was poor, and the yields deteriorated. Agricultural productivity kept falling.[106]

For successful commercial activities, France had the necessary prerequisites. It was located at the centre of European trade. It had fertile land, a good climate and a large number of manufacturers. Nevertheless, the country's manufacturing and commercial activities were not developed.[107] To appraise the current state of French commerce, Zinzendorf decided to talk to established merchants in Lorient, Nantes, St Malo and Paris. All of them, he noted, agreed that trade had declined since the peace treaty of Aix-La-Chapelle (1748).[108] The merchants suggested a variety of reasons: the war, in general, had depressed economic activity in France and had generated corresponding trade gains for its enemies; large domestic merchant houses in Lyon, Marseilles, Bordeaux and Nantes went bankrupt; and a number of traders did not have sufficient financial reserves to replace vessels which had been lost during the conflict. Also, Zinzendorf learned, French sailors had either been killed or made prisoners by the English. The few who remained in France demanded high wages which reduced profits for merchants. The war broke the lucrative trade networks with the American colonies. In general, France suffered from a dramatic fall in exports.

To these, Zinzendorf added two of his own observations. Both, he thought, were good evidence of a deceleration of French commerce. First, given that the Compagnie des Indes required debt financing for its operations, it was likely that small merchants were also short of money. Second,

[106] Ibid., fols 42v–51r.
[107] Ibid., fols 51v–52r.
[108] Ibid., fols 59v–60r.

the success of insurance companies reflected the general strength of commerce. If they were profitable, it was a sign that merchants were buying equipment for their ships. However, the new insurance company in Paris was making a loss, and for Zinzendorf, it was an indication that commercial activity was sluggish.[109]

These arguments on trade were very relevant since it was impossible to have an accurate knowledge of French commerce. Unlike in England where the balance of trade was published, France considered these activities to be a state secret. According to an expert with whom Zinzendorf had discussed the issue, the French balance of trade had decreased significantly.[110] The lack of expertise and skill among government officials, Zinzendorf thought, was partly to blame for the poor trading record. Individuals had bought for themselves positions in government. They had no understanding of commerce, finance and naval affairs and did not receive appropriate training for their administrative roles. In government, individual gain and jealousies were prevalent.[111]

Susceptible to domestic pressure groups, the government adopted policies without due regard to commerce. Zinzendorf gave the example of the use of tobacco, which had become widespread in France and which exceeded domestic production. The appropriate policy, he thought, would have been to develop the vast unexploited tobacco plantations in the fields of American Louisiana. However, domestic investors meddled in the policy to influence its outcome. They insisted on destroying the existing plantations and set up a new production. Their aim was to keep tight control of revenues. For France, the result was continuing dependency on imports of English tobacco from Virginia.[112]

As in agriculture, inappropriate taxation held back success in trade. The state, Zinzendorf thought, should apply low taxes on surplus products to encourage export and with low tariffs enable the import of commodities which were vital for domestic industry. However, it did just the opposite: for exports of some agricultural surplus, tariffs were kept high and the country suffered a loss of revenue. The Dutch bought French

[109] Ibid., fols 64v–65v.

[110] Even though still in surplus by 9m. liv., Zinzendorf had learned, it had fallen by 40 per cent from its peak: ibid., fols 66–68v.

[111] The *conseil de commerce* in Paris was a good example. It was a forum for the representatives of the 12 main commercial centres in France to coordinate policies. However, due to rivalries among the representatives, meetings did not take place: ibid., fol. 71v.

[112] Ibid., fols 70v–72; fols 73r–73v; fols 77v–78r.

salt, but mixed it together with salt from Portugal which did not incur tariffs and was more affordable. In addition, the ruler taxed English and Spanish linen yarn which were necessary for the domestic production of fine cloth. Between provinces, France kept an ancient system of high tariffs which distorted trade. It created confusion among tradesmen, and the government confiscated the produce of merchants who did not comply with the latest legislation put out by the local trade bureaus.[113]

On Zinzendorf's diagnosis, the structures of French trade were weak. The country did not have the same successful policies as England, where, through Cromwell's Navigation Act of 1651, commerce could only be undertaken using domestic vessels.[114] The Act, Zinzendorf thought, was the foundation of English '*grandeur*'.[115] Profits from navigation were not shared with other nations, and foreign merchants were given limited access to English ports: they could only sell their produce if it was brought in on their own ships and, in addition, had to load English merchandise equivalent to half of the value of their own goods. These restrictions made English tradesmen invest in their own vessels. It allowed them to sail abroad and buy produce cheaper directly from local sources. Without these measures, foreigners would have shipped the same products to England and would have sold them at significantly higher prices to the domestic customers.[116] France, on the other hand, allowed foreign ships to make full use of its harbours. The Dutch controlled the cabotage in France, and its merchants could sell freely in the country. The French, Zinzendorf maintained, hardly carried out any commerce in Europe: foreign merchants loaded produce from France and its colonies directly in French ports and traded them on.[117]

Other structural impediments to French navigation were the high costs of manning vessels and the failure by the government to recognise the increasing competition in commerce. Labour was more mobile and willing to move abroad to find employment. Whereas other countries understood the growing international dimension of trade, the greed of French officials

[113] Ibid., fols 73v–75v.

[114] Ibid., fols 78v–79r. 'Le commerce d'une nation n'approchera ou ne s'éloignera donc de la perfection, qu'autant que ces maximes seront plus ou moins conformes à celles de l'Angleterre. Or celles de la France y sont diametralement opposées; donc je me crois autorisé à affirmer que le commerce de cette Nation est vicieux dans sa Nature'.

[115] Ibid., fol. 78v.

[116] Ibid., fols 79v–80v; fol. 81v.

[117] Ibid., fols 79v–80r; fols 80v–83r.

and inspectors created a poor climate for business and prompted skilled workers to move abroad.[118] Moreover, the United Provinces and England had lower borrowing costs and were able to offer their produce at more advantageous prices.[119] Finally, Zinzendorf thought, elements in the Catholic religion and French culture clashed with trade considerations. The high number of public holidays was an economic disadvantage. Workers in Protestant countries, like England, could work at least 40 days more a year. For them, this translated into a direct price advantage of more than 14 per cent because, in addition to other costs, French traders had to absorb the holiday pay of their workers. French culture, Zinzendorf argued, perverted the '*génie national*'. If poor, Frenchmen were hard-working. But once affluent, they became only interested in luxury. It was an attitude, Zinzendorf thought, which was passed on in the family. Instead of teaching best commercial knowledge to subsequent generations, French merchants kept repeating the same mistakes in business. In England or the United Provinces, assiduous merchants could triple their fortunes over 30–40 years and thus contribute to an increase of national wealth. France suffered from an '*esprit de désinteressement*'.[120]

The second part of the 'Mémoire sur les richesses, le commerce et les finances de la France' dealt with money and credit. Both, Zinzendorf argued, were the lifeblood of commerce and thus needed to be examined in a French context.[121] Zinzendorf began by estimating the monetary base of France. Again, data were not readily available, but Zinzendorf had a stroke of good fortune when he did the research. He was able to review a private account which had been written in 1744 by Claude Dupin, a government official. The document belonged to the private papers of French noblemen, including Louis François de Bourbon, Prince of Conti and Louis de Bourbon, Count of Clermont. The starting point of Zinzendorf's calculation was Dupin's estimate of 1300 million of specie.[122] Between 1744 and 1752, Zinzendorf argued, the amount of money in the French

[118] Ibid., fols 83v–87r.

[119] The high rate of interest in France of 6 per cent, Zinzendorf argued, discouraged productive activities. Commercial opportunities were not pursued unless they yielded at least a 9 per cent return. In the United Provinces, the lower rate of interest of 2.5 per cent gave more incentives for commerce. So for Dutch traders, a 5 per cent return on a business enterprise was already attractive: ibid., fols 87r–89r.

[120] Ibid., fols 89r–93r.

[121] Ibid., fol. 93v.

[122] Ibid., fols 94–95v.

economy did not increase.[123] On the contrary, it decreased. Money was spent to subsidise Bavaria and Prussia, and to support military personnel stationed in Italy, Germany and the United Provinces. With the military expenses and the purchases of agricultural produce between October 1748 and March 1750, the aggregate loss of specie was 200 million. Thus by 1752, the monetary base had contracted to 1100 million.[124]

However, in comparison with other European nations, the monetary base was still very large. It was more than three times the amount of specie available in England and represented, Zinzendorf speculated, probably one-fifth of the monetary base in Europe. With such impressive monetary wealth, a country should surely dominate other nations. Previously, this would have been the case. But the introduction of credit, he argued, had changed the rules of the game.[125] Weaker nations, which understood the use of credit, could decisively strengthen their economies. Similarly, countries which failed to take advantage of credit lost power. So, to assess the power of a 'nation', credit had to be added to the monetary base. England was a very good example: it had a small amount of specie, and its territory and population were one-third the size of France. Through credit, the country increased its financial firepower, and during the War of the Spanish Succession it could muster a similar military force to France. State credit was upheld by public confidence. Public opinion, in turn, was guided by market forces of demand and supply and confidence in the rule of law. The easier public debt instruments circulated and traded, Zinzendorf argued, the higher was their usefulness for commerce.

In detailed tables, Zinzendorf provided an overview of the types of government borrowing in France. The latter included debt of the Hôtel de Ville, obligations raised on tax receipts, bonds by the Compagnie des Indes and miscellaneous debt on the collection of income taxes.[126] For

[123] For Zinzendorf, an increase in specie could only have resulted from trade since no new specie had arrived from abroad or had been minted domestically. However, from 1743 to 1748, the balance of trade was negative and, in any case, any positive effect would have been neutralised by the extraordinary military expenses for the War of the Austrian Succession: ibid., fols 96v–97r.

[124] Ibid., fols 96v–97r.

[125] Ibid., fols 97r–98v.

[126] Zinzendorf excluded *tontines* and the *rentes viagères*, both of types of life annuities, because they did not circulate. He also excluded *crédits des fermiers* and *revenus généraux*. Although these financial papers were traded, he did not consider them to be part of government borrowing, see ibid., fol. 108r. On the significance and performance of French Estates' debt issues, see Mark Potter and Jean-Laurent Rosenthal, 'Politics and Public Finance in

each type of debt, Zinzendorf specified the standard denomination and rate of interest. By comparing daily market prices with par values, he concluded that the borrowings traded at discounts of approximately 50–85 per cent to par value.[127] The low prices were the result of a lack in demand which translated into low trading volumes. Public paper recently issued by the current government was the exception. It traded above the issue prices because it had smaller denominations, and the French public had confidence in the economic policies of the *controleur général*.[128] In financial tables, Zinzendorf compared the market value of French debt instruments with their actual traded value. The differences were startling. The par value of government borrowing was 1702 million *livres*. The market value however was only 300 million *livres*, less than 20 per cent of the original value. In total, Zinzendorf concluded, France had a monetary wealth of 1400 million *livres*: 1100 million *livres* of specie and only 300 million *livres* of public debt which circulated.[129]

The same analysis for English government borrowing gave a radically different picture. Zinzendorf used financial data of December 1751 which he had received from the Charles François Thaon de Revel. The latter was a military official and close friend of Gaston-Pierre de Lévis-Mirepoix, the French ambassador in London, and had recently returned from England to Paris.[130] According to these figures, the monetary wealth in England, expressed in French currency, was approximately 2300 million *livres*: 300 million *livres* of specie and 2000 million *livres* of bonds in circulation.[131] This reflected the different dynamics of English state credit. England had a lower rate of interest than France, at 3 per cent versus 5 per cent, and different types of public borrowing. Government debt consisted mainly of bonds of the Bank of England, the East India Company and the South Sea Company. These institutions could lend money to the government which they had received as deposits from their shareholders. As they had profitable

France: The Estates of Burgundy, 1660–1790', *Journal of Interdisciplinary History*, 27:4 (1997), pp. 577–612.

[127] Zinzendorf, 'Mémoire sur les richesses', fols 103v–105v. The calculation of the discount was based on the difference between the rate of interest in France and the actual yield of the public debt instruments. The former was 5 per cent, and most of the government borrowing which was traded had yields of between 1 and 2.5 per cent: ibid., fol. 104r.

[128] Ibid., fols 105v–107r.

[129] Ibid., fols 107r–108v.

[130] Ibid., footnote, fol. 108v.

[131] Ibid., fols 111–112v.

operations, they could pay out a higher return to their shareholders than the interest of 3 per cent they would receive from the government on their money advances. English public debt instruments, supported by public confidence, traded on premiums of more than 20 per cent to par values.[132] In addition, they were liquid and could easily be converted into specie. Their liquidity created a strong velocity of circulation.[133] Hence, Zinzendorf observed, England had significantly more monetary wealth than France. Even though the latter had three times more specie than England, its '*masse circulante*' was 30 per cent less.[134] The French economy, in effect, had been overtaken by a rival nation.[135]

These arguments, Zinzendorf recognised, were not easy to follow. One important criticism was that public borrowing was, in effect, a sign of poverty rather than wealth. By extension, extensive state credit would eventually lead to national bankruptcy. To address this, Zinzendorf developed three separate arguments: on the nature of public credit, its application in France and its propensity for economic instability.[136] The example of England was proof that public debt instruments could be a solid foundation of wealth. Before the creation of the Bank of England and state credit, the government, even though virtually debt free, struggled to borrow at 16 per cent. Now, with established credit, the rate of interest in England had fallen to 3 per cent and the public debt instruments were priced at a premium to face values. This, Zinzendorf argued, was the relevant context to examine the purpose of credit.

He set out a model of two nations which were similar in terms of land, agriculture and commerce, but different in monetary wealth. The first country had 500 million of specie which was sufficient to support agriculture and industry. The second country had only half this amount of specie. Consequently, some of the productive activity in the second country could not be undertaken, and it had to send its produce abroad to be manufactured. Consider now, Zinzendorf continued, the same two countries with equal economies and the same amount of specie. If the second country

[132] Ibid., fols 109r–110v.

[133] On the theory of velocity in the context of eighteenth-century economies, see Joseph Vogl, *Kalkül und Leidenschaft. Poetik des ökonomischen Menschen* (Zurich: Diaphanes, 2008), pp. 223–34.

[134] For France, Zinzendorf calculated a total '*masse circulante*' of 1403m. liv., for England 2041m. liv.: ibid., fol. 112v.

[135] Ibid., fol. 112r.

[136] Ibid., fols 112v–113r.

doubled its monetary base to 1000 million, it will, as it has already been operating at full capacity before, attract labour from abroad who will want to take up work in its growing economy. The commercial activity of the second country will develop, and its international economic competitiveness will increase. Thereby, it should be able to promote its international standing and influence. The main beneficiary of this newly created wealth would be the country's ruler, who would find more scope for taxation among its citizens.[137]

The second nation in Zinzendorf's model was England. It first doubled, and then quadrupled its capital base. But rather than using conventional means of growing industry and commerce, which were slow processes, England chose credit. By 'fictitiously' doubling the fund deposited at the Bank of England and by increasing the velocity of public debt instruments, the government propelled the country forward to its current position of power. It resulted in the growth of commerce and hence in the growth of real wealth. The additional wealth, in turn, gave opportunity for more use of credit. It created a virtuous circle which catapulted the economy of England above France. It was, Zinzendorf thought, an incredible achievement that England, with merely a third of the population, land mass and money of France, could overtake its 'dangerous neighbour'. Without credit, Zinzendorf concluded, England's international standing and commercial activity would shrink to reflect its modest natural wealth.[138]

The paucity or abundance of money in an economy was determined by the rate of interest. Before the discoveries of the mines in the new world the rate of interest was, generally, 10 per cent. Following the large shipments of specie from Peru to Europe, the rate of interest had decreased by more than half. Variations in the rate of interest between nations in Europe were dictated by the amount of specie available. Poland and Hungary, with little use of money, had higher rates of interest of 8 per cent and 6 per cent respectively. In richer countries, the rate of interest was considerably lower: 3 per cent in England and, the lowest, 2½ per cent in the United Provinces. An increase of credit, Zinzendorf pointed out, had the same effect as the increase of specie and would drive down the rate of interest. France however, where specie was plentiful but the rate of interest high, was an exception to this rule. Zinzendorf examined its case in the second argument.[139]

[137] Ibid., fols 115r–116v.
[138] Ibid., fols 116v–117v.
[139] Ibid., fols 117v–118v.

To round off the discussion and get a full appreciation of the utility of credit in lowering the rate of interest, Zinzendorf proposed to examine the influence of the rate of interest on two key economic parameters: the value of land and the personal wealth of the population. In the *dixme royale*, Zinzendorf argued, Vauban had shown that the value of land was 100 times larger than the value of specie. The value of land was inversely correlated with the rate of interest. On this basis, the value of land would increase from 100 to 120 with a corresponding fall of the rate of interest from 5 to 4 per cent. Therefore, a fall of the latter would increase the value of land which represented a permanent and solid source of wealth.[140] Second, Zinzendorf thought, an increase in the monetary base with a corresponding reduction in the rate of interest would increase personal wealth. The landowners, on whom the government relied to service its debt, generated only a 3 per cent return from their assets. The *rentiers*, however, who were the creditors of the state, charged a rate of interest of 5 per cent. A larger quantity of money would enable the ruler to either redeem government debt or reduce the interest charges on the borrowing, and thereby ease the payment burden on the landowners.[141] These advantages applied to credit as well as to specie. However, credit offered additional economic advantages which money did not have.

Credit had four benefits. First, for a country, it was in general not possible to create commercial activities from scratch: it was too challenging for a nation to find enough capital to get commerce going, to create sufficient velocity of money and provide good income for the population. If commerce could be established, it would become the engine of the economy. But this, Zinzendorf thought, was a slow process. Profits could only grow at a modest pace due to the associated costs of undertaking commercial activities: commodity and production costs, international price competition, import penetration from other nations in exchange for export opportunities, and, generally, the jealousy of rival nations which sought to prevent a too-rapid rise of a new competitor. Based on these assumptions, France, Zinzendorf calculated, with its current amount of specie and positive balance of trade, would take 120 years to double its capital, whereas a well-administered system of credit could achieve in just

[140] As explanation, Zinzendorf provided a numerical example in a footnote: assuming land would yield 5000, its value would be 100,000 fr. at a rate of interest of 5 per cent. The value of the same piece of land would rise to 120,000 if the rate of interest would drop to 4 per cent: ibid., fol. 119v.

[141] Ibid., fols 118v–120v.

a few years what lucrative commerce could not accomplish in over a century. Credit, Zinzendorf argued, would triple and quadruple the national capital base and create swiftly continuous prosperity. It would have taken a long time to achieve the same outcome with commercial activities only, and it would have been a very costly undertaking.[142]

Second, paper as money equivalent was more common than specie. It was more convenient than specie to transport, to store and to use for larger transactions. For merchants, it removed the threat of money clipping and made it the payment method of choice for international transactions. Traders would not have to count specie any longer, and public paper could have an easy settlement mechanism. Large amounts of money in paper could be transferred by post between two geographic points of trade at much lower cost than specie. Also, the ease of use made it attractive to undertake transactions with comparatively small profits. Lower transactions costs, on aggregate, would make a very large difference to commercial profit and enable traders to sell at more advantageous prices.[143] Third, until a merchant was ready to start production and sell his produce, borrowing in specie created a net interest cost for him. Paper credit had a double advantage: it could become an instrument to finance production as a liquid bond, with a market price, generated interest income and capital gains. The merchant would also have a commercial benefit as, with lower production costs, he could sell his produce at more competitive prices.[144] Fourth, Zinzendorf argued, credit was a good way to provide a ruler with emergency financing. Traditional means of credit from landowners were slow to organise, and investors would only very reluctantly recall committed capital from established borrowers to lend, at short notice and without solid collateral, to a new government borrower. Moreover, creditors were wary of the administrative process involved with traditional government debt and were fearful of the haggling and chasing that was necessary to recoup money from a bankrupt state. This was different in a country where credit was established. Bonds, which were traded and had an active market, created confidence for investors and allowed an easy switch between paper and specie. They also opened up the market for emergency government financing. In this way, England had easy access to debt markets.[145]

[142] Ibid., fols 120v–122r.
[143] Ibid., fols 122r–123v.
[144] Ibid., fols 124r–125r.
[145] Ibid., fols 125r–126v.

In theory, France could introduce a system of credit like England, but, Zinzendorf thought, it was impossible in practice.[146] The government in France was the insurmountable obstacle to managing state credit like England. The form, but not the nature of government, Zinzendorf explained, was at fault. A monarchy, after all, was the most perfect system for producing the best credit arrangement which did not exist so far. In England, it was deficient because the nation was continuously defying its ruler. Yet, the French government was unable to exploit the advantages which a monarchy—as the preferential form of government—offered. The abuse of authority and the unlimited powers given to ministers had destroyed the public confidence which was necessary for the introduction of state credit. France did not follow regular political processes. Transparent political deliberations and guidelines for government departments on how to conduct business were the basis for public confidence. France did not have them. French ministers were despots in their departments and acted with self-interest. Often decision-making by force, intrigue and secret schemes prevailed, and no consideration was given for the public good.

The *parlement* was an admirable institution which could cement public confidence. It was created as a check and a sounding board for ministers and as the vehicle to make the voice of the people heard. But French ministers refused involvement by the *parlements*, convinced that they limited their freedom to govern. As the public understood that the institution which represented their interests was rejected, it was inconceivable that introduction of state credit, which assumed complete confidence in the government, would be successful. The French predicament, Zinzendorf thought, was the result of Richelieu's domestic policies which had promoted a government without checks and balances. What was needed was a functioning representative assembly with limited control. The English model was impractical: the powers of parliament, Zinzendorf thought, were too extensive.[147]

Zinzendorf's second concern was the legacy of excesses and abuses of the credit system. For many years, the twin pillars of financial management in France had been the increase of specie and the forced reduction of the rate of interest. Zinzendorf argued that the forced devaluation of 1726 was, in effect, a concealed national bankruptcy. It was an 'unjust policy measure' designed by the government to help debtors at the expense of creditors. It reduced the value of creditors' loans by approximately half from the time

[146] Ibid., fol. 139v.
[147] Ibid., fols 126v–129v.

when credit had been extended to Louis XIV.[148] The forced reduction of the rate of interest was even more detrimental to creditors. Government loans under Louis XIV, issued by the Hôtel de Ville at 5 per cent, currently only paid 2½ per cent. Even though the ruler could stop interest payments, he could not prevent the erosion of public confidence in his bonds. This pushed down the value of the papers and saw them trade at a loss. The market prices of the bonds of the Hôtel de Ville and the obligations on the government's tax receipts borrowing traded at half their par values.

Was it likely, Zinzendorf asked, that public confidence could be re-established in France? Could France have a financial system like England's? He was not convinced. The low number of French public debt instruments which were actively traded could not truly be referred to as state credit.[149] In France, the bonds in circulation represented only a quarter of the amount of specie. Also, out of 300 million bonds in circulation, only 60 per cent was direct state borrowing—the balance was debt issued by the Compagnie des Indes. In comparison, England's state credit, without bank bills, was more than five times as large as its total amount of specie. Moreover, Zinzendorf added, the French public credit 'in circulation' was not in reality circulating. Only a few shares a day, and this with much effort, were traded. Manipulation and intervention guaranteed that market prices could be maintained. The government had to orchestrate transactions through third parties which bought and sold according to the prescriptions of the state. There was no depth in the market. One larger sale of public bonds would, in all certainty, immediately depress prices. Zinzendorf gave the example of de Monmartel's sale of lottery tickets which, when recently executed, made the price fall by 40 per cent.[150] Public debt instruments were not held by investors for any length of time. At the first appearance of risk, they were sold straight away. The most pertinent reflection of the loss of confidence in French state credit was the persistent high rate of interest. Given France's abundance of specie, it should be lower than in other countries. However, it remained at 5 per cent. Investors demanded a higher risk premium to lend to the ruler. In comparison, commercial paper debt, which tended to be short-term and very risky, traded at a rate of interest of 6 per cent: only a 1 per cent premium over public debt.[151]

[148] Ibid., fols 129v–131r.

[149] 'La circulation mediocre des effets Royaux qui ce fait ici, ne merite pas d'être appellée de ce nom': ibid., fol. 132v.

[150] Ibid., fols 132r–133v.

[151] Ibid., fols 133v–135r.

So far, the lack of public confidence had been considered simply as an obstacle to introduce a good working system for general credit. But, Zinzendorf continued, the crisis of public confidence in France had deeper and more serious implications: it also eroded current state credit. A discerning public understood the terrible state of public finances. Despite the government's undertaking to repay its debt annually and run lotteries, abuse of government ministers, favouritism and personal interests were endemic to the system. An imminent increase of the *taille* would only hit the poorer parts of the population. As the ruler made no effort to fix these problems, investors, Zinzendorf argued, had given up hope, and there was despondency in France.[152] Among the public, there was a deep-seated expectation that government had to resort to drastic policy measures to deal with situations which were beyond its control. The opposition of stakeholders and *parlement* to ministers together with the personal animosities created a toxic atmosphere.[153] Zinzendorf illustrated the government's predicament with a set of examples: the clergy stopped giving charitable donations to the ruler and left a financial shortfall for the state; the provinces, refusing to pay the tax of the *vingtième*, did not submit their wealth declarations for assessment of their profitability; and the *fermiers généraux* were forced by government to have their accounts audited in order to assess their profitability. In this context, Zinzendorf held Monmartel's lending scheme in high esteem. During time of war, the astute and able statesman was able to keep the rate of interest down and was lending to the government with a rate of interest of 5 per cent. He set up a loan bureau under his name and offered lending for small amounts. As he paid the 5 per cent rate of interest one year in advance, the public had confidence in his debt scheme and used his bonds like specie. His paper had a very good take-up. Monmartel lent the government money at an interest rate of 7⅓ per cent, including charges, and thus provided a financial lifeline to the state. Despite the small amounts deposited, the good circulation of his bonds created a large lending volume. At any one time, more than 120 million of Monmartel's paper were in circulation. Monmartel's credit was good; the government's was bad.[154]

Zinzendorf also gave details of the most recent financial operation undertaken by the French government at the time he wrote the 'Mémoire sur les richesses, le commerce et les finances de la France'. The operation,

[152] 'L'abbatement des esprits est extrême': ibid., fol. 136r.
[153] Ibid., fols 135–138v.
[154] Ibid., footnotes: fols 136v, 137r, 137v–138r.

Zinzendorf thought, provided pertinent evidence of the government's poor credit standing and the lack of self-confidence it had in its debt-raising capabilities. The ruler was close to raising a debt amount of 45 million through an irregular procedure. The latter consisted of an *arrêt du Conseil du Roy* and would bypass the consent of the *parlements*. Half of the debt was raised in specie and the balance through bonds of the Hôtel de Ville which the government accepted at par values even though they traded at large discounts. Issued during peace time, Zinzendorf calculated that this debt carried a rate of interest of 6⅙ per cent which was higher than the rate of interest Monmartel managed to secure during the war years. However, it was noteworthy that even though public confidence in general was lacking, investors continued to participate in debt issues by the government. The reason, Zinzendorf thought, could be attributed to a certain amount of short-term confidence by the public in the current government and to the belief that public debt instruments could be easily swapped back into money.[155]

In his third argument, Zinzendorf refuted the claim that English credit had no stable foundation and could be easily destroyed due to its small money base.[156] The proponents of this view, he argued, were confusing state credit with personal credit. Typically, the value of the latter was much larger than the assets of an individual. The net worth corresponded to one-tenth of the size of personal credit. State credit, on the other hand, corresponded to deposits in banks which were revolving and employed in the economy.[157] Critics thought that there was not enough money in the economy to redeem the public paper in circulation, and that, therefore, the state was unable to repay the national debt: public bonds were artificially increasing the value of specie, and they represented merely 'imaginary wealth'. These critics, Zinzendorf argued, did not understand that public debt instruments were different to letters of exchange. The latter had a monetary value. State credit, however, represented national wealth which the state extended via public bonds to creditors. The concept was equivalent to a piece of real estate which was traded by investors and in circulation in the economy.[158]

[155] Ibid., footnote, fols 138v–139v.

[156] Ibid., fols 139v–140r.

[157] Zinzendorf gave the example of the Bank of Amsterdam: ibid., footnote, fol. 140r. See also the discussion 'The Survey of European Banks' in Chap. 5.

[158] Ibid., fols 140r–141v.

National wealth was larger than the amount of money in an economy, in the same way as the total value of land in a state was superior to its cash reserves. The value of an asset was equivalent to the amount of money which yielded the same revenue as the asset. In a country with a rate of interest of 5 per cent, Zinzendorf observed, 500 of revenue in bonds had to be worth 10,000 in specie. The same would hold true for land where revenue of 500 would produce a value of 10,000. English national wealth, Zinzendorf argued, had to be considered in this way and was as solid as the value of land. Here, public bonds gave a true representation of the value of state credit. The value of national debt owned by creditors was accurately reflected by the price of the public debt instruments in circulation. England had established a good legal framework for the circulation of public bonds, and had removed administrative hurdles for buying and selling them.[159]

Was the comparison, critics would argue, between a public bond and a letter of exchange not a valid argument given that the state, similar to a merchant, guaranteed payment? The ruler, Zinzendorf replied, did promise repayment of the debt, but, unlike in commerce, he could set his own repayment terms. The important advantage of an established system of state credit was that creditors were not looking for repayment of the borrowings. Credit was a useful tool for commerce and for the purchase of land. If required, public debt instruments could be easily exchanged for money. Provided that the government could credibly commit to a timely service of the interest payable, demand would exceed the supply of state credit. In this respect too, France was different to England. To reassure creditors, the French government had to be clear at the outset about the repayment terms of its borrowing. In England, there were no such constraints for the repayment of public credit.[160]

English state credit, however, would be affected by economic difficulties. A fall in tax revenues, a decrease in commercial activity or military conflict would lead to sudden variations in interest payments. A cessation of interest payment by the government would invariably trigger a fall of the prices of public bonds. If the causes of these events were transient, the disruption to credit would be temporary, and after the resumption of regular interest payments, public confidence would gradually return. The Bank of England as well as the Bank of Scotland had periods of discredit,

[159] Ibid., fols 141v–142v.
[160] Ibid., fols 143r–143v.

but succeeded to re-establish their creditworthiness with ease. If both banks could regain commercial credibility, then surely creditors would eventually regain confidence in state credit.[161]

Even if the ruler was forced to reduce the rate of interest of government borrowing, state credit in England would not be completely lost. A fall of the rate of interest by half would lead to a proportional fall by half of the value of debt. Such reductions would have much less of a sustained impact than in France.[162] The large value of public bonds in circulation, Zinzendorf thought, would keep England's wealth comfortably ahead of France. The English government was interested in maintaining a system of state credit which had served it well. So after political upheavals, it would seize the first opportunity to re-establish credit. The relationship between domestic debtors and creditors was strong. In England, there was no interest in destabilising individual market participants or threatening the entire political framework.[163]

The solid state credit in England was reinforced by the government's impressive conduct in financial affairs. Even though, Zinzendorf indicated, he hoped to develop his understanding of English finances, he nevertheless could highlight key aspects of English financial policy. The state used three institutions for its financial policy-making: the Bank of England, the East India Company and the South Sea Company. These institutions were managed by a sizeable number of England's wealthy commercial elite. In 1749, after the peace treaty of Aix-La-Chapelle, they offered a general redemption of public debt to achieve a voluntary decrease of the rate of interest on public borrowing to 3 per cent. This represented, Zinzendorf argued, a strong case against the third argument. Public debt instruments, he concluded, could be a solid foundation of wealth, and England provided the example of how it could be done successfully.[164]

In the conclusion of the 'Mémoire sur les richesses, le commerce et les finances de la France', Zinzendorf offered a progressive policy prescription for the monarchy. A country, he thought, had to have good natural resources to be able to exploit the power of state credit. At its basis, state credit required a big state like France, with a significant population, fertile

[161] Ibid., fols 143v–145v.

[162] Ibid., fols 145v.

[163] Ibid., fols 145v–147r.

[164] Ibid., fols 147r–148r. For Zinzendorf's fuller account of the Bank of England, see Chap. 5, particularly section 'The Survey of European Banks'.

land and the ability to conduct profitable commerce. If this state were to be governed by a ruler who had the confidence of the public, it could, with a system of state credit like the one found in England, become the leading power in Europe. Its industry would be re-invigorated and commerce would be profitable. Government income would increase, and the population could benefit from lower taxes. The country would have the economic resources to raise a stronger military force than England's and could swiftly become the dominant force in Europe.[165]

Zinzendorf's formative years in France were very productive. He collected valuable information on the French economy and the state, planned and undertook commercial travels and established important relationships with local experts. Zinzendorf made an impression: more than 15 years later, some of his contacts in France still had good memories of him.[166] Except for the anecdotes on the French court, Zinzendorf wrote his accounts for Kaunitz. The findings were new, important and detailed, and Kaunitz often sent copies to Maria Theresa and her husband Francis Stephen. Zinzendorf's main output, the 'Mémoire sur les richesses, le commerce et les finances de la France', should be read in the context of the monarchy's shifting geopolitical interests in Europe. It was an important piece of intelligence on a rival nation, and, in the light of Kaunitz's diplomatic manoeuvring to conclude a new defensive alliance with France, on a possible future continental ally.[167]

Kaunitz, however, had a low opinion of the French government. Soon after his arrival in France, Kaunitz complained about the practices in the administration.[168] In his account of the French court, he noted the sloppy and casual education of Louis XV. Kaunitz commented on the ruler's habit of yawning during council meetings and on Louis' timid nature which would make him shun contact with foreign dignitaries and the public, and prompt him to just move his lips, without talking, during audi-

[165] Ibid., fols 148v–151v.

[166] Letter of Ludwig Zinzendorf to Karl Zinzendorf, 11 February 1767, vol. 64, DOZA in Klingenstein et al. (eds.), *Europäische Aufklärung*, vol. 1, p. 16.

[167] On Kaunitz's efforts to conclude the new treaty with France, see Schilling, *Kaunitz* and William J. McGill, 'The Roots of Policy: Kaunitz in Vienna and Versailles, 1749–1753', *Journal of Modern History*, 43:2 (1971), pp. 228–44.

[168] 'A mesure que je vois de plus près cette cour et le gouvernement intime de cette monarchie, j'y découvre plus de défectuosités. C'est une charrue assez mal attelée et la plupart des choses ne se font que par intrigues et cabales'. Letter of Kaunitz to Koch, Paris, 11 December 1750 in *Correspondance Secrète*, ed. Schlitter, p. 50.

ences with ambassadors.[169] Zinzendorf, too, was highly critical of the government and its economic record. He strongly blamed the state's policies and incompetence for the poor state of the economy, the finances and the navy. Similarly, he criticised the attempts by officials to exert direct influence on the affairs of the Compagnie des Indes. In his notes on the court, under the heading 'commerce', Zinzendorf's succinctly remarked that 'those who govern have no knowledge whatsoever'.[170] But as much as French public officials made a poor impression, Zinzendorf took full advantage of the intellectual life in France. He developed his reading of political economy and sought direct contact with French scholars. In Zinzendorf's writing, the intellectual presence of French political economists can be clearly felt.

[169] Wenzel Anton von Kaunitz: 'Mémoire sur la cour de France 1752' in ed. Vicomte du Dresnay, *La revue de Paris*, 11 (1904), pp. 441–54 at pp. 447–47. It is an extract from Kaunitz's memorandum, 'sur la cour de Versailles', undated, fols 1r–28v, Frankreich Varia 1750–1752, Karton 22, HHStA.

[170] 'Notes on the French Court', undated, fol. 1r, Archive Zinzendorf, Karton 39, NÖLA.

CHAPTER 3

French Intellectual Influence: Melon and Gournay

From the beginning of their association, Kaunitz had encouraged Zinzendorf to develop the skills to understand and evaluate the most advanced economic ideas. In this respect, the 'Mémoire général des recueils des pièces de finance faites par Messieurs Fougerolles, Le Bret, de Vauban, du Guerin de Rademont, de la Jonchère, de M. Le Regent, d'un anonyme, de Boulainvilliers, de M. de Chevalier Renaut, de M. le Marquis de Silly, de M. l'Abbé de St.Pierre' is revealing.[1] The manuscript is part of Karl Zinzendorf's *Nachlaß* and was intended as a manual for economic administrators. Its provenance is unclear, and the author's name and date are not given. The document was probably written in the mid-1740s for Kaunitz while he served as the chief minister of the Austrian Netherlands.[2] At that time, Kaunitz was involved in discussions to reform the finances of the province and support its economy.[3] He probably gave the 'Mémoire

[1] [Anonymous], undated, 'Mémoire général des recueils des pièces de finance faites par Messieurs Fougerolles, Le Bret, de Vauban, du Guerin de Rademont, de la Jonchère, de M. Le Regent, d'un anonyme, de Boulainvilliers, de M. Chevalier Renaut, de M. le Marquis de Silly, de M. l'Abbé de St. Pierre, Tome premier', 159 fols, Cod. 14194, ÖNB. I could not locate other volumes of this document in the archives.

[2] The most recent figures in the document, on the finances of England, were from 1745: ibid., fol. 148r.

[3] William J. McGill, 'The Roots of Policy: Kaunitz in Italy and the Netherlands, 1742–1746', *Central European History*, 1:2 (1968), pp. 131–49, at p. 142.

S. Adler, *Political Economy in the Habsburg Monarchy 1750–1774*,
Palgrave Studies in the History of Finance,
https://doi.org/10.1007/978-3-030-31007-3_3

général' to Zinzendorf as a study guide. In 14 chapters, the document dealt with the French economy and covered the key activities of agriculture, commerce and state credit. It also had separate sections on tolls and taxation as well as two chapters on begging and the celibate which discussed the productivity of citizens. In addition, the author presented an overview of England's political system and its economy, and in the last chapter set out the operations of a new *bureau économique* to improve the French finances and commerce.[4] Throughout the document, he used references and quotes from other writers and included some of their names in the title.

The reason for compiling the 'Mémoire général', the author explained in the introduction, was to emphasise the significance of good financial management. With sound finances, a country could wage war, keep the peace and uphold law and order. The '*sciences économiques*' had a '*utilité indispensable*' and should be recognised as important remits of the state. To reinforce this point, the author used Melon. 'This modern author', he argued, had shown the critical impact of bad economic decision-making: for a country, Melon had argued, the loss of 100,000 men from political miscalculations was less severe than errors made in financial policy. The former could be confined to the initial loss of lives. The latter, however, would have a much wider impact. It could lead to the death of more than 500,000 people and would inevitably cause suffering to the entire nation. Due to a '*préjudice fatal*' in France, political economy had been neglected. It was treated with indifference, and thus major mistakes were unavoidable. It was essential, he argued, to encourage well-trained economic administrators into four key areas of economic policy: the adequate supply and circulation of money in the economy, the development of commerce, the good management of state finances and the growth of agriculture.[5] In addition to Melon, the arguments of Law, Charles-Henri Dutot and Deparcieux feature prominently in the document. Extracts from the latter's work on life expectancy were used in the chapter concerning the impact of a celibate priesthood.[6] Law's arguments on the difference between French and Dutch economic policies were included in the chapter on commerce. His financial scheme and its subsequent appraisal by Melon and Dutot were set out in the section on public credit. The bases

[4] The bureau would be a consultative body of 12 specialist advisers appointed by the ruler. Its operations were set out in 36 brief articles: 'Mémoire général', fols 151r–154v.

[5] Ibid., fol. 2r.

[6] Ibid., fols 113r–114r.

of Law's system, the author of the 'Mémoire général' concluded, had been sound, but the Scotsman had become the 'victim of a force majeure'.[7]

French literature on political economy was a significant intellectual reference point for Zinzendorf. In particular, Melon's *Essai politique sur le commerce* was a key intellectual source for his arguments. This already is evident in Zinzendorf's early essay on state credit: the 'Essai sur l'Établissement d'une Banque générale des États'.[8] His subsequent texts written in France, which were discussed in the previous chapter, also display the presence of Melon's ideas. A further strong influence on Zinzendorf's thinking was his contemporary Jacques Vincent de Gournay. The arguments of Gournay's translation of Sir Josiah Child, *Traités sur le commerce de Josiah Child*, were similar to Zinzendorf's.[9] Like Zinzendorf, Gournay was eager to gain a thorough understanding of the economic processes of other countries. As such, in 1752 he requested an information memorandum on the state of the monarchy's economy from the French embassy in Vienna.[10]

'Essai sur l'Établissement d'une Banque Générale des États'

In the 'Essai sur l'Établissement', a concise text of six folios written before leaving for France in September 1750, Zinzendorf attempted to address the problems of public finances in the monarchy. He completed it in six days.[11] Zinzendorf made the case for the use of circulating public debt instruments in the monarchy which should, he argued, spur the growth of commerce and reinforce the main source of the country's wealth, agriculture. The current credit system in Austria, Zinzendorf recognised, was not

[7] Ibid., fol. 67r.

[8] Ludwig Zinzendorf, 'Essai sur l'Établissement d'une Banque générale des États', 26 Septembre 1750, Nachlaß Zinzendorf, vol. 105, HHStA. The text is defective: it has a hole in the middle of the last page where wording is missing.

[9] For Gournay's translation, see Simone Meyssonnier (ed.), *Traités sur le commerce de Josiah Child suivis des Remarques de Jacques Vincent de Gournay* (Paris, 2008).

[10] [Anonymous], 'Mémoire d'information pour les pays héréditaires de la Maison d'Autriche en Allemagne', 10 August 1752, vol. 82, number 2, pp. 1–37, fonds Gournay, Bibliothèque municipale de Saint-Brieuc.

[11] Eduard Gaston von Pettenegg (ed.), *Ludwig und Karl Grafen und Herren von Zinzendorf. Ihre Selbstbiographien nebst einer kurzen Geschichte des Hauses Zinzendorf* (Vienna, 1879), p. 59.

working. Existing proposals to fix it were inadequate because they were rejected by creditors. He therefore proposed the creation of a new unified bond for the Estates which would satisfy the monarchy's creditors and create economic prosperity.

Zinzendorf began the 'Essai sur l'Établissement' by describing the different classes of state creditors and their economic utility. He then set out the existing proposals to reform the credit system and his reasons for thinking that they would not offer successful remedies for the state's finances. What was needed, he argued, was a new public debt instrument which earned the trust of creditors. The new instrument would not only re-energise state credit but also promote economic growth through an increase in the circulation and in the supply of money. Zinzendorf's analysis conveyed the need for a more radical proposal to reform public credit through the creation of a unified debt instrument.[12]

In setting out the different economic classes of creditors, Zinzendorf's concern was twofold. First, he wanted to show why existing bonds did not work and why his proposal for a new debt instrument was beneficial to creditors. Then, he pointed to a dynamic process between the monarch and the creditors which dictated how a ruler ought to behave towards the providers of capital. While the overall aim for a ruler was to provide happiness to all citizens, it was important that he recognised the different economic contribution, in particular to public debt, of each class of creditors. The appropriate attention and care a sovereign gave to his creditors depended on their respective utility to the state.[13]

Zinzendorf divided investors in public credit into three economic classes. The first and most important group included the landed nobility and the peasantry. Zinzendorf referred to them collectively as *terriers*. It was the largest class by numbers since it included the peasants. The latter, Zinzendorf argued, were virtuous citizens who were often unjustly treated with contempt. The nobility was important for the security and military defence of the state.[14] The second group, the *industrieux*, consisted of tradesmen and manufacturers. They were involved in commerce, and their skills in conducting trade and negotiations were unique assets which *terriers* were not readily able to master. In addition, success in commerce was dependent on access to cheap sources of finance. For the same types of produce, a country

[12] Zinzendorf, 'Essai sur L'Établissement', fol. 3v.

[13] Ibid., fol. 1v.

[14] Ibid., fol. 1r.

would succumb to a rival trading nation who could borrow money more cheaply at a lower rate of interest.[15] The third group were the investors or *rentiers*. Their only asset was capital, which they moved easily in and out of a country. Contrary to the other two economic classes, *rentiers* did not commit important longer-term or fixed assets to the state. For the ruler, they were the most unreliable source of wealth. Their activities were solely driven by profit and by the creditworthiness of borrowers.[16]

Creditor satisfaction, Zinzendorf recognised, was instrumental for the success or failure of public debt operations. Creditors were not willing to accept changes to existing public credit arrangements or consider alternative borrowing facilities which were commonly discussed. The annuity bond, as an alternative borrowing method as it was used in France, could not be implemented in the monarchy. The principle of the annuity as a de facto waiver of a repayment of principal as long as interest payments were met would, Zinzendorf surmised, be rejected by creditors as contravening common debt issue practices.[17] Moreover, a government intervention which would unilaterally lower borrowing costs was a change to existing public credit practices. It extracted advantages for debtors at the expense of creditors and, therefore, damaged public confidence. Investors would react immediately to such a measure by transferring liquid funds abroad with letters of exchange. The state did not gain anything by forcing a lower rate of interest on creditors.

Most of the existing bonds in the monarchy were not uniform debt instruments. They lacked credibility among creditors and were difficult to understand.[18] Their reimbursement mechanism was uncertain, and due to opaque legal requirements, transactions were generally cumbersome. Sometimes, creditors had to wait for years to receive interest and capital payments. These bonds lacked the solid administrative and legal framework which was essential for a borrower like the monarch who, suffering all too often from a poor credit record and a history of default, needed to build up confidence with creditors. The scarce use of bonds in commerce, Zinzendorf argued, was further convincing evidence of their inadequacy. Commercial traders preferred to use other public paper instead which, even though it traded at a discount, was transparent and functioned more like cash.

[15] Ibid., fol. 2r.
[16] Ibid., fol. 1v.
[17] Ibid., fol. 2v.
[18] Ibid., fol. 3r.

Zinzendorf's solution to the problem of state credit was the creation of a new bond issued by the Estates which offered creditors compelling advantages over existing types of public debt and compensated them for receiving a lower rate of interest. The new bond, which was more secure, liquid and therefore more readily tradable, would replace the existing public debt instruments.[19] The idea of a new debt instrument, Zinzendorf clarified, was adopted from somewhere else. He did not provide more details of the bond or of the mechanism of issue. The bond, he simply argued, would be advantageous to all citizens and restore trust in the credit system. Public confidence in state credit would lead to the acceptance by creditors of a lower rate of interest, or borrowing cost, for the government. It would halt the activities of financial speculators who, short of alternatives, would be forced to exchange the old debt instruments for the new bond.[20] Also, the forced loans with punitively high interest charges which the nobility had been obliged to take to meet the increasing cash demands from the monarch would become redundant. Those types of loans, Zinzendorf thought, presented an existential threat to those who had to subscribe to them.[21]

Financial credit was an issue of public perception, and the creation of a solid set-up for its execution was essential to success. The price and the demand of the new bond would be upheld by public confidence, and the bond used by investors as cash equivalent. It would therefore increase the supply of money in the economy and add to the amount of money in circulation. If set up correctly, public credit could provide additional liquidity to the economy.[22] The amount of money in proportion to the number of goods available influenced the price level in the economy. A doubling of the monetary base would lead to a doubling of the price of goods, which was beneficial to the manufacturing class. Conversely, Zinzendorf argued, doubling the number of goods in the economy by keeping the monetary base constant led to a price drop of manufactured produce. This would lead to a shortage of money in the economy, triggering a slowdown in economic activity.[23]

[19] 'Procurer aux créancier un nouveau genre d'obligations plus solide, plus circulant, plus conversible en argent et par la plus proper à en faire les fonctions, effectuer ces choses dis-je seroit donc le vrai moien pour amener les ésprits au but proposé': ibid., fol. 3v.

[20] Ibid., fols 3v–4r.

[21] Ibid., fol. 4v.

[22] Ibid., fols 5r–5v.

[23] Ibid., fol. 5v.

Zinzendorf concluded the 'Essai sur l'Établissement' with a discussion of the benefits of a lower rate of interest of the new bond for manufacturing and land ownership. A lower rate of interest, he thought, would rebalance the demand for debt and land. *Rentier* activities would become less profitable and hence less interesting to pursue, and, with lower borrowing costs in the economy, land purchases would become more attractive. A shift from money to land ownership was generally beneficial, given the stronger attachment and loyalty to the state that land ownership entailed.[24]

Finally, it should be noted that the title of the 'Essai sur l'Établissement' is misleading. In the text, Zinzendorf did not discuss the institution of the *Banque générale des États* mentioned in the title. He also did not refer to the Estates, which would own the bank or describe their roles in issuing the new bond. Zinzendorf only made one brief reference to a bank-like institution which *rentiers* would have to use to exchange their old bonds for new ones.[25] This short text could have been the beginning of Zinzendorf's ideas about the creation of a new bank for the monarchy. As argued in Chap. 5, he developed these arguments fully in his writings on state credit.

The Importance of Melon's *Essai Politique*

Despite its failure in 1720, the financial scheme of John Law triggered lively discussions among French intellectuals on political economy and on the benefits of state credit. Zinzendorf followed these very closely. For him, Melon's *Essai politique* was of great significance. Zinzendorf made copious notes for himself in his copy of the book and decided to translate the text into German.[26] Melon had been secretary to Law's large Mississippi holding company, and it was his knowledge and willingness to discuss aspects of Law's financial system that made his writing so attractive. In addition, the ambitious scope of Melon's *Essai politique* made it a valuable source for developing Zinzendorf's own ideas. Melon had covered a wide range of economic processes and provided a systematic account of a political economy. Following the failure of Law's scheme, he sought to re-establish

[24] Ibid., fol. 6r.

[25] '*Établissement salutaire*': ibid., fol. 4r.

[26] Letters of Ludwig Zinzendorf to Karl Zinzendorf, Vienna, 14 December 1759, vol. 63, DOZA; fragments of Zinzendorf's translation of Jean-François Melon, *Essai politique sur le commerce* can be found in Kartons 9 and 40, Archiv Zinzendorf, NÖLA.

France's economic power. In a methodical manner, Melon set out principles for an economic recovery in France and encouraged public discourse on policy matters to support the ruler in the decision-making.[27]

The *Essai politique* was reprinted four times between 1734 and 1735. In 1736, Melon published a revised edition with eight additional chapters. This expanded second edition was the result of the monetary debate with Dutot about currency manipulation and included new chapters on export and imports, money and exchange, the balance of trade and liberty of commerce, political arithmetic and 'systems'. There were an estimated 20 editions of Melon's book. It was widely disseminated in Europe and translated into several languages, including English, German, Italian, Spanish and Russian.[28]

Melon's concept of the economy was agriculture based and manufacturing driven. The starting point of his analysis had been a competitive trade model of three single product islands. The first island produced grain, the other two wool and drinks respectively. Trade resulted from mutual need, and surpluses were sold to other islands. The island producing grain, however, had a key advantage: grain was the essential commodity required by all; the other two islands were dependent on it for their survival. The first objective for the ruler, Melon had argued, was an adequate production of grain. Agriculture was the basis of economic activity, and more grain would enable population growth. Progress in agriculture and industry, which drove commerce, was linked to the size of the population or a more efficient use of agriculture and industry to increase output. In case of the latter, a surplus of people would be of good use to increase the variety of commodities produced or to colonise new territories to extend economic power. Increasing the size of the population, therefore, was the second objective of the legislator. A sufficient supply of money as the engine of commerce, was, by extension, the third objective.[29] For Melon, clever commercial activities were a better tool for national power than military conflict. Trade, even though

[27] Jean-François Melon, *Essai politique sur le commerce* (2nd edn, 1736), ed. Eugène Daire, *Économistes-Financiers du XVIIIe siècle* (Paris, 1843), Chap. 25: 'Des Systèmes', pp. 707–836, at pp. 827, 831. This edition of the *Essai politique* is equivalent to the second edition of 1736.

[28] Jesús Astigarraga, 'La dérangeante découverte de l'autre: traductions et adaptations espagnoles de *l'Essai politique sur le commerce* (1734) de Jean-François Melon', *Revue d'histoire moderne et contemporaine*, 57:1 (2010), pp. 91–118, at p. 92.

[29] Melon, *Essai politique*, Chap. 1: 'Principes', pp. 707–11.

intensely competitive, was a peaceful activity and a preferable alternative to wars in securing the place of a nation internationally.[30]

Political economy was a challenging and complicated science. To attain his three objectives, the legislator had to make policy choices by considering the various possible scenarios of labour productivity. Thus, he had to quantify the agricultural output and the population growth as well as assess the adequacy of the national monetary base. Precise calculations, Melon had maintained, would lead to a good grasp of the objectives and produce informed policy decisions. Political plans had to be workable, with realistic goals. Interference by influential groups to advance their vested interests was detrimental. For this reason, the plans had to be publicised, printed and discussed widely to filter out the good from the bad in the interest of the society.[31]

Agricultural output and agricultural consumption by province were easy to ascertain, and acquiring this knowledge was an essential task for the legislator. Abundance and degradation of agricultural produce was always followed by shortages of grain. Although this endangered both rich and poor, the poorer segments of the population, the peasants, were the backbone of the economy and were most severely hit by famine. To prevent such dangers to economic performance, and given that not all provinces were equally abundant, the legislator had to ensure freedom and ease of transport of agricultural produce between provinces. Freedom of transport had to be supplemented by ease of transport. It included the construction of roads and waterways, and had to be linked to sound financial decision-making by abolishing toll payments and internal tariffs. This, Melon had thought, was the basis of a good agricultural policy.[32]

In order to ensure the appropriate transfer of grain between provinces, the legislator had to know not only the agricultural output but also the number of people living in each of the provinces.[33] He had to keep records of births and deaths to track changes in the population. Population growth

[30] On trade as competitive activity in Melon, see Istvan Hont, *Jealousy of Trade: International Competition and the Nation-State in Historical Perspective* (Cambridge, MA, 2005), pp. 31–2; John Robertson, *The Case for the Enlightenment: Scotland and Naples 1680–1760* (Cambridge, 2005), p. 343.

[31] Melon, *Essai politique*, Chap. 24: 'De l'Arithmetique politique', pp. 810–11 and Chap. 25: 'Des Systèmes', p. 831.

[32] Melon, *Essai politique*, Chap. 24: 'De l'Arithmetique politique', p. 812 and Chap. 2: 'Du Blé', p. 712.

[33] Melon, *Essai politique*, Chap. 2: 'Du Blé', p. 713.

was the necessary basis for agricultural and commercial prosperity. The legislator had to know how much each worker could contribute economically to the state. As the majority of the population worked in agriculture, it was important to ensure that the peasants, who were often treated unjustly and with contempt, received special care which included appropriate medical treatment. Refusal by citizens to work and have children, as well as an excessive growth of clergy who took vows of celibacy, presented a threat to national prosperity.[34]

Commerce required liberty. But the latter had to be kept in check with a certain level of protection to safeguard the common good. A good example, as the basis for English trade supremacy, was the protection to national shipping granted under the English Navigation Act. The English government intervened strategically to help its domestic agricultural market by offering financial incentives for exports when grain prices were depressed, and financial subsidies for imports when grain prices were high.[35] Accurately assessing the success of commerce by calculating the balance of trade with other nations was difficult. The best proxy was the monetary exchange, measured over one year, which was required to conduct commerce. Even more important than quantifying commerce was identifying the factors which contributed to a nation's trading surplus. Melon had stated four key principles. The first principle was increasing the means for commerce by nurturing the domestic workforce and encouraging immigration. The second was increasing the '*fonds de commerce*' by enabling a good circulation of money and ensuring, through a reduced number of public holidays and a larger variety of manufactured products. The third principle was the creation of a good market framework which was conducive to commerce. It included monetary liquidity as well as the creation of hubs of specialist knowledge through advisory councils composed of merchants. Finally, it was important to respect commercial treaties and keep exports flowing so that foreign nations were incentivised to continue trading.[36]

Melon had recognised the importance of national trading companies for the development of commerce. The success of a trading company was not dependent on government support. Rather, it required a solid structure,

[34] Melon, *Essai politique*, Chap. 24: 'De l'Arithmetique politique', pp. 816–17, and Chap. 3: 'De l'augmentation des habitants', pp. 718–19.

[35] Melon, *Essai politique*, Chap. 11: 'De la liberté du Commerce', pp. 756–57, and Chap. 10: 'De l'Exportation et de l'Importation', pp. 755–56.

[36] Melon, *Essai politique*, Chap. 22: 'De la Balance du Commerce', pp. 793, 798–99.

sound management and a good capital base. The shares of the Compagnie des Indes gave instant market value to the physical produce which was shipped from port to port across continents and where, in the absence of any sales, value could often not be established. The shares were liquid and thus circulated well in the economy. As they were traded freely by investors, the shares were accurate representations of the value of the Compagnie's commerce. As a financial instrument, Melon had underlined, they were as valuable as public bonds.[37]

The circulation of money was the driving force of commerce. Money, Melon had argued, had to circulate throughout the whole economy, even in small amounts, to enable productive activity in the major commercial centres as well as in the provinces. Provincial administrators ought to be encouraged to lend money locally, particularly to small businesses, to make money work rather than hoard it: '*ainsi nulle circulation, nulle commerce*'. Importantly, the legislator had to target the right amount of money to support the economic activity in the country. Monetary inflation, which had been the death blow to Law's financial scheme, was detrimental to the economy and worse than a shortage of money. The latter would halt economic activity. An oversupply of money, on the other hand, would destroy the price setting capacity in the economy and require economic agents to revert to barter trading.[38]

Monetary matters and the defence of Law's financial system had been an important strand of Melon's argument. Money's intrinsic value, Melon had maintained, was its content of gold and silver which should not be altered. Using examples of previous French currency manipulations, Melon had warned of changes to the standard denomination of specie through changes of its gold and silver content. These changes, he had thought, were detrimental to the public and cause for complaint. Melon, however, had allowed for a devaluation of the currency by raising the nominal value of money as a means to help debtors, including the state, at the expense of creditors. In this instance, currency manipulation was a legitimate means to create an advantage for debtors.[39]

The state needed to ensure that it had adequate revenues to cover its outlays. The expenses of the state determined its revenues, and therefore borrowing was necessary to cover any financial shortfall. Public debt had

[37] Melon, *Essai politique*, Chap. 7: 'Des Compagnies exclusives', pp. 728–29.

[38] Melon, *Essai politique*, Chap. 24: 'De l'Arithmetique politique', pp. 819–20.

[39] Melon, *Essai politique*, Chap. 12: 'Des Valeurs numéraires', p. 763; Chap. 18: 'Réponses aux objections', p. 779, and Chaps. 13–15.

to be shouldered equally by the whole nation and should not be imposed only on certain parts of the population. Law's System, Melon had argued, had proposed the right remedies for France in the early eighteenth century: an increase in consumption, in the circulation of money and in the supply of money. Public debt was reduced. The old debt that had strangled agricultural production was replaced by a supply of money that was transparent and became a source of credit to the economy. Law's System ultimately failed because it had too much liquidity; in 1720, consumers rejected the use of the banknotes for daily payments.[40] Melon had approved of Law's strategy to encourage the use of paper money rather than specie but, referring to the *arrêt* of 27 February 1720, he had disapproved of the political means that were used to enforce it. If banknotes could be used responsibly and their use becomes established, they could be the basis of a solid credit system which would become a source of prosperity to the state. Paper debt which was easily tradable could be considered genuine sources of credit.[41]

The basis of monetary exchange was public confidence and a relationship of trust between the ruler and his citizens.[42] On that basis, public debt was beneficial to the economy. If the legislator could ensure a measured use of credit together with a stable political environment, all classes of society would contribute to state credit. With liquidity and a good circulation of money, public credit was, as Melon had argued in a metaphor, the right hand lending to the left. He had reinforced the argument by using the example of republics which, due to their public banks and system of solid credit, enjoyed prosperity and power.[43]

Melon had not been concerned by a rise in the general price level which followed from an increase in the supply of money. Higher prices would not have any impact on the majority of the public, as they were both consumers and producers. Debtors and manufacturers would benefit most from an increase in prices. Financial investors as well as the military would be disadvantaged, but soldiers had to be compensated, and their pay had to be adjusted in line with price increases. A higher price level, Melon had thought, via an increase in the monetary base was

[40] Melon, *Essai politique*, Chap. 16: 'Des Diminutions', pp. 770–72.

[41] Melon, *Essai politique*, Chap. 19: 'Diverses observations sur les Monnaies', pp. 781, 783.

[42] Melon, *Essai politique*, Chap. 23: 'Du crédit public', p. 801.

[43] Ibid., pp. 802, 804–5. Melon's metaphor of the hands has been referred to as the 'indifference theory of public debt': Fritz Karl Mann, *Finanztheorie und Finanzsoziologie* (Göttingen, 1959), p. 39.

beneficial to the economy: it would accelerate commercial activities, ensure that citizens would be prosperous enough to carry the tax burden with ease, and remove the threat to creditors of a loss of capital or late payments by the state. An increase in the price level was justified provided that there was not already a sufficient supply of money in the economy to adequately support the level of public debt.[44]

A lower rate of interest was an additional benefit of an increase in the supply of money. It was essential for conducting international commerce successfully since the manufacturer who borrowed more cheaply than his competitor would be able to sell at an advantageous price. For this reason, Melon had argued that it was important to have, at the very least, access to the same level of interest rate as rival commercial nations. In Europe, the rate of interest had decreased as the supply of money had increased. The price of money was dependent on the level of supply and demand. In an economic environment of high rates of interest, Melon had continued, the value of produce and hence also the value of land would decrease. Land ownership was the real source of wealth for the state. The landowner would become impoverished and would not be able to pay taxes. The debtor would be unable to service his debt and, eventually, would be forced to sell the land to his creditor for a low consideration. The creditor, however, would not have any incentive to cultivate the land and would leave it neglected. A high rate of interest, Melon had concluded, would suffocate the economy, and financial investors rather than the productive classes of society would receive preferential treatment. In terms of commerce, domestic activity would be destroyed and external trade would stop.[45]

Melon's views guided the thinking of Zinzendorf. The 'Essai sur L'Établissement', the Brittany travel account and the 'Mémoire sur les richesses, le commerce et les finances de la France' display a continuous engagement with the arguments of the *Essai politique*. In the 'Essai sur L'Établissement', Zinzendorf, like Melon, took the crisis of state finances as the starting point of his analysis on the monarchy's economy. The aim of his proposal to create a new debt instrument for the Estates was to repair the monarchy's inadequate and fragmented credit system. Zinzendorf then extended his analysis to describe what he thought were the dynamics of the monarchy's economy and suggested improvements.

[44] Melon, *Essai politique*, Chap. 17: 'De la cherté des denrées', pp. 773–74 and Chap. 18: 'Réponses aux objections', p. 780.

[45] Melon, *Essai politique*, Chap. 22: 'De la Balance du Commerce', pp. 795–96.

First, his classification of public creditors into economic classes with differing economic interests showed the difficulty the state had in achieving general creditor satisfaction and successfully managing public debt operations that involved parties who had competing economic interests. Second, it displayed Zinzendorf's awareness, like Melon's, of the importance of human capital for economic growth. Both economic classes of *terriers* and *industrieux* would work for the prosperity of the state provided the legislator guaranteed appropriate working conditions in the economy.

As landownership was the prime source of wealth, the *terriers* enjoyed precedence over other economic classes. Zinzendorf, like Melon, recognised the numerical importance of the peasantry in the economy and thought that the ruler owed them an adequate level of protection and care. The second class of citizens, the *industrieux*, were dependent on the *terriers*. Once the supply of agricultural produce was ensured, the *industrieux* could develop the manufacturing and commercial activities of the country. With a well-functioning economy, a nation could successfully embark on foreign trade.

The necessity for a sufficient supply of money in the economy was an important argument in Zinzendorf's 'Essai sur L'Établissement'. Money was required to conduct commerce. An increase in the monetary base, Zinzendorf argued, would lead to a higher price level in the economy and enable manufacturers to sell their produce more dearly. The additional money supply would be generated through public credit and the creation of easily tradable bonds. For Zinzendorf, the idea of money in circulation, rather than an absolute quantity of money, was crucial. He was guided by Melon's insistence on a good circulation of money in the whole economy, and as such he wanted to extend the mechanisms for bond transactions from the main cities to the provinces of the monarchy. Zinzendorf had to grapple with a variety of debt schemes in the monarchy which had become inappropriate for the state's financing needs and which were mostly trading at discounts to face value. A new and liquid bond was, therefore, a good mechanism to relaunch the broken debt system and unify it. Melon had proposed such debt instruments for France, and, aware of their successful use in England, Zinzendorf proposed them as an appropriate remedy for the finances of the monarchy.

Money supply, Melon had maintained, should be guided by the level of productive activity in the economy. An increase in the supply of money ought to be related to an increase in the aggregate demand for goods. For this reason, commerce was of prime importance to Melon since the economy had to have sufficient output for a productive use of the increased money supply. Similarly, Zinzendorf mentioned the importance of healthy economic activity, in terms of both ordinary and luxury trade, so that the economy could absorb the increased money supply. He underlined the benefits of a lower rate of interest for the monarchy's agriculture, commerce and state credit. Zinzendorf referred to the importance of public confidence for a successful functioning credit system and for ensuring that money circulated in the economy. The lack of public confidence, he argued, was the reason that existing credit arrangements were unsatisfactory. In this, the monarchy was comparable to France. The introduction of new bonds, which Zinzendorf proposed, would create creditor satisfaction and confidence.

Although Zinzendorf and Melon agreed on many issues related to economic reform, there were still significant differences of opinion. Currency manipulation was one important difference between the two. Currency devaluation, Melon had argued, was justified to help debtors manage their financial commitments and alleviate their debts. Zinzendorf disagreed. Creditor satisfaction, he thought, was the crucial element of a successful public credit system. There was no room for a preferential treatment of debtors over creditors, and therefore no justification for unilateral measures by debtors to change existing credit terms, including, to this end, a monetary devaluation. For Zinzendorf, the arguments over currency manipulation were of major importance: he discussed them again in some detail in his German translation of Law's *Money and Trade*.[46]

In the travel account of Brittany, Zinzendorf used Melon's arguments on national trading companies to evaluate the Compagnie des Indes. He commented on its structure and management, and provided detail on its financial set-up. Like Melon, Zinzendorf commented on the liquidity of the Compagnie's shares and its debt instruments. They circulated well and were beneficial because they added money to the economy. His analysis of the Compagnie followed the structure set out by Melon. Zinzendorf wrote in great detail on the Compagnie's financial structure since it was required to comprehend its current state and economic performance. Zinzendorf was encouraged by the liquidity of the Compagnie's shares which ensured a good supply of money in the economy. As in the 'Essai sur L'Établissement', Zinzendorf argued that it was important to add money to the economy by encouraging the use of paper through credit

[46] See Chap. 4 for a further discussion of Zinzendorf's views on currency manipulation.

rather than specie. However, he was concerned about the opaque decision-making processes by the Compagnie's directors. Like Melon in relation to political plans, Zinzendorf was convinced of the necessity for transparent decision-making processes and of the dangers of parties trying to influence and promote their interests.

Finally, in Zinzendorf's 'Mémoire sur les richesses, le commerce et les finances de la France', Melon's arguments were meticulously rehearsed and most explicit. At the beginning of the text, Zinzendorf acknowledged Melon's direct influence on his thinking. Zinzendorf's analysis of the French economy was driven by the country's three sources of wealth or, as Melon had argued in the first chapter of the *Essai politique*, in terms of the three policy objectives for a legislator. As prescribed by Melon, Zinzendorf attempted to quantify the three objectives which were required for good and informed policy-making. The 'Mémoire sur les richesses, le commerce et les finances de la France' was, in effect, a direct test of Melon's arguments on French economic policies of the late 1740s and early 1750s. Zinzendorf followed Melon in setting out necessary measures to reverse the French population decline. He encouraged gainful economic activity for the population, especially in rural areas, marriage to create domestic stability and offspring, and immigration of skilled labour as well as checks on the growth of the clergy. The failure of the French government, Zinzendorf thought, to accurately determine the number of citizens and thereby to calculate the required level of national agricultural output exposed the country to famines. His diagnosis of the shortcomings of French agricultural policies was close to Melon's.

Strategic policies were necessary for commerce and, like Melon, Zinzendorf admired the protection to national shipping under England's Navigation Act. His starting point in assessing commerce was to look at the balance of trade, but he understood that the results of commercial activities were more important than simply quantifying the components that made up the trade itself. They dictated what kind of economic policies were appropriate. This was in line with Melon's *Essai politique*. Zinzendorf's analysis of French commerce followed the four principles which Melon had set out in Chap. 22 on the balance of trade. The importance of skilled labour and open borders for migration of workers corresponded to the first principle. The emphasis on the importance of money and credit in circulation, with a corresponding lower rate of interest, as well as the criticism of the large number of public holidays and the lack of commercial continuity among generations of French merchants reflected the second principle of having to grow the domestic '*fonds de commerce*'. Zinzendorf's description and condemnation of bad commercial policy decisions related to the third. The requirement for the government to account of the changing character of international commerce was in line with Melon's last principle.

At its core, successful commerce required money. As with Melon, money and credit were essential elements of Zinzendorf's argument. He devoted the entire second part of the 'Mémoire sur les richesses, le commerce et les finances de la France' to calculations of the monetary base and the value of the various types of public credit instruments in France and England and discussed in detail the contrasting financial policies of both countries. England was the prime example of a nation which used state credit to its full economic advantage. Zinzendorf set out a model of two nations to show how England, with much more modest natural wealth than France, successfully used public credit to overtake its continental rival. For Zinzendorf, like Melon, the supply of money through public debt was the engine of commerce. It made weaker nations more powerful. Unlike France, England had created general confidence in its system of government. State credit, based on public confidence, was the beneficial instrument for a swift growth of commerce and amounted to, as Melon had argued, the right hand lending to the left. Zinzendorf also agreed with Melon on the benefits of a lower rate of interest for agriculture, commerce and the market price of public debt instruments following an increase in the money supply. Both argued that agricultural activities would become unprofitable and only financial investors would benefit at higher rates of interest. Without competitive financing terms, France was unable to create an advantage over rival trading nations. A lower rate of interest was essential for economic prosperity and, in terms of the country's second source of wealth, would increase the value of produce and the value of land.

Jacques Vincent de Gournay

During Zinzendorf's stay in France, Gournay (1712–1759) rose to prominence in French economic and political life. In 1751, he became *Intendant* in the *Bureau du Commerce*.[47] At the same time as Zinzendorf wrote the

[47] See Chap. 5 for an account of Gournay's very original programme to form a circle of individuals who would translate and publicise European writings on political economy and of the operations of the *Bureau du Commerce*.

'Mémoire sur les richesses, le commerce et les finances de la France', Gournay translated Sir Josiah Child's *Treatise on Trade*. Like Zinzendorf, he completed his text in late 1752.[48] The basis for Gournay's translation was the fifth English edition of Child's book which had been published in Glasgow in 1751.[49] The edition included a new introduction addressing the criticism of his first pamphlet, *Brief Observations concerning Trade and interest of money*, published in 1668; a revised *Brief Observations*, expanded with ten new chapters; and Thomas Culpeper's short brochure, *A tract against usury*.[50] Child, who was the son of an English merchant and had started his career as a merchant apprentice, became a member of parliament in 1659. He was also a director and subsequently governor of the East India Company, and by the late seventeenth century, he had amassed a considerable personal fortune.[51] Child had played a leading part on the trade committee of the House of Lords which examined developments in trade as well as in the Council of Trade. The latter had been a new body, composed of merchants and statesmen, which advised the king on commerce and economic policies. Child's book was an influential publication which set out the relationship between trade, interest rate and money circulation. For Child, the most convincing explanation of Dutch prosperity was the country's low rate of interest. For this reason he had advocated an interest rate reduction from 6 per cent to 4 per cent in order for England to compete successfully with the Dutch and re-invigorate commerce. The ruler, the landed nobility, the peasants and the merchants, he had argued, would all be the beneficiaries of this financial policy.[52]

When Child had written the *Treatise on Trade*, England, Gournay thought, was in a difficult economic situation. It was like France's predicament in 1750. Gournay sought to use Child's arguments to educate government officials and persuade them to follow the examples of the successful English and Dutch economies.[53] Gournay undertook the translation on the advice and with the support of his superior, Daniel Trudaine, the *Intendant*

[48] At the end of September 1752, Gournay had only two chapters of Child's book left to translate and comment on. The commentary followed the translation. I am grateful to Simone Meyssonnier who pointed this out to me.

[49] Meyssonnier (ed.), *Traités sur le commerce*, p. xxii.

[50] Ibid., p. xlv.

[51] Henry C. Clark (ed.), *Commerce, Culture and Liberty: Readings on Capitalism Before Adam Smith* (Indianapolis: Liberty Classics, 2003), p. 371.

[52] 'Cinquième Objection', pp. 47–8 in Meyssonnier (ed.), *Traités sur le commerce*.

[53] On Gournay's policy objectives, see ibid., pp. xxxix, xlii–xliii.

des Finances, who understood that France was rapidly losing ground to rival trading nations. However, the publication of the translation was delayed. The *controlleur général* Jean-Baptiste Machault D'Arnouville considered the timing for a publication to be inappropriate. In 1753, he faced strong domestic opposition to the *vingtième* income tax which he had introduced in 1749. Only in 1754, when D'Arnouville resigned from office, was Gournay's text, without commentary, finally published.[54]

The translation was a good example of the Gournay circle's collaborative nature. Various commentaries on the manuscripts by Véron de Forbonnais (1722–1800) and other unidentified collaborators were evidence of the intellectual exchanges of the writers. Gournay's annotations to the text showed how his own arguments evolved through these discussions.[55] He wrote a separate commentary (*Remarques*) to almost all chapters of Child's book, as well as to Culpeper's tract on usury, and added a short introduction (*Avertissement*) as well as a conclusion to the translation.[56] He sought to identify the elements which could unlock the economic potential of France and develop the permanent sources of national wealth: agriculture and commerce.[57] France, Gournay argued in the *Remarques*, had to implement four economic measures to reform its economic policy: first, it needed a prudent reduction in the rate of interest; second, a comprehensive Navigation Act; third, a system of public credit which would naturally follow from growing agricultural activity, commerce and shipping; and, finally, a *Conseil de Commerce* to coordinate and guide nationally the various commercial enterprises.[58] In annotations to Child's text, Gournay added that monarchies were better suited than

[54] Ibid., pp. xviii–xxv.

[55] Ibid., pp. xliii–xliv, xlviii; Simone Meyssonnier, 'Vincent de Gournay, un intendant du commerce au travail. L'apport du fonds de Saint-Brieuc a l'intelligence de ses textes' in Loïc Charles, Frédéric Lefebvre and Christine Théré (eds.). *Le Cercle de Vincent Gournay. Savoirs économiques et pratiques administratives en France au milieu du XVIIIe siècle* (Paris: Institut National D'Études Démographiques, 2011), pp. 89–110, at pp. 89–92; Loïc Charles, 'Le Moment "Vincent de Gournay": Réflexions à propos des *Remarques* sur les Traités sur le commerce de Josiah Child editées et préfacées par Simone de Meyssonnier', *Cahiers d'économie Politique*, 56:1 (2009), pp. 205–11 at pp. 206–7.

[56] Gournay did not write commentaries to Chap. 2: 'Du soulagement et de L'emploi des Pauvres' or to Chap. 6: 'De l'établissement d'une Juridiction marchande'. The *Remarques* were only published after Gournay's death: Meyssonnier (ed.), *Traités sur le commerce*, p. xxi.

[57] Gournay, 'Avertissement', p. 3, in Meyssonnier (ed.), *Traités sur le commerce*.

[58] Gournay, 'Conclusion des Remarques', p. 307, in Meyssonnier (ed.), *Traités sur le commerce*.

republics to support commerce. Once commerce was recognised in monarchies as '*affaire principale*', he argued, the decision to remove the obstacles to trade could be more readily implemented than in republics.[59]

The need to lower the rate of interest in France was a key element of Gournay's argument, which he reiterated throughout the *Remarques*. The high rate of interest was choking economic activity, and it was hindering the circulation of money. It was also preventing the ruler from making prompt repayment of existing borrowing and thus curtailing the government's ability to raise additional finance for the military and for public investments. It led to a misallocation of resources away from preferred investments in commerce and agriculture and towards financial transactions which yielded a higher short-term return.[60] The unfavourable high rate of interest was also the chief reason for France's poor balance of trade and contributed, as Forbonnais added in Gournay's text, to its loss of competitiveness. Despite France's large monetary base and the steady progress of commercial activities over the previous 20 years, the numerous restrictions on commerce suppressed the circulation of money in the economy. Reducing the rate of interest, Forbonnais commented, would entice the holders of capital to lend more readily as they feared greater loss of income through further decreases of the rate of interest.[61]

The high rate of interest made a Navigation Act, similar to the English one, a relevant policy objective for France. It would enable the country to rebuild its navy, increase the number of sailors and compete successfully in trade.[62] As such, a Navigation Act for France, with freedom for merchants

[59] Gournay, 'Des colonies', pp. 269–70, in Meyssonnier (ed.), *Traités sur le commerce*.

[60] Gournay, 'Avertissement', p. 3; 'Remarques sur la Préface de Child', pp. 32, 35; 'Remarques sur le Discours sur le Commerce', pp. 57–8; 'Remarques sur le chap. 9 touchant la Balance du Commerce', pp. 218, 228, 238; 'Remarques sur le Traité contre l'Usure', p. 301, all in Meyssonnier (ed.), *Traités sur le commerce*. See also: Vincent de Gournay, undated, 'Pièce détachée sur l'intérêt de l'argent', pp. 89–90 in ed. Takumi Tsuda, *Mémoires et lettres de Vincent de Gournay*, Economic research series, no. 31, The Institute of Economic Research, Hitotsubashi University (Tokyo: Kinokuniya Co., 1993). On the role of money and the rate of interest in Gournay's thought, see Gilbert Faccarello and Philippe Steiner, '"Philosophie économique" and Money in France, 1750–1776: The Stakes of a Transformation', *European Journal of Economic Thought*, 19:3 (2012), pp. 325–53, at pp. 330–32.

[61] Gournay, 'Remarques sur le ch. 9 touchant la Balance du Commerce', p. 222, in Meyssonnier (ed.), *Traités sur le commerce*.

[62] Gournay, 'Remarques sur le ch. 4 touchant l'Acte de Navigation', p. 143, in Meyssonnier (ed.), *Traités sur le commerce*.

to ship from any domestic port, was a prerequisite to support maritime trade and commerce as well as a source for domestic prosperity. Gournay was critical of the treaties between France and the United Provinces which allowed the Dutch free access to French ports to control cabotage. Commenting on various articles of commercial treaties concluded between the two countries between 1713 and 1739, he argued that the Dutch, despite being a simple intermediary, were keeping the largest share of trading profits. Often, Gournay complained, the costs of transport were higher than the value of produce, and so these treaties could never be economically advantageous for France. They were part of a historical legacy and no longer served a strategic rationale. Moreover, the Dutch had progressively lost their political influence in Europe, and since 1748 they had been under the military tutelage of England. For this reason, relationship with the United Provinces no longer required careful management.[63]

Commerce itself was the foundation of economic prosperity. It enabled population growth and the development of agriculture and manufacturing. At the most basic level, commerce required monetary support to the productive forces in the economy.[64] This England had recognised, and had successfully used public credit to develop its economy. France, Gournay thought, having a larger stock of national resources and more specie, should profit more from the use of public credit than England. The country needed to make changes to its financial policies, however. As a first step, government paper should be made more easily tradable, as was already the case in Lyon. Gournay conceded that the second step, the establishment of a national system of state credit similar to England's, was more difficult to implement. It required changes to existing outdated legislation which did not reflect the growing importance of international trade.[65] Commerce and state finances were closely linked. Once trade was well-entrenched as a national economic activity, the ruler would recognise its invaluable contribution. The public would become convinced of the ruler's commercial ambitions and would have assurance that public confidence would not be abused. This was important for state credit. Once the confidence of market participants to trade with each other was restored,

[63] Ibid., pp. 144–45; also 'Remarques sur le ch. 9 touchant la Balance du Commerce', pp. 243–44; 'Conclusion', pp. 307–22, in Meyssonnier (ed.), *Traités sur le commerce*.

[64] Gournay, 'Remarques sur le ch. 9 touchant la Balance du Commerce', p. 217, in Meyssonnier (ed.), *Traités sur le commerce*.

[65] Gournay, 'Remarques sur le ch. 5 touchant le Transport des Dettes', pp. 161–63, in Meyssonnier (ed.), *Traités sur le commerce*.

market prices for both old and new public debt instruments would increase due to the better circulation of funds.[66]

Gournay criticised the restrictive administrative practices for trade.[67] He deplored the lack of a commercial tradition in France and the general ignorance and indifference of decision-makers, and of the Parisian public in particular, towards the merchant profession.[68] Commerce was a vital economic activity and should be treated as an '*affaire d'État*'. It required a specialist '*Conseil de Commerce*', which would pursue commercial activities for the benefit of the whole country rather than solely for a city or province. The new institution should maintain a regular dialogue with other trading nations. It should also monitor the quality of French produce and uphold good business conduct as well as make decisions about imports based upon an analysis of the French balance of trade. A further remit for the new institution would be to identify local families with entrepreneurial acumen whose knowledge could be gainfully used for the state. Typically, these families would have built successful businesses and through international experience have a command of foreign languages.[69]

Other important economic measures which fed into Gournay's four main policy objectives included: facilitating immigration to compensate for the loss of population following emigration, war and desertion; encouraging the settlement of foreign skilled labour; making employment conditions in France less stringent to keep the productive labour force in the country and stem depopulation in the provinces; carefully managing trade with grain and, as Forbonnais added, establishing granaries; and decreasing the number of public holidays to avoid a competitive disadvantage with rival trading nations because of a standstill in economic activity.[70]

[66] Gournay, 'Remarques sur le ch. 9 touchant la Balance du Commerce', pp. 234–37, in Meyssonnier (ed.), *Traités sur le commerce*.

[67] Gournay, 'Remarques sur le ch. 8 concernant la Laine et les Manufactures de Laine', p. 200, in Meyssonnier (ed.), *Traités sur le commerce*.

[68] Gournay, 'Remarques sur le ch. 9 touchant la Balance du Commerce', pp. 225–27, in Meyssonnier (ed.), *Traités sur le commerce*.

[69] Gournay, 'Conclusion', pp. 322–25, 329–30, in Meyssonnier (ed.), *Traités sur le commerce*.

[70] Gournay, 'Remarques sur le ch. 7 touchant la naturalisation', pp. 177; p. 179; 'Remarques sur le ch. 9 touchant la Balance du Commerce', p. 224; 'Remarques sur le ch. 10 touchant les colonies', pp. 271, 273; 'Remarques sur Quelques Endroits de la Préface de M. Child', pp. 35–7; 'Remarques sur le ch. 1 touchant les considérations sur le Commerce et l'interêt de l'argent', pp. 85, 96; 'Remarques sur le ch. 9 touchant la Balance du Commerce', pp. 239–40 with Forbonnais' calculations of the financial loss associated with a day of public

There is a striking similarity between the arguments of Zinzendorf and Gournay. This is reinforced by their geographic proximity at the time when Zinzendorf wrote the 'Mémoire sur les richesses, le commerce et les finances de la France' and Gournay published the *Traités sur le commerce*. Both writers made the same assessment of the French economy in the early 1750s: despite its large reserves of natural wealth, France was losing the economic race with rival trading nations. Inadequate government institutions and outdated commercial arrangements were to blame for the country's poor economic performance. In the conclusion to the *Remarques*, Gournay criticised the trade agreements with the United Provinces. But as an *Intendant*, he had to be cautious with his attacks on French policies. Gournay had to find ways to work around the more conservative officials in the *Bureau du Commerce*.[71] Zinzendorf, on the other hand, could be more direct with his criticism of French government practices. Throughout the 'Mémoire sur les richesses, le commerce et les finances de la France', he blamed the French administration for the country's economic problems and considered it an obstacle to the introduction of appropriate economic policies.

Both Zinzendorf and Gournay argued that a monarchy was better suited to adopt commercial policies than a republic. The policy remedies, they agreed, should follow the arguments of Melon and concentrate on growing the real economic resources: population, agriculture and commerce, supported by credit and a good circulation of money.[72] Gournay had developed similar ideas. However, given the way that Gournay's translation was published, with extended annotations to individual chapters, his arguments appeared less structured and included repetition with respect to the argument for a decrease in the rate of interest. In his conclusion, Gournay reiterated the four key policy elements which, if implemented by the ruler, would enable the growth of French economy. Zinzendorf also highlighted them in the 'Mémoire sur les richesses, le commerce et les finances de la France': state credit and a low rate of interest were important. Also, Zinzendorf concluded, the absence of a Navigation Act and of

holiday, footnote 20, p. 240. On the importance of agricultural prosperity for the writers of Gournay's circle, see John Shovlin, *The Political Economy of Virtue: Luxury, Patriotism and the Origins of the French Revolution* (Ithaca, NY, and London: Cornell University Press, 2006), pp. 54–5.

[71] Meyssonnier (ed.), *Traités sur le commerce*, p. xli.

[72] On Melon's influence on Gournay, see Meyssonnier, *La Balance et l'Horloge: La Genèse de la pensée libérale en France au XVIIIe siècle* (Paris, 1989), pp. 198, 204, 207.

commercial policy coordination were significant weaknesses of the French economy. Despite the similarity of arguments, it is important to be mindful of the different types of audiences which the writers addressed. Gournay sought to create '*une nation de commerçants*' and promote economic knowledge among the French public.[73] Zinzendorf wrote primarily for Kaunitz, the ruling elite in Vienna and the Estates.

Zinzendorf and Gournay not only shared ideas. They also had similar ways of working. They both commented on economic developments in other European countries to identify ideas and practices which might be useful and could be implemented domestically. Zinzendorf, of course, had more authority than Gournay since he worked in a smaller government administration and was closer to the centre of power. Gournay used economic accounts, both domestic and international, to help address commercial issues in France. During his travels in Europe between 1746 and 1747, he had identified capable officials in the French embassies and consulates who reported to him on economic progress and who helped advance his political agenda.[74] The archives of fonds Gournay in St Brieuc contain several mémoires on the economies of other nations.[75] Gournay also asked for information on the Habsburg monarchy's economy: written in Vienna and dated 10 August 1752, the 'Mémoire d'information pour les pays héréditaires de la Maison d'Autriche en Allemagne' was set out as a sequence of more than 40 short questions and answers on the Austrian economy.[76]

Gournay had sent questions to officials in Vienna seeking information on the monarchy's finances, commerce, agriculture and tariff system. His first set of questions related to the cost of money and to the financial administration. The government of the monarchy, the official reported, borrowed at 6 per cent. In peacetime, the rate of interest was 5 per cent at

[73] Meyssonnier (ed.), *Traités sur le commerce*, p. xxxiv.

[74] Sophus A. Reinert, *Translating Empire: Emulation and the Origins of Political Economy* (Cambridge, MA: Harvard University Press, 2011), p. 147.

[75] For a list of mémoires on individual countries, see Simone Meyssonnier, 'Annexe 1, Inventaire analytique du fonds Gournay de la Bibliothèque municipale de Saint-Brieuc' in Loïc Charles, Frédéric Lefebvre and Christine Théré (eds.). *Le Cercle de Vincent Gournay. Savoirs économiques et pratiques administratives en France au milieu du XVIIIe siècle* (Paris: Institut National D'Études Démographiques, 2011), pp. 303–43, at pp. 307–30.

[76] Fact finding by embassy officials was commonplace. In 1765, Lord Stormont wrote an outline of the Austrian hereditary lands and promised London a separate account of the monarchy's commercial activities: 'Appendix A: Lord Stormont's report on the Austrian Monarchy', in P.G.M. Dickson, *Finance and Government under Maria Theresia 1740–1780* (2 vols, Oxford, 1987), vol. 1, pp. 389–98.

most and the government was ready to redeem debt if creditors refused to accept a rate of interest as low as 4 per cent. The Vienna City Bank was the main finance entity but was unjustly called a 'bank'. Established during the War of the Spanish Succession to guarantee the assets of the city and of the Austrian hereditary lands, it acted more like a *caisse d'emprunt* for citizens to invest and redeem capital. The bank was headed by Count Rudolf Chotek and a group of officials who, swiftly and cost effectively, administered the sale and purchase of debt obligations. After the monarchy lost the province of Silesia, whose revenues had been assigned to the city of Vienna to cover annual interest payments and repayment of capital, public paper had lost 30 per cent of its value. When subsequently the government agreed to transfer up to 10 million *florins* of cameral revenue a year to the bank as compensation for the loss of the territory, the bonds traded again at par values. Currently, the official argued, in order to build up the confidence of the public, the government was seeking to reduce the rate of interest to 4 per cent.[77]

An important part of Gournay's inquiry on the monarchy covered industry and trade. He wanted to have a good understanding of manufacturing, the tariff regime and the administrative framework including measures to protect against fake produce. Manufacturing generally, the official in Vienna reported, had improved, and he provided Gournay with an overview of the main produce. The monarchy manufactured cloth, velour and silk, all of which, the author maintained, were of inferior quality to produce from other countries. Linen and canvas, produced close to Linz and used for army tents, blankets and shirts, had good sales. However, the same items from the United Provinces, Saxony and Silesia were of superior quality and colour and were in higher demand. Francis Stephen was closely involved in developing the country's manufacturing base. With the help of Baron de Toussaint, his financial councillor, the emperor had established a production facility for painted cloth on the border with Moravia and one nearby for earthenware. The latter was of good quality, and due to its reasonable prices, it was popular in the monarchy. The raw materials were imported from various countries including Tuscany, Turkey and India. They were necessities and so not subject to any import duties.

The Austrian–Bohemian lands had a tariff system for foreign and for domestic produce coming from other provinces, including Hungary. To promote internal commerce, in 1749 the empress had published an *avertissement*

[77] [Anonymous], 'Mémoire d'information pour les pays héréditaires', pp. 1–3.

which had reduced internal tariffs on domestic produce and had established an orderly trading framework for public market days. However, to protect Austrian–Bohemian industries, the government kept high tariffs for cloth and linen. Unlike France, the monarchy did not publish its tariffs and only merchants knew what the payment demands were. Nevertheless, the author provided tariff estimates for a range of produce and reported the whimsical manner of import practices: a 30 per cent tariff on imports of cloth from the United Provinces, Saxony and Prussian Silesia was ostensibly based on the value of produce. However, the latter was arbitrarily decided by customs officers together with the importing merchants and gave rise to much complaint.[78] Even though each province of the Austrian–Bohemian hereditary lands had an *inspecteur* who reported to Chotek, it was not possible, the officials argued, to know if they followed any policy guidelines. There was, for example, no government regulation on the sale of fake produce as most of the domestic production was sold in the home market. All commercial activities, including tariffs, were directly administered by Chotek, but it was not possible to discern what policy objectives he followed. Commercial treaties between the monarchy and other trading partners, European as well as African nations, were kept confidential. It was only through bribery that information on them could be obtained.[79]

The exports of the monarchy were limited because industrial produce was not plentiful or of high enough quality to be attractive for foreign markets. Even though the empress made efforts to support domestic manufacturing, it was doubtful, the official noted, if the monarchy's produce would ever reach a sufficiently high standard. While manufactured produce was deficient, agricultural produce, mainly from Hungary, was considered suitable for selling abroad. Hungary had a good stock of horses and cattle and had the potential to become an important exporter of grain. Despite this, the government failed to recognise commercial opportunities and, more generally, the benefits of actively managing the land. Hungarian peasants were enslaved and only working for their subsistence. They had not been educated to recognise the benefits of increasing production for the use in commerce. The sporadic recruitment and resettlement of agricultural labour from Alsace and Lorraine to Hungary by government agents had not been a successful undertaking. The inhospitable terrain and the lack of good infrastructure prompted most foreign workers to

[78] On tariff policies in the monarchy, see Gustav Otruba, *Die Wirtschaftspolitik Maria Theresias*, Österreich Reihe 192/194 (Vienna: Bergland Verlag, 1963), pp. 142–51.

[79] [Anonymous], 'Mémoire d'information pour les pays héréditaires', pp. 4–20, 28.

return home. The prospects for the sale of Hungarian wines abroad were limited. The poor quality of the bottles made them unsuitable for maritime transport via Trieste, and this limited their sale to neighbouring countries via overland routes. Hungary's natural resources, which included reserves of gold, silver and iron were also poorly exploited.[80]

Gournay was particularly interested in both the market for sugar and the trade between the monarchy and the Ottoman Empire.[81] Foreign nations, the officials reported, could freely sell sugar to Austria. It was imported via Trieste from England and Portugal, but it was impossible to know if sugar was also bought from France. The empress had granted permission to the Compagnie de Trieste to build a sugar refinery in Trieste, but it was not large enough and was barely producing enough white sugar for domestic consumption. Through the Compagnie, Maria Theresa sought to develop the ports of Fiume and Trieste as trading hubs for the monarchy. Both now had good storage facilities. Produce which arrived via Trieste on days of commercial trade fairs was granted free entry. An exception was produce where the monarchy had a surplus production. The merchandise which entered via Trieste was exempt from transit duties and consumption tariffs, and it was only taxed once to pay towards the upkeep of the domestic road network. Austria's trading efforts through the Compagnie were not successful. The shareholders of the trading company, two-thirds of whom were from the United Provinces with the remainder from Austria, could not reach an agreement on how to use shareholders' funds. The Compagnie, therefore, was not able to fully develop its activities, and foreign merchants seized upon this weakness to increase their business in Trieste. The empress, who most likely held shares in the Compagnie, was alarmed and had sent an official on a fact-finding mission to Trieste. He returned to Vienna with a glowing report on the city's development. Maria Theresa, together with Francis Stephen, the official speculated, could decide in the autumn of 1753 to travel to Trieste to receive a first-hand account of the challenges surrounding the Compagnie's activities, inspect the port's new installations and tour the city's new quarters.[82]

[80] Ibid., pp. 23–6.

[81] Ibid., pp. 20–1. As *Intendant*, Gournay was interested in trade opportunities with the Levant: Loïc Charles, 'Annexe 3: Résultat de la tournée de M. de Gournay en Languedoc relativement aux draps pour le Levant' in Loïc Charles, Frédéric Lefebvre and Christine Théré (eds.). *Le Cercle de Vincent Gournay. Savoirs économiques et pratiques administratives en France au milieu du XVIIIe siècle* (Paris: Institut National D'Études Démographiques, 2011), pp. 345–49, at p. 345.

[82] [Anonymous], 'Mémoire d'information pour les pays héréditaires', pp. 21–3.

In agricultural activities, the official reported, there was a large disparity between Hungary and the Austrian–Bohemian hereditary lands. Hungary suffered from a lack of manpower, and its vast agricultural fields lay idle. This lack of population meant that it was doubtful, in the official's view, that any surplus could be successfully exploited for export, despite potential access by either river or land to the country's commercial ports. Like Bohemia, Hungary had plenty of cattle and sheep, but the quality of wool was poor. In contrast, the agricultural output in the Austrian–Bohemian hereditary lands exceeded domestic consumption. The lands were farmed with great care and in case of agricultural shortage, which was rare, produce was moved between provinces. The government did not offer incentives to encourage output. Peasants were driven by self-interest, and the good production yields ensured that they would not leave farm land idle. As the monarchy had few export opportunities, surplus production was kept in storage. The relative agricultural abundance enabled low prices of meat and bread. Unlike in France, bread prices had not increased, even after periods of bad harvests. The government, the official maintained, had opted instead for reductions in the weight of bread and hence avoided peasant revolts which had threatened other countries in Europe.[83]

Tax collection was undertaken by the Estates and was comparable to the mechanisms used by some provinces in France. The Estates met on specific days during the year to decide on administrative matters. Before their meetings, they would receive the payment requests of the government representative and set the tax demands for their cities and towns accordingly. The system worked well. Their methods of tax collection had also been successful in provinces where the government feared opposition. Thus, the official argued, either the total amount payable was reasonable or the government had taken the necessary precautions against excessive taxation demands by the Estates. The taxes were comparable to the French *tailles*. While it was not possible to give a precise figure of the amount collected, estimates of tax income varied between 23 and 24 million *florins* annually. Large sums were paid by individuals in professions, which was comparable to the *capitation* tax in France, and by the cities for the use of their gates early in the morning and late in the evening.[84] The empress often made changes to the system of central tax collection. Central tax farming, the official thought, only existed for tobacco. In the Austrian–Bohemian hereditary lands the

[83] Ibid., pp. 33–5.
[84] Ibid., pp. 28–31.

rights over the sale and distribution of tobacco had been regulated for some time. Raw tobacco could only be imported by the officially appointed *fermier* who sold it domestically for the highest possible price. The *fermier* paid an annual fee to the government. His profits from this activity were not disclosed.[85] Gournay had also sent queries on salt farming, currency seigniorage and the circulation of foreign specie in the monarchy. Since the official in Vienna could not readily provide answers, Gournay was promised separate memoranda on these issues.[86]

In general, the conclusions of the 'Mémoire' were similar to Zinzendorf's views. Like Zinzendorf, the author identified the disorder of state finances and the limited usefulness of the Vienna City Bank for the economy. Also, like Zinzendorf, he highlighted the monarchy's weak commerce. Its industrial produce was not suitable for export markets, and the Compagnie de Trieste was unable to compete successfully in international trade.[87] Exports of agricultural produce were not encouraged by the government. For importers, the tariffs were not readily accessible. Trade policies were opaque. Gournay read the account on the monarchy closely. He made six brief annotations in the margin of the text. He added the exchange rate between the French and Austrian currencies.[88] He also questioned the assertion that import tariffs were not made public as, he argued, traders had to have reference points to evaluate their business opportunities.[89] On tariff-free import of *drogues* for dying, he remarked that the same was policy was followed in France; and on agriculture, that the low prices of meat from Hungary were beneficial for workers and made the domestic economy more competitive.[90] Finally, Gournay was surprised that breaking the monopoly of tobacco farming merely carried a financial penalty and was not enforced with a more severe prison sentence.[91]

[85] Ibid., pp. 31, 36–7.

[86] Ibid., pp. 33, 37. I could not locate the additional memoranda in the index of the fonds Gournay in Saint-Brieuc. Two other *mémoires* of 1750 and 1751 gave trade figures between France and the Austrian Netherlands, vol. 86, fonds Gournay for which see Meyssonnier, 'Annexe 1, Inventaire analytique du fonds Gournay' in Charles, Lefebvre and Théré (eds.), *Le Cercle de Vincent de Gournay*, pp. 303–43, at p. 324.

[87] On Zinzendorf's ideas for a new trade company, see Chap. 6, particularly the section 'Projectors'.

[88] [Anonymous], 'Mémoire d'information pour les pays héréditaires', pp. 3, 37.

[89] Ibid., p. 16.

[90] Ibid., pp. 28, 35.

[91] Ibid., p. 36.

Gournay's set of questions on the monarchy, emphasising the permanent sources of national wealth and credit, reflected the ideas which he had developed in his translation of Child's text. He was keen to find new French export channels to Austria and identify economic practices which could be adopted in France. Gournay was interested in systematic inquiries. As such, for the monarchy, he requested numbers and facts on the economy. In the *Traités sur le commerce*, too, he worked with a series of figures to compare the costs of building and equipping vessels in France and the United Provinces.[92] Like Zinzendorf, Gournay attempted to estimate the wealth of England, and, for a comparison with France, calculated the quantity and cost of English and German productive and unproductive labour.[93]

Gournay had direct exposure to business dealings and had received his initiation into commerce from his father. For more than 15 years, he worked in the family business in Cadiz. In 1744, during the War of the Austrian Succession, he was asked by the Comte de Maurepas, the Secretary for the Navy, to move to Paris to help secure the assets of merchants in the French colony in the Antilles.[94] Zinzendorf and Gournay were both practical men. Through extended travels, they sought to broaden their experience and understanding of business activities. They did not want to reinvent economic processes. Rather, they looked to have a dialogue with economic experts and merchants in order to expand their knowledge of applied economic theory. A quote from the *Essai politique*, which the author of the 'Mémoire général des recueils' used at the end of his introduction, summarised this approach to political economy: '*Vous ne pouvez pas tout penser*'. Since it was 'impossible to know everything', often, the most elusive of projects could become beneficial, and, rather than reject ideas from other thinkers, it was valuable to learn from them.[95] There was, he continued, as much merit in implementing good ideas as there was in devising them.[96] Gournay promoted translations of important economic texts. Zinzendorf set out to do the same.

[92] Gournay, 'Remarques sur le Chapitre 4', pp. 149–155, in Meyssonnier (ed.), *Traités sur le commerce*.

[93] Vincent de Gournay, 1753, 'Mémoire (sans titre)', pp. 39–63, in ed. Tsuda, *Mémoires*; Vincent de Gournay, 1752–53; 'Estimation des richesses de L'Angleterre dans quatre époques servant à en faire voir les progrès jusqu'à aujourd'hui tirée d'une brochure intitulé: *Essai sur la dette de la nation*, 2e édition', pp. 35–8 in ed. Tsuda, *Mémoires*.

[94] Meyssonnier (ed.), *Traités sur le commerce*, p. vii.

[95] [Anonymous], 'Mémoire général', fol. 3r.

[96] Melon, *Essai politique*, last paragraph of Chap. 25: 'Des Systèmes', p. 832.

CHAPTER 4

The German Translation of Law's *Money and Trade*, 1758

In 1746, during his university studies in Leipzig, Zinzendorf developed his interest in translations. Leipzig was a centre for language reform, and Zinzendorf made plans to produce German translations of important financial literature.[1] As part of some general advice to his younger brother Karl on the skills he needed to acquire, apart from learning how to dance, Zinzendorf emphasised the importance of mastering languages. He mentioned in particular English, Italian and French. The simplest method, he advised, to learn languages was to work at least one hour a day from a book translated from French and compare the result to the French original.[2] Zinzendorf himself translated a large number of texts on finance and commerce.[3] Translations were also among the first pieces of work he

[1] Eduard Gaston von Pettenegg (ed.), *Ludwig und Karl Grafen und Herren von Zinzendorf. Ihre Selbstbiographien nebst einer kurzen Geschichte des Hauses Zinzendorf* (Vienna, 1879), p. 62. On language reform, see Grete Klingenstein, *Der Aufstieg des Hauses Kaunitz, Studien zur Herkunft und Bildung des Staatskanzlers Wenzel Anton* (Göttingen, 1975), pp. 210–14. On the importance of Leipzig in the book trade with France, see Mark Lehmstedt, 'Über den Anteil des Leipziger Buchhandels am literarischen Austausch zwischen Frankreich und Deutschland. Das Beispiel der Peter Philipp Wolfschen Buchhandlung in Leipzig (1795–1803)', in Hans-Jürgen Lüsebrink, Rolf Reichhardt, Annette Keilhauer and René Lohr (eds.), *Kulturtransfer im Epochenbruch. Frankreich-Deutschland 1770 bis 1815* (2 vols. Leipzig, 1997), vol. 1, pp. 403–43.

[2] Letter of Ludwig Zinzendorf to Karl Zinzendorf, 20 March 1758, vol. 63, DOZA.

[3] Pettenegg (ed.), *Selbstbiographien*, p. 66.

S. Adler, *Political Economy in the Habsburg Monarchy 1750–1774*, Palgrave Studies in the History of Finance,
https://doi.org/10.1007/978-3-030-31007-3_4

produced for Kaunitz.[4] For the government, Zinzendorf did paid translations of legal texts into French, Italian and Latin.[5] Among his personal papers, there are fragments of translations of European writers, including Child, Melon, Hume, Plumard de Dangeul and Forbonnais.[6] Other works have been lost.[7] An important text, which appeared in print in 1758, was the German translation of Law's exceptional economic treatise of 1705: *Money and Trade Considered, with a Proposal for Supplying the Nation with Money*. It was published with the title *Gedanken vom Gelde und von der Handlung, nebst einem Vorschlage dem Geldmangel in Schottland abzuhelfen*,[8] and was printed in octavo format, but without the author's name. The publisher was Johann Thomas von Trattner, who owned the most successful and privileged printing business in the monarchy, with offices in Vienna, Prague and Trieste.[9] By printing Zinzendorf's text, Trattner was responding to a general interest for economic titles.[10] It also followed the French trend from 1750 onwards which saw a rapid rise in the production of French language economic publications due to an

[4] Ibid., p. 59.

[5] Grete Klingenstein, 'Between Mercantilism and Physiocracy. Stages, Modes and Functions of Economic Theory in the Habsburg Monarchy, 1748–63' in Charles W. Ingrao (ed.), *State and Society in Early Modern Austria* (West Lafayette, IN: Purdue University Press, 1994), pp. 181–214, at p. 197.

[6] In addition to Melon's *Essai politique*, Zinzendorf translated Sir Josiah Child, probably *Brief Observations Concerning Trade and the Interest of Money*; David Hume, *Political Discourse*; Louis-Joseph Plumard de Dangeul, *Remarques sur les avantages et les désavantages de la France et la Grande Bretagne*; Véron de Forbonnais, *Elémens de Commerce*, all in Karton 38, Archiv Zinzendorf, NÖLA. Karl read Ludwig's translation of *Elémens*: see Diary of Karl Zinzendorf, 6 August 1762, HHStA.

[7] Ludwig Zinzendorf, 'Übersetzung aus dem Englischen des Locke Geld und dessen Ausmünzung und Erhöhung der Münzen, auch die diesfällige Meinung des Herren Lowndes betr.', Nachlaß Zinzendorf, vol. 93, HHStA. The document is missing from the files.

[8] [Ludwig Zinzendorf], *Gedanken vom Gelde und von der Handlung, nebst einem Vorschlage dem Geldmangel in Schottland abzuhelfen. Aus dem Englischen übersetzt. Gedruckt bey Johann Thomas Trattnern* (Vienna, Prague and Trieste, 1758). For Law's original text, I have used the reprint in Antoin. E. Murphy (ed.), *Monetary Theory: 1601–1758* (6 vols, London, 1997), vol. 5, pp. 3–70.

[9] On the success of Trattner, see Ursula Giese, 'Johann Thomas Edler von Trattner. Seine Bedeutung als Buchdrucker, Buchhändler und Herausgeber', *Archiv für Geschichte des Buchwesens* (Frankfurt/Main, 1961), vol. 3, col. 1013–1454.

[10] Other economic publications published by Trattner included a translation of Forbonnais' criticism of physiocracy: *Principes et observations économiques* (Paris, 1767) and *Des Herrn von Fourbonnais Sätze und Beobachtungen aus der Oekonomie, aus dem französischen übersetzt von Wilhelm Ehrenfried Neugebauer* (Vienna, 1767).

increasingly free press.[11] Copies of Zinzendorf's translation are held today at the National Library in Vienna, at the Hitotsubashi University in Tokyo and at the Research Library Olomouc.[12]

John Law wrote *Money and Trade* for the Scottish Parliament during the debate in Scotland about a union with England. For the Scots, economic factors were key considerations in the discussion of their relations with England. In the late seventeenth century, their small economy had suffered both from agricultural shortages following harvest failures and from decreasing commerce with Europe and North America. The economy was weak, and by 1700 it was heavily dependent on exports to England.[13] Law set out to convince Parliament that Scotland did not need to join forces with England. The Scottish economy, he thought, was paralysed by a chronic monetary crisis. With limited access to gold and silver mines, metallic money was in short supply and therefore the Bank of Scotland was of limited use. Also, in general, the value of silver money varied frequently. Without a supply of money, Law argued, the economy would not be able to become more sophisticated and build its manufacturing base. *Money and Trade* was Law's radical proposal to expand the supply of money with a new monetary standard that would circulate in the economy and support trade.[14] Paper money, he argued, based on land as collateral, would be a suitable standard as it could be managed to address the needs of commerce and increase the domestic level of employment.[15]

[11] For the growth of publicity of economic titles in France, see Christine Théré, 'Economic Publishing and Authors, 1566–1789' in Gilbert Faccarello (ed.), *Studies in the History of French Political Economy: From Bodin to Walras* (London, 1998), pp. 1–56.

[12] Copies can be located as follows: Cod. 232596-A, ÖNB; Cod. 128049192, Carl Menger collection, Hitotsubashi University, Tokyo; and Shelf mark: 13.531, Research Library Olomouc. I have used the copy in Olomouc which belonged to Johannes Schulz, a pupil of Josef Sonnenfels. I am grateful to Grete Klingenstein for having pointed out the provenance.

[13] John Robertson, *The Case for the Enlightenment: Scotland and Naples 1680–1760* (Cambridge, 2005), pp. 90–2; T.C. Smout, 'The Road to Union' in Geoffrey Holmes, *England after the Glorious Revolution 1689–1714* (London: Macmillan, 1969), pp. 176–96, at pp. 182–83, 187–88.

[14] It was a development of his arguments in *The Essay of a Land Bank* (c.1704) where he had discussed monetary issues only and, for the first time, had proposed the use of land-based paper money: see Antoin E. Murphy, *John Law: Economic Theorist and Policy-Maker* (Oxford, 1997), pp. 51–3.

[15] Law, *Money and Trade*, ed. Antoin E. Murphy, *Monetary Theory: 1601–1758*, pp. 8–9, 34, 45–6, 50–1, 56–9. Law thought that land had a stable value, was of limited supply and recognised as a valuable commodity by the general population.

Zinzendorf was very influenced by Law's ideas. He wrote accounts, which are now lost, of Law's financial system and of its favourable reception by scholars.[16] Zinzendorf sought to introduce *Money and Trade* to as wide a German-speaking public as possible since, as he wrote to his brother, there was no German book of comparable sophistication.[17] In this, he differed from other writers who, in their translations, omitted any references to Law. Due to the failure of Law's financial scheme in France, the ideas were considered by some as too dangerous for public dissemination.[18]

Law implemented his scheme in the early eighteenth century. At the death of Louis XIV in 1715, France was virtually bankrupt. The country, in Law's view, was suffering from a shortage of money and a fiscal crisis. The shortage of money had caused unemployment and low levels of output, and the fiscal crisis was the result of the substantial state debt and the corresponding high rates of interest that France had to offer on its bonds. Law proposed, as a first step, the creation of a General Bank which would expand the supply of money. The second and more radical step was an ambitious debt reduction programme through the conversion of the state debt into equity by means of a large, state-sponsored, conglomerate trading company. In 1718, the entire colonial trade of France was part of a single, large holding company backed by the state and directed by Law. Law recognised that an enterprise of this scale required more financing, and he began to use the General Bank, which he had established in 1716, as an instrument to facilitate the plans for growth. In December 1718, by a state declaration, he succeeded in converting the General Bank into a Royal Bank. The state bought out the bank's private shareholders and increased the scale of banking operations. The bank provided liquidity for the purchase of shares in the company. At first, the scheme was extraordi-

[16] The two documents are indexed as Ludwig Zinzendorf, '4 Memoiren über Banken und das System des Law', vol. 106 and 'Système de Law. Sentiments de quelques auteurs célèbres en faveur du papier' in 'Système de finances', vol. 25, both in the index of Nachlaß Zinzendorf, HHStA.

[17] 'L'autre qui vient de paraitre dans ce pays cy depuis peu et qui contient de bonnes choses qu'on ne trouve ordinairement dans les livres allemands. L'original est anglais.' Letter of Ludwig Zinzendorf to Karl Zinzendorf, 7 November 1759, vol. 63, DOZA.

[18] In the 1743 Spanish edition of Melon's *Essai politique*, the translator, Teodoro Ventura de Argumosa, left out all references to Law: Jesús Astigarraga, 'La dérangeante découverte de l'autre: traductions et adaptations espagnoles de *l'Essai politique sur le commerce* (1734) de Jean François Melon', *Revue d'histoire moderne et contemporaine*, 57:1 (2010), pp. 91–118, at pp. 100–1.

narily popular. With strong demand, the value of the company's shares increased dramatically. The success of the financial operation encouraged Law to pursue the ambitious plan of exchanging the entire French national debt of 1.5 billion *livres* for shares. However, the economy was not strong enough to absorb the large supply of money, and the price of shares and banknotes tumbled during the summer of 1720. The system collapsed in the second half of that year. In December, Law was forced to flee the country with the help of the regent and never returned to France.[19]

Zinzendorf was a supporter of Law's economic theories. *Gedanken vom Gelde* was published anonymously, but soon after Karl's arrival in Vienna, Zinzendorf confirmed his authorship to his brother.[20] Earlier, Zinzendorf had sent it to him, urging him to read the book while cautioning that the content might appear very 'abstract' at first.[21] There was a long time lag between the publication of Zinzendorf's book and the first German translation of *Money and Trade*, which had appeared in Leipzig in 1720.[22] The latter had coincided with Law's popularity, his appointment as Controller General of Finances and the extraordinary power Law wielded in French politics from 1718 to 1720.[23] The translation of 1720 had followed the structure of Law's text. In the preface, the English printer had deplored

[19] Antoin E. Murphy, *The Genesis of Macroeconomics: New Ideas from Sir William Petty to Henry Thornton* (Oxford, 2009), pp. 62–70. On Law's financial scheme, see also Michael Sonenscher, 'The Nation's Debt and the Birth of the Modern Republic: The French Fiscal Deficit and the Politics of the Revolution of 1789', *History of Political Thought*, 18:1 (1997), pp. 64–103, and Marc Cheynet de Beaupré, *Joseph Pâris-Duverney. Financier D'État (1684–1770). Les sentiers du pouvoir (1684–1770)* (Paris, 2012), pp. 611–784. For Law's assessment on his scheme, see Fritz Karl Mann (ed.), 'Justification du Système de Law par son Auteur', *Revue D'Histoire Économique et Sociale*, 6:1 (1913), pp. 49–103.

[20] Diary of Karl Zinzendorf, 8 February 1761, HHStA; also Pettenegg (ed.), *Selbstbiographien*, p. 72.

[21] Letter of Ludwig Zinzendorf to Karl Zinzendorf, 14 December 1759, vol. 63, DOZA; Diary of Karl Zinzendorf, 3 December 1759, HHStA.

[22] [Anonymous], *Herrn Laws, Controlleur general der Financen in Franckreich Gedancken vom Waaren und Geld Handel, nebst dem erst in Schottland, hernach in Frankreich vorgestellten und angenommenen neuen project und Systemate der Financen, wobey einige curieuse Fata des Autoris zu lesen. Nach dem französischen und Englischen Exemplar* (Leipzig: bey Jacob Schustern, 1720). Both this translation and Zinzendorf's *Gedanken vom Gelde* are catalogued in Kenneth E. Carpenter, *Dialogue in Political Economy. Translations from and into German in the 18th Century* (Boston, MA: Kress Library Publications No. 23, 1977) pp. 28–9.

[23] Fritz Karl Mann, 'Der politische Ideengehalt von John Laws Finanzsystem', *Jahrbuch für Nationalökonomie und Statistik*, 113 (1919), pp. 97–122, at p. 105.

Law's treatment in England and Scotland where his monetary theories became unpopular. The justification of the new publication had been the relevance and sophistication of Law's ideas and the concern that now they were beneficial to a rival nation.[24]

Zinzendorf's translation, which was published almost 40 years later, had three advantages over the earlier German text. First, it was a closer and more nuanced translation of the English original. The version of 1720 had omitted many of the italics which Law had used to emphasise text passages. It also had left out some of the arguments which Law had made in *Money and Trade*, including Law's criticism of Hugh Chamberlen's proposal to issue notes backed up by land.[25] Law had argued that Chamberlen, who had been his main rival, had a flawed financial plan and had failed to take into account the calculations on the time value of money and the benefits of compound interest.[26]

The second advantage of *Gedanken vom Gelde* was the effort Zinzendorf undertook to expound arguments for the benefit of the reader. Law had written in a concise style, and Zinzendorf often added examples to explain ideas and clarify calculations. As Law had reduced Chamberlen's money proposal to two sentences, Zinzendorf provided a numerical illustration so that the reader would appreciate more fully its significance. For example, Chamberlen had envisaged issuing notes upon land security and cancelling 2¼ per cent of the issue each year over a period of 45 years. Assume, Zinzendorf added, that the revenue generated by the land is £1000 and the owner, in order to be able to borrow money, assigned the land to the bank as collateral. He would then receive from the bank freely circulating notes, equivalent to silver money, worth £45,000.[27] There would be no interest charge since the bank would keep the revenue of the land and cancel each year 2¼ per cent of the loan. After 45 years, the loan would be amortised, and the land would be transferred back to its owner. The ben-

[24] 'So wurde er gezwungen in fremde Lande zu flüchten, und da siehet man in jetzt als hohen Minister, nachdem er die Bosheit seiner Feinde auf unterschiedliche Art empfunden. Man siehet ihn an solchem Ort die gleichen Sachen ausführen, welche die vorherigen Zeiten nicht zu sehen bekommen, die unsrigen nicht begreiffen, und die späte Nachwelt nicht wird glauben können': [Anonymous], *Herrn Laws*, p. 2.

[25] Ibid., p. 93.

[26] Chamberlen had proposed the establishment of a land bank, and Law had rushed the publication of *Money and Trade* to pre-empt a favourable proposal by the Scottish parliament on Chamberlen's scheme: see Murphy, *John Law*, p. 76.

[27] Based on the land's yearly revenue of £1000 divided by the redemption of 2¼ per cent.

efit of this financial operation was greatly to increase the value of land and, in addition, increase the supply of money in the economy. Based on the prevailing rate of interest of 5 per cent, the value of the same plot of land would have been much lower and only worth £20,000 in silver money.[28]

Finally, Zinzendorf sought to reaffirm the relevance of Law's arguments by adding references and 'paratext' of mostly more contemporary French, German and English writers. By providing a coherent set of arguments which extended over 60 years, Zinzendorf attempted to rehabilitate Law's theories. Unlike the translation of 1720, but following Melon's *Essai politique*, Zinzendorf's translation never mentioned Law by name. He probably sought to remove as far as possible any lasting negative connotations of Law's reputation and keep the reader's attention firmly on the value of the economic theory. *Gedanken vom Gelde* is heavily annotated with long footnotes running over several pages. It is more than three times the length of the German translation of 1720. In addition to numerical examples, Zinzendorf's footnotes included references to relevant technical questions set out by other writers. In general, Zinzendorf gave precise references and added the edition and the page numbers of the publications he used. Sometimes in the main text of the translation, he included short additions, emphasised meaning through the use of bold type style and made small variations to Law's numerical examples. As in the earlier German version, the content and the structure of Zinzendorf's translation follow Law's text, and a summary table of contents of the book's eight chapters is included at the end.[29]

The exposition of *Gedanken vom Gelde* below follows the chapters in the book. The section headings introduce Law's arguments to which Zinzendorf added comments and gave references to publications by other writers. In Chaps. 1 and 2, Zinzendorf reinforced Law's idea on the nature of money and developed the discussion of the link between trade and exchange rates. In the next two chapters, he described the banking systems necessary for good credit management and explained the effects of domestic currency manipulations. Here, in order to emphasise the concerns about currency manipulations, he inserted an account of the technical debates between financial specialists from France and Germany. Chapter 5 contained historical calculations on changes in currency values

[28] Zinzendorf, *Gedanken vom Gelde*, pp. 289–90.

[29] Zinzendorf, *Gedanken vom Gelde*, pp. 443–44. As in Law's original text, Zinzendorf repeated the section headings at the beginning of each chapter.

and agricultural prices in France, England and Germany, and Zinzendorf's assessment of their respective economic policies. Finally, in the chapter on Law's proposal, Zinzendorf set out his arguments for implementing an issue of paper money.

Qualities of Money

Zinzendorf emphasised Law's idea concerning the function of silver as a measure of value.[30] It reflected the value in the exchange of produce and varied in relation to demand.[31] It was a voucher for buying produce. So, as a means of exchange, Law had argued, silver was not unique and could be replaced by a different medium with comparable qualities.[32] Gold and copper had been suitable replacements. Zinzendorf added that Portugal, which was short of silver, used gold while Sweden resorted to the use of copper.[33]

Trade and Money

In the second chapter, Law had discussed the influence of money on trade and employment. Population growth, he had underlined, depended on commerce which, in turn, required a sufficient supply of money. Zinzendorf added that among European trading nations, the Dutch were able to sell and ship produce at the most competitive prices. As such, the Dutch merchant benefitted from a capital base which was 20 times the size of his Scottish rival, who was forced to use his entire profit to pay for subsistence. The merchant in the United Provinces was able to keep a large amount of his profit as money reserves. Thus, he could defend his competitive advantage over the Scottish merchant.[34]

Zinzendorf was in agreement with Law that an increase in the supply of money in proportion to the demands of commerce would not lead to a decrease in the value of money. He had also refuted the arguments of some contemporary writers according to which an increase of the monetary base of a country would lead to a loss of its competitive advantage in commerce. For Zinzendorf, only if the supply of money was larger than

[30] Ibid., p. 15.

[31] For a discussion of Law's analysis of money and his use of supply and demand to set a price, see Murphy, *John Law*, pp. 53–9.

[32] Zinzendorf, *Gedanken vom Gelde*, pp. 11, 13, 21–2, 24.

[33] Ibid., p. 25.

[34] Ibid., pp. 37–8.

the demands of commerce would the value of money decrease and the general level of prices increase.[35]

The discussions of exchange rates were important. Zinzendorf expanded on Law's arguments of commerce and exchange rate variations between Scotland, England and the United Provinces. A depreciation of the Scottish money versus the English *pound sterling*, he thought, had no impact on the intrinsic value of Scottish produce. It only affected the relative values. Abroad, Scottish merchants could sell their produce at lower prices. Domestically, with everything else being equal, they were able to buy the same amount of produce as before the currency depreciation.[36]

In relation to Law's discussion of the market value of exchange rates as an indication of the balance of commerce, Zinzendorf added references to two French texts. These sources, Zinzendorf argued, gave the reader a comprehensive exposition of the variations of exchange rates.[37] The first was Charles de Ferrare Dutot's publication *Réflexions politiques*.[38] In 1735, Dutot had written three lengthy anonymous letters addressed to his former colleague Melon. They had formed the basis of Dutot's book which had been published in two volumes in 1738. A further four editions had been printed between 1740 and 1755.[39] Zinzendorf referred to the third chapter, which constituted the entire second volume, where Dutot had examined the impact of exchange rate changes on the balance of trade.[40] Dutot, who liked statistics, had reinforced his arguments with

[35] Ibid., pp. 431–32.

[36] Ibid., pp. 81–2.

[37] Ibid., p. 59.

[38] Charles de Ferrare Dutot, *Réflexions politiques sur les finances et le commerce* (2 vols, Paris, 1738); see also Charles de Ferrare Dutot, *Réflexions politiques sur les finances et le commerce*, ed. Paul Harsin (2 vols, Paris, 1754; reprint, 2 vols, Liège, 1935). On Dutot's first name, see *Réflexions politiques*, ed. Harsin, vol. 1, p. xi. On Dutot's intellectual debates and influences, his admiration for Law and assessment of the financial scheme, see Antoin E. Murphy (ed.), *Du Tot. Histoire du Systême de John Law (1716–1720)* (Paris: Institut National d'Études Démographiques, 2000), Introduction, pp. xi–lxxvii, as well as 'The Enigmatic Monsieur Du Tot' in Gilbert Faccarello (ed.), *Studies in the History of French Political Economy. From Bodin to Walras* (London, 1998), pp. 57–77. On Dutot's life, see François R. Velde, *The Life and Times of Nicolas Dutot*, Working Paper No. 2009–10, Federal Reserve Bank of Chicago (November, 2009).

[39] *Dutot, Réflexions politiques* (ed.) Harsin. vol. 1, p. xxii.

[40] Dutot, 'Chapitre III. Dans lequel on examine si le surhaussement des Monnoies est avantageux à notre Commerce en suivant le cours du change étranger qui en est le véritable Baromètre et la seule route qui puisse nous le montrer avec certitude et avec clarté', *Réflexions politiques*, vol. 2, pp. iii–427. This is found in Harsin's edition, pp. 146–291.

empirical data.[41] He had set out the variations of exchange rates from 1709 to 1734 between France, England and the United Provinces and had calculated the ensuing profit or loss for France and the impact on its commerce. In the preface to his work, Dutot had underlined the importance of this chapter in providing detailed calculations which were reliable and intelligible to the general reader. He also had noted that he had been able to establish a method which made it possible to assess the balance of commerce and calculate exchange rates.[42]

The second French work of relevance was Forbonnais' *Elémens du Commerce* which, in Chap. 8, presented a sophisticated and technical discussion of exchange rates.[43] Zinzendorf had recommended this chapter as useful reading to his brother.[44] Forbonnais' book had developed the ideas of Melon, and Zinzendorf read the second, expanded edition of 1754. Most of the chapters of the book, as Forbonnais had pointed out in the introduction, had been published before in the *Encyclopédie* of Diderot and d'Alembert. In this book dedicated to the economy, Forbonnais had been able to establish commerce as a recognised science and to reproduce relevant ideas of other writers in a clear and coherent manner. Forbonnais had chosen a concise presentation and had decided to forego detailed arguments.[45]

Forbonnais had begun Chap. 8 by arguing that only two types of exchanges were allowed in commerce: either the exchange of currencies or negotiation between merchants to move funds at a fixed price from one country to another. Such negotiation had two purposes: first, to decide on the transport of funds and, second, to settle its cost. Forbonnais had referred to identical values of currencies from two countries as *pair du prix de change* and variations of these values as *le cours du prix de change*. Exchange rates of currencies had resulted from the international transport of funds. As commerce developed, physical movement of specie had become cumbersome and risky. Hence, a 'mercantile contract', or letter of exchange, had been developed to avoid the transport of money and facilitate commercial transactions within a country and between countries.[46]

[41] Dutot, *Réflexions politiques*, p. xxiv.

[42] Ibid., vol. 1, pp. 1, 15–20, 23–6.

[43] Véron de Forbonnais, *Elémens du Commerce*, 2nd edn (2 vols, Leiden, 1754), vol. 2, pp. 74–117.

[44] Letter of Ludwig Zinzendorf to Karl Zinzendorf, 14 December 1759, vol 63, DOZA.

[45] Forbonnais, *Elémens*, 'Avertissement'.

[46] Ibid., pp. 74–82.

Gold and silver specie, Forbonnais had continued, were used for commerce. However, necessity or bad faith led people to clip coins while keeping their denominations. As the reduced specie content of the coins did not reflect any longer the original denominations, countries had to have a *monnaie réelle* and a *monnaie idéale*. The latter was kept for ease of use and as reference values for economic transactions. The different variations of these *monnaies* in various countries demanded the calculation of exchange rates, which had an influence on the development of commerce. It was nevertheless possible, Forbonnais had argued, to establish the precise exchange rate, *pair réel du change*, between two currencies if important factors, including the content of specie and the denomination, could be accurately determined and then compared between the currencies.[47]

Forbonnais had calculated the *pair réel du change* between the French and the English currencies and had argued that variations in the value had been driven by two factors. The first was a variation between a country's *monnaie réelle* and *monnaie idéale* which would reduce the value of state credit, assign new arbitrary values to property and investments and so affect public confidence. The second variation recognised financial pressures which state finances had exerted on the economy. The latter, Forbonnais had argued, had been the result of excessive debt requirements with foreign creditors. Because of the demands of war finance, debt levels had grown and had led to an outflow of money. However, they had also been an expression of the different costs of public debt in various countries, and a country with a lower rate of interest on public debt would experience an outflow of money to a country which had offered a higher rate of interest on state finances. Money had become a commodity and had been paid by investors to those countries which had offered the highest return. Hence, the *balance du commerce* between countries had been an assessment of the countries' reciprocal debts as well as a reflection of money transfers to repay loans. Variations in the cost of state finances had contributed to it.[48]

The variations, Forbonnais had continued, of the *cours du prix de change* had reflected changes in commercial activities and movement of money. Therefore, it also had been an expression of the state of the balance of trade between countries. The instability of the exchange rates had led to sudden changes in the exchange of monies between countries and

[47] Ibid., pp. 82–5.
[48] Ibid., pp. 85–8.

had created opportunities for financial trading that involved merchants following the developments of exchange rates between major commercial centres to anticipate potential profits or losses by moving funds. This type of commerce had consisted in taking advantage of exchange rate differences between cities which traded with each other. Profit opportunities disappeared if the variations of the *pair du prix du change* between commercial centres were of identical proportion. Forbonnais had referred to the identical *cours du prix du change* between trading places as the *pair politique*. In situations, he had maintained, where the *pair politique* had been broken, exchange rate operations would be most lucrative in countries which had kept the rate of interest low. In those countries, investors would be incentivised to undertake exchange rate transactions since the opportunity cost to seek alternative investments domestically would be low. This type of trade had been closely linked to decisions by governments on setting a national rate of interest.[49]

At the end of the analysis, Forbonnais had drawn five general conclusions. First, the average exchange rate of a country with its commercial partners could show if over a period of time its balance of trade had been positive. Second, a higher level of public debt than in rival trading nations had resulted in a loss to the economy as money had been sent abroad, so it followed, third, that the commerce with the rival trading nations had suffered and that produce had been exported at lower prices. Also, money from these transfers had been lost to the domestic industry and represented a gain to the creditor country. Fourth, if one country owed money to a foreign creditor, it would be preferable to make money transfers rather than to seek adjustments via the exchange rate because the latter would harm commerce. In this respect, finally, it would have been pointless to restrict the outflow of specie to foreign nations. Without foreign debt, money transferred abroad would have been repaid with interest, and the gain would have been reflected in the exchange rate.[50]

For Zinzendorf, these two sources were useful. They clarified terminology and showed how exchange rate variations provided an indication of the economic competitiveness of a country. Also, they were a good fit to the arguments which Zinzendorf had developed in his earlier works, the 'Essai sur l'Établissement d'une Banque générale des États' and the 'Mémoire sur les richesses, le commerce et les finances de la France', on the positive impact of trade and a low rate of interest on the economy.

[49] Ibid., pp. 103–14.
[50] Ibid., pp. 114–17.

Zinzendorf concluded the discussion of exchange rates by drawing the readers' attention to the monetary discussion in Montesquieu's influential work *De l'Esprit des Lois*. Montesquieu's argument, Zinzendorf thought, was significant. It complemented Law's analysis and explained the real effect that commerce exerted on changes in exchange rates.[51] Thus, instead of using a simple text reference, Zinzendorf provided a loose translation of Montesquieu's entire passage. He inserted it at the end of the chapter so as not to cut off the flow of Law's argument. The discussion Zinzendorf was interested in covered the relative values of money between countries rather than, as Montesquieu had explained at the beginning of the chapter, arbitrary variations of the rate of exchange triggered by a change of law. The passage of *L'Esprit des Lois* which Zinzendorf translated began with an example of the exchange rate adjustment between the French *écu* and the Dutch *groschen* when the rate fell below par: from 1 *écu* for 54 *groschen* to 1 *écu* for 50 *groschen*. As the Dutch were able to buy more French produce following the adjustment in the exchange rate, French exports to the United Provinces increased and, conversely, Dutch imports to France fell. The French state lost as a buyer, but gained as a seller. Because of the depreciation of its currency, France had to send more money abroad to buy the same amount of goods. However, Montesquieu had argued, the forces of commerce redressed the movement of the exchange rate. The change in demand and supply of produce, based on the self-interest of French and Dutch merchants, moved the prices of produce back to par. Following the rate change, French prices, expressed in Dutch currency, decreased. French merchants might have preferred to increase their prices, but they were prepared to share their gain with Dutch traders to secure their profit. Dutch prices, expressed in French currency, increased in an opposite, neutralising effect. In this way, French merchants purchased less produce, and Dutch merchants, with fewer exports, lost accordingly. Commerce, Montesquieu had argued, had induced a self-regulatory process to counteract variations in exchange rates where, in the end, nations gradually gravitated back to equilibrium.[52]

[51] Charles-Louis de Secondat, Baron de Montesquieu, *L'Esprit des Lois* (1748), ed. Victor Goldschmidt (2 vols, Paris: Garnier-Flammarion, 1979), vol. 2, book XXII, Chap. 10: 'du change', pp. 84–5.

[52] Zinzendorf, *Gedanken vom Gelde*, pp. 104–7.

Banks

Like Law, Zinzendorf considered banks to be important institutions which facilitated the supply of money to the economy. In the same year as the publication of *Gedanken vom Gelde*, Zinzendorf also wrote an extensive and detailed survey of major European banks. The survey, which is analysed in Chap. 5, further illustrated Law's arguments. Law had mentioned various European countries which were using banks, and in *Gedanken vom Gelde*, Zinzendorf added Italian examples of public banks: St Ambrosio of Milan, St George of Genoa, Bank of Venice and the credit schemes, the 'Monti', of Rome and Naples. As an extension of Law's example of the Bank of Sweden which allowed for the safekeeping of specie, Zinzendorf described in a footnote the procedure of bookkeeping which banks ought to follow to extend credit to customers. Recording transactions with *Folios* and *Banco Geld* were important aspects of good banking practice.[53]

For Law, the Bank of Amsterdam had provided a double benefit to the country: first, by lending money, it had increased trade and commerce; and second, by adding to the supply of money, it had contributed to the output of the economy and thus enabled a fall in the cost of borrowing. The bank itself also had 'benefitted' from these activities, and Zinzendorf emphasised Law's argument by adding 'considerable' to 'benefit' in the text. Zinzendorf explained that the money which was deposited for free could be lent by charging a rate of interest, hence generating an income for the bank.[54]

In relation to the banking practices in England, Zinzendorf clarified the role of goldsmiths. The latter, who were the precursors to the Bank of England, provided money changing services. They differed from typical money changers in other countries in that, similar to public banks, they accepted money for deposits and issued bills which were payable at sight. The goldsmiths thus acted as a clearing institution and, in addition, were free to trade in gold and silver commodities with other countries. Zinzendorf admired the operations of the Bank of England and corrected Law, who had argued that the banknotes of the Bank of England had traded at a discount. Zinzendorf translated 'discount' as 'a little below par' and explained that for over 60 years since the creation of the bank, the

[53] Zinzendorf, *Gedanken vom Gelde*, pp. 110–14. See also in Chap. 5, particularly the section 'The Survey of European Banks'.

[54] Zinzendorf, *Gedanken vom Gelde*, pp. 119–20.

market price had only been two or three times below par. These price falls, he added, were very rare; they were of very short duration and resulted from periods of domestic unrest. In normal times, the notes of the Bank of England were solid instruments, accepted nationally and traded directly among investors.[55]

Currency Variations

In France, domestic currency manipulations had been frequent occurrences in the early eighteenth century. To appreciate the extensive discussions Law and Zinzendorf devoted to currency manipulations, it is useful to provide a summary of the financial mechanism. European economies had a bimetallic system of gold and silver. The money of account gave a common set of prices through which the various gold and silver coins in circulation in the country could be evaluated. To express economic values such as wages or the price of debt, France used the *livres tournois* as the money of account. The medium of exchange was the *louis d'or*. The ruler could vary the domestic exchange rate between the money of account and the metal coins. An augmentation of the currency raised the value of *louis d'or* in terms of *livres tournois*. It was, therefore, a devaluation of the money of account and a revaluation of the medium of exchange. Conversely, a diminution of the currency was a devaluation of the medium of exchange in terms of money of account. A devaluation of the *livres* was advantageous for debtors and employers because they required less specie to make payments. For the French state, in particular, devaluations were attractive. They alleviated the burden of public debt and created through the alteration of coins seigniorage tax gains for the state. Creditors and employees were opposed to devaluations in the domestic exchange rate. Their loan and wage agreements were expressed in money of account and, following a devaluation, they would receive less specie.[56]

Even though, Law had argued, money and commerce were interdependent, adjusting domestic exchange rates would not positively and sustainably influence commerce. Law gave France and the United Provinces as examples of countries where the rulers had used changes in the domestic exchange rates to quickly fix their domestic finances. Also, he had noted, the level of price adjustment in the economy had been slow to track any

[55] Ibid., pp. 122–23, 124–25.

[56] This is based on Murphy, *John Law*, pp. 150–52.

variation in the domestic exchange rate. In Scotland, Law had assumed that an augmentation of the currency by 20 per cent would not lead to a proportional increase in the price of produce, and the value of money would fall by only 10 per cent. Zinzendorf, adding his own calculation, gave a slightly higher loss of 12 per cent.[57]

Changing the denomination of the currency had required a new minting which, Law had argued, had been a redistribution of wealth to the ruler from his people. The ruler levied charges for minting coins. In the case of France, this had amounted to 20 or 25 million *livres* or more depending on the quantity of money in the economy. These currency operations, Law had pointed out, stopped the circulation of money. The French had reacted by sending their money to the United Provinces. In return, via bills of exchange, they had received the same value of money as before the change in the exchange rate. Zinzendorf explained that Law had been alluding to the French currency manipulation of 1693 and added details of the French devaluation. His source was Forbonnais' *Recherches et Considérations sur les Finances de France*.[58] Forbonnais' compendium of French financial operations between 1595 and 1721 was published in the same year as *Gedanken vom Gelde*. It was an extensive publication in two volumes in which Forbonnais had examined the reasons for French public finance decisions and their impact on the economy.[59] With respect to the currency change of 1693, Forbonnais had argued, the French ruler only succeeded in receiving just over half of the expected income. The difference had been sent abroad and foreigners instead of nationals had benefited from half of the money received.[60]

Like Law, Zinzendorf thought that the value of produce could not be influenced by variations in the currency. An augmentation of the currency would not make produce more profitable for export. Law had supported the argument with an example of a Scottish merchant. It was, he had argued, as if the merchant were to end up financially worse off in order to show the same higher profit across his entire range of produce. Out of 100 different items, the merchant could have sold only 90 varieties at a 30 per cent profit. The remaining ten varieties were much less attractive to purchasers, and the

[57] Zinzendorf, *Gedanken vom Gelde*, pp. 161–63.

[58] Véron de Forbonnais, *Recherches et Considérations sur les Finances de France depuis l'année 1595 jusqu'à l'année 1721* (2 vols, Basel, 1758), vol. 2, pp. 96–7.

[59] Ibid., vol. 1, p. 4.

[60] Zinzendorf, *Gedanken vom Gelde*, pp. 169–70.

profit would have been significantly lower. To show the same higher level of profit for all items, the merchant would have had to adapt the systems he used to determine weight and measurement of produce, which would increase the quality. However, in total, with sales prices unchanged but with higher costs of produce, the merchant would have earned less. To clarify, Zinzendorf added two tables of calculations: if, in order to sell the entire range of produce for the same profit of 30 per cent, the Scottish merchant decided to increase his reference values for measurement of produce by one quarter in value without increasing the sales price, his revenue after cost of produce, or gross profit, would have dropped correspondingly by one quarter. He would now also earn less on his 90 varieties, and thus less in aggregate. The same, Zinzendorf continued, would hold true for a country such as Scotland. If it sought to promote the sale of a small part of its domestic produce, it would be at the expense of losing important profits from the bulk of its exports.[61]

Law's text, Zinzendorf noted at the end of the chapter, had not provided an exhaustive enough analysis of the disadvantages of monetary devaluations. Therefore, he provided the reader with additional references of publications in a footnote. These, Zinzendorf thought, were important texts which had been published after *Money and Trade* and offered good discussions of the problems associated with currency variations. The first set of texts by Dutot, Forbonnais and Law had examined monetary changes in France; the second set were German publications written in the context of the Prussian currency reform of 1750. Zinzendorf did not provide translations or commentaries of these texts. However, he gave their full titles and, for the French works where applicable, specified edition, volume and page numbers.[62]

Zinzendorf's first reference was *Réflexions politiques*, Dutot's direct response to the monetary arguments of Melon's *Essai politique*.[63] There, Dutot had disagreed with Melon on the benefits from changes in the domestic exchange rate of the currency where, in case of monetary devaluations, debtors had been favoured at the expense of creditors. Dutot had set out three scenarios of devaluation of the *livres*: the first was an increase

[61] Ibid., pp. 175–77.

[62] Ibid., pp. 197–98. Zinzendorf never directly referred to Law. Here, in a footnote, referring to the French *Mémoire* as 'written by our author', he made an indirect reference to the Scotsman.

[63] Article 7 of Chap. 1, in Dutot, *Réflexions*, vol. 1, pp. 123–64. This is found in Harsin's edition, pp. 43–56.

in prices equivalent to an increase in the money of account; the second, an increase in prices which was less than the increase in the money of account; and in the third, Dutot had assumed no change in prices, but an increase in the money of account. The first scenario, he had argued, was detrimental to wage earners. They were more numerous than debtors and faced higher prices without a higher income to compensate. Scenarios two and three led to a deterioration of the terms of trade with competing nations. Other nations rapidly entered the domestic market to buy up local produce as they needed less specie than before, and local traders had to pay more for foreign goods.

To *Réflexions politiques*, Zinzendorf added a summary of the discussion between Melon and Dutot. Forbonnais had included this in Chap. 9 of *Elémens* where he discussed the circulation of money.[64] The text was technical and not easily comprehensible for the general reader. This was also Karl's impression. He subsequently noted in his diary that the dispute between Melon and Dutot in *Elémens* had been very abstract.[65] Forbonnais had come out in favour of Dutot's views. Given that *Réflexions politiques* was relatively unknown compared to Melon's *Essai politique*, it was, Forbonnais had argued, necessary to set out again the exchange between the French writers. Moreover, he thought, the partisans of Melon had claimed that the two writers were in agreement on the benefits of monetary adjustments. This perception, which Forbonnais had thought was widely held, ought to be changed.[66]

Both Melon and Dutot, Forbonnais had argued, were in agreement that changes in domestic exchange rates could not be made without affecting public confidence. An augmentation of the currency for the benefit of the ruler had been pernicious and, because of a disproportion between old and new monies, had led to confusion in monetary affairs. Dutot had presented detailed calculations to support this argument. He had made the case that in order to stabilise the resulting disorder of the circulation of money, it had been necessary to move the values of both monies together again, either by decreasing the new or increasing the old specie. Dutot had also shown that Melon's preference for an augmentation of the currency was detrimental to the state and against the interests of the ruler and his people.[67]

[64] Forbonnais, *Elémens*, vol. 2, pp. 191–218.

[65] Diary of Karl Zinzendorf, 22 February 1762, HHStA.

[66] Forbonnais, *Elémens*, vol. 2, pp. 191–92.

[67] Ibid., vol. 2, pp. 192–95.

To summarise the arguments, Forbonnais, like Dutot, had introduced three scenarios: first, an increase in prices proportional to an increase in the money of account; second, an increase in prices greater than a change in the money of account; and third, a change in the money of account superior to a variation in prices. The first scenario would not create any advantages to people engaged in industry or agriculture as expenses would increase in line with revenues. But, using Melon's argument, if the number of debtors in an economy were larger than the number of creditors, '*raison d'état*' might prompt the ruler to act in the interest of the majority. It would be, Forbonnais had continued, a bad policy decision as it had shown a lack of understanding of the nature of creditors. The latter had been the owners of either money or produce. They had chosen to introduce money into the economic system because they had had confidence in its orderly management. Increasing the money of account would punish their trust in the economy. It would prompt them to offer money at higher rates in the future which would negatively impact the circulation of money. The requirement, Forbonnais had thought, was to ensure that a broader and more equitable distribution of funds was available in the economy. There had been a circular flow of money and produce between debtors and creditors such that, through consumption, market participants had been both debtors and creditors at the same time. Therefore, one group had not been larger than the other, and it had been impossible to favour debtors over creditors. Changing domestic exchange rates would only benefit foreign debtors who would pay less to reimburse their old debts.[68]

If the state had been a debtor, an augmentation of the currency would not only diminish the state's credibility versus its creditors, but it would also result in a real loss to the economy. By receiving less from the state, the creditors, who themselves had been part of economic transactions, would be able to contribute a mere fraction of what they were able to give before to productive activities in agriculture and industry. Importantly, they would offer new credit at more onerous terms. It would restrict the availability of money for commerce and hence curtail its circulation. On balance, Forbonnais had thought, if the ruler had decided to change the economic terms and thus had accepted a loss of public confidence, it would have been preferable to decrease the interest payable to creditors rather than to increase the money of account. The ensuing confusion among economic agents would not have been as wide-

[68] Ibid., vol. 2, pp. 195–201.

spread, and confrontation could have been contained to the state and its creditors. In general, an increase in prices equivalent to an increase in the money of account had only created confusion in the economy and had not provided any tangible advantage for the ruler or his citizens.[69]

The same conclusions would apply under the second scenario, except that the rentier class would be at a greater disadvantage and consume even less. In terms of commerce, rising prices might affect exports and lead foreign nations to buy less domestic produce. However, the effects on the economy of an augmentation of the currency and a stronger rise in prices had been gradual. The people became poorer as prices and taxes had continuously increased. The work, Forbonnais had added, of the Abbé de Saint-Pierre and Dutot on the income of several French rulers had supported this conclusion.[70]

The third scenario had been the most favourable to Melon. With a money increase of 50 per cent and a rise in prices for labour and produce of 25 per cent, a peasant would not be better off as the larger disposable income would be offset by the increase in the expenditure on subsistence. In addition, profits from commerce would have decreased: assuming values of exports of 48 and imports of 36, the balance of trade would have been 12. Following the increase of prices, domestic produce would sell at 60, and after the devaluation of the money of account, the price for imported produce would rise to 54.[71] The net effect would have been a profit halved to six which had been equivalent to a paltry gain of four before the currency adjustment.[72]

Moreover, debts owed by foreigners would be worth 50 per cent less and, correspondingly, debts due to foreigners would have increased by the same amount. Domestic merchants would face financial hardship which would have given the advantage to their foreign rivals. The risk of domestic bankruptcies might stifle the supply of money and increase the rate of interest. The consequences for the economy would be disastrous: the circulation of money and the supply of credit in the economy would stop because, in addition to the commercial risks borne in relation to normal trade activities, economic agents would also have to contend with the

[69] Ibid., vol. 2, pp. 201–5.

[70] Ibid., vol. 2, pp. 205–7.

[71] A 25 per cent increase in the value of exports and 50 per cent increase in the value of imports.

[72] Forbonnais, *Elémens*, vol. 2, pp. 208–10.

negative effects of currency variations. The economy, Forbonnais had argued, would be choked by persistent high rates of interest and the propensity for usury.[73]

One significant argument in favour of currency variations had been that the stronger rise in the money of account had produced an increase of exports of domestic produce.[74] However, Forbonnais had cautioned the effects of price changes would not necessarily generate a corresponding boost to commercial activities. In this respect, three observations were important.[75] First, the consumption of some produce had a natural ceiling so that sales would not increase in the same proportion as the fall in price. Also, the additional profit from exports might not automatically flow back to the economy and benefit the country. Merchants might decide to keep profits and refrain from increasing their spending pattern. Second, due to the loss of confidence in the economy, the cost of money would remain expensive. After a currency variation, the higher rate of interest would counteract any increase of profit.[76] Third, the decrease in the price level, generally, had been of short duration. As prices adjusted upwards over the medium to long term, sales would fall again. In essence, Forbonnais concluded, the higher cost of money had been the root of the problem. It had had negative effects on the supply of money, the amount in circulation and the level of employment in the economy. The level of the rate of interest had been the measure of prosperity of a nation.[77]

[73] Ibid., vol. 2, pp. 210–11.

[74] With an increase of prices of 25 per cent and a rise of the money of account of 50 per cent, a price fall of a quarter would lead to a corresponding increase of exports of a quarter. Sales of 72 minus the value of export of 54 would net a surplus of 18: a 50 per cent increase on the initial profit in the third scenario of 12: ibid., vol. 2, pp. 211–12.

[75] Ibid., pp. 212–15.

[76] Forbonnais had provided numerical example using the assumption of the second scenario: 100 liv., equal to 150 liv. after the currency variation, would purchase 125 liv. of produce. With a rate of interest of 6 per cent, the cost of money was 9 liv. which had to be deducted from 150 liv. So, 141 liv. were available to purchase produce which cost 125 liv. after the change of prices. Hence only 16 liv. worth of additional produce could be purchased. Following the currency manipulation, the higher interest charge of 3 liv. (6+3) on 150 liv. directly offset the 25 liv. of additional purchase power which the people had hoped to achieve. These calculations, Forbonnais had added, could be refined further. They could incorporate the principle according to which merchants always had been targeting a level of profit which had to be at the least twice as much as the potential investment income based on the prevailing rate of interest in the country: ibid., vol. 2, pp. 213–15.

[77] Ibid., vol. 2, p. 217.

Zinzendorf agreed with Forbonnais' analysis and like him came out in favour of Dutot. It was important, Zinzendorf thought, to remind readers of the debate and highlight that Melon, despite his well-known book in defence of Law's ideas, offered a different and mistaken view on currency manipulation. So, as a further proof against Melon and as his third key source for additional reading, Zinzendorf provided a reference to Law's *Mémoire sur l'usage des Monnoyes* (1706), presented by Law in the following year to the future French regent, Philippe Duke of Orléans.[78] There, Law had set out arguments against currency variations. The version of Law's *Mémoire* which Zinzendorf used was that printed in Forbonnais' *Recherches*. The text was part of the fifth and final section of Forbonnais' book which covered the period after the death of Louis XIV to Law's financial scheme. Forbonnais had chosen to insert it between a *Mémoire* on the reduction of the rate of interest and a general assessment of Law's financial system.[79] The third part of the *Mémoire* in which Law dealt with monetary variations, was of particular interest to Zinzendorf.[80]

Law had applied his monetary principles to France and had argued that a weakening of the currency was unjust and damaged the interests of the state.[81] He had associated an augmentation of the currency with the cost of producing new money, in particular with the seigniorage tax, a decrease in the content of specie and a change in the money of account. A weakening of the currency, Law had argued, would lead to a decrease in the supply of money and trigger an outflow of specie as well as produce to rival trading nations. France, he had estimated, had a seigniorage tax of 3 per cent whereas England had none. The French could easily evade their own tax by sending specie to England and accessing the funds in France via letters of exchange. However, contrary to popular arguments, an augmentation of the currency would not lead to an inflow of foreign money. Specie had been sent abroad only once an opportunity for profit had been identified. The same applied to the use of letters of exchange. If the English were to depreciate their money of account by one quarter, the French or Dutch, Law had argued, would not send 8000 écus to England to receive,

[78] *John Law: Oeuvres complètes*, ed Paul Harsin (3 vols, Paris, 1934), vol. 1, p. xxiv.

[79] In Forbonnais, *Recherches*, 'Mémoire sur la réduction des Intérêts', vol. 2, pp. 528–41, and ibid., 'Vue Générale du Système de M. Law', vol. 2, pp. 574–644.

[80] The third part of John Law's *Mémoire*, 'Mémoire sur l'usage des Monnoyes et sur le profit ou la perte qu'il peut y avoir pour un Prince et pour un Etat, dans l'altération du titre de ses Monnoyes, et dans l'augmentation ou la diminution de leur prix, par rapport aux Etats voisins' can be found in Forbonnais, *Recherches*, vol. 2, pp. 542–73, at pp. 560–69.

[81] Ibid., p. 542.

in return, 10,000 écus in weak money. The inflow and outflow of foreign currencies was based on the quality and availability of specie.[82]

Law had proceeded to counter two arguments in support of currency augmentations. According to the first, following a devaluation of the English money of account, the French and Dutch would send money abroad to buy additional English produce. Even though, Law had conceded, the English merchants would benefit in the short term, a currency augmentation would not produce any lasting benefits for the economy. Assume, he had argued, the French had bought 50 million *livres* worth of English produce. After the currency change, they could buy the same amount of produce for 40 million *livres* by either sending specie to England or through the use of letters of exchange. The English, conversely, who previously had been able to buy for 50 million *livres* worth of produce in France, had their purchasing power reduced to 40 million *livres*. They had to add an additional 10 million *livres* to make up for the shortfall. Suppose that the French and Dutch merchants doubled their purchases in England to take advantage of their stronger currencies. The English merchants would receive 80 million *livres* for the exports of produce which was worth 100 million *livres* prior to the devaluation. The gain in sales volume, however, which had to compensate for the loss in value, would be short lived. As demand and consumption in France and the United Provinces would not have risen proportionally to the variation in the currency, both countries would begin to store the extra produce. In England, following the high level of exports, there would be a shortage of produce for domestic consumption. Price levels, Law had thought, would eventually adapt and reverse any advantages from currency manipulations: prices in England would increase, and prices abroad would fall.[83]

A further disadvantage of currency augmentations had been the indiscriminate reduction of prices across all categories of produce, which had been to the detriment of the state. The price sensitivity of foreigners for domestic produce had varied. For some produce which had been necessities, prices could be readily increased, but among the categories of produce where prices could be lowered, price adjustments had not been uniform. They had varied according to demand. For Law, currency variations had not taken account of such important differences, and they had been a method to induce bankruptcies.[84]

[82] Ibid., pp. 560–62.
[83] Ibid., pp. 562–64.
[84] Ibid., pp. 564–65.

The second argument in favour of currency variations had postulated that an increase in the money of account would prompt a rise in prices for produce and hence generate more profit for domestic merchants. In any case, Law had conceded, over the long term, prices tended to rise irrespective of monetary changes. Produce which required raw materials from abroad would have been the first to increase in price. However, generally, prices and wages took longer to adjust and did not reflect immediately an augmentation of the currency. In terms of commerce and direct revenues to the state, an augmentation of the currency had led to a fall of real income from tariffs and duties.[85]

According to some, an increase in the money of account had been equivalent to an increase in the supply of money, and for this reason it had represented an appropriate remedy to address the financial requirements of the state. For Law, this argument had been flawed. The logic had been equivalent to saying that 300 *aunes* of fabric which had been available to decorate a room would yield more fabric if the unit of measurement arbitrarily had been changed to 400 *aunes*. Government ministers, Law had argued, had understood that currency variations had not created wealth but had merely supported the finances of the ruler. They had been, however, unaware of the harmful consequences of manipulating the currency. In creating money, the ruler had been supposed to guarantee the immutability and stability of specie. Out of justice and respect for his citizens, he ought to have refrained from currency variations. If, nevertheless, for the benefit of the state, a change in the money of account had been required, existing financial transactions had to be executed on the basis of the old exchange rates. The content and the amount of specie had bestowed value, not the denomination set by the state.[86] Finally, Law had argued, changing only a few types of the specie was worse than a general increase in the money of account. The imbalances between the domestic exchange rates would produce crime and encourage the use of counterfeit money.[87]

After providing references on French currency discussions from Dutot, Forbonnais and Law himself, Zinzendorf turned to Germany. He was remarkably well informed about discussions in Europe on monetary matters and added the German perspective to the French arguments. For German

[85] Ibid., pp. 565–66.

[86] Ibid., pp. 567–68.

[87] Ibid., p. 569. Law had assumed that only the coin of 10 sols had altered and that the other specie had remained unchanged.

readers, this was highly relevant, given the different approaches of German states to currency manipulations. Zinzendorf's final two references related to the forceful debate which took place in the wake of the creation of a new system of coins and exchange values in Prussia. The system had been devised in 1750 by Johann Philip Graumann, who had been a merchant by training. Zinzendorf did not agree with Graumann's ideas. Rather, he praised two texts by Julius Melchior Strube, a local government official in Hannover and strong critic of Graumann's plans, who had warned of the drawbacks ensuing from currency changes in domestic exchange rates. Strube had published his works, *Gründliche Prüfung* in 1751 followed by *Untersuchung der Frage* in 1752, as direct responses to two pamphlets written by Graumann on currency reform.[88] Strube had questioned the need for a new currency standard, and the debate with Graumann, in the framework of a bimetallic system of gold and silver, had centred on establishing relative values which would be favourable for silver coins.

The context of their exchange was the declining availability of silver coins for daily transactions. Since 1730, this had led to increased currency clipping. A large variety of lower quality coins had appeared in circulation. German merchants could not exchange silver coins for foreign coins and refused to accept them for payment. So, gold had functioned as a parallel currency, and Spanish, Dutch and especially French gold coins had been used for commerce. Following the example of the French gold coins, *louis d'or*, Frederick William, the father of Frederick II, had started to mint his own gold coins, *friedrich d'or*. Faced with rising war expenses, Frederick II had wanted to stem the loss of silver coins and stop arbitrage activities between gold and silver coins. To this end, he had instructed

[88] The titles of Graumann's and Strube's publications and the sequence of their exchange had been: 1. C.I P. G[raumann], *Abdruck von einem Schreiben, die deutsche und anderer Völker Münzverfassung und insonderheit die Höch-Fürstl. Braunschweigische Münze betreffend* (Braunschweig, 1749); 2. Anonymous [Julius Melchior Strube], *Gründliche Prüfung des Schreibens, die Teutsche und anderer Völker Münzverfassung und insonderheit die Höchfürstl. Braunschweigische Münze betreffend* (Hannover, 1751); 3. Anonymous [Johann Philipp Graumann], *Vernünftige Vertheidigung des Schreibens die Teutsche und anderer Völker Münz-Verfassung betreffend, der sogenannten gründlichen Prüfung desselben entgegengesetzt. Nebst einem Anhange worin die in der Erfahrung gegründete Ursachen von dem Steigen und Fallen des Gold und Silberpreises, und dem darauf sich gründenden Steigen und Fallen des Wechsel Courses angehandelt werden* (Berlin, 1751); 4. Anonymous [Julius Melchior Strube], *Untersuchung der Frage: Ob das Silbergeld zu erhöhen sey? Worin die sogenannte Vernünftige Vertheidigung des Schreibens: die Teutsche und anderer Völker Münz-Verfassung betreffend beantwortet wird* (Hannover, 1752).

Graumann, previously commissioner for monetary affairs of the duke of Braunschweig, Frederick's brother-in-law, to devise a new, autonomous Prussian coin standard.[89]

The new standard had to address the loss of silver coins. It would thus revise the nominal values of gold and silver coins which had been fixed since 1737 and had determined the proportion between gold and silver specie. Graumann's currency proposal had been based on gold (*friedrich d'or*) and silver coins (*thalers*). It had redefined the values of both and was the first step towards the German monetary reform of 1871. However, Graumann had made important mistakes. In the belief that gold would always have good availability, he had fixed a value of gold to silver which was too low, and the newly minted *friedrich d'or* coins had been quickly bought by foreigners. He also had made promises to the Prussian ruler which he could not keep. He had predicted that by replacing the Dutch *ducats* with the *friedrich d'or*, the Dutch would be ousted from the trade in the Baltics. Also, he had assured Frederick of significant income streams from seigniorage. Prussian commerce, however, had been too weak to exert any influence on the trade of specie. It could not keep the prices of gold and silver specie low enough to enable the newly established mint units to operate profitably. Therefore, a large number of the units which had competed directly against each other had been forced to close down. Frederick had lost faith in Graumann, and had dropped him in 1754.[90]

The exchange between Graumann and Strube had been technical and heated. The debate had started with Graumann's pamphlet *Abdruck von einem Schreiben*. While still working for the duke of Braunschweig, Graumann had published it and had proposed to renew the existing currency standard. In his reply, *Gründliche Prüfung*, Strube had set out a threefold criticism of Graumann's arguments: first, Strube had disagreed with Graumann's idea to raise the denomination of silver coins in relation to gold; second, he did not see the need to remint an old silver coin, the *albertusthaler*, which was used by the Dutch, but was not common any-

[89] For an account of the Prussian currency reforms, see Friedrich Freiherr von Schrötter, 'Die Münzverwaltung Friedrichs des Großen' in Paul Seidel (ed.), *Hohenzollern Jahrbuch*, vol. 15 (Berlin and Leipzig, 1911), pp. 91–9, at p. 92. Schrötter was a historian and numismatist who worked at the *Münzkabinett* in Berlin.

[90] Ibid., pp. 93–4. On the establishment of Graumann's system in 1750, see Friedrich Freiherr von Schrötter, 'Das preußische Münzwesen im 18. Jahrhundert', *Acta Borussica, Münzgeschichtlicher Theil. Die Begründung des preußischen Münzsystems durch Friedrich d.Gr. und Graumann* (Berlin, 1908), vol. 2, pp. 74–90.

more in Germany[91]; finally, he had warned against minting the small denomination silver coins (*scheidemünze*) with a lower specie content than the other silver specie currency. Strube reinforced his arguments by referring to the arguments of other writers, including Law, Melon, Dutot and Montesquieu. He was particularly complimentary about Dutot and had recommended the reading of *Réflexions politiques* in order to apply the book's conclusions to policy-making.[92]

For Strube, money had been a symbol used for commerce and a means to exchange goods. It had to be based on trust, and no gain could be had from changing the content of the currency or its denomination. Money, Strube had continued, also had been a sign in relation to other currencies and had depended on commerce between nations. Foreign nations had determined the value of coins according to their specie content and their commercial interests, and had not been guided by the monetary denomination (*gesetzmäßiger Preis*). Therefore, Graumann's first proposal to raise the value of silver had been misguided.[93]

Second, Strube had not identified any good reasons for minting the *albertusthaler*. The existing currency standard, Strube had maintained, had not been the reason for the coin not being available any longer. But, if one had insisted on having it again, the Dutch, who had produced currency for foreign nations, could mint additional coins for Germany. Strube had also rejected Graumann's argument that the lack of the *thaler* had prevented Germany from undertaking direct trade with Spain and the Baltics. He pointed out that most German provinces, with the exception of the Hanseatic states, had not been well placed geographically to trade with these nations. If, however, the availability of the coin was crucial for their commercial enterprises, trading centres such as Hamburg would have minted the *thaler* themselves or made concerted efforts to purchase it. In practice, the Hanseatic city states had followed the *rouble* exchange rates as most produce from the Baltics had originated in Russia. In addition, Strube had noted, most of the Russian trade had not been driven by the United Provinces, which had the *thaler*, but by England which, using a variety of coins to conduct commerce with Russia, had benefited from having established first a direct presence in Russian commercial harbours.[94]

[91] It was a silver coin which was first minted in the early seventeenth century and named after Albert VII, the sovereign of the Habsburg Netherlands and Archduke of Austria.

[92] Strube, *Gründliche Prüfung*, p. 10.

[93] Ibid., paragraphs 1–4, pp. 4–9.

[94] Ibid., paragraphs 28 and 29, pp. 72–6.

The third criticism in *Gründliche Prüfung* had related to Graumann's proposal to lower the silver content of *scheidemünzen* which typically had been used for small, low value transactions. Even though their metal content had been lower than their denomination, Graumann had argued that they could be minted again with lower specie content as their use had been relatively modest. For Strube, however, these coins had performed an important economic function, and therefore their proportion to other silver coins in circulation had to be kept the same. It had been a line of argument similar to his first criticism of Graumann's gold and silver specie manipulation.[95]

In the introduction to *Untersuchung der Frage*, his response to Graumann's reply, Strube had repeated the warning that wrong decisions in relation to currency standards could have severe repercussions for both the ruler and the people. Due to the complexity of the issues and the specialist knowledge required to conduct commerce, ministers had not felt competent enough to decide on monetary policy. They had chosen, Strube had argued, to delegate decision-making to specialists like Graumann who, by hiding behind a veil of technical terminology, had tried to exclude public discussion and influence decisions to further their personal financial gain. Strube had repeatedly referred to Graumann as his 'adversary' and had drawn attention to the vitriolic and personal tone of the exchange. This, he had thought, was a disguise for a lack of good supporting evidence in Graumann's arguments. Contrary to Graumann, Strube's only remit had been to clarify questions in relation to Prussia's new currency standard and publicise them as widely as possible.[96] Strube's text had been a discussion of Graumann's argument, which Graumann had reiterated in his second pamphlet, *Vernünftige Vertheidigung*, for changing the domestic exchange rate between silver and gold currency. A currency standard, Strube had thought, had to provide stability by fixing the proportion between gold and silver, specifying the specie content of coins and creating a framework for the use of money in the economy. A change would create uncertainty in the economy. Graumann, Strube had maintained, had not convincingly shown why the proportion between silver and gold in foreign countries had been more accurate than in Germany and how, by altering the currency standard, the value of silver coins could be increased.[97]

[95] Ibid., paragraphs 30 and 38, pp. 76–8, 95–7.

[96] Strube, *Untersuchung der Frage*, Introduction, pp. 4–6, 15–18.

[97] Ibid., p. 9.

Nevertheless, in *Untersuchung der Frage*, Strube had softened his stance and conceded that a new exchange rate between gold and silver might be appropriate. Contrary to Graumann however, he had argued for a decrease in the value of gold. In line with a general increase in Europe, the quantity of gold available in German states had risen, and the specie commanded less value than in the 1730s when the previous currency standard had been established. Also, as commerce sometimes had required payment in predetermined currency, it would be possible to avoid the usury of money changers who had demanded hefty commissions for currency in short supply. Finally, Strube had speculated, it had been tactically wise to play to the prevailing public sentiment and offer a concession to the articulate critics who had worried about the outflow of silver coins.[98]

In his second pamphlet, Strube had also developed his arguments against Graumann's proposal to increase the value of silver rather than to decrease the value of gold. Referring to the debates between Melon and Dutot on currency manipulation, Strube had argued that an increase in silver, which would bestow an advantage to debtors over creditors, would lead to a loss of public confidence. Moreover, raising the denomination of silver had been neither in the ruler's nor in the people's interest. The ruler would generate less income from taxes, duties and rents whose value had been set before the currency change. The people, including landowners, peasants and soldiers would receive less silver content as payment and hence less income. If, Strube had argued, a change of proportion between gold and silver had been required, adjusting the value of gold had been preferable. As gold had not been the primary means of exchange, it would not disrupt economic activities. Silver coins, on the other hand, had been used for daily transactions. Silver money had been the benchmark for setting prices in the economy and had been used to express the values of important categories of agricultural produce. To have a robust currency standard, it had been necessary to keep its foundation, the silver coins, stable and adjust the gold value accordingly.[99]

Stability of silver had important implications for commerce. An increase in silver would not translate into an economic advantage since merchants

[98] Ibid., pp. 22–4, 33. Gottfried Achenwall, German philosopher and economist, had also taken part in the debate and, like Graumann, had argued for an increase in the denomination of silver coins: 'Entwurf einer politischen Betrachtung über die Zunahme des Goldes und Abnahme des Silbers in Europa' in *Hannoverischen Gelehrte Anzeigen*, 1751, pp. 343–51.

[99] Strube, *Untersuchung der Frage*, paragraphs 24–25, 29, 40 at pp. 55–6, 73–5, 90–3.

had been guided by the intrinsic value of produce. Also, it generated suspicion and insecurity among trade partners and creditors. Therefore, it had been harmful to state credit and to the growth of money supply which had been important for the growth of commerce. Creditors had valued monetary stability and had preferred to transact with countries where laws and lending arrangements had been respected. Strube had refuted arguments that it would be favourable if the thaler moved closer to the currency standards of foreign trading nations, in particular France. It had not been necessary, he had thought, to follow the monetary vagaries of neighbouring countries and, in any case, the previous currency arrangement had been more comparable than the current one to the French currency standard.[100]

For Zinzendorf, policies which advocated a currency debasement were misguided and Strube provided the arguments for why Graumann's system for the new Prussian currency standard could not be successful. Nevertheless, Prussia kept to its policies of currency manipulations. During the Seven Years War, refusing to take on foreign debt, Frederick resorted to a debasement of English bullion, which he received as subsidy from England, and decided on three debasements of the Prussian coinage. Approximately 40 million, one-third of the war costs, were paid with lower quality specie. After the war, Frederick continued the debasements of foreign coins, including Austrian, Polish and Russian, and used them as payments to other countries. Even though he recognised that these manipulations were harmful to the domestic population, he argued that they were a violent, yet essential, remedy to save the state.[101]

The monarchy's strategy on currency was very different. It was in line with Zinzendorf's ideas. In the late 1740s, the monarchy had adjusted its coinage and harmonised all silver coins to exclude lower quality specie.[102] In 1752, it had created the silver *Maria-Theresien-thaler* which was also extensively used for commerce with the Levant.[103] In late 1753, through

[100] Ibid., paragraphs 24, 49, pp. 79–83, 124–25.

[101] Christopher Duffy, *The Army of Frederick the Great* (Vancouver, 1974), pp. 130–31; Günther Probszt, *Österreichische Münz- und Geldgeschichte* (2 vols, Vienna, 1994), vol. 2, pp. 502–3. For an account of the Prussian currency debasements during the war, see also August Octavian Ritter von Loehr, 'Die Finanzierung des Siebenjährigen Krieges', *Numismatische Zeitschrift*, 18 (1925), pp. 95–110, at pp. 98–103.

[102] Probszt, *Münz- und Geldgeschichte*, vol. 2, p. 496.

[103] The financier Johann Fries was involved in selling the silver *thaler*, see Chap. 6, 'Projectors'. On the use of the Maria-Theresien-thaler in commerce, see Probszt, *Münz- und Geldgeschichte*, vol. 2, pp. 506–10.

a coinage treaty (*Münzkonvention*), the system had been extended to Bavaria. The currency standard guaranteed the free circulation of coins minted under the new convention.[104] It had been created as a rival currency standard to Prussia. Despite Frederick's efforts to discredit the new arrangement, most of the South German states joined. During the Seven Years War, the government refusal to manipulate its coins gave the monarchy currency stability and after the war, the success of the system attracted other German states, including Saxony.[105]

The Disadvantages of Silver Money and Advantages of Land

Zinzendorf highlighted several passages where Law had argued that silver money was simply a measure of value in commerce and that substitutes could be found that were more appropriate to support economic activity and employment.[106] Law had also noted that over time the supply of money in Europe had increased more than the demand and that, consequently, the value of silver had fallen and prices for internationally traded produce had risen substantially. Even though, on Law's analysis, Scotland had an insufficient supply of money, as a small open economy the domestic price level could not withstand the forces of international supply and demand for produce. The prices of traded produce in Scotland had to adjust to international price levels and thus also had reflected the general increase of prices for produce in Europe.[107]

Law had also argued that land, following agricultural development, had increased in value and had been subject to greater demand. In an extensive footnote running over 18 pages, Zinzendorf reinforced the point of fluctuating prices. He provided price data for agricultural produce covering 150 years for France, England and 'Germany'.[108] The prices of produce, Zinzendorf argued, were driven by two factors: first, by changes in the

[104] Dickson, *Finance and Government*, vol. 2, p. 34; on the currency standards, conversion and exchange rates used in the monarchy, see ibid., Appendix F, pp. 369–71, and Probszt, *Münz- und Geldgeschichte*, vol. 2, p. 498.

[105] For a comparative account of the different currency policies in Prussia and the monarchy during the Seven Years War, see Loehr, 'Die Finanzierung'.

[106] Zinzendorf, *Gedanken vom Gelde*, pp. 202–5.

[107] For a discussion, see Murphy, *John Law*, pp. 97–8.

[108] Zinzendorf, *Gedanken vom Gelde*, pp. 227–44.

demand or supply of produce or of money; and second, by a change in the content of specie or in the denomination of money. Based on this data, he analysed and compared trends and price developments in the three countries.[109]

Zinzendorf's choice of France and England was a direct extension of Law's arguments where he had referred to both countries in the text. Zinzendorf added 'Germany' as a third example to make the argument more relevant to German-speaking readers and to complement the discussion on the currency reform in Prussia.[110] Zinzendorf set out a data table for each country which included between 10 and 20 data points. The data for France was based on Nicholas-François Dupré de Saint Maur's *Essai sur les monnoyes, ou rapport entre l'argent et les denrées*.[111] For the English currency, Zinzendorf used William Lowndes' *A report containing an essay for the amendment of the silver coins*.[112] English data on agricultural produce was derived from the price index published by the English bishop William Fleetwood.[113] The German prices were taken from Johann Friedrich Unger's *Von der Ordnung der Fruchtpreise, und deren Einflusse in die wichtigsten Angelegenheiten des menschlichen Lebens*.[114] Unger (1714–1781) was an important German agricultural economist, statistician and practitioner of political arithmetic. He was a man of considerable economic experience and the first to study German price mechanisms affecting agricultural produce. His political appointments included mayor of Göttingen and posts in the duchy of Braunschweig.[115]

[109] Ibid., pp. 228.

[110] Zinzendorf used the monetary standard of Hannover (*Hannoverischer Münz-Fuss*), previously the standard of Leipzig, for his calculations: ibid., p. 243. He did not clarify which states he included in 'Germany'.

[111] Nicholas-François Dupré de Saint Maur, *Essai sur les monnoyes, ou rapport entre l'argent et les denrées* (Paris, 1746).

[112] William Lowndes, *A Report Containing an Essay for the Amendment of the Silver Coins* (London, 1695).

[113] William Fleetwood, *Chronicon Preciosum: or An Account of English Money, the Price of Corn and Other Commodities, for the Last 600 Years* (London, 1707).

[114] Johann Friedrich Unger, *Von der Ordnung der Fruchtpreise, und deren Einflusse in die wichtigsten Angelegenheiten des menschlichen Lebens* (Göttingen, 1752).

[115] On Unger's activities and the importance of *Von der Ordnung der Fruchtpreise*, see Günther Schmitt, 'Johann Friedrich Unger (1714–1781). Arithmetiker und erster bedeutender landwirtschaftlicher Marktforscher deutscher Sprache', *Agrarwirtschaft*, 16 (1967), pp. 201–6.

The starting point of each of the three tables was the end of the fifteenth century when supply of silver specie accelerated with imports from the mines of the Americas. The end point, depending on the availability of data, was the 1740s. For the three countries, Zinzendorf compared the change in the value of money to the change in the prices of agricultural produce by indexing the values for 150 years to 1000.[116] In several subfootnotes, he explained his calculations.[117] The first and most extensive data table consisted of the price movements in France. From the data, Zinzendorf drew five conclusions. First, over more than 250 years, the denomination of the French currency had either increased almost fivefold (2760 to 13,038) or the content of silver had been reduced. Second, prices of agricultural produce had increased by a factor of almost 35 (137 to 4680). Third, in terms of unit of silver, the increase was only sevenfold (1000 to 7241). Fourth, in the sixteenth century alone, the price of produce, in terms of silver, had risen almost ninefold (1000 to 8795). Fifth, from 1649 to 1746, the prices of produce had only increased by more than 30 per cent (3480 to 4680). For several reasons, Zinzendorf thought, the price increase over the previous century was striking. Over the same period, the price of produce, measured in silver units, had not increased, but decreased (10,160 to 7241) even though the value of silver coins had soared (6884 to 13,038). Also, strong commerce had triggered a growth of the supply of money by almost half, but production output of agricultural produce had generally been lower. Under normal circumstances, Zinzendorf speculated, the combination of these factors would have led to a more pronounced price increase of at least 150 per cent since, according to contemporary scholars of political economy, every augmentation of the denomination of the currency was followed, after a time lag, by a more

[116] The reference value was applied to the first data point of each series. For France and England, the first entry was the value in 1495; for 'Germany' it was in 1325.

[117] The first three columns of each table consisted of the raw data for Zinzendorf's calculations: the first column set out the years, the second and third, respectively, gave the values at which a unit of silver was minted and the prices of agricultural produce. The fourth and fifth columns indexed the values of coins and the prices of produce each year to the reference value at the beginning of the data series. The sixth column, finally, combined the values of the previous two columns and was an expression of the proportional changes in both the content of specie and the prices of produce. For France, Zinzendorf gave numerical examples, using the beginning and end of the data series, 1495 and 1746, to show the proportional change. For 1746, the values were as follows: column four: $2760/13{,}038 = 0.2117 \times 1000 = 212$; column five: $4680/137 = 34.16 \times 1000 = 34{,}160$; column six: $212/1000 = 0.212 \times 34{,}160 = 7241$: Zinzendorf, *Gedanken vom Gelde*, pp. 229–31.

substantial increase in the general price level. Therefore, Zinzendorf concluded, the actual increase of the prices of produce by a paltry 30 per cent was the result of the government's poor economic policies. Before Colbert, France had pursued a liberal trade policy. Colbert, however, he explained, was misguided not only to disallow the export of grain, but also to restrict its internal movements between provinces. This artificial reduction in sales, which was upheld until 1754, forced French merchants to sell their produce below market value.[118] It was a charge that Zinzendorf had forcefully made previously in the 'Mémoire sur les richesses, le commerce et les finances de la France'.

The data for England gave a very different picture. Over the same period, from 1495 to 1740, the value of the English currency had barely doubled (487 to 804). Meanwhile, the price of produce, measured in silver units, had increased eightfold (1000 to 7995) with, from the fifteenth to the sixteenth century, a more pronounced price increase of eleven times. In the mid-seventeenth century, these price increases reversed, and, until 1726, Zinzendorf calculated price decreases for produce of 30 per cent. This was a very unusual trend given that the strong increase in the supply of money from commercial activities coupled with the introduction of paper debt in the economy had led to an increase in the general level of prices. For Zinzendorf, therefore, the uncharacteristic price development of agricultural produce must have been the result of targeted government policies. The Act of Parliament of 1689 had actively encouraged the commerce of grain by offering the merchants a cash award for foreign trade as long as their sales price had remained below a ceiling determined by the government.[119] This policy, Zinzendorf argued, was an export subsidy to increase the competitiveness of English produce versus foreign trading nations. The effects of the government measure on the economy were positive as it increased the production yield of English agriculture. Whereas 100 years previously, England had to buy grain abroad for domestic consumption, it was now able to earn more than £1 million a year from the export of grain. Zinzendorf supported his argument by quoting two important French texts which drew similar conclusions. The first publication was Louis-Joseph Plumard de Dangeul's loose translation of Josiah

[118] Ibid., pp. 234–36.

[119] The cash award was, at the maximum, 10 per cent of the price ceiling set by the government.

Tucker's *Remarks on the Advantages and Disadvantages of France and Great Britain* which Dangeul had published under the pseudonym of John Nicholls. In particular, Zinzendorf referred to the chapter on agriculture in which Dangeul had provided data on the growth of English agricultural production and had applauded the country's agricultural self-sufficiency.[120] The second publication, which had followed a similar line of argument, was Forbonnais' *Elémens du Commerce*.[121]

In France and England, Zinzendorf concluded, the price decreases of grain had not only different causes, but also very different effects. In England, the subsidy was a stimulus for the economy. It reduced domestic prices for consumers and encouraged export activity. In France, however, low profit expectations and high taxation discouraged agricultural activities.[122]

The price developments in 'Germany' differed yet again from those in France and England.[123] On the German data, Zinzendorf made four observations. First, over 250 years, the value of the *mark* had doubled. It was a smaller increase than the French currency, but a more pronounced rise than the English *pound sterling*. Second, the same applied to agricultural produce, where prices increased more than tenfold (14.5 to 160). Third, prices of produce, in terms of silver units, had risen slightly more than fivefold (627 to 3340) which was less than the corresponding price increases over the same period in France and England. The explanation, Zinzendorf argued, was that 'Germany' had evidently a more restricted access than France and England to the supply of specie from the Americas. Fourth, therefore, over the sixteenth century, the rise in the price of grain, in terms of silver units, was less pronounced than in France and England. Finally, over the previous century, unlike in France and England, prices of agricultural produce rose continuously as a result

[120] Louis-Joseph Plumard de Dangeul, 'Des bléds et de la culture en général' in *Remarques sur les avantages et désavantages de la France et de la Grande Bretagne par rapport au Commerce et aux autres sources de la puissances des États*, 3rd edn (Leiden, 1754), pp. 82–101.

[121] Forbonnais, *Elémens*, vol. 1, pp. 112–30. Forbonnais began the passage with: 'Les peuples qui n'ont envisagé la culture des terres que du côté de la subsistance, ont toujours vécu dans la crainte des disettes et les ont souvent éprouvées. Ceux qui l'ont envisagé comme un objet de commerce ont joui d'une abondance assez soutenue pour se trouver toujours en état de suppléer aux besoins des étrangers. L'Angleterre nous fournit tout à la fois l'un et l'autre exemple': ibid., pp. 112–13.

[122] Zinzendorf, *Gedanken vom Gelde*, pp. 236–41.

[123] Zinzendorf used German data from Unger, *Von der Ordnung*, p. 268.

of the increase of the supply of money to the economy. In addition, 'Germany' did not follow active economic policies to guarantee low prices for agricultural produce.[124]

In concluding the chapter, Zinzendorf emphasised the weakness of silver as a currency and the arbitrary value that was given to it. He added the translation of a passage of Forbonnais' *Recherches* which, Zinzendorf argued, was a good description of the effects of an increase in the supply of money on government income, consumption and on the prices of domestic produce. Forbonnais had compared the money supply in France of 1683 with the monetary base at the time of writing in 1754. From 1683 to 1754, he had noted, the money supply had soared from 500 *livres* to 1700 *livres* or, if the important money outflows due to the war effort are taken into account, to 1500 *livres*. But even though the amount of fine silver had also almost doubled to 30 million *mark* over the same period, government income was lower than in 1683. The financial burden on farmers seemed less because the government taxes, *tailles* and *capitation*, measured as a percentage of the monetary base, had fallen by more than 40 per cent. However, it became evident, by examining the change in income in both years of the *Aides* (an excise tax levied on the sale of items including wine and tobacco), that in France consumption had decreased over the period. For this deterioration, Forbonnais had argued, three explanations were plausible: first, fewer people in 1683 were exempt from paying government taxes than in 1754; second, farmers were more affluent and kept more cattle; and third, as the price of grain dropped, so did the income of farmers.[125]

For both Zinzendorf and Law, the stability of silver content was important. The content of specie and more generally, the level of demand in the economy influenced the prices of agricultural produce. The comparative historical data for France, England and 'Germany' which Zinzendorf provided emphasised this argument. It also made it possible to evaluate the agricultural policies of the three countries. French policies were harmful to both domestic producers and consumers: the government, Zinzendorf argued, was too restrictive on the internal and external movement of agricultural produce. England, by contrast, pursued a good output-orientated and export-led strategy. In 'Germany', by comparison, the development was steadier and the result of a non-interventionist economic policy.

[124] Zinzendorf, *Gedanken vom Gelde*, pp. 243–44.

[125] Ibid., pp. 281–87. The original text is in Forbonnais, *Recherches*, vol. 1, pp. 297–99.

Law's Proposal to Issue Paper Money

Law had proposed a commission appointed by Parliament to issue paper money backed up with land. The type of money, Law had argued, which should be established had to have a stable value and serve the domestic economy. It would not be subject to the vagaries of international supply and demand. For Law, the aim had been for employment, agriculture, industry and commerce to be undertaken with the appropriate supply of money: the wealth of a nation should only depend on the success of commerce. In the main text, Zinzendorf emphasised Law's argument.[126]

For Zinzendorf, Law's idea of paper money with an inherent stable value was sophisticated. However, in terms of execution, it represented a somewhat 'metaphysical proposal'. The aim of ensuring the growth of employment, industry and commerce could also be achieved with an appropriate supply of money, which had simpler characteristics. It was sufficient, Zinzendorf thought, for the paper money to have the same value as land, as expressed in silver money, and for it to circulate in the economy so as to facilitate economic transaction and being freely redeemable in all public *caisses* in the country. If paper money was backed up with land and, in addition, the Scottish Parliament could supervise the notes' issuance of the commission, public confidence would be upheld and supply of money would not exceed demand. Paper money, Zinzendorf conceded, would have served a good purpose even if, as was the case for silver money, it would lose some of its value over a long period of 100 years.

Zinzendorf suggested that the execution of Law's proposal would have been easier if Law had restricted it to a simple issue of notes not backed up by the whole value, but only by one half or two-thirds of the value of land. The monetary operation would have been much easier to administer. Given that the value of land steadily kept increasing, it provided sufficient collateral for the issue of paper money. In addition, as public debt, similar to the paper money, would freely circulate in the economy, Zinzendorf also envisaged the possibility to re-issue the notes which were redeemed.[127]

A significant objection to Law's proposal for the use of paper money had been that it had never been tried in Scotland before. Law had replied that, as a matter of principle, a wise nation had no need to follow the lead of other countries. Nevertheless, France, Law had pointed out, had been

[126] Zinzendorf, *Gedanken vom Gelde*, pp. 370–72.
[127] Ibid., pp. 402–6.

using paper money for economic transactions and could serve as an example. Zinzendorf illustrated Law's reference to France with an additional translation of a section from Forbonnais' *Recherches*.[128] Forbonnais had given a verdict of the issue of *billets de monnoye* in 1701 and had argued that this new credit mechanism could have been advantageous for the state if the French administration had used it in a measured manner. A successful issue of *billets* would have required thorough preparatory work which included the creation of a dedicated fund of silver money to exchange the *billets* which holders wanted to redeem. The size of the fund ought to be set according to the intended volume of *billets* to be issued and the anticipated amount of redemptions. In order to enable the circulation of money, the system of exchange should be convenient to use, and the *billets* ought to be accepted at sight at all public *caisses* in the country. This system, Forbonnais had argued, would give the *billets* the intended cash-like character and sustain public confidence. It would furthermore avoid a shortage of money in the economy which would trigger a rise of the general price level and of domestic wages.

Forbonnais, however, had criticised the French government for making its sole objective that of addressing the shortage of money and raising funds as swiftly as possible. The French administration, he thought, had not been sufficiently concerned with the process and the details of the monetary operation. It had made three errors. First, the government had decided on a high rate of interest of 7½ per cent which it could not repay. The *billets*, Forbonnais had thought, should have been issued, like silver money, without any rate of interest, so that people would use them for daily transactions. Instead, because of the rate of interest, they had been perceived as investment opportunities which had promised a financial return. The anticipation of interest payments had restricted the circulation of the *billets* and had prompted holders to demand swift payouts. The second mistake had been that the government had not set up a redemption fund for repayment. The third mistake had been that it had allowed the volume of money to increase to a level that caused the public to lose confidence in the currency. The French administration had used *billets* for all its payments, and the large volume of money in the market had been proof that neither the principal amount nor the interest could be repaid.[129]

[128] Forbonnais, *Recherches et Considérations*, vol. 2, pp. 140–41.
[129] Zinzendorf, *Gedanken vom Gelde*, pp. 396–401.

Bringing Law's Thinking up to Date

With *Gedanken vom Gelde*, Zinzendorf attempted to give authority to Law's arguments and bring them to the attention of a wide readership. For Zinzendorf, Law's *Money and Trade* was a highly relevant work on political economy. It offered the theory as well as the policies required for a well-functioning economy. Zinzendorf made few changes to Law's text, but with new references to other texts and with calculations, he reinforced and clarified Law's arguments. Like Law, Zinzendorf believed in the importance of money for output, trade and employment. But Zinzendorf cautioned against the excessive growth in the use of paper money. Rather, its use should be increased gradually to keep a stable value and the confidence of the public.

Through the translation of Law's arguments and by supplementing them with new ideas from economic writers, notably from Gournay's circle, Zinzendorf built up his own thinking. It shows how closely he worked with French economic writers. It is interesting to compare Zinzendorf's *Gedanken vom Gelde* with the translation of a work on political economy of another prominent Scotsman by a member of Gournay's circle: the Abbé Le Blanc's French translation of David Hume's *Political Discourses* published as *Discours politiques de Monsieur Hume*.[130] Le Blanc's book was in two volumes and was printed four years before Zinzendorf's translation. Out of the three French translations of *Political Discourses*, Le Blanc's, which was the second, was the most influential.[131] Rather than simply provide a translation of the text, Le Blanc attempted to insert Hume into the context of French economic thought. He added a long introduction and many footnotes to the text. Le Blanc also provided two bibliographies: the first of notable English works, the second of recent French translations mainly from other writers of Gournay's circle.[132]

[130] Abbé Jean-Bernard le Blanc, *Discours politiques de Monsieur Hume traduits de l'anglois* (2 vols, Amsterdam, 1754).

[131] For Le Blanc's French translation of Hume's *Political Discourses*, I follow the interpretations of Loïc Charles, 'French "New Politics" and the Dissemination of David Hume's Political Discourses on the Continent, 1750–70', pp. 181–202, at pp. 186–95, and Istvan Hont, 'The "Rich Country–Poor Country" Debate revisited. The Origins and French Reception of the Hume Paradox', pp. 243–323, at pp. 267–74, both in Carl Wennerlind and Schabas Margaret (eds.), *David Hume's Political Economy* (London: Routledge, 2008).

[132] Le Blanc, *Discours politiques*, vol. 2, pp. 383–96, 397–417.

He did not modify Hume's text, but added lengthy notes from French writers, in particular from Melon, Forbonnais and Dangeul.

Le Blanc was from an older generation and had been a friend of Melon. In his view, Melon had developed French political economy into an advanced science, and in his translation, quoted him the most. But, supporting Dutot's views, Le Blanc criticised Melon's views on currency manipulations.[133] For Le Blanc, Melon had a significant intellectual influence on Hume, and he showed the closeness of their arguments on trade. However, he had to recognise that Hume's criticism of the use of public debt and of the concept of the circulation of money represented an irreconcilable difference with the views of Melon and the French writers of Gournay's circle. His way to circumvent this difficulty was to isolate and weaken Hume's rejection of public credit by placing it in the context of party politics in England. Le Blanc did not attempt to explain Hume's position. He left it to Forbonnais and other members of Gournay's entourage to refute Hume's monetary analysis and make it compatible with the circle's economic programme.

There are clear similarities between Zinzendorf and Le Blanc. For one, both considered Hume's *Political Discourses* to be of major significance and translated the book. Only a few draft pages of Zinzendorf's translation of Hume's work are in the archives and these do not allow a comparison of the texts.[134] However, it is instructive to examine the similarities between *Gedanken vom Gelde* and *Discours politiques*. In their translations, both Zinzendorf and Le Blanc followed a similar structure. They did not modify the original text, but chose to work with peritext. They both promoted Melon's ideas and those of the writers of Gournay's circle. Both rejected currency manipulations. However, unlike Le Blanc, Zinzendorf did not have to explain substantial differences in arguments. His ideas were generally in line with those of Law. Zinzendorf's aim was to make Law's arguments accessible and relevant to German readers. Unlike Gournay's initiative, he did not have a larger national political agenda into which *Gedanken vom Gelde* had to fit.

[133] Ibid., vol. 1, pp. xxi–xxii.

[134] See note 6.

CHAPTER 5

The Development of Zinzendorf's Thinking on State Credit

In early 1756, Zinzendorf returned from a diplomatic mission to Russia, Sweden and Denmark.[1] At that time, Kaunitz was engaged in diplomatic efforts to build the monarchy's strategic alliance with France and was aware that a new military conflict with Prussia was approaching. He asked Zinzendorf to devise a mechanism which would allow Austria to quickly raise additional funds. Zinzendorf wrote a proposal which was printed in 1757 as *Pro Memoria an eine ständische Deputation einen Vorschlag zur Erleichterung des ständischen Credites betreffend.*[2] Even though only intended as a temporary measure to raise war finance, Zinzendorf presented a thorough and innovative financial system. His hope was that it would be recognised as a valuable mechanism with equal relevance for war and peacetime.[3] The *Pro Memoria* was the first substantial result of Zinzendorf's intellectual engagement with reforming the state credit of the monarchy.[4] Importantly, it was Zinzendorf's starting point for creating more robust economic structures for the monarchy. Printed in quarto,

[1] Eduard Gaston von Pettenegg (ed.), *Ludwig und Karl Grafen und Herren von Zinzendorf. Ihre Selbstbiographien nebst einer kurzen Geschichte des Hauses Zinzendorf* (Vienna, 1879), p. 71.

[2] Ludwig Zinzendorf, *Pro Memoria an eine ständische Deputation einen Vorschlag zur Erleichterung des ständischen Credites betreffend. Im September 1757*, vol. 33, fols 181r–253r, Nachlaß Zinzendorf, HHStA.

[3] Ibid., fol. 230r.

[4] The earlier text was Zinzendorf's 'Essai sur l'Établissement d'une Banque générale', 26 September 1750, vol. 105, Nachlaß Zinzendorf, HHStA: see above, Chap. 3.

S. Adler, *Political Economy in the Habsburg Monarchy 1750–1774*,
Palgrave Studies in the History of Finance,
https://doi.org/10.1007/978-3-030-31007-3_5

the *Pro Memoria* was intended for a wider dissemination so that government and Estates officials could become familiar with the new financial operation. A revised version was printed in 1759 as *Finanz-Vorschläge zur Fortsetzung des gegenwärtigen Krieges. Allerhöchst Ihro Röm- Kais.-König. Apostolischen M.M.. Alleruntertänigst übergeben von Ludwig Grafen und Herrn von Zinzendorf und Pottendorf; dero wirklichen geheimen Rathe, Cämmerern und Assessore in denen Directoriis in publicis et cameralibus. Im Monat Jul.1759.*[5] In 1758, Zinzendorf had a written manuscript version, 'Projet de Finance pour la continuation de la Guerre'.[6] In the French text, Zinzendorf replaced the Estates of Lower Austria as the issuer of the bonds with the Vienna City Bank and tripled the issue size of the financial operation to 6 million *florins*.[7] The other elements of the *Pro Memoria* remained largely unchanged.[8] The use of the Vienna City Bank was a concession to Count Rudolf Chotek, its president, and to other officials in government who voiced strong opposition to Zinzendorf's plan.[9] Over four years, Kaunitz relentlessly pursued his plan to have Zinzendorf's

[5] Ludwig Zinzendorf, *Finanz-Vorschläge zur Fortsetzung des gegenwärtigen Krieges. Allerhöchst Ihro Röm- Kais.-König. Apostolischen M.M.. Alleruntertänigst übergeben von Ludwig Grafen und Herrn von Zinzendorf und Pottendorf; dero wirklichen geheimen Rathe, Cämmerern und Assessore in denen Directoriis in publicis et cameralibus. Im Monat Jul.1759*, B.E. 6.O.46, ÖNB. A copy is held at the National Library of France; see also, Pettenegg (ed.), *Selbstbiographien*, p. 73. In the title of the document, 'Directoriis' in plural, rather than 'Directorium', might indicate that Zinzendorf wrote the document for a wider audience in several departments within the 'Directorium in publicis et cameralibus'. In particular, Zinzendorf might have intended it for the bureau of trade where he had worked and which operated from within the 'Directorium'. See also Chap. 6, particularly 'The Institutions for Commercial Affairs'.

[6] Ludwig Zinzendorf, 'Projet de Finance pour la continuation de la Guerre', 1758, vol. 18, unfoliated, Nachlaß Zinzendorf, HHStA.

[7] For summaries of *Finanz-vorschläge*, see P.G.M. Dickson, *Finance and Government under Maria Theresia 1740–1780* (2 vols, Oxford, 1987) vol. 2, p. 133; Johann Schasching, *Staatsbildung und Finanzentwicklung: Ein Beitrag zur Geschichte des österreichischen Staatskredites in der 2. Hälfte des 18. Jahrhunderts* (Innsbruck, 1954), pp. 12–16; Hans Gross, 'Die ständische Kredit-Deputation und der Plan eines erbländischen Nationalkredites (Ein Beitrag zur Finanzpolitik unter Maria Theresia)' (PhD dissertation, University of Vienna, 1935), pp. 12–19; Adolf Beer, 'Die Staatschulden und die Ordnung des Staatshaushaltes unter Maria Theresia', *AÖG* 82 (1894), pp. 1–135, at pp. 7–9. To ensure a large take-up of the operation, Zinzendorf sought to overcome linguistic barriers by printing the banknotes in German, Hungarian and Czech: Gross, 'Die ständische Kredit-Deputation', p. 16.

[8] For a concise summary of the changes in the revised manuscript proposal, see Franz A.J. Szabo, *Kaunitz and enlightened absolutism 1753–1780* (Cambridge, 1994), p. 121.

[9] Ibid., pp. 120–21.

ideas accepted by government.[10] Eventually, in 1761, the empress authorised the creation of an Estates Credit Deputation of Austrian and Bohemian lands and appointed Zinzendorf as its first president.[11]

The monarchy, Zinzendorf was convinced, urgently needed new processes, and the Estates of the hereditary lands could play an important role. They could be instrumental in restoring state credit which had been damaged by the country's existing institutions, in particular the Vienna City Bank. In 'Geschichte und Beschreibung der Wiener Stadt Banco',[12] written in 1758, Zinzendorf explained why the monarchy's most important financial institution was not working. In 1761, as part of the wider discussions in government about administrative reforms, he proposed to join the operations of the Estates of the Austrian and Bohemian lands with the bank. This was, Zinzendorf thought, the quickest and most direct way to create a unified credit for the monarchy. Zinzendorf's ideas on the reorganisation of the financial administration will be covered in the next chapter.

Ultimately, Zinzendorf's thinking on state credit was guided by the works of European economic writers and by the examples of foreign financial institutions. In 1758, he began to write a survey of 12 European banks entitled 'Beschreibung der vornehmsten Europäischen Bancken von Ludwig Friedrich Julius Grafen und Herrn von Zinzendorf und Pottendorf, Ihrer kaiserl. König. Apostol. Majestät wirklichen geheimen Rat, Kämmerern und Assesore des Directoriums in publicis et cameralibus'. Two identical copies are in the archives.[13] The document, which he completed in 1763,

[10] Between 1757 and 1761, Kaunitz made no less than four forceful attempts to rally support for Zinzendorf's scheme: ibid., pp. 120–26.

[11] This credit operation, in which the amount of paper issued was trebled again to 18m. fl., is well covered in the literature: Schasching, *Staatsbildung*, pp. 18–24; Dickson, *Finance and Government*, vol. 2, pp. 134–38; Szabo, *Kaunitz*, pp. 127–30; and William D. Godsey, *The Sinews of Habsburg Power: Lower Austria in a Fiscal-Military State, 1650–1820* (Oxford, 2018), pp. 240–45. Maria Theresa's letter appointing Zinzendorf is printed in Beer, 'Die Staatsschulden', p. 11, and in Friedrich Walter (ed.), *Vom Sturz des Directoriums in Publicis et Cameralibus (1760/61) bis zum Ausgang der Regierung Maria Theresias: Aktenstücke*, II. Abteilung, vol. 3 (Vienna: ÖZV, 1934), p. 165.

[12] Ludwig Zinzendorf, 'Geschichte und Beschreibung der Wiener Stadt Banco', undated, unfoliated, vol. 101, Nachlaß Zinzendorf, HHStA. Based on references in the text, the date of the manuscript is probably 1758.

[13] Ludwig Zinzendorf, 'Beschreibung der vornehmsten Europäischen Bancken von Ludwig Friedrich Julius Grafen und Herrn von Zinzendorf und Pottendorf, Ihrer kaiserl. König. Apostol. Majestät wirklichen geheimen Rat, Kämmerern und Assesore des Directoriums in publicis et cameralibus', Vienna 1758, Nachlaß Zinzendorf, vols 103 and 104, HHStA.

was remarkable not only because of the level of analysis it offered on the operations of European banks but also because it decisively shaped Zinzendorf's financial proposal of 1767 for the creation of a stock exchange together with a political bank for the monarchy entitled 'Allergnädigst, abgeforderter Vorschlag, die Einrichtung einer Börse zur Verhandlung der öffentlichen Papiere und eines Banco di Credito betreffend, Februar 1767'.[14] It was Zinzendorf's most developed plan for the new financial institutions which followed an earlier proposal of June 1763 on the stock exchange, the bank and uniform bonds.[15]

Except for the *Pro Memoria* and *Finanz-vorschläge*, Zinzendorf's memoranda on credit reform were folio manuscripts. They were not printed. However, as they were intended for circulation among senior officials, several identical copies of documents were written. The multiple manuscript copies of 'Beschreibung der vornehmsten Europäischen Bancken' show that the intention was the rapid dissemination of information so that discussion in government could take place.[16]

Better Credit for War Finance

The *Pro Memoria* was already an elaborate text and consisted of several parts. The core proposal extended to over 100 pages. Two additional documents were intended for official use: the *Hofdecret* from the ruler to the Estates of Lower Austria, and the *Patent* written by the Estates of Lower Austria for the public. Neither were dated.[17] Both explained again the mechanics of the financial operation and, to the core text, Zinzendorf

[14] Ludwig Zinzendorf, 'Allergnädigst, abgeforderter Vorschlag, die Einrichtung einer Börse zur Verhandlung der öffentlichen Papiere und eines Banco di Credito betreffend, Februar 1767', Nachlaß Zinzendorf, vol. 20, HHStA.

[15] Ludwig Zinzendorf, 'Finanzvorschläge', 1 June 1763, vol. 19, fols 179r–237r, Nachlaß Zinzendorf, HHStA. For a summary, see Dickson, *Finance and Government*, vol. 2, pp. 43–4. It is also covered in Szabo, *Kaunitz*, pp. 132–33.

[16] According to Szabo, *Kaunitz*, pp. 120–21, notes 23 and 29, there are German versions of Zinzendorf's 'Projet de Finance' in Staatskanzlei 'Vorträge', Karton 84 and 81, HHStA. However, I could not find these texts there. In Karton 81, X–XII, fols 22–29, ibid., there is a 'Vortrag' by Kaunitz to the empress on Zinzendorf's plan dated 14 October 1757.

[17] *Entwurf eines allergnädigsten Hof-Decretes welches von Ihro Majestät an die R.D. drey oberen Heren Stände wegen des von denenselben anzubegehrenden Darlehens von 2,200,000 Gulden abzulassen*, in Zinzendorf, *Pro Memoria*, fols 232r–238r; *Entwurf eines von den oberen dreyen Herren Ständen Patent an das Publicum zu erlassenden Patentes*, in ibid., fols 238v–251v.

added a detailed repayment schedule for a bond issue together with two financial tables setting out the variations of bond prices and the calculation of the repayments.

For the war effort of the monarchy, Zinzendorf proposed to raise 2.2 million *gulden* from the Estates of Lower Austria at a rate of interest of 5 per cent. Under the current credit arrangements, the Estates had to pay higher rates of interest on their debt and had to take up forced loans, *subsidia praesentanea*, to supplement government revenues. Therefore, Zinzendorf argued, it was important to have a more cost-effective mechanism in place which would facilitate voluntary credit and the timely availability of funds for war-related expenses. He wanted to avoid imposing new financial burdens on the 'public' and sought to remove the state's dependence on expensive debt which was offered by financial speculators. There were two fundamental elements to Zinzendorf's financial plan: first, an increase of the supply of money; and second, as part of the voluntary bond, the issuance of paper money so that funds could be made available immediately to the state.[18]

The increase of the supply of money would be achieved by broadening the monarchy's investor base for public debt. The largest pool of liquid funds, Zinzendorf thought, was not concentrated among the wealthy landowners and industrialists, but rather among the broad mass of the less prosperous 'public' living in towns and villages.[19] Successfully accessing these funds from a new, hitherto unused, investor base would increase the money supply to the Estates and remove the problem of forced loans. To tap this new investor base, Zinzendorf argued, it was necessary to adapt the way public debt was issued in the monarchy. Existing debt instruments had been tailor-made for wealthy investors and were cumbersome in their administration: they were only issued in high denominations of 100 *florins* or 500 *florins*, were not readily transferable and had a difficult method for calculating interest payments. Zinzendorf proposed a simplified financial operation. It consisted of short-dated debt instruments, *Coupons-Obligationen*, in small denominations of 30 *florins* only. The new bonds were endorsable bearer documents with detachable premium certificates. They would be issued by the Estates in several *caisses*, which would be located in cities as well as in the countryside. The interest would be paid once a year, on the same date. The low nominal value would make the

[18] Ibid., fols 182r–183r.

[19] On the monarchy's social structure, see Dickson, *Finance and Government*, vol. 1, pp. 41–58.

bonds easily tradable. To further simplify transactions, sale and purchase prices would be published daily. Success would depend on publicity, simplicity and transparency. To maximise demand for the debt issue, the 'Patent' document for the public ought to be distributed in print as widely as possible. In sum, Zinzendorf argued, the voluntary bond issue offered four important advantages to state credit: first, additional funds became available from a new investor base; second, it added money to the economy; third, the bearer format of the bonds enticed holders of undeclared funds to invest anonymously; and fourth, the format of the bonds might also attract the interest of speculators.[20]

War finance required swift access to funds. In the second part of his proposal, Zinzendorf argued, money could be made available quickly to the state through the issue of paper money (*Zahlungsstatt Obligationen*). These were also bearer bonds but, in addition, with cash-like qualities, they were comparable to paper money. Zinzendorf envisaged creating 1 million *florins*, almost half of the total debt issue, as paper money with a nominal value of 30 *florins*. He recommended their use for cameral and salary payments and wanted them to be visibly stamped with *Zahlungsstatt*. Like the *Coupons-Obligationen*, they were also suited for use in daily transactions. To ensure widespread acceptance, the *caisses* in all hereditary lands as well as in Hungary would accept the bonds and would have their interest and payments refunded by the Estates of Lower Austria. The sale and purchase of the paper money would be transparent and based on daily published rates. For Zinzendorf, it was critical to support the value of the bonds by ensuring liquidity. He therefore proposed the establishment of stock exchanges in town halls, where buyers and sellers would meet to trade face to face. To enlist the support of the Estates of the hereditary lands for the creation of such exchanges, the government, Zinzendorf recommended, should cover the administrative expenses. He also envisaged the creation of cash funds, *Umsetzungskassen*, financed by government, as support for unsuccessful stock exchange trades. To guarantee their independence, the administration of the cash funds should not be undertaken by the Estates, but by private individuals or other suitable public funds. Zinzendorf's ideas on this were not fully developed, and as such he did not explain the mechanism by which the funds would operate. He recognised this himself and used it as the justification for not having included the *Umsetzungskassen* in the *Patent*.

[20] Zinzendorf, *Pro Memoria*, fols 183r–191v.

Zinzendorf was convinced that he had devised a mechanism which would ensure a successful issue of paper money. However, he underlined that the issue was a strictly temporary measure. Immediately after a peace treaty, the Estates should cease issuing new paper money, and bonds already in circulation would only be redeemed at public *caisses* up to one year following the end of the war.[21] To underline the advantage of his scheme, Zinzendorf compared it to similar paper money issues which had, he argued, weaker structures. In particular, Zinzendorf referred to the financing operations of Sardinia. In 1745, the Italian kingdom was in need of capital for its war effort and resorted to three successful issues of cameral bonds. The *Biglietti di Credito* were comparable to *Zahlungsstatt Obligationen*, and were also accepted in all public *caisses*. However, their financial mechanism was not as robust as the one he had proposed for the debt issue of the Estates. Repayment of the *Biglietti di Credito* took as long as five years. Rather than interest payments, they offered fixed capital increases of 1 per cent every quarter, payable at maturity, and had very limited liquidity.[22]

Governments, Zinzendorf thought, had to refrain from creating new indefinite debt burdens to finance their war campaigns. Therefore, as an important confidence building measure for creditors, he proposed the establishment of a redemption fund which would enable a detailed repayment schedule for the bond issue. This was an integral part of Zinzendorf's plan. The size of the fund would be set at 154,000 *florins* to cover interest payments as well as the repayment of the principal. As transparency was essential, payment dates and amounts had to be communicated in advance to investors. Over a period of 25½ years, Zinzendorf calculated, the entire debt would be amortised.[23] The system ensured the commitment of the state to reduce the size of the outstanding debt. Zinzendorf also wanted the bonds that had been redeemed to be burnt in public every six months to reinforce the public's confidence in the Estates' financial management.[24]

France and England were examples of two countries that had followed different strategies in regard to debt repayment plans. France, since 1735,

[21] Ibid., fols 191r–195v.

[22] Ibid., fols 196v–198r.

[23] About 110,000 fl. would cover the yearly interest expense of 5 per cent. And 44,000 fl., or 2 per cent of the value of issued debt, was earmarked for the repayment of the principal. The bond issue was split into 73,333 bonds of 30 fl., and the repayment period was set from 1759 to 1784: fol. 199r. Zinzendorf provided a detailed repayment plan: ibid., fol. 252r.

[24] Ibid., fols 195v–203v.

had used dedicated funds for the repayment of each new debt issue. The disciplined approach of the French, Zinzendorf speculated, should lead by 1760 to a repayment of the state debt which was raised during the War of Austrian Succession. England also used a redemption fund, but had failed to fully repay its old debts before taking on new credit. English debt repayments were dependent on Parliament whose consent was arbitrary. Zinzendorf preferred the French model. To obtain lower rates of interest on state debt, it was important, he argued, to use only the funds already dedicated to servicing the debt obligations. Taking money out of existing funds to cover new expenses would lead to a loss of public confidence.[25]

The bonds should be redeemed in one single payment to investors, and the capital of the paper money should be paid back first. The redemption dates should be decided by lottery and communicated to investors six months before. Zinzendorf preferred this mechanism which was based on the calculations of the French mathematician Antoine Deparcieux and had been used in France since 1749.[26] The advantage of the French method, Zinzendorf argued, was that investors had their entire capital returned to them in one payment. They could then decide to reinvest the money and would continue to have an interest income. The English system of 'annuities', on the other hand, was inferior. It provided payments of smaller fixed amounts over many years without additional income.[27]

Most of the financial proposals, Zinzendorf argued, had been devised solely for the benefit of the landed aristocracy. His plan however was designed to address equally the requirements of all three parties involved in the transaction: the Estates, the treasury and the state (*gesammter Staats-Cörper*).[28] For the Estates, the new plan did not present any drawback to their current financial arrangements. It merely involved a different administrative set-up. The important 'novelty' of the issue was the clear commitment to investors to repay the debt. For the Estates, this did not create any financial uncertainties since the redemption fund was provided for by the state. To show that these concepts had been tried and tested

[25] Ibid., fols 202r–203v.

[26] Antoine Deparcieux, *Essai sur les probabilités de la durée de la vie humaine* (Paris, 1746). For a recent edition, see *Antoine Deparcieux, Essai sur les probabilités de la durée de la vie humaine (1746). Addition à l'Essai (1760). Réédition en fac-similé avec une introduction et des notes de C. Behar, accompagnée de contributions de G. Gallais-Hamonno, C. Tietsch, J. Berthon* (Institut National D'Études Demographiques, Paris, 2003).

[27] Zinzendorf, *Pro Memoria*, fols 203v–205v.

[28] Ibid., fol. 223r.

before, Zinzendorf used the example of a similar operation undertaken in 1756 by the Estates of Moravia. Unable to supply enough finances to the government, the Estates paid in natural produce instead. They, in turn, paid their local providers by issuing interest-bearing bonds.[29]

Also, the execution of the bond issue would not interfere with their existing administrative processes, and price increases of the new *Obligationen* would not trigger a fall in the prices of existing bonds. On the contrary, the use of paper money avoided forced credit and, as it was readily accepted by the government as currency, it did not carry any risk. Zinzendorf pointed out that the denominations of bonds issued by the Estates had decreased over time from 500 *florins* to 100 *florins*. A new bond issue with a smaller denomination would not interfere with the existing state credit. He envisaged, however, that holders of old bonds would buy new ones and provided a mechanism of how they could be swapped.[30] The new debt issue would allow the Estates to draw on a much wider potential investor base and create prosperity for a large number of the 'public'. The stock exchange, as the anchor for direct trades between investors, would create a more liquid market and remove the Estates as intermediary in transactions. Finally, the entire administrative system for managing the issue was simpler and demanded less time and paperwork.[31]

For the state treasury, small retail investors were an important new source of credit as the landed aristocracy was generally cash poor. Also, unlike in France and England, the monarchy did not have wealthy financiers and industrialists who could offer financial support. Zinzendorf's system offered cheaper debt and, alongside existing credit arrangements, a significant increase in the supply of money to the economy. As the mechanism of the bond issue was transparent, it added to the credibility of the state and made its public debt operations less dependent on success and luck on the battlefield. The system, Zinzendorf maintained, was robust and its use could be readily extended to other provinces of the monarchy where the population did not have large enough money reserves to invest in existing bonds.

Zinzendorf argued that this system was based on tried and tested mechanisms used in Europe. From France, Zinzendorf borrowed the idea of using detachable coupons, the repayment method through lottery and the

[29] Ibid., fols 207v–208r.

[30] Ibid., fols 206v, 210v–211r.

[31] Ibid., fols 206v–211v, 229v–230r.

burning in public of bonds. He used the English exchequer bills as a model for the issue of paper money. From Sweden, Zinzendorf copied the idea of using printing techniques to guard the bonds against forgeries. France and England already had a mechanism where buyers and sellers of bonds could trade directly. The stock exchange, where investors would meet on a daily basis, was an extension of this and was, in addition, necessary for the growth of commerce Zinzendorf thought. Other improvements which he claimed were new and not used by foreign nations included the issuance of bonds with very small denominations of 30 *florins*; possibilities for investment across cities, towns and villages; the publication of daily bond prices; and a new numbering system for bonds to conveniently administer the payment of interest and cancellation of the debt.[32] The paper work required for the sale of bonds would follow administrative procedures used by the banks in Amsterdam and London. As an addition, without providing detail, Zinzendorf envisaged setting up a *Depositen Amt* where bonds would be held for safekeeping against fire and other hazards. His idea was based on the *Bureau de Dépot* in France which was holding the shares of the Compagnie des Indes.[33]

These advantages were equally relevant to the state, which would benefit from a stronger domestic economy. As the debt issue was primarily a domestic financial operation, the interest payments would be made to domestic investors and hence would benefit investments in the monarchy.[34] In addition, paper money was a convenient way to undertake large payments. By offering a financial return, investors could be enticed to hold paper rather than coins and reinvest their savings in the economy. For the first time, the 'public', especially those who were less well off, would be able to generate an income from their savings. As the bonds were liquid instruments with the cash funds as money guarantees, citizens could swiftly sell their investments if they required money. Eventually, as the examples of foreign countries showed, new financial systems would be adopted. The same would be possible in the monarchy if the citizens were led by the 'enlightened class' (*erleuchtetern Classe*). Rejection by the public would be unlikely if the Estates, with their reputation for prudence and concern for the general well-being, would propagate the plan.[35] The appeal of the

[32] Ibid., fols 211v–225v.

[33] Ibid., fols 225r–225v.

[34] Zinzendorf estimated that, over 30 years, as part of the monarchy's credit arrangements, 20–30m. fl. had been paid out to foreigners in interest: ibid., fols 225r–225v.

[35] Ibid., fols 223r–230v.

bond issue, Zinzendorf thought, was reinforced by the previous success of the Viennese lottery, which had operated as a private enterprise without state guarantees. The lottery had been run for over 25 years, and participation, with a ticket price of 500 *florins*, was very costly. Nevertheless, the popular attraction of the lottery had been strong despite widespread financial uncertainty in Europe following large losses in the wake of the collapse of Law's scheme in France and the South Sea Bubble in England. The lottery in Genoa had also benefitted from a wide appeal.[36]

In a letter to Kaunitz of 24 July 1756, Zinzendorf summarised the advantages of the *Pro Memoria*.[37] The scheme to issue voluntary bonds, Zinzendorf boasted in the letter, established the 'true principles of state credit' which the monarchy should follow. Adapted to the needs of the monarchy, it represented a development and 'perfection' of the French system. It improved the use of existing amortisation funds and included a repayment schedule which was modelled on Deparcieux's calculations and his empirical observations on life expectancy. His new financial proposal, Zinzendorf pointed out, offered three important advantages. First, it was based on tried and tested principles and an in-depth study of European financial institutions. Second, having been revised several times, its argument had been reinforced by taking account of the objections of government ministers. Third, the text was very detailed. This, Zinzendorf made clear, was intentional as it would facilitate a quick implementation of the scheme.[38]

As in his earlier writings, Zinzendorf borrowed the ideas of foreign thinkers to develop his arguments. However, in the *Pro Memoria*, Zinzendorf took his argument in a new direction. He supplemented the ideas with European models. Zinzendorf introduced existing credit arrangements, notably debt repayment plans, from foreign countries. Their application, he wrote to Kaunitz, was a key advantage of his plan. Like financial practices elsewhere, notably in England, Zinzendorf's mechanism was based on confidence building and transparency. In particular, Zinzendorf appreciated the dominant role of the Estates which was interposed between the government and the creditors. Also, he understood the

[36]Ibid., fols 231r–231v. On the Genoa lottery, introduced in November 1751, see Dickson, *Finance and Government*, vol. 1, p. 138, note 84.

[37]Letter of Ludwig Zinzendorf to Kaunitz, 24 July 1756 in Pettenegg (ed.), *Selbstbiographien*, pp. 67–8.

[38]As examples, Zinzendorf included templates of bearer bonds with their detachable interest coupons: Zinzendorf, *Pro Memoria*, fol. 253r.

importance of directly involving the numerous small and often rural investors in the capital-raising operations of the state.

Zinzendorf's *Pro Memoria* was not the only proposal on war finance which was presented to the government,[39] but it was certainly the most developed and sophisticated. Also, it was important in terms of the development of Zinzendorf's thinking on credit. For the first time, Zinzendorf set out the key elements of the financial system which he would develop in his subsequent writings. These included the use of a stock exchange and the application of transparent banking mechanisms. The systems of the *Pro Memoria*, Zinzendorf argued, were a preparation for an improved public credit system in the future.[40]

The Vienna City Bank

The system of the *Pro Memoria* had to offer new and different arguments to match Zinzendorf's diagnosis that the existing financial structure of the monarchy was weak. In particular, the Vienna City Bank had lost its original function of providing independent support to state finances. It needed urgent reform. In 1758, in 'Geschichte und Beschreibung der Wiener Stadt Banco', Zinzendorf set out his thinking on the bank.[41] At the outset, the Vienna City Bank had operated as a public fund. It had received funds from the state to make the interest payments and the quarterly capital payments to creditors. The city of Vienna had also agreed to issue bonds to creditors at a rate of interest of 5 per cent. Redemption funds for capital repayments were set up for a maximum of 15 years. Their life span could

[39] Other proposals included: [Anonymous], undated, 'Das bei Abgang des baren Geldes in Vorschlag gebrachte Münz-Surrogatum betreffend'. It was a plan to issue bonds without interest payments and to offer repayment after 16 years. The small denominations of the bonds would enable a good circulation in the economy. The plan followed a French model: Gross, 'Die ständische Kredit-Deputation', p. 19.

[40] 'Es sind vielmehr die wichtigeren Vortheile anzusehen, so dieses System, als eine Vorbereitung zu einem verbesserten Credit-Wesen, auf die zukünftigen Zeiten verschaffet': Zinzendorf, *Pro Memoria*, fol. 219v.

[41] Karl Zinzendorf closely read his brother's memoir and transcribed a long passage: Diary of Karl Zinzendorf, 22 November 1761, in Maria Breunlich and Marieluise Mader (eds.), *Karl Graf von Zinzendorf, Aus den Jugendtagebüchern 1747, 1752–1763. Nach Vorarbeiten von Hans Wagner*, Veröffentlichung der Kommission für Neuere Geschichte Österreichs 84 (Vienna, 1997), pp. 246–47.

not be shortened, and they could not be used for other purposes.[42] A Deputation of the Estates of Lower Austria had been created with the intention of supervising the correct administration of the funds and of guaranteeing the bank's independence from the state. It had been designed, Zinzendorf argued, to act as a trusted body which could mediate between the bank, the treasury and the public. The Deputation would ensure that the bank's credit was kept in good order, that the relationship with creditors was sound and transparent and that none of the parties was put at a disadvantage.[43]

Gradually, however, this arrangement had been abandoned. The bank, Zinzendorf pointed out, became a *Schulden Caße* providing *Activ-Credite* to the state.[44] First, the bank used its deposits to cover war-related expenses. The latter were generally larger than the deposits and, for a period of time, the bank had to refuse creditors the right of redemption. Second, the bank frequently gave loans in secret to the ruler. It was unknown, Zinzendorf noted, whether or not the bank assumed the credit risk for these advances or insisted on receiving additional deposits from the ruler. Finally, the institution extended credit to the government by using miscellaneous state income as collateral. As a last resort, if money reserves were not sufficient, it assigned its bonds to the state.[45] The bank had turned into an agency of the state. The *Hofdeputation* replaced the city of Vienna as administrator of the credit operations but kept the mayor of Vienna, in a largely ceremonial role, as signatory of the bonds.[46] The *Hofdeputation*, Zinzendorf argued, was not accountable to anybody except the ruler, and it followed arbitrary and secretive processes. As such, the operations of the bank, including the sizes of its debt and reserves, were only known to its president and a small group of his advisers.[47]

[42] Zinzendorf, 'Wiener Stadt Banco', pp. 2–12. Various documents on the Vienna City bank are in 'Miscellenia den Banco betreffend von 1704–1755', vol. 100, Nachlaß Zinzendorf, HHStA.

[43] Zinzendorf, 'Wiener Stadt Banco', pp. 15–21.

[44] Ibid., pp. 21, 24.

[45] Ibid., pp. 34–9. In a reply to Chotek's first objection to the creation of the Estates Credit Deputation, Zinzendorf summarised how the Vienna City Bank was transformed into a more dependent institution of the state: Zinzendorf, 'Projet de Finance', pp. 65–71. See also Chap. 6, particularly 'Debates Within Government'.

[46] Zinzendorf, 'Wiener Stadt Banco', pp. 39–41. On the *Hofdeputation*, see Dickson, *Finance and Government*, vol. 1, pp. 223–25.

[47] Zinzendorf, 'Wiener Stadt Banco', pp. 44–6.

Despite the secrecy surrounding the operations, Zinzendorf thought that it was possible to get an idea of the bank's financial health by comparing the loans of 1748 with those of March 1758. In 1748, the loans had amounted to 56 million *florins*, and the bank had received an income of 4.9 million *florins*. Of the latter, 3.9 million *florins* had been used to service the debts: 2.8 million *florins* to cover interest payments, and 1.12 million *florins* to repay capital. By March 1758, even though there had been peace for eight years, the bank's debts had increased to 59 million *florins*. This was proof, Zinzendorf concluded, that the yearly repayment fund of 1.12 million *florins*, which could have been used to reduce the debt outstanding by more than 10 million *florins*, had been deployed elsewhere.[48]

Zinzendorf highlighted several important shortcomings in the bank's operations. Contrary to other public funds, it remained continuously open for new deposits. Offering a comparatively high rate of interest, even during peacetime, the bank attracted foreign capital. However, it could not repay deposits early since foreign creditors did not disclose their true identities. Domestic investors were attracted by the high rate of interest, too, and thus domestic capital, Zinzendorf argued, was diverted from productive use in the economy. Merchants in need of financing had to resort to expensive foreign credit with rates of interest as high as 8 or 9 per cent. The Vienna City Bank's rate of interest was higher than the rates in other European countries. A previous attempt to reduce it to 4 per cent had been unsuccessful.[49]

Moreover, Zinzendorf continued, the bank closed itself to the large pool of potential domestic investors living in the countryside and in smaller cities. It did not accept sums below 500 *gulden* and only allowed deposits to be opened in Vienna.[50] This, for Zinzendorf, was a fundamental weakness. The right of creditors to redeem their deposits, *Aufkündigungsfreiheit*, was a further shortcoming.[51] Zinzendorf conceded that the right of redemption was not a unique practice of the Vienna City Bank. Other domestic funds as well as credit institutions in Germany operated according to the same principle.[52] During peacetime, the bank

[48] Ibid., pp. 46–51.

[49] Ibid., pp. 56–9, 62–4, 67. The reduction to 4 per cent did not amount to very much. It only yielded a very small annual saving. So, during the war, the bank swiftly offered a rate of 5 per cent again: ibid., pp. 68–9.

[50] Ibid., pp. 69–71.

[51] Ibid., pp. 76–7.

[52] Ibid., p. 77.

had to keep large capital reserves to cover potential cash withdrawals. This money, therefore, was blocked and could not be used productively for commerce or manufacturing. As a deterrent to investors against redeeming their funds at short notice, the bank refused to pay interest on money which had been deposited for less than three months. In wartime, when the state relied the most on financial support, the bank was unable to provide assistance as it could not grow its capital base. Creditors who had lost redemption rights on their deposits refused to add money.[53]

Direct market transactions between buyers and sellers of the bank's bonds were rare. The bonds, issued with large and different nominal values by name to creditors, had a cumbersome transfer mechanism. It was thus easier for the bondholders to redeem the paper directly with the bank rather than to seek interested parties in the market. The administrative burden had two components. First, the bank had to record the details of each of its 83,000 creditors as well as any subsequent transactions. Even if only 1000 creditors added to their deposits or transferred bonds each year, the workload was overwhelming. Second, based on the number of creditors, the bank had to process more than 300,000 interest receipts and ensure that they were archived correctly. It was a system, Zinzendorf noted, which was prone to error. There had been cases when the interest was paid out twice, once to the new owner and once to the seller of the bonds. Zinzendorf referred to comments by Count Philipp Kinsky (1700–1749), the former president of the bank, who had acknowledged that the institution had lost 15,000 *gulden* over several years.[54]

The bank's main weakness was its opaque processes.[55] This, too, was the conclusion of an assessment of various external knowledgeable observers.[56] Zinzendorf reiterated his criticism of the bank's loss of accountability as a result of being under the direct influence of the state. Having been reduced to a simple *Schulden Caße* of the state, Zinzendorf argued, the bank did not follow the more sophisticated processes which institutions elsewhere in Europe were using.[57] It was no longer possible for outsiders to verify its

[53] Ibid., pp. 79–80.

[54] Ibid., pp. 85–96.

[55] Ibid., pp. 96–7.

[56] Zinzendorf did not name them. He specified, however, that they were proficient in credit and financial affairs: ibid., p. 96.

[57] The Hôtel de Ville in Paris, Zinzendorf argued, a comparable institution to the Vienna City Bank, would not take on new debt without issuing a royal patent and making it available to the public. The patent would include the size of the new credit facility and identify the fund which would be used as collateral: ibid., pp. 105–6.

accounts, and suspicion arose that it would lead to a misuse of funds.[58] It was, Zinzendorf emphasised, the only large public fund which kept the state of its finances a secret. Therefore, even if the bank did follow good administrative practices, the public had to be distrustful of its operations.[59] As part of this, the most imminent danger was the issue of bonds to the state. It was done in secret, and the public knew nothing about the bonds nor about the funds which would be created by the bank as collateral. Thus, Zinzendorf argued, it was understandable that the public should fear the worst, including the total collapse of the bank's credit.[60] Details of the bank's other bond issues were also kept from the public, but the potential for their manipulation was limited given that they were fully covered by deposits. However, the danger of abuse through an unlimited issue of bonds to the state remained large. The example of Saxony, Zinzendorf argued, gave real reason for concern. There, the secret administration of tax income by one government official had triggered the collapse of the entire state credit. *Steuer Scheine* had been issued without cash collateral, and holders of older government paper had lost half of their investment as well.[61]

Two changes, Zinzendorf thought, were critical to improve the operations of the bank. First, the redemption funds ought to be dedicated to specific portions of the debt. Also, the bank should commit publicly to repay the debt over a predetermined period of time. This was the first principle of *Staatswirthschaft*, and its application the only remedy against the reckless financial management practices of a ruler. However, the new management had discarded this 'cardinal rule' originally followed by the bank. As a result, the bank lost millions and also the confidence of the public.[62] The second change would be to open the bank up to public scrutiny.[63] It would include the disclosure of capital reserves and accounts as well as the use of a new system for the administration of the contribution. The latter was managed by the bank for its own advantage and hence yielded poor results. An outside party, Zinzendorf proposed, would be more diligent in recruiting able and honest officials to administer the contribution and would strive to avert embezzlement. Like tobacco farming,

[58] Ibid., pp. 102–5.

[59] Ibid., pp. 106–7.

[60] Ibid., pp. 107–9.

[61] Ibid., pp. 110–15. Zinzendorf probably was referring to Count Heinrich von Brühl, the chief minister of Saxony. Brühl was accused of financial mismanagement and corruption, and after his death in 1763 tried in court.

[62] Ibid., pp. 121–24, 127–28.

[63] Ibid., pp. 132–34.

it could produce superior results.[64] The good administration of public revenues, he concluded, was an art which was not yet widely enough practised in the monarchy.[65]

The Vienna City Bank had been created in 1706 as the successor of the *Banco del Giro*. Set up in 1703 to improve the general situation surrounding state credit, its remit had been to increase the value of government debt by increasing liquidity. However, it could not gain the confidence of the public. It was perceived as a government agency which extended preferential treatment to some creditors over others.[66] To increase the public confidence, its operations were transferred to the city of Vienna.[67] Like the *Banco del Giro*, the Vienna City Bank assumed the state debt and received state revenues. Nominally independent, it was managed from the city hall in Vienna.[68] The Vienna City Bank was the largest single creditor to the government, and its income was significantly smaller than the level of debt it held.[69] In 1721, it also assumed an additional 25 million *florins* of debt of the *Universal-Bancalität* which collapsed in 1720.[70] During the Seven Years War, the Vienna City Bank played an active part in generating funds to cover military expenses. In 1762, it issued 12 million *florins* in *Banco Zettel*, which was non-interest-paying paper money and could be used for partial payment to the state. In 1766, as part of a programme to reduce the bank's debt, most of them were burnt.[71] In the 1770s, subsequent issues followed, and *Banco Zettel* were increasingly accepted by the public.[72]

[64] Ibid., pp. 137–43. On Zinzendorf's proposal for tobacco farming, see Chap. 6, particularly 'Projectors'.

[65] Ibid., pp. 143–44.

[66] On the 'Banco del Giro', see Ignaz Bidermann, 'Die Wiener Stadt-Bank, ihre Entstehung, ihre Einteilung und Wirksamkeit, ihre Schicksale', *AÖG* 20 (1858), pp. 341–445, at pp. 350–56.

[67] Ibid., pp. 357–58.

[68] Dickson, *Finance and Government*, vol. 1, p. 220.

[69] From 1721 to 1748, debts carried by the bank were 78m. fl. versus 3m. fl. in income: Rudolf Fuchs, *Die Wiener Stadtbank: ein Beitrag zur österreichischen Finanzgeschichte des 18. Jahrhunderts* (Frankfurt-am-Main: Peter Lang, 1997), pp. 90–91. On the level and structure of the bank's debts and its cash balances, deposits and advances to the state between 1740 and 1756, see Dickson, *Finance and Government*, vol. 2, table 1.3, p. 32.

[70] Set up in 1714 by the Treasury as a rival to the Vienna City Bank, the *Universal-Bancalität* failed because it could not attract enough deposits: Dickson, *Finance and Government*, vol. 1, p. 220; see also ibid., vol. 2, pp. 80–1.

[71] Ibid., vol. 2, pp. 54, 137–38, table 4.7, p. 140. On *Banco Zettel*, see also Fuchs, *Die Wiener Stadtbank*, pp. 129–31.

[72] Dickson, *Finance and Government*, vol. 2, pp. 74–5; on the circulation of 'Banco Zettel', ibid., table 2.5, p. 377.

Over time, the government had progressively increased its influence over the Vienna City Bank. In 1749, the emperor made Chotek the bank's new president and through him took control of the institution.[73] For Zinzendorf, too, as he highlighted in 'Wiener Stadt Banco', the closeness between the bank and the state was of major concern. But in other areas, it is interesting to note the differences between Zinzendorf's observations on the bank and later scholarly judgement. Friedrich Walter noted the links between the bank's management and the state, but argued that through the good work of its presidents, the bank succeeded in keeping the confidence of the public in the institution.[74] For Ignaz Bidermann, the bank's purchases of land and manufacturing units in Carinthia and the Banat on behalf of the state were no cause for concern. The bank's bonds were used for the transactions, and in order to reassure creditors, the financial institution was the nominal owner of the assets. However, Bidermann did not see these as indications of the bank's secret financial support to the state.[75] More recently, Thomas Winkelbauer argued that the Vienna City Bank helped to significantly widen the circle of creditors and access domestic cash reserves.[76] Zinzendorf reported the opposite. Concerned with the narrow investor base in the monarchy, he proposed in the *Pro Memoria* to specifically target the broader base of small domestic creditors in future financial operations.

The Survey of European Banks

For Zinzendorf, an improvement of the monarchy's state credit was impossible without the creation of a functioning banking system. The best way, he concluded, to create a respected public bank in the monarchy was to follow established European banking models. Zinzendorf decided to consolidate his considerable knowledge of European banking into one comprehensive document where he would provide an analysis

[73] Ibid., p. 30.

[74] Friedrich Walter, 'Die Wiener Stadtbank und das Staatsbankprojekt von Grafen Kaunitz aus dem Jahre 1761', *Zeitschrift für Nationalökonomie*, 8 (1937), pp. 444–60, at p. 453.

[75] Bidermann, 'Die Wiener Stadt-Bank', pp. 444–45, note 102.

[76] Thomas Winkelbauer, 'Nervus Rerum Austriacarum. Zur Finanzierungsgeschichte der Habsburgermonarchie um 1700' in Petr Mat'a and Thomas Winkelbauer (eds.), *Die Habsburgermonarchie 1620–1740. Leistungen und Grenzen des Absolutismusparadigmas* (Stuttgart, 2006), pp. 179–215, at p. 203. I am grateful to William Godsey for having brought this to my attention.

of banking systems in several countries. It would serve as the basis for his subsequent ideas about a public bank.

The survey of 12 European banks, 'Beschreibung der vornehmsten Europäischen Bancken von Ludwig Friedrich Julius Grafen und Herrn von Zinzendorf und Pottendorf, Ihrer kaiserl. König. Apostol. Majestät wirklichen geheimen Rat, Kämmerern und Assesore des Directoriums in publicis et cameralibus' written in Vienna in 1758, was an elaborate and remarkably well-informed text. Zinzendorf had collected some of the information on the banks and their regulation during his diplomatic travels in France, Germany and Northern Europe. He had been adept at creating a network of international correspondents in the monarchy's embassies, which, as in the case of England, would keep him informed about local developments and would regularly supply documents and publications which had potential value.[77] Karl, too, kept reading Zinzendorf's document as it developed and noted that, due to its exceptional level of detail, it deserved to be printed.[78] But Zinzendorf's survey was only intended for the ruling elite in order to provide a good level of knowledge of other banking systems and help with the financial decision-making. In 1763, when the government evaluated the financial proposals of Hermann von Caratto, which included the creation of a public bank, Zinzendorf gave the document to the ruler and to key ministers.[79]

The survey had 136 folios with a long preface followed by individual chapters on 12 European banks.[80] In the preface, Zinzendorf divided the institutions into three groups. Each group, he argued, reflected the different political aims of the governments that had created the banks.[81] Except for the bank of Rome and the banks of Naples, each bank was included in one of the three groups. The historical description of the banks, Zinzendorf

[77] For example, see Letters of Anton von Zöhrern, an Austrian diplomat at the embassy in London, to Ludwig Zinzendorf: 20 January 1753, 30 August 1754, 23 November 1754, 2 December 1754, 20 January 1755, Karton 38, NÖLA.

[78] Diary of Karl Zinzendorf, 22 and 23 February 1761; 19 March and 27 March 1763, HHStA; Pettenegg (ed.), *Selbstbiographien*, p. 72.

[79] Zinzendorf, 'Allergnädigst, abgeforderter Vorschlag, die Einrichtung einer Börse zur Verhandlung der öffentlichen Papiere und eines Banco di Credito betreffend, Februar 1767', fol. 174v, Nachlaß Zinzendorf, HHStA. For Zinzendorf's working relationship with Caratto, see Chap. 6, particularly the section on 'Projectors'.

[80] The order of the chapters is as follows: Amsterdam, Hamburg, Genoa, Mantua, Venice, Rome, Naples, Scotland, Sweden, Copenhagen, England, France: Zinzendorf, 'Beschreibung', fol. 3r.

[81] Ibid., fol. 4r.

pointed out, was based on scholarly writing, reliable documents, charters and personal experience. Given that some of the historical facts from eight or ten years ago were outdated, he asked his readers for forbearance. The main remit for which the banks had initially been set up remained unchanged even though their operations were continuously evolving.[82]

Zinzendorf provided a detailed account on each institution. He showed how financial policy aspirations of governments in Europe differed and how successful the various banks, within their political framework, conducted their operations. The most efficient and sophisticated bank, Zinzendorf thought, should serve as the model for the monarchy. In the section below, I will provide an account of Zinzendorf's arguments on the types of banks and will illustrate each of the three groups with one example from 'Beschreibung der vornehmsten Europäischen Bancken'.[83]

Banks for the Expansion of Commerce

The Swedes had conceived the first and most basic type of bank. Its aim was to facilitate daily financial transactions and the conduct of commerce. They used specie made of copper for monetary transfers which proved to be impractical for large transactions. As an alternative, they created a banking institution which allowed the safekeeping of specie and the issuance of paper for use in daily transactions. This type of bank followed a set procedure to extend credit to customers. The bank opened for each customer a numbered page, a *Folio*, in its books. It was used to record the individual transactions. This administrative procedure was an important aspect of good banking practice, and Zinzendorf elaborated by providing a numerical example. He set out where and how credits and debits had to be recorded on the *Folio* and also indicated the German terms, *Abschreiben* and *Zuschreiben*, which ought to be used consistently to make credit and debit entries.[84]

This rigorous process, Zinzendorf explained, had two advantages. First, it was a convenient way to transfer money without having to move it physically and incur transport and cashier costs. It significantly reduced the risk

[82] Ibid., fols 22v–23r.

[83] For concise summaries of Zinzendorf's bank groups, see Schasching, *Staatsbildung*, pp. 63–65; and Christine Lebeau, *Aristocrates et grands commis à la Cour de Vienne, 1748–1791. Le modèle français* (Paris, 1996), pp. 170–73.

[84] Zinzendorf, 'Beschreibung', fols 4r–6r.

of counterfeit money and theft. It also increased the speed of transactions as the physical presence of customers was no longer required. It was sufficient for a client to sign a pre-printed *ordre* on which the bank would enter the amount to be transferred and the name of the recipient. The second advantage consisted in neutralising the frequent changes in the value of specie, both in terms of denomination and in precious metal content, instigated by provincial nobility. The bank would keep its record consistently in a reference value, *Banco Geld*, which represented the value of specie at the time that the bank was set up. *Current Geld*, different to *Banco Geld*, varied according to supply and demand. The reference value applied both to domestic money and to currencies received from abroad, and it thus removed the uncertainty of specie changes for the conduct of commerce. The banks of Amsterdam, Hamburg and Genoa were examples of the first type. Their economic impact however, Zinzendorf concluded, was limited. Their business was local, and they generally were only able to facilitate commerce between merchants of the same city.[85]

Early examples of this first type were the banks of Naples. However, Zinzendorf explained, they were not included in the first category because, like the Bank of Rome, they had not been set up as public banks with methods to increase the supply of money and promote commerce. Rather, their origins were charitable causes. The banks of Naples were created to lend to the poor and eventually were allowed to become public banks with mechanisms to facilitate financial transactions.[86]

Naples had not one, but seven banks of equivalent standing. Between 1539 and 1640, they were established by charitable institutions.[87] The bank's credit mechanism was *billets* or *fedi di credito* which were issued against deposits of specie. The *billets* became negotiable instruments through which the owner could make payments and where he could specify the conditions for the transfer of money.[88] The most important advantage, Zinzendorf argued, was that the *fedi di credito* could be used for partial payments until the entire amount for which the paper had been

[85] Ibid., fols 6v–8r.

[86] Ibid., fols 54v–55r.

[87] Zinzendorf listed the banks: Monte e Banco dei Poveri (est. 1660); Monte e Banco della Pieta (est. 1539); Banco di Santa Maria del Popolo (est. 1623); Banco del Santissimo Salvado (est. 1640); Banco del Spirito Santo (est. 1591); Banco di San Giacomo (est. 1593); and Banco di San Eligio (est. 1592): ibid., fol. 55r.

[88] Ibid., fols 58r–59v.

issued was transferred.[89] Also, in support of commerce, the banks accepted foreign specie as deposits. They would lend the equivalent sum in local currency interest-free, but with a discount, to domestic merchants.[90] The *billets* circulated in the entire kingdom, and most banks accepted the paper of others as payment.[91] However, without permission of the court, the banks were barred from supporting each other financially.[92] The court nominated the administrators of the banks, but it could not interfere in their daily operations.[93]

The systems of the Bank of Amsterdam were more advanced and more representative of the type-one banks. The Bank of Amsterdam recorded credit operations initially by issuing a 'receipt' for deposits and, secondly, by opening a *Folio* for depositors. The receipt was the basis for the bank charge levied every six months to investors. The bank applied the charge for safeguarding both domestic and foreign currency, and it varied between 0.125 and 0.5 per cent depending on the type of coins. In the presence of the depositor, the money was sealed, and the receipt was issued as proof of deposit. The receipt stated the amount and type of coins received as well as the exchange rate of the coins to the bank's reference value.[94] The bank also made the corresponding entry in the *Folio*. After six months, the depositor could choose either to withdraw the money, and settle the bank charges, or to renew his deposit for a further six months. Renewals were recorded on the receipt, and deposits could be rolled forward on a half-yearly basis. Even though the receipt was issued to the depositor, it was a bearer document which could be used by any holder to either withdraw money or renew deposits.[95]

[89] Ibid., fos 59v. Instructions of the owner to the bank on various payments were noted on a separate piece of paper, the *Zahlungs Polize*, and then transferred by the bank to its books. The *billet* was kept by the owner. The *Zahlungs Polize* was given to the recipient who, before receiving the money, had to prove to an official notary that all conditions for payment had been met: ibid., fols 59v–60r.

[90] Ibid., fols 61r–62r.

[91] Ibid., fol. 62v. The Banco della Pieta and Banco dei Poveri were not permitted to accept *billets* of other institutions: ibid., fol. 63r.

[92] Ibid.

[93] Ibid., fol. 63v.

[94] The current difference between the two values, Zinzendorf added, was 5 per cent: ibid., fol. 24r.

[95] Ibid., fols 23r–25v. In a footnote, Zinzendorf provided an example of the text of a receipt. The receipt was dated 20 May 1759 and recorded a deposit of French *louis d'or*: ibid., fol. 25r. For a discussion of the Bank of Amsterdam and its role in the economy, see

For the Bank of Amsterdam, only domestic coins had the intrinsic function of money. The value of foreign coins merely reflected their use in commerce. As the value fluctuated with the supply and demand of foreign trading nations, the bank could generate substantial profits by storing foreign coins until demand exceeded supply. For the bank, Zinzendorf thought, it was a very lucrative income with very modest expense.[96]

Folio entries were the second important mechanism to record bank transactions. They were undertaken either by the accountants of the bank, by the owner of the *Folio* or by an appointed representative who could show a letter of authorisation. On the stock exchange, depositors had the opportunity to make small payments which had been refused by the bank. Via designated brokers, either parts of or entire *Folios* could be exchanged for money. To facilitate negotiations and ensure secure payments between individuals, it was decided to settle transactions via entries into the bank's *Folios* which involved letters of exchange above a value of 300 *florins* and produce of the East India Company.[97]

Terms of Exchange of *Folio* against cash reflected not only the 5 per cent difference between *Banco Geld* and *Current Geld*, but also the supply and demand of money for the conduct of commerce. The difference between the two values would become more pronounced following the increased use of letters of exchange or following strong demand for *Banco Geld* to purchase produce which the East India Company was selling in Europe.[98]

Clients of the bank could have four types of credit arrangements. The first, coins, could be deposited and, correspondingly, a *Folio* which recorded the value in *Banco Geld* was opened by the bank. Second, transfers could be made in *Current* and *Banco Geld*. A depositor could sell a part of his *Folio* to a third party at a value expressed in *Current Geld*. The

Lucien Gillard, *La Banque d'Amsterdam et le Florins Européen au temps de la République néerlandaise (1610–1820)* (Paris, 2004).

[96] Zinzendorf, 'Beschreibung', fols 25v–26v.

[97] A careful reader of Zinzendorf's manuscript, who had underlined the passage of the use of the bank's *Folios*, had added in the margin of the text a sentence of Cornelius Oudermeulen's book: *Recherches sur le Commerce ou Idées relatives aux intérets des différents peoples de l'Europe* (2 vols, Amsterdam, 1778), vol. 2, part i, Chap. 3, p. 52. There, Oudermeulen indicated that letters of exchange above a value of 600 fl. had to be settled through the bank's books, and that this practice had been changed on 16 Dec. 1643. The reader had added the exact reference from Oudermeulen's book to his remark: Zinzendorf, 'Beschreibung', fol. 28r.

[98] Ibid., fols 28r–29r.

seller's *Folio* would be debited by the value expressed in *Banco Geld*, and the purchaser would receive the corresponding credit on his *Folio*. Third, merchants could use letters of exchange. Fourth, payment for produce could be made with an appropriate entry into the bank's *Folio* and without coins exchanging hands. In case the seller was not a client of the bank, he could readily open a *Folio* by paying a small fee.[99]

Given the large number of contracting parties and transactions to guarantee orderly and accurate recordings in its books, the bank had to follow detailed internal procedures. Every six months, the bank was closed for business so that its balance sheet could be calculated, and new books created. Depositors had to rectify any discrepancies in the records within six weeks of the bank opening again, otherwise they were required to pay 25 *florins*. Fines were also levied on ongoing transactions to ensure that there was no discrepancy between the bank's records and those of its depositors. If a client had given instructions to make a payment which was larger than his credit limit at the bank, he would be charged a 3 per cent fine on the excess amount. In addition, subsequent transactions, even for amounts which fell within the limit, would not be executed by the bank until the depositor decided to add the money to his *Folio*. In a footnote, Zinzendorf illustrated the bank's mechanism with a numerical example: a depositor had a *Folio* worth 20,000 *florins*. Based on his personal records, he assumed, however, that he had credit of 21,000 *florins*. He therefore instructed the bank to make a number of transfers which, in aggregate, amounted to 20,950 *florins*. The bank would levy a penalty charge, payable in coins, of 29.5 *florins* and would not undertake any transfers until the *Folio* was credited with the outstanding balance of 950 *florins*. Depositors who were uncertain about the accuracy of their records could use the services of the banks. For a fee of 12 *stuiver* for each *Folio* page consulted, the bank's accountants would cross-check the entries. To avoid larger costs and keep the records accurate, it was thus advisable to compare entries once a *Folio* page had been written out in full.[100]

The bank's main purpose, Zinzendorf argued, in particular for commercial transactions, was to facilitate payments. As the bank's operations had been consistently reliable, it had earned the trust of the public. This had become particularly apparent during the Dutch War of the late seventeenth century. In 1672, when the French had invaded the Dutch

[99] Ibid., fols 29r–29v.
[100] Ibid., fols 29v–31v.

Republic, the population had rushed to the bank to withdraw money for safekeeping. Despite such testing times, the bank had been able to keep important money reserves and had continued to undertake payments with accuracy and in a timely manner. Having weathered this crisis, the bank never again had to face large cash demands from its depositors.[101]

The size of the bank's deposits was kept confidential and, as such, it was only known to the mayor of Amsterdam who had a supervisory role at the institution. Melon's estimate of the deposits, Zinzendorf speculated, which was 300–400 million *gulden*, was exaggerated.[102] The figure had to be smaller, he thought, given that the bank only extended credit to the city of Amsterdam. The best way, Zinzendorf argued, to estimate the size of the deposits was to take the use of money by local merchants as the basis of the calculation. Even though the population of London was four times larger than Amsterdam, the latter had a larger number of merchants. Zinzendorf estimated that 3000 merchants lived in Amsterdam, compared with 2800 in London. If the average value of bank deposits of each merchant was 10,000 *florins*, or at most 20,000 *florins*, the total value of deposits would not exceed 60 million *florins*. This value was a more accurate estimate than the figure Melon had provided.[103]

Banks for the Increase in the Supply of Money

The second type of bank played a more prominent role in the economy. It not only facilitated commerce through the safekeeping of specie, but it also sought to increase the supply of money in the economy. Such banks, Zinzendorf argued, had to use their own type of debt instruments. *Folios*, which operated according to a set of administrative formalities, were too restrictive. For this reason, banks of the second type issued *billets* for monies deposited by customers. The *billets* were issued as bearer certificates and for small amounts so that they could be used for day-to-day transactions. They were easily tradable and could be immediately redeemed for specie in public *caisses* nationwide. The security of the *billets* against counterfeits and the provision to exchange them against new ones should the

[101] Ibid., fols 31v–32r.

[102] Jean-François Melon, *Essai politique sur le commerce* (2nd edn, 1736), ed. Eugène Daire, *Économistes-Financiers du XVIIIe siècle* (Paris, 1843), Chap. 23: 'Du Crédit public', p. 805.

[103] Gillard, *La Banque D'Amsterdam*, p. 75, plots the number of accounts against the average value of deposits from 1610 to 1820. According to his calculation, the value of deposits in 1760 was around 16.5m. fl.

paper wear off gave them the same security and longevity as specie. As they were a direct substitute for cash, they would only be redeemed if the bearer required specie. This meant there was no risk of a 'run on the bank', a situation in which all *billets* would be exchanged at the same time and the bank would be depleted of specie.[104]

This type of bank had a continuous stream of specie exchanged for *billets* and *billets*, conversely, were redeemed for specie. These two flows, Zinzendorf thought, were more or less in equilibrium, and the bank knew from experience the amount of specie that was required for the ongoing redemption of *billets*. Therefore, instead of remaining idly in the bank, the balance of specie could be used elsewhere. Extending credit to merchants and manufacturers was the main use. Credit operations required prudence, of course, and money was only lent against collateral, including produce, so as to provide a maximum level of security to the owners of the *billets*. Through these operations, the bank was able to stimulate commerce and achieve its aim of increasing the supply of money in the economy. A simple numerical example, Zinzendorf thought, offered a good illustration of the argument: for a deposit of 3 million in specie, the bank would issue 3 million of *billets* which would be in circulation in the economy. If the bank decided to use 2 million of specie for credit operations, the money supply in the economy would rise to 5 million.[105]

The founders of such banks were privileged shareholders. They provided capital, *Fonds*, to the government in return for the right to manage the bank through a dedicated company set up with shares. The capital provided consisted of a loan to the government which served as a security for the creditors against a misappropriation of the *Fonds* by the bank. The shares of the company were issued in bearer form, in small, equal denominations to facilitate circulation among investors. The shares also paid an income in the form of yearly dividends and thus provided two streams of income: an interest payment from the government for the use of the *Fonds*, and a profit share from the bank's operations.[106] The dividends were paid out on presentation of the coupons, which were attached to the shares. Zinzendorf used the example of the shares of the Compagnie des Indes. Based on Jacques Savary des Brûlons' *Dictionnaire Universel de Commerce*, he set out, in a footnote, the six months' coupon payments of the Compagnie

[104] Zinzendorf, 'Beschreibung', fols 8r–9v.
[105] Ibid., fols 10r–12r.
[106] Ibid., fols 12v–13r.

between 1720 and 1722. The dividends, Zinzendorf argued, represented generally a higher income than other forms of investments. The market price of the shares, therefore, reflected both the value of the capital and of the dividends. Hence, a share with a nominal value of 1000 *guilders* and a dividend of 70 *guilders* would, assuming a prevailing rate of interest in the economy of 5 per cent, be traded at 1400 *guilders*. Shares, he concluded, had a significant wealth effect for the economy: they not only contributed in volume terms to an increase of the supply of money in the economy, but their market price also represented a higher value than the underlying *Fonds* originally committed by the shareholders.[107]

As shares could be easily traded, they, rather than specie, should be the preferred medium of exchange in commerce. The shares could swiftly be sold in case of cash requirements by merchants, and, through the dividends, they provided an additional income which could be used to develop commercial enterprises. The shares, Zinzendorf added, were also useful in making commerce competitive. In a detailed footnote, Zinzendorf reinforced his analysis with an example. His starting point was the assumption that a merchant required 20,000 *guilders* as working capital. With a 5 per cent rate of interest in the economy, the merchant would increase the sale price of his produce by 1000 *guilders* to make up for the interest he would have earned had he invested the capital instead. If, however, with an equivalent 5 per cent dividend payout, he would have kept half of his working capital in shares, the amount of foregone interest would have been only 500 *guilders*, and the merchant could thus have offered his produce at a more competitive price. Since the shares were important for commerce, appropriate precautions had to be taken against theft or destruction. One method was not to hand out shares to investors and, following the example of England, only record the transactions in the bank. Alternatively, as practised in other countries, the shares could be held physically in *bureaux de depots* and *Folios* would be used to record sales and purchases.[108]

The banks of this second type also provided important economic functions to the state. Their first benefit related to commerce. Their activities expanded commercial credit and the circulation of money. The banks could lend against produce, land or personal guarantees and purchased bills of exchange before maturity at a modest discount rate of 0.5 per cent.

[107] Ibid., fols 13r–14r.
[108] Ibid., fols 14r–16r.

The second benefit included a lower cost of capital: the rate of interest at which the banks provided credit was, at 3 per cent, significantly lower than the national rate of 5 per cent. This would, Zinzendorf thought, generate more competition among providers of capital who would be forced to adjust their rate of interest downwards. Given that the credit facilities generally were extended only for short periods of time, the banks had regular inflow of capital and could thereby sustain their credit activities. Importantly, the lower rate of interest would become the reference rate for the economy, and investors would be prevented from again charging a higher rate. The ensuing economic benefits included an increase in the money supply, an increase in the value of land and a shift away from investment activities into value-added commercial undertakings. Internationally, the state would be able to compete successfully in commerce.[109]

Zinzendorf developed the idea of the general economic benefits of a lower rate of interest. He showed how the value of land was inversely related to the rate of interest in the economy and how, therefore, the true wealth of a nation increased as the price of money fell. With a 1 per cent reduction of the rate of interest, from 5 to 4 per cent, the value of land would increase by 20 per cent. In commerce too, a lower rate of interest was advantageous. Comparing merchants in France and the United Provinces, Zinzendorf assumed that both set out to make twice as much profit from commerce as from passive financial investment activities. In France, with a rate of interest of 6 per cent, a commercial investment of 30,000 *guilders* would have to earn the merchant a return of 12 per cent, or 3600 *guilders*. In the United Provinces, however, Zinzendorf argued, where the rate of interest was 3 per cent, a merchant would accept a lower profit of 1800 *guilders* and could thus sell his produce in both France and the United Provinces at more competitive prices than his French rival. Even if, Zinzendorf continued, the French merchant were to lower his target return to 10 per cent, the Dutch trader would remain more competitive because the national rate of interest in the United Provinces, which was the basis for reference, was significantly lower.[110] These arguments were similar to the ones Zinzendorf had set out previously in the 'Essai sur l'Établissement d'une Banque générale des États' and the 'Mémoire sur les richesses, le commerce et les finances de la France'.

[109] Ibid., fols 15v–18v.

[110] Ibid., two footnotes: fols 17v–20v.

The banks also played a specific role in supporting local manufacturing. Given that they accepted produce as collateral, they represented a valuable source of financing for industrialists. Without having to wait for the cash flows from their sales activities to arrive, the industrialists, with the support of the bank, were able to proceed swiftly with investments to develop their operations. Other benefits included lower administrative costs in relation to the use of bills of exchange, which otherwise suffered from the high charges levied arbitrarily by rapacious investors. The Bank of Scotland, the Bank of Denmark and the Bank of Mantua were examples of this second type of bank, as was the Bank of France.[111]

The French bank, Zinzendorf argued, was an important example, since it had enjoyed an excellent reputation throughout Europe. Even though the bank, founded in 1716, had only lasted for a short time and had disappeared together with Law's system, commentators who had studied it had recognised that its collapse was not attributable to its own systems. Rather, Zinzendorf thought that the French bank would have been considered to be one of the most 'complete credit institutions in Europe' if *Parlement* and some of the provincial estates had adopted its first constitution of 1716. From the beginning, the bank was run by a company created by private shareholders. However, they could not provide the security which was necessary to create public confidence in the institution and avert malpractice. The downfall of the bank, Zinzendorf argued, was caused, first, by its attachment to Law's scheme and, second, by its transformation into a royal institution. The bank's link to a system which was 'defective, unfavourable and dangerous', together with its total dependence on the demands of the ruler, represented the reason for its eventual demise.[112]

The original *Banque Générale* of 1716, however, was a solid institution and a relevant example. For this reason, Zinzendorf translated a *Mémoire* written by Law in 1717 in which the Scotsman described the workings of the bank. It was, Zinzendorf claimed, a *Mémoire* which had never before been published. Law's original text included extracts of the two *lettres patentes* of the ruler, 2 and 20 May 1716, declaring the establishment of the bank as well as the patent of 10 April 1717 which stipulated the acceptance of the bank's *billets* in the *caisses royales* and their cash-like use. Zinzendorf added to his translations an example of a *Banco Billet* as well as an extract of the patent of 4 December 1718 which transformed the

[111] Ibid., fols 19r–20v.

[112] Ibid., fols 118r–118v.

General Bank into a Royal Bank.[113] The last addition was significant, as Zinzendorf considered political banks, which he introduced subsequently, to be the most developed. The translations excluded the *Préambules* of the original declarations but were, otherwise, similar to the original French texts.

Setting out the arguments that Zinzendorf repeated in the introduction of 'Beschreibung der vornehmsten Europäischen Bancken', Law had begun the *Mémoire* by pointing out the cumbersome and slow process of shipping specie between two locations. Using the example of merchants in Lyon and Paris wanting to trade, he showed how transactions through letters of exchange facilitated by private banking services in their respective locations enabled commerce.[114] Zinzendorf omitted from his translation a section in which Law had included examples of English and French private banking services, had mentioned their large number of bankruptcies and reluctance to engage in commerce and thus had argued for the establishment of public banks in Paris and London. Zinzendorf probably never seriously considered these private services as 'banks', and they were thus not relevant to his argument.[115] Law's banking system had been more ambitious than simply creating banking services for local use. He had envisaged a system of banks which would encompass the main commercial trading hubs in Europe.

The appropriate evaluation of a relevant banking system required the distinction between private and public credit. In commerce, the term 'credit' referred to a paper which contained the promise of a cash payment. The payment was either immediate or undertaken at some date in the future. The paper replaced specie and was much easier to use. Law had differentiated between *credit à vue* and *credit à terme*, and Zinzendorf

[113] Ibid., fols 118v–119r. Law's original *Mémoire sur la Banque générale* is included in *John Law: Oeuvres complètes*, ed. Paul Harsin (3 vols, Paris, 1934), vol. 3, pp. 11–20. Harsin states that the authorship might seem unclear. He nevertheless attributes the memoir unequivocally to Law due to its content and to Law's habit to refer to himself in the third person. Harsin suggested a publication date of mid to end 1717 because the most recent text reference was 10 April 1717 and the transformation to *Banque Royale* was not mentioned. See ibid., vol. 1, pp. liii–liv.

[114] Ibid., vol. 3, p. 11. In the French original these banking services are referred to as 'banques particulières'. Zinzendorf's translation was 'Privat Wechsler': Zinzendorf, 'Beschreibung', fol. 119v.

[115] Ibid., fols 119r–119v.

included this distinction in his translation.[116] If a merchant was wealthy and followed good business practice, Law had reasoned, he was considered to have 'private credit'. He was trusted and could engage in commerce with paper without having to pay or offer specie as security.[117]

Public credit was represented by a paper which had assurances from the state or from a company backed by the state that the principal borrowed and the interest accrued would be repaid, either immediately or in the future after a predetermined period of time. For a nation engaged in commerce, public credit was preferable to private credit. Public banks were more secure credit institutions, with the additional advantage that they operated without the associated costs of the private banking services. They also could increase the scope and the growth of commerce, and could offer good payment services within Paris as well as between Paris and the provinces. The banks offered convenient access to funds, both locally and internationally, through bills of exchange, and ensured access to liquidity for foreigners travelling to France to buy local produce.[118]

The *Mémoire* had ended with descriptions of issuance and remittance mechanisms of *billets*, on their use in public *caisses*, and on counterfeit provisions.[119] These again were arguments which Zinzendorf repeated in the introduction to the document on European banks. The appendix of the *Mémoire* had consisted of the official government declarations regarding the bank. The two *letters patentes* of May 1716 had set out various provisions for the French bank, including a 20-year monopoly for Law to operate the *Banque Générale* under the 'protectorate' of the ruler, an encouragement to deposit specie for free as protection against frequent exchange rate changes and a capital base limitation of 6 million *livres* consisting of 1200 shares. They also stipulated that the bank should be headquartered in Paris with trading hours on weekdays in the morning and in the afternoon, that balance sheet reporting should be undertaken twice a year and that the bank could engage in discounting letters of exchange,

[116] *Credit à terme* is limited to one year and inferior to *credit à vue*, *John Law*, ed. Paul Harsin. vol. 3, p. 14. According to Harsin, this passage was probably later added by Law and is missing from one edition of the *Mémoire*: ibid., footnote 1, p. 14.

[117] Zinzendorf, 'Beschreibung', fols 120r–120v.

[118] Ibid., fols 120v–121v. On the General Bank of 1716, Lüthy argued that even though, at first, it was a useful institution, its scope was limited. See Herbert Lüthy, *La Banque Protestante en France de la Révocation de L'Edit de Nantes à la Révolution* (2 vols, Paris: S.E.V.P.E.N., 1959), vol. 1, p. 306.

[119] Zinzendorf, 'Beschreibung', fols 122r–128v.

but had to refrain from conducting commerce herself. Shareholder meetings were scheduled twice a year and decisions were taken by majority vote. The *arrêt* of 10 April 1717, which established a direct connection between the bank and the state, had declared that *billets* were a legal tender in the payment of taxes. Finally, the declaration of 4 December 1718 had turned the *Banque Générale* into the official state bank. The ruler would acquire the entire share capital of the bank, and the director would directly report back to him on a daily basis. The bank's *billets* would now receive the official stamp of the ruler.[120] As the *Banque Royale*, it joined the third category of 'political banks'.

Political Banks

The last and most sophisticated type of bank was very similar in terms of structure and set-up to the second. It also used *billets* for credit operations, issued shares and sought to increase the supply and the circulation of money in the economy. The important additional purpose of this type of bank was the use of financial liquidity to support the government. However, the intention was not to offer sustained credit to the state. The banks of this third type, Zinzendorf emphasised, would offer short-term finance to the ruler before more permanent funds became available.[121] The state credit was secured on the *Fonds* of the bank or on future streams of state income.[122]

The political bank offered state credit at a low rate of interest and thereby kept the reference rate in the economy competitive. For the government, the advantages of these credit terms were twofold: first, it received much needed financial liquidity at a rate of interest which was below the national rate; and second, investors could no longer dictate onerous credit terms to the ruler. Hence, especially in times of crisis, the rate of interest could be kept low and eventually, Zinzendorf thought, even speculators would invest their funds with the bank. It was a worthwhile operation for the bank, too. Even though the profit for its shareholders would be smaller due to the lower interest income, the money which otherwise would have remained unemployed in the bank's coffers was put to good use. The bank's profits would be bolstered by

[120] Ibid., fols 128v–136v.

[121] In the text, Zinzendorf emphasised 'sustained' and 'short-term': ibid., fol. 21r.

[122] Ibid., fols 20v–21r.

the usual financial operations of supporting commerce and discounting bills of exchange. In addition to the Bank of France, examples of 'political banks' included the Bank of England, the Bank of Sweden and the Bank of Venice.[123]

Of all of the 'political banks' he identified, Zinzendorf felt that the Bank of England was the most effective institution of its type. For this reason, it is the focus of the following discussion. It was founded in 1694 when English finances were in disarray. Even though Parliament granted funds to William III for the continuation of the war with Louis XIV, they were not paid out swiftly enough to cover the expenses of the state. The king, therefore, had to rely on private credit to bridge the shortfall in finances. Creditors took advantage of the government's vulnerable position and, through usurious practices, charged rates of interest on loans of between 20 and 30 per cent. These profits were so important that the creditors refused to consider other financial operations. Even though, at that time, the amount of state credit was not important, it was clear that, under these circumstances, England would not be able to sustain its war effort.[124]

The English government, Zinzendorf argued, therefore required a political bank which, in addition to facilitating commerce, had as its main remit the provision of credit to the state. A company of private individuals offered the government a loan of £1.2 million at a rate of interest of 8⅓ per cent repayable after 13 years. In return, the state granted the company the exclusive right to run the operations of a bank over the period of the loan. The latter was allowed to receive money deposits from private individuals and thus could conduct operations to encourage commerce. The share capital of the bank consisted of 12,000 shares with a nominal value of £100. The shareholders could trade the shares, and Zinzendorf added the details of share transfers in England. Unlike in France, share certificates were not used. Rather, in the presence of both creditor and debtor, the transfer was recorded as *Zu- und Abschreiben* in the *Folio* of the 'credit book' of the public fund.[125]

[123] Ibid., fols 21v–22v.

[124] Ibid., fol. 89v. For a concise account of Zinzendorf's chapter on the Bank of England, see also Schasching, *Staatsbildung*, pp. 65–7.

[125] Zinzendorf, 'Beschreibung', fols 90r–91r. On the establishment of the Bank of England and its immediate important cash contributions to the state, see P.G.M. Dickson, *The Financial Revolution in England. A Study in the Development of Public Credit, 1688–1756* (London: Macmillan, 1967), pp. 48–9, 54–7.

In order to appreciate the advantage which the bank provided to the state, it was important, Zinzendorf thought, to gain an understanding of its operations. The bank was allowed to receive deposits on the condition that no fees for safekeeping and no rate of interest were levied on the money. For the deposits, the bank issued *billets* or opened a *Folio* in its books. The *billets*, issued as bearer documents in any amount larger than £5, were payable at sight. They were engraved into copper, and the name of the first depositor and the relevant amount were added. To safeguard against forgery, the amounts on the *billets* were crossed out with a knife. These operations, Zinzendorf noted, were similar to the Bank of Amsterdam. However, transactions were more accurate and less cumbersome than at the Dutch bank.[126]

Transactions were recorded by a bank's official both in the bank's *Folio* as well as in a dedicated book which was given to the depositor for safekeeping. Given that only one person, who was an expert, was involved in the record taking, the system removed any risk of discrepancies in the figures and hence the need, as at the Bank of Amsterdam, to impose a system of fines on depositors. Also, transfers could be made without the physical presence of depositors. To record the transactions, it was sufficient to fill in the coupons contained in the 'draws', *Anweisungsblätter*. The bank kept the coupons and would issue new 'draws' to depositors once all coupons were used up.[127]

As the bank could not issue more *billets* than the amount of money deposited, the billets could be exchanged for cash and were accepted in all public *caisses*. Thus, Zinzendorf argued, it was not surprising that the English public, which had been accustomed to transact with less secure paper issued by goldsmiths and private bankers, swiftly supported the new paper of the bank. For years, like money, the *billets* circulated in the economy, and investors were reassured that they could redeem them instantaneously for cash. The bank was able to use its deposits for lucrative transactions and could pay its shareholders a profit each year, distributed in the form of a dividend. Transactions also undertaken by the bank included discounting short-term letters of exchange, which produced an annual profit of 4 per cent, and the exclusive trade in bullion.[128]

[126] Zinzendorf, 'Beschreibung', fols 91r–91v.

[127] Ibid., fols 92r–93r.

[128] Ibid., fols 93r–95v. Unlike foreign coins, the export of English specie was not permitted. Thus, the bank bought bullion cheaply when it was imported and sold it at a profit when

The most important remit of the bank was the provision of state credit at rates of interest below the prevailing rates in the economy. The revenue to fund any extraordinary government expenses had first to be authorised by Parliament and thus, generally, was not available in time. The Exchequer, therefore, issued Bills which could be exchanged for money in all the public *caisses*. The Exchequer Bills were short-term borrowings, and they were drawn on revenues which the government received within the year. They were individually numbered bearer documents with denominations of £100 and, occasionally, up to £5000. Their rate of interest was 3 per cent and payments were made quarterly. However, the payment dates were not fixed. The repayment of the principal amount as well as the interest payments were only undertaken once revenues became available.[129]

Given that the denominations were large and the timing of payments was unpredictable, the Bills were not useful instruments for daily transactions. They were hoarded in the public *caisses* and did not circulate in the economy.[130] Here the bank intervened to support the finances of the state. The Exchequer often transferred the Bills to the bank and in return received money or *billets*. As soon as the government transferred the revenues to the bank to cover both the principal and the interest payments, the bank returned the Bills. The state, Zinzendorf remarked, took the obligation for repayment very seriously. Officials of the Exchequer were personally held responsible for repayment in full, and in case of financial irregularities, they were threatened with dismissal. The benefit to the state from working closely with the bank was obvious: the government received much needed funds in advance, and the bank's *billets* could be used like money.

The bank and the state also devised mechanisms to address extraordinary funding requirements. In case where the financial demands of the state were too large for conventional issues of Exchequer Bills, the bank would take against a small premium the additional Bills issued by the state.

it was required for payments to foreign trading nations and domestic demand was high: ibid., fols 95r–95v.

129 On volumes of less than £1m., the rate of interest was reduced to 1 per cent. The denominations of the bills had been steadily increased, and by 1750, the only denomination was for £1000: see Dickson, *Financial Revolution*, pp. 383, 384. For the system of short-term borrowing by Exchequer Bills, see ibid., pp. 365–92.

130 In contrast, Zinzendorf added, the Estates Credit Deputation of 1761, which he devised, operated with a simpler payment mechanism and ensured a good circulation of the paper money: Zinzendorf, 'Beschreibung', fol. 97r.

The bank would then allocate them to wealthy merchants and share the premium with them. A second short-term emergency funding mechanism included the provision of state credit without the transfer of Exchequer Bills. The government could repay its credit to the bank as and when it received revenues. In addition, the bank would also issue *billets* without having money deposits to cover them and redeem the *billets* when it received the revenues from the state.[131]

For longer-term funding to the state, the bank could issue *Appels* to its shareholders. They were equivalent to a capital increase, and shareholders were expected to supply the additional funds in proportion to their shareholding. If they failed to add capital, the bank could charge fines: it could stop dividend payments and, in addition, for the period where the payment was not made, levy a penalty of 6 per cent on the amount outstanding. Between the end of the seventeenth century and the mid-eighteenth century, Zinzendorf noted, national debt due to the bank increased almost tenfold to £11 million. More generally, the bank was able to support state finances by using its strong credibility with the public. In 1752, national debt due to and managed by the bank had increased to £40 million.[132]

For Zinzendorf, a remarkable example of how the bank served the financial interest of the state was the interest rate reduction in 1749 on long-term government debt. At the end of the War of the Austrian Succession, state credit had risen to £79 million. Given the substantial interest payments, it was impossible for the state to also repay the principal of the debt, so the English government followed a plan of interest rate reductions in order to be able to service its debt. It decided to reduce the rate of interest on £58 million from 4 per cent to 3 per cent and use the resulting savings of close to £600,000 to pay down the outstanding debt. The reduction in the rate of interest was to be managed prudently, in two stages, so as not to damage the confidence of creditors.[133] The first stage, from Christmas 1750 to Christmas 1757, saw a decrease of the rate of interest to 3.5 per cent. In the second stage, the rate of interest was finally

[131] Ibid., fols 97r–99v.

[132] Ibid., fols 99v–100r. For the end of September 1749, Dickson *Financial Revolution*, Table 26, p. 232, provides a figure of £37.3m.: £11.7m. was due to and £25.6m. managed by the bank.

[133] For an account of this episode, see Dickson, *Financial Revolution*, pp. 228–41. Dickson gives a national debt in September 1749 as over £70m.: ibid., p. 232. His calculations on servicing the debt are like Zinzendorf's: ibid., p. 239.

reduced to 3 per cent. Thus, for the first seven years, the yearly payments into the government's sinking fund were reduced to £290,000.[134]

In a footnote, Zinzendorf compared the English sinking fund, established in 1717, with its equivalent in France. State credit in England, by the late 1740s, had risen noticeably. Despite a long period of peace of over 20 years, the fund was not able to contribute to a reduction in debt. Over seven years, the growth of the fund had slowed, and in 1757 the value was approximately £2 million. The reason, Zinzendorf thought, for the fund's poor performance was that it had not been earmarked for the repayment of specific portions of the national debt. Also, the involvement of Parliament which had to authorise contributions to the fund, was not helpful as it ultimately stood under the strong influence of the king. The French mechanism, on the other hand, was more useful. Since 1735, France had a dedicated repayment fund for every issue of new debt. Each fund was also provided with a patent by the ruler which was a guarantee for both the payment schedule of interest as well as for the repayment of the principal. So, by 1760, the entire debt which had been raised for the country's war effort in the Austrian War of Succession had been repaid. A country which had chosen to repay its debt from a dedicated fund, and had thereby gained the confidence of the public, could more readily raise new money. The discipline of dedicating funds to specific portions of national debt, Zinzendorf concluded, resulted in a better management of state credit.[135]

In the mid-1750s, the Bank of England took advantage of its good reputation with the public to actively support the state in the reduction of the rate of interest on the national debt. The bank made money available to the government so that the latter could meet payment obligations to investors who refused to accept the lower rate of interest. Also, following the reduction in the rate of interest, the financial institution used its credit to support the price of public paper. Without receiving collateral deposits from the state, the bank issued *billets* to buy public paper. A strong market for public paper developed, and investors who had sold paper for *billets* were keen to repurchase the paper to profit from the rising prices. The

[134] For the plan of Henry Pelham, First Lord of the Treasury, to reduce rate of interest in two stages, see ibid., p. 233.

[135] Zinzendorf, 'Beschreibung', fols 101r–103r. On the conversions acts which established the English sinking fund, its use as collateral for new debt and the temptation for abuse by ministers, see Dickson, *Financial Revolution*, pp. 85–9.

price of public paper was stabilised, and the reduction of the rate of interest was successfully implemented. In order to terminate the financial operation, the bank repurchased its *billets* at a profit and destroyed them. The support of the English public was essential for the success of the interest rate reduction. The public understood, Zinzendorf argued, that lower interest rates were important to establish a sound basis for state credit. It also realised that the short-term financial loss would protect their long-term wealth as the state again was able to begin repaying its debt. The positive sentiment was reflected in the financial market: not only did the price of public paper not fall, it even increased by up to 5 per cent above its nominal value.[136] Between 1757 and the end of the Seven Years War, Zinzendorf added in a footnote, the situation of English state credit deteriorated again. In 1763, the national debt had risen to £140 million. Again, the government had to offer a rate of interest of 4 per cent to raise the new money. The sinking fund, with a value of close to £2 million, was not sufficiently large enough to service the growing debt. Unless, after a peace treaty, England would be able to grow its commerce and thereby raise additional taxes, it would have to raise new public funds to guarantee the interest payments on the loans.[137]

In summary, through its active involvement in the financial operations of the government, the bank could end reliance on expensive credit. The bank contributed to a fairer system of commercial transactions by charging moderate fees for discounting letters of exchange. Financial operations were more secure, and the state enabled the bank to run a commercial operation by granting it the privilege to receive funds which were deposited for free. In return, the bank provided funds to the state. Zinzendorf provided details on the terms of the loans: the privilege which the state had given to the Bank of England in 1694 was initially limited to 13 years. It was extended to 1719, and subsequently to 1742 and 1764. For each extension, Zinzendorf explained, the bank had to make new cash advances to the state. The first loan had amounted to £1.2 million, and the interest income paid by the government was 8 per cent, or £96,000. In 1719, the bank had made an additional payment of £400,000 to the state. As the interest income on the new payment was limited to the same amount, the effective rate of interest of the national debt had been reduced to 6 per cent. In 1742, with a new loan of

[136] Zinzendorf, 'Beschreibung', fols 101r–105r.
[137] Ibid., fols 105r–105v.

£1.6 million to the government and the interest payment capped at £96,000, the effective rate of interest on total debt of £3.2 million was halved to 3 per cent. Moreover, the bank had raised additional funds for the state from *Appels* to its shareholders. In total, state credit amounted to £11 million which had to be repaid in full before the government could remove the privileges it had granted to the bank.[138]

Most of the influential business community in England, Zinzendorf pointed out, including the directors of the bank as well as the wealthy merchants, were financially dependent on the state. Therefore, they had to have the interests of the state in mind when they sought to impose their business terms onto the rest of the financial community. Zinzendorf counted 110 influential people in England: the bank was managed by one governor, one deputy governor and 24 directors. On a yearly basis, 8 out of the 24 directors were replaced and could rejoin the bank one year later. The governor and his deputy were required to own 50 shares each, or £500 worth of capital in the bank. A director had to hold 30 shares, or 300 of capital. Shares could not be sold as long as the managers remained active in the bank. Also, the South Sea Company and the East India Company were other important economic institutions. Like the bank, the South Sea Company had one governor and one deputy governor, but 30 directors. The East India Company, on the other hand, operated without a governor or a deputy governor and had 24 directors. All three institutions had a combined management of 82 people and, with an identical rotation mechanism, meaning that 28 people in total had to take a one-year sabbatical. Adding 28 to 82 gave the total number of 110. This financial arrangement was very different to other countries where creditors were 'adversaries' of the state, waiting for the ruler's financial distress to make large profits.[139]

Towards the end of the Seven Years War, however, the English state could no longer take advantage of its preferential borrowing terms and had to raise money at higher rates of interest. The money supply in England, Zinzendorf argued, was depleted: £2 million in subsidies and as support for armies stationed in Germany were sent abroad. Also, money was spent on large-scale naval refurbishments and on financial transfers to

[138] Ibid., fols 107r–108r. On the negotiations for the extension of bank's charter, see Sir John Clapham, *The Bank of England. A History, 1694–1914* (2 vols, Cambridge, 1970), vol. 1, pp. 93–101.

[139] Zinzendorf, 'Beschreibung', fols 105v–109r.

America. Nevertheless, the bank continued to play an important role for the state. It provided, insofar as it was able, cash advances to the government and, through its influence on investors, succeeded in keeping the financial profiteers at bay. This was, Zinzendorf remarked, a better outcome than elsewhere. In other countries engaged in war, investors would have taken advantage of the money shortfall and immediately demanded a significantly higher rate of interest on the first war loan of the state.[140]

To fully appreciate the significant role of the Bank of England for the economy, it was important to know its capital reserves. As the level of capital was not disclosed, Zinzendorf proceeded, as he did for the Bank of Amsterdam, to provide an approximation. The starting point of his calculation was £11 million which the bank had lent to the state.[141] The annual government receipts from the public amounted to £7.7 million. It was the figure for 1752 which Zinzendorf took from Forbonnais' translation of the *British Merchant* published by Charles King in 1721.[142] Against those receipts, the bank issued *billets* which were in circulation in the economy. They provided a triple benefit: the shareholders of the bank received an interest income, the state had credit, and therefore, the tax burden on the public was alleviated. Using 'reliable' sources, Zinzendorf estimated further that the bank kept approximately £4 million as cash deposits and was able to draw on a wide pool of funds which included contributions from individuals and from the state treasury as well as the East India and South Sea trading companies.[143]

[140] Ibid., fols 108v–110r.

[141] See footnote 132 above.

[142] Véron de Forbonnais, *Le Négociant Anglois, ou Traduction libre du livre intitulé: The British Merchant, Contenant divers Mémoires sur le Commerce de l'Angleterre avec la France, le Portugal et l'Espagne. Publié pour la premiere fois en 1713* (2 vols, Paris and Dresden, 1753), vol. 1, discours préliminaire du traducteur, p. clxix. The revenues for 1752 included: £4.5m. from income taxes, from papier timbre and other taxes from before the war, £0.9m. from new taxes, £1.5m. from land taxes and £0.75m. from taxes on corn threshing. Then, after setting out of the expenses of the state (pp. cl–cliii), he concluded (p. cliii) that in 1752 there was a small surplus for the government. For a discussion of Forbonnais translation, see Antonella Alimento, 'Beyond the Treaty of Utrecht: Véron de Forbonnais's French Translation of the *British Merchant* (1753)', *History of European Ideas*, 40:8 (2014), pp. 1044–66. Forbonnais, Alimento argued, refused to tie the French economy to England. Instead, he wanted France to emulate the economic success of England and use statistics to establish a national trade balance. He also examined the role of the Bank of England and its paper money operations.

[143] Out of the reserves of £11m., *c.*£7m. were lent to the state.

The bank, Zinzendorf argued, used two mechanisms to increase the supply of money in the economy. First, it added liquidity through the issue of *billets*. Second, its own shares were in circulation and were regularly used for payments of large sums. As the shares paid a dividend of 5 per cent, the supply of money by the bank was closer to £15⅔ million.[144] When the government deposits of more than £7 million were added, the total amount of funds in circulation reached £23 million. This, Zinzendorf concluded, exceeded by far the more common estimates of £18 million. He also pointed out that the bank's role in supplying money was enhanced given that £4 million, held as deposits, were not circulating in the economy. Coins were evenly used in London and the provinces, but the *billets* were mostly traded in the capital.[145]

Controls had been put in place to ensure that the bank's credit would not become a threat to the economy. First, the cash deposits of £4 million were foremost an emergency fund in case of sudden liquidity shortages. It was considered a large enough reserve given that only £120,000 were required to cover the daily circulation of *billets*. Second, the cash advances to the government through the issue of *billets* were always intended as a short-term measure. And third, the banks only released money to the state which was secured on funds that had been authorised by Parliament. The latter provided an additional level of control and kept in regular contact with the bank to exchange information and compare numbers.[146]

The credit of the bank, both in peace and in times of war, was so well established that demand for it always exceeded supply. It was only ever in jeopardy when political events shook the country. During the Jacobite rebellion of 1745, it relied on special mechanisms to receive extra funds. However, the best support for the bank's credit was the confidence of the public: the promise by merchants and financiers to keep using *billets* for their daily payments instead of reverting to coins. It bought the bank time to await the end of the political unrest when it could replenish its reserves. For Zinzendorf, the 'new circulation' was an example of a special measure. It was a reserve of £1 million made up of individual subscriptions of £1000 each. The first cash payment of £100 carried a high rate of interest of 10

[144] The basis for Zinzendorf's actual calculation was the year 1752 when the dividend had fallen to 4.5 per cent.

[145] Zinzendorf, 'Beschreibung', fols 111v–113v.

[146] Ibid., fols 113v–115v. Zinzendorf's statement on the role of Parliament contradicted his previous observation on the influence of the king upon Parliament.

per cent. Subsequent subscriptions offered a reduced rate of interest of 4 per cent. The interest on the first payment would be lost if the investor failed to make further contributions towards his subscription. However, additional cash calls were unlikely to occur. Due to the high interest on the initial payment, there was strong demand among investors for the subscription.[147]

For Zinzendorf, the Bank of England was an extremely effective political bank which facilitated commerce and had implemented systems to provide both short-term and long-term credit as well as emergency funding to the state. Its internal operations were transparent and its administrative tasks were performed accurately. This gave confidence to the public. Importantly, in the 1750s, the Bank of England had delivered significant interest-rate reductions on government debt and had used its good credit record to support the price of public paper. Generally, the interests of the influential domestic business community and the state were aligned. With the support of the Bank of England, Zinzendorf observed, the English government 'often made the impossible possible'.[148]

Intellectual Stock-Taking: A Stock Exchange and Political Bank for the Habsburg Monarchy

In 1767, in 'Allergnädigst, abgeforderter Vorschlag, die Einrichtung einer Börse zur Verhandlung der öffentlichen Papiere und eines Banco di Credito betreffend', Zinzendorf set out his ideas for a stock exchange and political bank in the monarchy. The state credit of the monarchy, Zinzendorf noted, had significantly improved since the end of the Seven Years War. The interest rate on the debt of the Vienna City Bank had decreased to 4 per cent, and most of the public bonds were trading at par.[149] The cash redemption fund of the government, he recognised, was a guarantee that interest rates could remain low. However, it was not large enough to guarantee the redemption of the entire value of the debt.[150] There was still room for financial speculators to provide finance, and for some loans, including investment credits, they demanded interest rates as

[147] Ibid., fols 115v–117v. See also Clapham, *The Bank of England*, pp. 68–72.
[148] Zinzendorf, 'Allergnädigst, abgeforderter Vorschlag', fol. 176r.
[149] Ibid., fols 6r–7r.
[150] Ibid., fols 7v–9r.

high as 6 per cent.[151] During the Seven Years War, the financial support and good supply of money from the Austrian Netherlands and Italy to the monarchy was a fortunate turn of events. It could not be counted on again in the next military conflict. One should not forget, Zinzendorf argued, that forced credit and heavily discounted bonds had to be used during the last war.[152] Therefore, new financial institutions were necessary which had been successfully tried and tested by other European nations.[153]

In 'Allergnädigst, abgeforderter Vorschlag', Zinzendorf began by presenting his plan for the stock exchange which he had first introduced in the *Pro Memoria*. The new stock exchange should provide an orderly market place where letters of exchange and government paper were traded via official and recognised stockbrokers. The aim was to provide competition and liquidity in the market and ensure that paper could be exchanged at advantageous prices.[154] Currently, the exchange did not create transparent pricing. The negotiations were conducted arbitrarily, often without recognised brokers. The terms of transactions were set by influential bankers. There were no official prices.[155]

A new stock exchange had to address these shortcomings. The institution for the monarchy, Hungary excluded, would be in Vienna with branches in the main cities of the hereditary lands. It should operate according to three principles.[156] First, it should generate sufficient demand so that prices of public paper would rise. The state, therefore, should attract all available capital to the exchange and, using a system of fines, should ensure that it was the only place where transactions would be undertaken. The *Coupons Obligations* could be easily traded on the bourse as they would be issued in small denomination. These measures, Zinzendorf thought, would help to increase investor demand. In addition, to maximise the circulation of the bonds on the exchange, it would be important to restrict their supply. The second principle was the direct intervention of

[151] Ibid., fols 8r–8v.

[152] Ibid., fols 9v–10r.

[153] Ibid., fol. 10r.

[154] Ibid., fol. 10v.

[155] Ibid., fol. 11v. As evidence, Zinzendorf included a memoria by Brabbé, a trader at the stock exchange, who had described the arbitrary buying and selling methods of middle men who were transacting for their own financial gain, 'Pro Memoria des Sensalen Brabbé', in ibid., fols 364r–370v. On the unsuccessful bourse which was created in August 1761, see Dickson, *Finance and Government*, vol. 2, p. 136.

[156] I follow here Schasching's interpretation, *Staatsbildung*, pp. 58–60.

the state to support the prices of public paper. The danger, Zinzendorf thought, of having to resort again to a system of forced loans justified the government's active part in influencing and controlling the prices of public paper. To absorb any excess demand of bonds, the state would use a unified amortisation fund controlled by the Estates Deputation. The size of the fund was 3 million *florins*, and it would be exclusively used for transactions on the stock exchange. The use of the fund's money would be twofold: first, to repurchase bonds and reduce the size of the national debt; and second, to support state debt by offering prices to sellers of between 0.25 and 1.5 per cent above market rates. The third principle for the operation of the exchange was the use of a political bank as lender of last resort. In cases where the amortisation fund was not large enough to prevent a collapse of the prices of government debt, the bank would intervene with its capital reserves. In addition, the bank could lend directly to the state and would ensure that the bonds circulated in the market.

For a model of the stock exchange, Zinzendorf looked abroad. He used the patent for the Paris bourse of 24 September 1724 and added an extract of the patent, consisting of 41 articles, as an appendix to his plan of 1767. The extract, Zinzendorf clarified in the text, was taken from the '*Dictionnaire de Commerce de Monsieur Savary*'.[157] In addition to the exact location in Paris as well as the opening hours of the exchange, the patent stipulated the creation of entry passes for access to the bourse. In case of unauthorised entry, monetary fines would be issued. Parisian business professionals as well as foreigners who had commercial dealings in France could use the institution. Women were excluded. To guarantee privacy of trades, prices could not be announced aloud to other market participants. There would be 60 accredited *Agens de Change* working at the Paris bourse, and their appointments would be vetted by local merchants. During the opening hours of the exchange, the brokers would have to be physically present and would be required to keep a daily register of their trades. During transactions, they would be the sole recipients of money and, as intermediaries, would subsequently credit the trading

[157] 'Extrait de l'arrêt du Conseil du Roy du 24 Septembre 1724 qui ordonne l'établissement d'une Bourse dans la ville de Paris' in Zinzendorf, 'Allergnädigst, abgeforderter Vorschlag', fols 180r–187v. The first 16 articles of the appendix were listed in the *Dictionnaire* under the entry '*Bourse*' and described the operations of the bourse. The subsequent 25 articles appeared under the entry '*Agens de Change*' and described the work of the stockbrokers, fol. 180r, ibid. See Jacques Savary des Brûlons', *Dictionnaire Universel de Commerce* (3 vols, Geneva, 1742), vol. 1, lettres A–C, *Agens de Change*, pp. 49–51; *Bourse*, pp. 520–22.

accounts of their clients. Negotiations had to be conducted face to face, and stockbrokers would be prohibited from making direct commercial arrangements. Also, so as to avoid conflicts of interest, accountants or treasurers working for merchants would not be permitted to be nominated as *Agens de Change*. The identity of clients would have to be kept confidential, and brokers could face the death penalty if they transacted for principals who were known to be financially bankrupt. Finally, the patent regulated the fees which the brokers would receive. It also required the names of those who contravened these rules to be made public at the bourse so that market participants would not use their services any longer. These measures were clear and enforceable. The system of fines would ensure discipline of market participants and the success of the exchange.

The bank of the monarchy, the second important institution within Zinzendorf's economic system, should support the operations of the stock exchange. It should be based in Vienna with branches in Prague, Brno, Linz, Graz and Trieste.[158] Its operations should combine the best practices of foreign banks. As a foundation, it would have systems to increase commerce. These would include book transfers with *Folios* and its own reference value to keep the records consistent.[159] Like the banks of Amsterdam and Naples, it should safeguard foreign coins to generate additional income.[160] For depositors, this represented a double advantage: first, they could have immediate access to the money and readily withdraw the coins; and second, they would be able to wait for a good exchange rate before using the coins for domestic commercial transactions.[161]

Moreover, like the financial institutions of the second group in 'Beschreibung der vornehmsten Europäischen Bancken', the bank's operations should increase the supply of money in the economy. Zinzendorf intended to issue *billets* to help the economy to grow, and to improve state credit by reducing the rate of interest. *Billets* worth 4 million *florins*, backed by a cash reserve, should be issued as bearer certificates in five denominations, ranging from 10 *florins* to a maximum of 500 *florins*. The main challenge of this operation, Zinzendorf recognised, would be the

[158] I follow largely the interpretation of Schasching, *Staatsbildung*, pp. 68–76. For a summary of Zinzendorf's bank project of Feb. 1767, see also Dickson, *Finance and Government*, vol. 2, pp. 66–7 and Pettenegg (ed.), *Selbstbiographien*, pp. 113–18.

[159] Zinzendorf proposed a silbermark worth 24 fl.: Schasching, *Staatsbildung*, p. 68.

[160] Foreign coins should be deposited for six months for a fee of a one-quarter per cent of the value deposited: Zinzendorf, 'Finanzvorschläge', 1 June 1763, vol. 19, fol. 198r.

[161] Ibid., fols 198r–198v.

initial introduction of the *billets* into the economy without having the confidence of the public. Therefore, at the outset, the creation of bank deposits should be a forced measure, and one-third of public and private transactions should be made by using the notes. In time, Zinzendorf argued, voluntary credit would replace the forced one. In addition, Zinzendorf thought, the bank could provide short-term financing to individuals. He anticipated that those who had to make immediate tax payments, but only held public paper that had significantly lost value, would take advantage of this offer. In support of commerce and industry, the bank could discount bills of exchange and provide financing to manufacturers against two-thirds of the value of non-perishable goods. Similarly, and provided that it could be kept separate from its core activities, the bank should also be allowed to offer long-term finance for large and more comprehensive agricultural investments through the issue of notes.

Ultimately, Zinzendorf wanted to create a 'political bank' in the monarchy, one that provided direct financial support to the state and was the most sophisticated type of bank. Zinzendorf's model was clearly the Bank of England. The important advantage of this bank, he argued, was that it had succeeded in creating a well-managed credit system which was supported by the total confidence of the public. Thus, the Bank of England's *billets* could circulate readily in the economy and replace money in private transactions.[162]

During peacetime, the new political bank in Vienna would support state credit and the circulation of money. It ought to keep the prices of public bonds at par and should use its branches to ensure that the bonds issued by the various provinces could be freely exchanged for cash. Once public bonds traded at par value and circulated readily in the country, financial speculators would no longer have a domestic market for their expensive loans. However, still seeking a financial return, they would have to invest through the stock exchange and thus would contribute to a strengthening of state finances. In case of emergency funding requirements, the bank could lend directly to the state at the lower rate of interest of 3 per cent. To prevent the abuse of the system and to avoid an 'unrecorded and hidden increase in credit', the bank should be allowed neither to open *Folios* for the state nor to issue interest-free *billets* to the govern-

[162] Ludwig Zinzendorf, 'Vorschlag um die Unzulänglichkeit der bisherigen Finanzmittel auf einen künftigen Krieg zu ersetzen', 18 January 1769, fols 341v–342r, vol. 21, Nachlaß Zinzendorf, HHStA.

ment. Zinzendorf specified that any emergency funding intended solely as a short-term measure had to be made from the bank's cash reserves rather than through a new credit facility. These rules, Zinzendorf argued, should be incorporated into the articles of incorporation of the bank and its content should be publicised as widely as possible.[163] He was determined to avoid the institution being degraded to another *Schulden Caße* of the state.

A solid financial system would facilitate war finance by enabling individuals to make larger contributions to the state. In wartime, Zinzendorf expected the bank to perform additional tasks. It should raise an additional 3 million *florins* to be able to fund critical operations.[164] However, he conceded, the bank would again have to resort to forced credit. It would have to issue 6 million *florins* of coupon-type loan bonds, *Darlehensobligationen*, to ensure that important payments, including salaries to the military and pensions, would continue to be made. Even though its *billets* were in circulation and the stock exchange was functioning, the prices of government paper, Zinzendorf thought, would be in danger of collapse. Therefore, as a precaution, the bank should keep a reserve of 2.2 million *florins* to support the market on the bourse. As liquidity support to the government, an additional 4 million *florins* in cash should be kept aside to readily buy provisions for the military and thus prevent agricultural prices from increasing. For this amount, the state would issue *Darlehensobligationen* to the bank which the latter could trade on the stock exchange and, if required, use 1.5 million *florins* of its money reserves to support their prices.

As in previous wars, Zinzendorf thought, forced loans to pay the war taxes would again become necessary, and individuals would be forced to incur debts at higher rates of interest.[165] Here, he argued, the bank could play a pivotal role by mitigating the financial damages to those who would

[163] 'Sicherheiten der Bank', fols 80v–83r in Zinzendorf, 'Allergnädigst, abgeforderter Vorschlag'.

[164] Zinzendorf assumed that, during peacetime, out of the 10m. fl. worth of *billets*, 6m. fl. were in regular circulation. Therefore, the bank had to keep a reserve of 4m. fl. to cover potential redemptions. With additional 3m.–6m. fl. already in circulation, the state would have a total money reserve of 9m. fl. Given that the loan periods were limited to a maximum of six months, the total fund circulated twice a year. Hence, the amount available for war finance was equivalent to a value of 18m. fl., circulating once a year. See Schasching, *Staatsbildung*, p. 73.

[165] For a list of war taxes used in the monarchy in the late 1750s and early 1760s, see Dickson, *Finance and Government*, vol. 2, pp. 128–30. The taxes, Dickson argued, were 'partly interchangeable with forced loans', ibid., p. 128.

be forced to finance the war. The bank could permit partial tax payments, and, in return, issue loan bonds which individuals could sell immediately on the bourse. The sale of the bonds would raise the extra money to make the subsequent tax payments. The bank could also inject liquidity to the stock exchange to support the market of the loan bonds. As direct financial support for the government, it would keep a cash reserve of 3.5 million *florins*, of which 1.5 million *florins* would be intended for emergency funding. A central albeit finite financial reserve, rather than the repeated cash calls to its citizens, should force the state to follow a tighter control of its war-related expenses.

To perform its operations well, the bank needed a robust foundation. The best arrangement, Zinzendorf argued, would be share capital provided by private investors. However, the economy of the monarchy, he recognised, was significantly less developed than England. It was thus highly unlikely that a group of domestic individuals could be found to provide the required capital for the new bank. Given that the capital structure of the Bank of England could not be replicated, Zinzendorf suggested, as the second-best option, that the Estates of the Austrian and Bohemian lands should act as guarantors to the institution.[166] They could create the necessary and important public confidence in the bank and thus could ensure that its operations would be successful both in times of peace and war. Without the ruler's consent, the Estates could also decide to liquidate the bank.[167] However, in case of financial turmoil, there would be a role for government in supporting the bank and in offering guarantees.

The bank's management, Zinzendorf argued, had to be independent of the state. The president of the bank would be appointed by the Estates for six years and would only be accountable to them. He had to follow the bank's main laws (*Fundamentalgesetze*) and was not allowed to accept conflicting orders from the ruler.[168] The other five directors, also appointed by the Estates, should be carefully selected. To minimise their dependence on the state as much as possible, those with government, clerical or military careers should be excluded. Moreover, to increase public confidence in the new institution, Zinzendorf envisaged the involvement of the busi-

[166] 'Sicherheiten der Bank', fols 78v–79r in Zinzendorf, 'Allergnädigst, abgeforderter Vorschlag'. On the involvement of Estates in Zinzendorf's bank proposal, see Godsey, *The Sinews of Habsburg Power*, pp. 270–71.

[167] 'Sicherheiten der Bank', fol. 81r in Zinzendorf, 'Allergnädigst, abgeforderter Vorschlag'.

[168] Ibid., fols 83r–83v.

ness community: two representatives, one nominated by a future trading company and one by domestic wholesalers would be allowed to examine the bank's operations and its books.[169] The new bank, Zinzendorf thought, had to win public trust right from the beginning. The level of public confidence would determine how quickly the bank's operations could become successful.[170]

The Estates Credit Deputation of the early 1760s, Zinzendorf added, should remain separate so that, as additional security, it could offer investors its payment bonds. In the event that the bank would be unable to redeem its own *billets*, creditors could request these bonds as alternative payment and could sell them in the *public caisses*. The bank could issue up to 10 million bonds which would pay an interest rate of 4 per cent to creditors.[171] It was, Zinzendorf argued, a precautionary measure against financial abuse by the state. The threat of payment bonds flooding the *public caisses* was designed to prevent the state from drawing down too much of the bank's capital reserve or delaying repayment of short-term loans. Alternatively, withholding part of the contribution would be a further measure the Estates could use to shield the bank from the unwanted interference by the government.

At the end of 'Allergnädigst, abgeforderter Vorschlag', Zinzendorf summarised the advantages of the new stock exchange and the bank for the monarchy's economy.[172] The Parisian bourse provided the appropriate model for the stock exchange and would make it a success. The idea of setting up branches in other cities, Zinzendorf argued, was a novelty without precedents in Europe. It would strengthen the operations of the monarchy's exchange. The latter, Zinzendorf was convinced, provided the best mechanism to support the market prices of bonds, both in peacetime and war.[173]

[169] Ibid., fol. 85v. During wartime, Zinzendorf acknowledged, when the bank would be heavily involved in trading paper, it was potentially dangerous to give business people full information on the institution's cash reserves. A compromise, Zinzendorf thought, would be for the bank itself to be involved in selecting the two representatives. The trading company and the wholesalers would nominate three candidates each and the bank would choose one from each group. The representatives would be elected for a period of five years and, like the deputies of the Estates, would take the oath on the bank. See ibid., fols 85v–86r.

[170] Ibid., fols 86v.

[171] Ibid., fols 79r–79v.

[172] 'Schluss', fols 173r–177v in Zinzendorf, 'Allergnädigst, abgeforderter Vorschlag'.

[173] Ibid., fols 173r–173v.

The bank played an important role in commerce and in war finance. Its set-up was an important element of its success. It should be independent of the state and should be created immediately, in a calm period of peace, to swiftly gain the confidence of the public.[174] Other nations, Zinzendorf thought, would be envious of the monarchy's new financial institution. England would take note of the new bank, as would France and Prussia. France still regretted the demise of its political bank and would recognise the benefits of the monarchy's bank in supporting state credit and reducing the cost of debt. Prussia would feel humiliated. Frederick II knew of the monarchy's precarious financial situation after the end of the Seven Years War. He would be resentful that with the new bank, Austria would be able to 'double' its resources and that Prussia, unable to create something similar, would be left behind.[175] The transparency of the bank's operations, leaving no room for abuse, would impress European nations. It would improve the country's international standing, and the increase of confidence in the monarchy's finances would provide better access to credit abroad.[176]

Zinzendorf was very excited about his proposal in which he had invested a great deal of effort.[177] He quickly set out his responses to criticisms of his plan. Within the government, Hatzfeld was a forceful voice against Zinzendorf. In 'Allergnädigst, abgeforderter Vorschlag', Zinzendorf devoted a long section to explain the shortcomings of Hatzfeld's counter-proposal.[178] For Hatzfeld, the mechanism of *Aufkündigungsfreiheit*, the right of creditors to redeem their deposits at government *caisses*, could

[174] Ibid., fols 175r–175v.

[175] Ibid., fols 175v–176v. Zinzendorf was critical of the new Prussian bank created in 1765 and which operated in Berlin. The latter, Zinzendorf argued, was clearly inferior to the monarchy's bank. The Prussian institution was only guaranteed by the king, did not issue banknotes and restricted the payment of specie to those who had cash deposits with the bank: ibid., fols 176v–177r. On the operation of the Prussian bank, see Markus von Niehbur, *Geschichte der Königlichen Bank in Berlin. Von der Gründung derselben (1765) bis zum Ende des Jahres 1845. Aus amtlichen Quellen* (Berlin, 1854).

[176] Zinzendorf, 'Allergnädigst, abgeforderter Vorschlag', fol. 176v.

[177] Over 12 days, Zinzendorf spent several hours a day developing his arguments. See letter of Ludwig Zinzendorf to Karl Zinzendorf, Vienna, 17 December 1766, vol. 64, DOZA. It was part of a long intellectual process which was already well under way in July 1766: Pettenegg (ed.), *Selbstbiographien*, p. 103.

[178] Zinzendorf, 'Allergnädigst, abgeforderter Vorschlag', fols 116v–140v. On Hatzfeld's counter-proposals of 1768, all based on Zinzendorf's work, and the ensuing discussions in government, see Dickson, *Finance and Government*, vol. 2, pp. 68–72; Schasching, *Staatsbildung*, pp. 80–3.

improve state finances and lift the market price of bonds back-up to par. Zinzendorf disagreed. Rather than repay creditors, it was preferable, he thought, to use the funds to buy paper on the stock exchange. *Aufkündigungsfreiheit* had not worked during peacetime and would certainly be inadequate during war, when conditions were even more challenging and investors demanded higher returns. In any case, Zinzendorf continued, the various *fonds d'amortissement* were not sufficiently large to repay 80 million *florins* of state credit. Conversely, the stock exchange was a large clearing system that included all investors of domestic public paper. Thus, it was much better suited to return capital to government creditors and support market prices.[179]

Zinzendorf also disagreed with Hatzfeld's arguments on war finance. Unlike Hatzfeld, Zinzendorf thought that forced credit remained a critical measure to finance the growing expense of the military. Even wealthy nations with a larger monetary base than the monarchy, Zinzendorf pointed out, had to resort to forced credit. As evidence, he used the monarchy's experience during the Seven Years War: total war expenses had been 165 million *florins*, and more than 70 per cent had been covered by forced credit. The monetary base of the monarchy had been far too small to pay for military outlays, and foreign loans had been quickly used up. Therefore, forced credit had been the only option to ensure that funds had become available in time.[180] Zinzendorf was also sceptical of Hatzfeld's proposal to issue 17 million interest-free *Bancozettel*. The Seven Years War had shown that the paper overhang in the economy would be too important, and the creation of *Umsetzungscassen* to support the prices of the paper was not practicable. Also, Zinzendorf dissented from Hatzfeld's idea of exchanging the paper into bonds of the Vienna City Bank. The amount of paper was too large to buy back, and for this kind of important financial operation, the monarchy would have to borrow money abroad. Zinzendorf again referred to the Seven Years War. After the war, he argued, it had taken the government more than two years to convert 7 million of paper into bonds with a 5 per cent interest rate. If the monarchy would undertake such a large operation now, the value of existing government

[179] Zinzendorf, 'Allergnädigst, abgeforderter Vorschlag', fols 119r–127v. Zinzendorf encouraged ministers to get familiar with the operations of the stock exchange during peacetime when the political situation was not so challenging. Delaying the creation of the stock exchange to more turbulent times to help with war finance, he cautioned, would fail: ibid., fols 126v–127r.

[180] Ibid., fols 128r–129v.

debt could be reduced and there would be a real risk that creditors would again demand a higher rate of interest on state debt.[181]

Other objections to Zinzendorf's plan also dealt with the role of the bank during military conflicts. The paper traded by Zinzendorf's bank would suffer larger discounts than in the Seven Years War. In his reply, Zinzendorf referred to the solid financial foundation of the bank and the increasing confidence in domestic credit generated by his new system. The reserves of the new institution, he underlined, were more important than the total amount of paper it would support. So, the bank could afford to wait for enough investor demand to buy its bonds and would not have to accept large discounts on the paper.[182] During the last war, critics argued, the prices of government bonds decreased by 40 per cent, and foreign creditors feared the possibility of a state bankruptcy. With the new stock exchange and bank, Zinzendorf postulated, the price decrease during war could be narrowed to 20 per cent: this discount was moderate enough to continue to attract new investors to buy government bonds.[183]

Zinzendorf not only engaged with domestic critics, but also closely followed the arguments presented by foreign writers. He reacted forcefully to French assessments about the monarchy's financial administration. In February 1767, when discussions in the *Staatsrat* about his financial plans were moving in his favour, he took up a comment in Forbonnais' newly published *Principes et observations économiques.* There, Forbonnais wrote that Vienna had a bank.[184] Zinzendorf wanted to clarify, however, that the Vienna City Bank was a bank in name only. In reality, it was a '*caisse d'emprunt*', and Forbonnais, Zinzendorf suggested, had been misled about the nature of the bank by the *Dictionnaire* of Savary. Anxious that his new project would be erroneously perceived as the copy of an existing Austrian bank and not receive the appropriate recognition it deserved, Zinzendorf urged his brother, who was travelling in Europe, to take this matter up personally with Forbonnais.[185]

[181] Ibid., fols 131r–136v. Only with great effort did the government succeed in reducing the rate of interest on its bonds to 4 per cent. Zinzendorf feared that after a large paper issue, investor would again demand 5 per cent interest payments to compensate for financial risk: see ibid., fols 136r–136v.

[182] Ibid., fols 141r–142v.

[183] Ibid., fols 144r.

[184] Véron de Forbonnais, *Principes et observations économiques* (Paris, 1767), Chap. 7: 'Des papiers représentant l'argent', p. 159.

[185] Letter of Ludwig Zinzendorf to Karl Zinzendorf, Vienna, 28 February 1767, vol. 64, DOZA.

The Significance of Zinzendorf's Writings

For Zinzendorf, his financial plans presented a radically new perspective: nobody before had consistently sought to apply foreign ideas and models to public credit issues in the monarchy. Zinzendorf drew his intellectual inspiration from the ideas of Law and Melon, and the French writers of Gournay's circle. A good supply of money, Zinzendorf argued, would have a double effect. First, through the issue of paper money, it could support state credit. Second, liquidity could increase the welfare of the public and grow commerce. This was a direct beneficial effect for the real economy. A strong domestic market would offer a solid basis from which the state could manage its finances and more readily raise public debt.

But the foreign influence on Zinzendorf's ideas went beyond the use of theoretical arguments. The institutions of the monarchy, Zinzendorf thought, should follow established and successful banking and stock exchange practices in Europe. The Bank of England was Zinzendorf's most important model. In addition to its direct functions as a political bank, Zinzendorf admired the English set up with private shareholders contributing share capital to the bank. The shareholders and the wider domestic business community, he maintained, had established a mutually beneficial working relationship which had accelerated the growth of English commerce. Moreover, the shares of the bank had added liquidity to the economy.

Zinzendorf summarised his thinking on financial policy and credit in 12 brief 'Maximes'.[186] Finance, he argued in the first 'Maxime', was the basis for all the operations of the state. The ruler, therefore, had to make it a priority of policy. This included strengthening the position and authority within government of the financial expert. The good management of taxes and revenues was important, as was clear planning of ordinary expenses for the state and the military. Extraordinary expenses required dedicated funds. As these funds were set up for a specific purpose, they should only be temporary measures. State credit, Zinzendorf argued, was built on public confidence and on keeping financial promises to creditors. So, a good management of public finances should unite credit funds, rather than keep them separate, and ensure a good circulation of money to be able to make timely interest and capital payments.

[186] Ludwig Zinzendorf, undated, 'Maximes sur L'État des Finances', Karton 39, NÖLA.

Political events in Europe dictated Zinzendorf's work. His financial system was driven by war finance. Thus, as an immediate measure, state credit ought to cover the extraordinary war-related expenses of the state. In the longer term, by adding liquidity, state credit could support agriculture, industry and commerce. Zinzendorf's aim was to reduce the cost of public debt and bring it in line with other European countries. Like England and the United Provinces, the monarchy should have access to long-term financing at reduced rates of interest. State credit, Zinzendorf argued, could become more permanent if the right of debt redemption (*Aufkündigungsfreiheit*) was abolished. A stock exchange would fulfil the crucial role of supporting the prices of government paper. The government, too, should play an active role and, if required, buy bonds on the bourse to prevent their prices from falling. Zinzendorf was very precise about the operations of the institutions. His guiding principles were transparency and accountability. He was very clear that the new system had to be workable for the state, the Estates and the public.

Zinzendorf understood the dynamics of the monarchy's financial system. He understood that the Vienna City Bank was no longer autonomous. It was under the control of the emperor and no longer able to keep the trust of the public. Its systems were secretive, its credit operations unwieldy and its bonds not suitable for the large group of small investors. Zinzendorf recognised the significance of the Estates as an intermediary power in negotiating and collecting taxes and in securing state credit. He also saw the problems of having a fragmented market for public bonds. The latter were issued in the provinces and thus had very different characteristics. Zinzendorf sought to unify the country's public debt to increase its circulation and liquidity, and was closely involved in simplifying the types of government paper. In 1767, he reformed the *Ständische Aerarial Schulden*. This was a large portion of debt which the state had raised during the previous war, and it was owed to the Estates of the Bohemian–Austrian provinces. Zinzendorf issued one single type of government bond to each province with a rate of interest of 4 per cent and replaced the more than 200 types of obligations which were previously in existence.[187]

The constraints and weaknesses of the monarchy's economy compelled Zinzendorf to keep forced credit as a significant element of his system. The heavy financial demands of the Seven Years War, he thought, would

[187] Dickson, *Finance and Government*, vol. 2, p. 58; see also Schasching, *Staatsbildung*, pp. 42–51.

arise again in future military conflicts. Therefore, so as to minimise the economic burden on the country, the financial demands should be spread more evenly among a larger number of citizens. In addition, the political bank could play an essential part by offering direct financial help to the state, supporting domestic taxpayers and adding liquidity to the stock exchange. This credit system, Zinzendorf was convinced, represented the most original and best financial recipe for the monarchy. Other proposals subsequently presented in Vienna, he made clear, were but mere variations of his financial plan.[188]

[188] 'Le dirai-je enfin c'est moi qui le premier ai fait sentir la nécessité d'un plan général de crédit, préparant des resources pour la guerre. Les projets qui ont été présentés depuis ne sont que des combinaisons différentes des parties qui composaient mon sistème.' Ludwig Zinzendorf, 'Sur l'utilité de la Chambre des Comptes et la nécessité de la conserver', October 1771, fol. 615r, vol. 4, Nachlaß Zinzendorf, HHStA.

CHAPTER 6

The Financial Expert of the Habsburg Monarchy

The preceding chapters presented the depth of Zinzendorf's financial knowledge and how it developed. This chapter examines how Zinzendorf took part in the wider European intellectual discourse on political economy and how he adapted to the circumstances of the monarchy. The approach in this chapter will be synthetic and assesses the significance of Zinzendorf's achievement from a variety of perspectives. The first section examines Zinzendorf's intellectual formation. It sets out the type of economic thinker he was, his contributions to the political economy in the monarchy, and suggests explanations for his ability to shape domestic debates and institutions. Zinzendorf's intellectual achievements and proficiency in financial matters attracted a small group of like-minded individuals. The circle around Zinzendorf, its composition, activities and writings are the subject of the second section which compares and contrasts it with the initiative of Gournay's circle in France in the 1750s. Sections three and four set out Zinzendorf's significance for the debates within government: first, how he interacted with and differentiated himself from projectors who had a continuous presence at court; and second, how Zinzendorf influenced the discussions on reforming the financial administration and stimulated intellectual decision-making in government. Administrative restructuring and economic questions were an important feature of Maria Theresa's reign. The debates on reform were long-winded and complicated, and departments were often abolished, resurrected or moved around. An overview of institutional change during

S. Adler, *Political Economy in the Habsburg Monarchy 1750–1774*,
Palgrave Studies in the History of Finance,
https://doi.org/10.1007/978-3-030-31007-3_6

Zinzendorf's time and the examples of the administration of commercial affairs do much to illustrate these differences of political opinions. The conclusion draws again on France and compares the *Bureau du Commerce* with the monarchy's own central institutions for commerce. The penultimate section discusses the extent to which a public sphere existed in Austria in the 1760s and 1770s and leads to an appraisal of Zinzendorf's ability to engage with the public and disseminate his ideas beyond the confines of inner government. The final section of the chapter emphasises the distinctiveness of Zinzendorf's ideas by comparing them to the cameralist arguments of Justi and Sonnenfels.

Zinzendorf's Formation

Zinzendorf followed a process of conscious self-education in political economy. From the mid-1740s, he read the works of European thinkers, in particular French and English, assiduously, and began to write economic texts.[1] However, his biography does not make any reference to a formal education in economic theory. Cameralism did not play a part in his intellectual formation. Zinzendorf's courses at the University of Leipzig were mainly on law and history. It is not clear why he developed his interest in economic questions, and finance in particular. It may have been linked to the practicalities of having to manage his estate in Lower Austria.[2] The latter prompted Zinzendorf to study new accounting methods from France. As a member of the Estates of Lower Austria, he became acquainted with general estate finances.[3] With Kaunitz's sponsorship in Paris and back in Vienna, Zinzendorf could concentrate on his self-education and systematically develop his understanding of economic questions. He took advantage of freedom to travel in Europe to meet leading thinkers and foreign officials in order to see at first-hand how other economies were organised.

[1] Eduard Gaston von Pettenegg (ed.), *Ludwig und Karl Grafen und Herren von Zinzendorf. Ihre Selbstbiographien nebst einer kurzen Geschichte des Hauses Zinzendorf* (Vienna, 1879), pp. 70, 59.

[2] For Zinzendorf's university studies and role in the government of Lower Austria, see Chap. 2.

[3] Grete Klingenstein, 'Between Mercantilism and Physiocracy. Stages, Modes and Functions of Economic Theory in the Habsburg Monarchy, 1748–63' in Charles W. Ingrao (ed.), *State and Society in Early Modern Austria* (West Lafayette, IN: Purdue University Press, 1994), pp. 181–214, at p. 185.

Zinzendorf advanced to become the most sophisticated financial expert in the monarchy. His abilities and knowledge were generally recognised by other government officials.[4] Both Francis Stephen and Maria Theresa sought his advice directly: from Paris, Zinzendorf gave his first briefings on the French economy and court to the emperor. His recommendations to Maria Theresa in 1763 included summaries of financial strategies for the state.[5] Eventually, as minister, the empress held weekly meetings with Zinzendorf.[6] Among Austrian state officials, 'he became an object of jealousy'.[7]

Zinzendorf was very meticulous and analytical in his work. It was useful, he thought, to follow a daily routine of recording new ideas.[8] The conclusions Zinzendorf presented in his texts were supported by well-informed observations on economic, social and fiscal developments and by detailed data.[9] In 1752, his assessment of the state of French agriculture and calculations of the French and English monetary bases, both set out in the 'Mémoire sur les richesses, le commerce et les finances de La France', were good examples. In the translation of Law's *Money and Trade*, Zinzendorf's comparison of agricultural policies in France, England and the German states was based on historical price data over a period of 250 years. Zinzendorf was a pragmatic thinker. He sought to understand how systems operated and looked for a dialogue with practitioners and merchants. In his analyses of the Austrian economy and finances, he gave a careful assessment of why its existing operations did not work. He then proposed new ideas and policies which had been

[4] Alfred Ritter von Arneth, 'Graf Philipp Cobenzl und seine Memoiren', *AÖG* 67 (1885), pp. 1–181, at p. 105.

[5] Ludwig Zinzendorf, 'Examens des offres présentées à sa Majesté Imperiale pour la ferme générale du Tabac dans les pays héréditaires en Allemagne', Diary of Karl Zinzendorf, 19 June 1763, HHStA. For Zinzendorf's views on farming, see the section 'Projectors'.

[6] Zinzendorf met with Maria Theresa every Tuesday at noon. Letter of Maria Theresa to Countess Enzenberg, 6 October 1770, in *Briefe der Kaiserin Maria Theresia an Ihre Kinder und Freunde*, ed. Alfred Ritter von Arneth (4 vols, Vienna, 1881), vol. 4, p. 500. On one occasion, Zinzendorf's discussions with the emperor lasted almost the whole day. It began at 5:30 in the morning and ended at 2 o'clock in the afternoon: Diary of Karl Zinzendorf, 22 July 1763, HHStA.

[7] 'On me reproche d'avoir des principes, de la theorie, d'avoir beaucoup lû, je suis devenu un objet de jalousie', in Pettenegg (ed.), *Selbstbiographien*, p. 66.

[8] Diary of Karl Zinzendorf, 27 March 1762, HHStA.

[9] Zinzendorf would often share with his brother economic statistics which he collected: Diary of Karl Zinzendorf, 3 and 20 May 1763, HHStA.

tested before elsewhere. Along these lines, Zinzendorf developed his arguments on credit institutions. First, in the text on the Vienna City Bank, he set out the operational shortcomings of the bank. These, Zinzendorf argued, became even more apparent when compared to the superior operations of foreign banks. Therefore, Zinzendorf thought, the processes of foreign institutions should be implemented in the monarchy. However, he knew that the domestic economy was not diversified and developed enough to readily adopt other banking systems. Also, it did not have common institutions for commercial and fiscal self-government. The main economic activities were conducted on a regional level. For this reason, he used the Estates of the Austrian and Bohemian lands to adapt foreign models for the monarchy. Zinzendorf understood that the good performance of the Estates' debt in 1748 and before, as well as their importance in collecting taxes, made them a reliable source of credit for the government.[10] As intermediary power, the Estates were trusted, and they played a key role in the economy. Thus, Zinzendorf thought, they were well qualified to act as guarantors of the new bank, and it represented the best workable alternative to the Vienna City Bank. In other areas of his work his pragmatic approach was also visible: it guided his discussions with projectors.

Zinzendorf's most visible political contributions were his presidencies of the Estate Credit Deputation and Audit office, *Hofrechenkammer*, as well as his work on reducing the country's borrowing costs and consolidating its various types of bonds. However, his impact on the monarchy's political economy extended well beyond that. Zinzendorf was the expert who wrote most of the financial plans which Kaunitz presented to the ruler, and for this reason it can be argued that he was instrumental in reshaping the financial administration. Intellectually, too, Zinzendorf's input was significant. It was through Zinzendorf that members of the ruling elite in Vienna, as early as the 1750s, were introduced to the most advanced economic ideas from Western Europe. Together with Kaunitz, he worked assiduously to open up the government to new and more radical ways of thinking about the economy and public finance. For Zinzendorf, foreign ideas, and in particular those of Melon, Montesquieu and Law,

[10] On the Estates' financial role during the War of the Austrian Succession, see William Godsey, *The Sinews of Habsburg Power: Lower Austria in a Fiscal-Military State, 1650–1820* (Oxford, 2018), pp. 193–95.

were essential for a good understanding of political economy.[11] Like these thinkers, Zinzendorf recognised that commerce was becoming more competitive and that growing the domestic economy was ultimately more critical for a country's international standing than military strength.[12] Zinzendorf translated the *Essai politique*, and as I have suggested earlier, his works displayed the direct intellectual presence of Melon. Law also decisively influenced his thinking. Zinzendorf wrote three large texts on Law.[13] *Gedanken vom Gelde*, his translation of *Money and Trade*, was a full engagement with economic theory where he supplemented the ideas of Law with the arguments of Montesquieu and those of more recent French and German writers. On state credit, Zinzendorf's diagnosis of two crises in the monarchy, monetary and fiscal, mirrored Law's verdict of French finances in 1716. Zinzendorf attempted nothing less than to recreate the building blocks of Law's scheme.

Zinzendorf showed clearly the relevance of European systems and ideas for the economy of the monarchy. He stressed the importance of looking abroad to identify those methods which would possibly work in his country. Best practice, Zinzendorf thought, had to be imported from Europe's most advanced nations so that the monarchy could keep up with the fierce international economic competition.[14] For commerce, the facilities and operations of the French trading company in Lorient provided a useful model. In finance, too, given the complexity of operations and the long preparation involved, he thought that it was preferable to build on proven systems. For the Estates' credit operation, he used and refined foreign financial practices and those which already had been implemented in certain provinces of the monarchy. Tried and tested methods, Zinzendorf

[11] Letter of Ludwig Zinzendorf to Karl Zinzendorf, Vienna, 7 November 1759, vol. 63, DOZA. He sent copies of Melon's *Essai politique*, Montesquieu's *De l'Esprit des Lois* and his German translation of Law's *Money and Trade* to Karl, who was studying in Jena. Karl received the books on 3 December 1759. He immediately started reading them: Diary of Karl Zinzendorf of 1759, summary for that year, second page and final entries at the end of the diary, HHStA.

[12] On Melon and Montesquieu, see Istvan Hont, *Jealousy of Trade: International Competition and the Nation-State in Historical Perspective* (Cambridge, MA, 2005), pp. 29–33.

[13] See Chap. 4, footnotes 16 and 17.

[14] The Seven Years War, Hont argued, was a largely commercial conflict 'fueled by jealousy of trade': Hont, *Jealousy of Trade*, p. 34.

made clear, were preferable to theoretical considerations.[15] The analysis of French and English monetary policies in the 'Mémoire sur les richesses, le commerce et les finances de la France' and, ten years later, the extensive review of the banking systems in Europe, prepared the ground for his recommendation of a new Bank of England-type political bank. Nevertheless, guided by pragmatism, he recognised that first the monarchy needed an adjustment period with a less developed financial institution before it could implement the operations of the most sophisticated type of bank. With regard to establishing a stock exchange, Zinzendorf followed a similar logic. The regulations of the Parisian bourse, he argued, were clear and well developed and most relevant for the creation of a similar institution in the monarchy. The final patent of the Austrian financial bourse issued on 1 August 1771 was based on his ideas.[16] For a considerable period, Zinzendorf's findings remained authoritative documents. More than ten years after Zinzendorf's first journey, his brother made three visits to France in 1765, 1767 and 1769. For Karl, his brother's accounts and conclusions on the Compagnie des Indes and the French navy were still relevant, and he incorporated both texts into his travel reports on France.[17] For the government more generally, the documents of both Zinzendorf brothers were important. In his will, Karl left his and his brother's writings to the *Hofbibliothek*. The *Staatsrat*, however, considered the documents, in particular those on administration, economics and finance, to be too sensitive to be given to the library. Instead, it designated a room in the imperial palace where 242 of the Zinzendorf volumes and Karl's diaries were to be kept, and access was restricted. Except

[15] 'Nachdem dasjenige, was die Erfahrung bewähret, den Vorzug vor dem verdienen muß, so sich auf bloße theoretische Sätze gründet': Ludwig Zinzendorf, *Pro Memoria an eine ständische Deputation einen Vorschlag zur Erleichterung des ständischen Credites betreffend. Im September 1757*, fol. 222v.

[16] P.G.M. Dickson, *Finance and Government under Maria Theresia 1740–1780* (2 vols, Oxford, 1987), vol. 2, p. 76.

[17] Both 'Mémoires differens sur la Compagnie des Indes écrites en 1752 par M le Comte de Zinzendorf, actuellement controlleur général des finances, a Mr le Comte (depuis Prince) de Kaunitz Rittberg; alors ambassadeur de ses Maj.Imperiales Royales apostoliques près de sa Maj. très chrétiennes', vol. 1, fols 176r–191v, and 'Extrait d'une letter sur la Marine de France écrite à Brest en 1752 par le Comte Louis de Zinzendorf à present Ministre de L'Etat de ses Maj. Imperiales', vol. 2, fols 165r–170v, are preserved in Karl Zinzendorf, 'Mémoires rassemblés par le Comte Charles de Zinzendorf pendant ses voyages par la France 1764, 1767 et 1769', vol. 1, Hs. Suppl. 954–W918, and ibid., vol. 2, Hs. Suppl. 960–§922, HHStA.

for the diaries, these documents remained part of the *Staatsrat*'s archives until 1867.[18]

The bedrock of Zinzendorf's self-education was extensive reading and the ability to obtain copies of the latest and relevant writings of European thinkers swiftly. To get a sense of where Ludwig Zinzendorf placed his intellectual emphasis, Karl's diaries and the personal correspondence of the brothers are good sources. In the early 1760s, Karl recorded books which his brother gave to him to read. The reading list was wide and included François-Marie Voltaire's *L'Histoire de l'Empire de Russie sous Pierre le Grand* and *Essai sur l'Histoire generale et sur les moeurs et l'esprit des Nations*, Jakob Friedrich Freiherr von Bielefeld's *Institutions politiques*, Gottfried Achenwall's *Grundsätze der europäischen Geschichte zur politischen Kenntnis der heutigen vornehmsten Staaten*, Victor Riqueti marquis de Mirabeau's *L'Ami des Hommes* and Justi's *Vollständige Abhandlung von den Manufakturen und Fabriken*.[19] Zinzendorf also read poetry to his brother, including Voltaire's *Pucelle D'Orleans*.[20] Using the diary, Christine Lebeau has undertaken an extensive quantitative review of Karl's readings, including those on political economy. According to this analysis, in the early 1760s, after arriving in Vienna, Karl mostly studied Forbonnais' *Elemens du Commerce*.[21] In fact, Ludwig Zinzendorf had strongly recommended the book to him, in particular the section on 'exchange'.[22] Also, during the same period, Karl repeatedly consulted Melon's *Essai Politique*, Hume's *Political Discourses* and Mirabeau's *Théorie de l'Impot*.[23]

[18] Grete Klingenstein, Eva Faber and Antonio Trampus (eds.). *Europäische Aufklärung zwischen Wien und Triest: die Tagebücher des Gouverneurs Karl Graf von Zinzendorf, 1776–1782*, Veröffentlichung der Kommission für Neuere Geschichte Österreichs, 103 (4 vols, Vienna, 2009), vol. 1, pp. 22–3, 25. When the *Staatsrat* was dissolved in 1867, the papers, together with other writings of Zinzendorf's *Nachlaß*, went to the general state archives: *Haus-, Hof- und Staatsarchiv*, ibid., p. 25. For a full history of the *Nachlaß*, see ibid., pp. 22–38.

[19] Diary of Karl Zinzendorf, 8 February 1761, 16 October 1761, 14 and 24 March 1762, HHStA.

[20] Diary of Karl Zinzendorf, 21 February 1761, HHStA.

[21] Lebeau, 'Ludwig et Karl von Zinzendorf, administrateurs des finances. Aristocratie et pouvoir dans la Monarchie des Habsbourg, 1748–1791' (PhD dissertation, 2 vols, Université de Paris IV—Sorbonne, 1991), Annex 11.

[22] Ludwig Zinzendorf to Karl Zinzendorf, 14 December 1759, vol. 63, DOZA.

[23] Christine Lebeau, 'Ludwig et Karl von Zinzendorf', Annex 11.

Zinzendorf used correspondents in the monarchy's European embassies to keep him informed about new publications.[24] But as he became more involved in political life, he was unable to devote as much time to follow the latest developments and discussions on finance. As a government minister, Zinzendorf's time was increasingly consumed by daily affairs and policies in the audit office.[25] He took advantage of his brother's extensive travels to keep abreast of European economic debates and, through him, continued to engage with foreign writers. He repeatedly sent Karl lists of books which he wanted to acquire.[26] And in order to know the provenance of ideas, he asked his brother to investigate the authorship of anonymous publications.[27] Karl acted as his brother's eyes and ears in Europe. As such, Ludwig helped Karl plan his travel itineraries and gave specific recommendations on individual countries. Zinzendorf was closely involved in Karl's first commercial trip to Saxony and Königsberg from August to November 1763, and he kept guiding his brother's subsequent visits to other European countries.[28] London, Zinzendorf pointed out, was deserted during the summer months and a visit then was not worthwhile.[29] In France, he thought, Fontainebleau was uninteresting and a 'place for lazy life'.[30] Paris was preferable by far, and French cities with manufacturing activities, including Rouen, Caen and Lille, were very interesting.[31] Similarly, in Portugal and Spain, Zinzendorf

[24] See ch 5, footnote 77.

[25] Letters of Ludwig Zinzendorf to Karl Zinzendorf, Vienna, 27 March 1767 and 14 November 1767, vol. 64, DOZA.

[26] One such 'small list' of books, which is lost, contained 32 titles: letter of Ludwig Zinzendorf to Karl Zinzendorf, Vienna, 4 January 1768, vol. 65, DOZA, in Christine Lebeau, *Aristocrates et grands commis à la Cour de Vienne, 1748–1791. Le modèle français* (Paris, 1996), p. 144.

[27] Zinzendorf wanted confirmation on the authorship of Nicolas Baudeau, *Idées d'un citoyen sur l'administration des finances* (Amsterdam, 1763). He speculated, based on the style of writing, that it was written by Forbonnais: letter of Ludwig Zinzendorf to Karl Zinzendorf, Vienna, 22 September 1764, vol. 63, DOZA in Lebeau, *Aristocrates*, p. 144, footnote 15.

[28] Diary of Karl Zinzendorf, 30 July, 1 and 2 August 1763, HHStA. Zinzendorf, for example, approved Karl's plan to go to the United Provinces and England, and then return to France: letter of Ludwig Zinzendorf to Karl Zinzendorf, Vienna, 8 April 1767, vol. 64 Vienna. Also, on Karl's travels, Lebeau, *Aristocrates*, pp. 125–27.

[29] Letter of Karl Zinzendorf to Ludwig Zinzendorf, Paris, 26 April 1767, vol. 53, DOZA.

[30] Letter of Ludwig Zinzendorf to Karl Zinzendorf, Vienna, 16 May 1767, vol. 64, DOZA.

[31] Ibid.

suggested visits to Lisbon and the port of Cadiz, which he considered more significant for international commerce than the harbours in France.[32]

As well as a travel itinerary, Zinzendorf gave recommendations on whom to meet and asked Karl to investigate financial policies and the operations of financial institutions. This was reflected in Karl's action plan, drawn up for his visit to Paris in 1767. He intended to have discussions with leading French thinkers, including Mirabeau, Forbonnais, D'Alembert and Diderot, and to collect the royal patents on financial operations which had been issued since Law's scheme. Moreover, Karl set out to gain an understanding of how French public papers were traded on the stock exchange and how the amortisation fund for state credit was administered.[33] These questions, of course, were of direct relevance to Zinzendorf who, back in Vienna, was pushing to have his financial plans accepted. As planned, Karl met with Mirabeau and Forbonnais. He also saw the liberal economist and friend of Gournay, Anne-Jacques-Robert Turgot.[34] In 1763, he had translated Turgot's *Questions importantes sur le commerce*.[35] Another member of the Gournay's circle whom Zinzendorf encouraged his brother to meet was Plumard de Dangeul, advising him to reread the Frenchman's adaption of Josiah Tucker's *Remarks on the Advantages and Disadvantages of France and Great Britain* as it 'provided a very useful comparison of the French and English economies'.[36]

[32] Letter of Ludwig Zinzendorf to Karl Zinzendorf, Vienna, 28 June 1767, vol. 64, DOZA.

[33] Letter of Karl Zinzendorf to Ludwig Zinzendorf, Paris, 9 January 1767, vol. 53, DOZA, in Christine Lebeau, 'Des aristocrates à la croisée des mondes. Politique aristocratique et pouvoir administratif en Europe dans la deuxième moitié du XVIIIe siècle' in Gabriele Haug-Moritz, Hans Peter Hye and Marlies Raffler (eds.), *Adel im 'langen' 18. Jahrhundert* (Vienna: Verlag der österreichischen Akademie der Wissenschaften, 2009), pp. 187–204, at p. 190.

[34] Lebeau, *Aristocrates*, pp. 128–29; Pettenegg (ed.), *Selbstbiographien*, p. 181. Karl met with Forbonnais several times.

[35] Grete Klingenstein, 'Between Mercantilism and Physiocracy', pp. 181–214, at p. 190. The title of the German translation was: *Einige wichtige Fragen den Handel betreffende bey Gelegenheit der Widersprüche, die die letzte Bill zu Naturalisation der Ausländer in Großbritannien erlitten, aufgeworfen durch Josiah Tucker, Rectoren des S.Steffens Collegii zu Bristol und Caplan des dasigen Bischoffs, London 1755. Aus dem Französischen ins Teutsche übersetzt druch Carl Christian Heinrich Grafen und Herren von Zinzendorff und Pottendorff, Wien 1763.* Karl finished the translation on 15 January 1763: Diary of Karl Zinzendorf, 15 January 1763, HHStA.

[36] Letter of Karl Zinzendorf to Ludwig Zinzendorf, Vienna, 23 April 1767, vol. 64, DOZA. It was first on Karl's reading list in 1761: Diary of Karl Zinzendorf, 8 February 1761, HHStA. Zinzendorf himself translated Dangeul's text: see Chap. 4, footnote 6.

England was a further important intellectual reference point for Zinzendorf. He requested details on the English system of accounting which proved difficult to find.[37] Also, Zinzendorf closely followed the publications of economic texts in English.[38] Of those, the works of David Hume had made a particular impact. Zinzendorf had translated Hume's *Political Discourses*, but it is unclear which version of the book he used as his reference.[39] Given his strong interest in the writings of the Gournay circle, it is quite possible that he was guided by the French translation of Abbé Le Blanc. In London, Karl had several discussions with Hume, including a '*grande conference*' on 3 April 1768.[40] During one of their first encounters, Karl made a point of explaining his brother's work to Hume. The latter, he noted, was pleasantly surprised by Zinzendorf's achievements.[41] Hume, Karl remarked, was at ease in the conversations. He showed Karl a new edition of his *Essays and Treatises*, and they talked at length about political economy. For Karl, some of Hume's work was new. He was not familiar with the essay *Of Jealousy of Trade*, originally published in 1758, and had not fully appreciated Hume's arguments in *Of the Balance of Trade* on the flexibility and ease with which the banks of Edinburgh extended credit. This banking model, Karl thought, should be of great interest to his brother.[42] Hume, in turn, also gained from the discussions with Karl. Six months later, during another meeting, Hume read Karl's notes from 1767 on Portugal and Spain and copied a historical

[37] Letter of Karl Zinzendorf to Ludwig Zinzendorf, London, 18 September 1768, vol. 53, DOZA. In his letters, Karl replied to Ludwig's queries.

[38] On England, Karl wrote, 'Me voici donc en Angleterre dans ce pays de liberté, au milieu d'une nation pensante.' Letter of Karl Zinzendorf to Ludwig Zinzendorf, London, 7 February 1768, DOZA.

[39] See Chap. 4, footnote 6.

[40] Diary of Karl Zinzendorf, 25 February, 15 March, 1 May, 23 May and 25 October 1768, HHStA. On the '*grande conference*' with Hume, see letter of Karl Zinzendorf to Ludwig Zinzendorf, London, 4 April 1768, vol. 53, DOZA.

[41] 'Nous causames longtemps et utilement, il s'étonne de tout ce que mon frère a fait': Diary of Karl Zinzendorf, 15 March 1768, DOZA.

[42] Letter of Karl Zinzendorf to Ludwig Zinzendorf, London, 4 April 1768. The passage which Karl referred to is David Hume, 'Of the Balance of Trade', pp. 189–90, in David Hume, *Of the Balance of Trade (1752)* in ed. Eugene F. Miller, *David Hume: Essays Moral, Political, Literary* (Indianapolis: Liberty Classics, 1987), pp. 184–93. Previously, Karl had read Hume's essays on the Balance of Trade, Luxury and Public Credit: Diary of Karl Zinzendorf, 8, 10 and 11 July 1763, HHStA.

account on the import of specie from Peru into Spain. Subsequently, he gave this piece of information to Adam Smith.[43]

Zinzendorf built up a significant library and soon after his brother arrived in Vienna, he made Karl rearrange and put his books in order. It was seemingly a time-consuming assignment, and Karl made several diary entries about the work.[44] On one day, he recorded no less than 100 different publications on law, administration, finance and commerce.[45] After Zinzendorf's death, Karl incorporated his brother's library into his own collection of books. Both have been lost. In 1775, his personal secretary compiled a catalogue and in 1781 Karl began to put together an alphabetical index. However, as they are also lost, so it is impossible to know how many works the library contained.[46] In Karl's obituary, the Viennese newspaper *Vaterländische Blätter für den österreichischen Kaiserstaat* noted that 'the library, which was remarkably well arranged, comprised several thousand volumes of all strands of sciences.'[47] In her analysis of the diaries, Lebeau also attempted to convey the content of Karl's library. The latter, she concludes, was a collection of works dominated by French, English and German texts.[48] The thematic emphasis of his readings was political economy followed by history and literary subjects.[49]

The Circle Around Zinzendorf

Zinzendorf's formation showed a strong engagement with other economic thinkers and their ideas. Zinzendorf was interested in discourse. He closely followed the debates in France and the German states on currency debasements and the different arguments and intellectual approaches of

[43] Diary of Karl Zinzendorf, 25 October 1768, HHStA. Ian Simpson Ross mentions this episode, but erroneously speculates that Hume received the information in Vienna from Ludwig Zinzendorf: Ian Simpson Ross, 'The Emergence of David Hume as a Political Economist: A Biographical Sketch' in Carl Wennerlind and Margaret Schabas (eds.), *David Hume's Political Economy* (Abingdon and New York: Routledge, 2008), pp. 31–48, at p. 43.

[44] Diary of Karl Zinzendorf, 13, 14, 16 October, 19 November 1761, HHStA.

[45] Diary of Karl Zinzendorf, 18 November 1761, HHStA.

[46] Klingenstein et al. (eds.), *Europäische Aufklärung*, vol. 1, p. 19.

[47] *Vaterländische Blätter für den österreichischen Kaiserstaat*, Wednesday, 27 January 1813, p. 46 in 'Nekrolog auf das Jahr 1813. Karl Graf und Herr von Zinzendorf', pp. 43–6, HHStA. See also Klingenstein et al. (eds.), *Europäische Aufklärung*, vol. 1, pp. 49–50.

[48] Lebeau, *Aristocrates*, pp. 142–43.

[49] Ibid., p. 150. Karl was also an avid reader of international newspapers: ibid., p. 149.

the writers of the circle of Gournay. While working in government, Zinzendorf looked for intellectual collaboration.[50]

He attracted a small circle of like-minded individuals with whom he would discuss his ideas and seek support to implement them. Like Zinzendorf, the members of the circle came mostly from aristocratic families, were career politicians with senior positions in government and had close connections with Kaunitz. They had direct involvement in economic policies, and some had interests in industry. The circle around Zinzendorf was a loose association of individuals which developed without patronage. The circle had an important social function and discussions were conducted on the same level. From Karl's diaries, it seems that exchanges were often oral, taking place over lunches and dinners.[51] It is probable that Zinzendorf and his friends also held informal discussions at work and at the *salons*.[52] Clearly, Karl Zinzendorf was a key intellectual partner for his brother, as was Kaunitz, who also often hosted dinners. With Count Philipp Josef Sinzendorf (1726–1788), the head of the commerce agency of Lower Austria, Zinzendorf debated questions of state credit. Sinzendorf was also well read and familiar with European economic thought, including the writing of Melon.[53] Other important individuals were Count Franz Xaver Wolf Rosenberg, Count Georg Adam Starhemberg and Baron Friedrich Binder von Krieglstein. Like Zinzendorf, they were writers of memoranda, proposals and reports for government purposes who spoke several languages and endeavoured to introduce proven foreign practices into the monarchy. Rosenberg and Binder also became close friends and advisers of Karl Zinzendorf.[54]

Rosenberg (1723–1796) was a cousin of Kaunitz and came from a distinguished aristocratic family in Carinthia with interests in local iron production facilities.[55] At a young age, Rosenberg moved to Vienna and, after

[50] See the section 'Projectors', where this is clear from Zinzendorf's engagement with Caratto.

[51] For an example of a typical lunch in July 1779, its attendees and the topics of conversations, see Klingenstein et al. (eds.), *Europäische Aufklärung*, vol. 1, pp. 169–70.

[52] See ibid., pp. 171–75, for a description of three significant Viennese *salons*.

[53] Diary of Karl Zinzendorf, 21 November 1761 and 20 March 1763, HHStA. On Sinzendorf's free trade efforts, see Adolf Beer, 'Studien zur Geschichte der österreichischen Volkswirtschaft unter Maria Theresia. Die österreichische Industriepolitik', *AÖG* 81 (1895), pp. 1–133, at p. 74.

[54] Klingenstein et al. (eds.), *Europäische Aufklärung*, vol. 1, pp. 161–62.

[55] Ibid., p. 162.

his studies, entered the Austrian diplomatic service. His junior posting in London shaped his liberal economic thinking. Rosenberg's extensive career in politics included ambassadorial appointments to Copenhagen and Madrid, and the position of minister of Grand Duke Leopold in Florence. His last appointment was as lord chamberlain in charge of overseeing the household of Joseph II and in managing the court theatre. Rosenberg's easy-going personality and cosmopolitan outlook earned him the trust of Maria Theresa, Joseph and Leopold.[56] Zinzendorf also admired his good disposition and talents.[57] During his posting in Florence, Rosenberg was mindful to keep close relations with the government in Vienna.[58] With Kaunitz, he discussed ways to improve Tuscan state credit through the issue of public paper and to increase trade in agricultural products. He was, Klingenstein surmised, a discreet yet pivotal figure for the diffusion of physiocratic ideas among the ruling elite in Vienna.[59]

Starhemberg (1724–1807) was a close friend of Rosenberg.[60] He, too, was a relative of Kaunitz,[61] from a family of diplomats and decorated Austrian soldiers.[62] His father had served as the emperor's envoy to the English court, and the English king George I was Georg Adam's godfa-

[56] Adam Wandruszka, *Leopold II. Erzherzog von Österreich, Grossherzog von Toskana, König von Ungarn und Böhmen, Römischer Kaiser* (2 vols, Vienna, 1965), vol. 1, pp. 173–74.

[57] Letter of Ludwig Zinzendorf to Karl Zinzendorf, Vienna, 8 January 1765, vol. 64, DOZA.

[58] Wandruszka, *Leopold II.*, vol. 1, pp. 180–82.

[59] Klingenstein et al. (eds.), *Europäische Aufklärung*, vol. 1, p. 163. Rather than trade, the physiocrats emphasised the primacy of agriculture and advocated radical economic policy plans to achieve in the long-term self-sufficiency. For a discussion of physiocracy, see Loïc Charles and Philippe Steiner, 'Entre Montesquieu et Rousseau. La Physiocratie parmi les origines intellectuelles de la Révolution française', *Études Jean-Jacques Rousseau*, 11 (1999/2000), pp. 83–159.

[60] Wandruszka, *Leopold II.*, vol. 1, pp. 174–75.

[61] Kaunitz's wife, Maria Ernestine Starhemberg, was a granddaughter of Georg Adam's great-uncle, Gundaker Thomas Graf von Starhemberg. The latter was president of the Court Chamber of Charles VI and held in high regard by Kaunitz, l. See the letter of Kaunitz to Ignaz Koch, Fontainebleau, 24 October 1751, in *Correspondance Secrète entre le Comte A.W. Kaunitz-Rietberg, ambassadeur imperial à Paris, et le Baron Ignaz de Koch, secrétaire de l'Impératrice Marie-Thérèse, 1750–1752*, ed. Hans Schlitter (Paris, 1899), p. 139.

[62] Reinhard Eichwalder, 'Georg Adam Fürst Starhemberg (1724–1807), Diplomat, Staatsmann und Grundherr' (University of Vienna, 1969), p. 11. More recently, Georg Heilingsetzer, 'Aristokratie, Aufklärung und Architektur. Fürst Georg Adam Starhemberg und die Neugestaltung des Schlosses Eferding durch Andreas Zach', *Mitteilungen des oberösterreichischen Landesarchivs*, 13 (1981), pp. 249–87.

ther.[63] Like Kaunitz and Zinzendorf, Starhemberg studied law in Leipzig. He also developed an interest in questions of trade.[64] In 1750, Starhemberg began his diplomatic career in Lisbon and was held in high esteem by diplomats there.[65] From Portugal, he moved to France where he worked with Zinzendorf. There, Starhemberg became an *élève* of Kaunitz.[66] He was also mentored by Kaunitz, who took promising young men like Starhemberg and Zinzendorf under his professional wing and moulded them into skilful officials of the Habsburg monarchy. In 1754, Starhemberg was appointed minister to France and in 1756, in recognition of the *renversement des alliances*, he was promoted to ambassador.

In addition to political affairs, Starhemberg was interested in the economy. In 1757, he wrote a proposal about extending commerce between France and the monarchy and in 1763 negotiated with a French group to get them involved in farming the tobacco tax revenues of Lower Austria.[67] He also summarised the key elements of a 'very popular' and 'clever' French health scheme to get the government in Vienna interested in implementing a similar system.[68] Maria Theresa admired Starhemberg's abilities, and so did Leopold II.[69] In 1766, he was set to progress further professionally and replace Kaunitz in the *Staatsrat*. Kaunitz, however, did not move aside. In 1770, after Cobenzl's death, Kaunitz negotiated for Starhemberg to become minister plenipotentiary in the Austrian Netherlands. While working in Brussels, Starhemberg pursued his interest in commerce, in particular with North America. He followed a liberal trade agenda and rejected general import and export restrictions. Joseph, a critic of Starhemberg, made every effort to remove him from his post. Due to Maria Theresa's resistance, it took until 1783 before Starhemberg finally left Brussels. He came back to Vienna and was given the title of first

[63] Hans Schlitter, 'Starhemberg, Georg Adam Fürst von/seit 1765', p. 471, in *Allgemeine Deutsche Biographie*, vol. 35 (1893), pp. 471–473.

[64] Eichwalder, 'Starhemberg', p. 16.

[65] Ibid., p. 21.

[66] Letter of Ignaz Koch to Kaunitz, Vienna, 26 August 1752 in *Correspondance Secrète*, ed. Hans Schlitter, pp. 269–70.

[67] Eichwalder, 'Starhemberg', pp. 111–12.

[68] Starhemberg called it 'Plan d'une maison d'association, dans laquelle au moyen d'une somme très modique chaque associé s'assurera dans l'état de maladie toutes les sortes de secours qu'on peut désirer': letter of Georg Adam Starhemberg to Kaunitz, Paris, 19 August 1754, Karton 92, Frankreich Berichte 1754, HHStA.

[69] Wandruszka, *Leopold II.*, vol. 1, p. 329.

Obersthofmeister.[70] The same year, he was gifted extensive estates in Lower Austria from his older brother, Count Johann Ernst Starhemberg. He added them to his existing landed possessions and, like Zinzendorf, implemented detailed accounting methods to improve the management of his large estate.[71]

Binder (1708–1782) was Kaunitz's closest friend and confidant. He studied law in Giessen and met Kaunitz in the late 1730s. The latter made him his personal secretary and over the years Binder became Kaunitz's indispensable aide. He became *Staatsreferendar* in the State Chancellery and drafted memoranda and working papers for Kaunitz. In 1762, he was promoted to membership of the *Staatsrat*.[72] There, he took a strong interest in the monarchy's activities in commerce.[73] In 1771, he was forced out by Joseph II and moved to the Chancellery of State.[74] Fiercely loyal, he remained with Kaunitz and continued to support as well as influence his policies.[75] Binder was open to foreign ideas. He was a proponent of the Oriental Academy, created in 1754, to teach oriental languages to future government diplomats. He also wrote about aspects of the history of the monarchy and on religion.[76]

In government, Kaunitz argued forcefully for the adoption of Zinzendorf's ideas. So did Binder and Starhemberg, who defended Zinzendorf's peacetime proposals on finance.[77] In 1767, during discussions on finance in the *Staatsrat*, Zinzendorf noted Starhemberg's support and 'friendship'. After having reviewed in detail Zinzendorf's

[70] Schlitter, 'Starhemberg', pp. 472–73. On Starhemberg's career, see also Szabo, *Kaunitz and enlightened absolutism 1753–1780* (Cambridge, 1994), pp. 61–5.

[71] Eichwalder, 'Starhemberg', pp. 203, 206–7.

[72] Alfred Ritter von Arneth, 'Friedrich Binder von Krieglstein', in *Allgemeine Deutsche Biographie*, vol. 2 (1875), pp. 648–49.

[73] Letter of Ludwig Zinzendorf to Karl Zinzendorf, Vienna, 13 September 1766, vol. 64, DOZA.

[74] Szabo, *Kaunitz*, p. 108.

[75] See, for example, in 1780 Binder's influence on Kaunitz in backing the plan for a new navy, ibid., pp. 301–2.

[76] Birgit Strimitzer, *Die Freiherrn Binder von Krieglstein. Studien zur Genealogie und Besitzgeschichte einer elsäßisch-österreichischen Adelsfamilie unter besonderer Berücksichtigung der Bedeutung einzelner Familienmitglieder in der Zeit Maria Theresias und der Ära Metternich* (Graz, 1998), pp. 84–5. Binder's book on the monarchy was: Johann Friedrich Binder von Krieglstein, *Abhandlungen über die Vorzüge des durchlauchtigsten Erzhauses Österreich bey Reichsbelehnungen* (Vienna, 1780).

[77] Letter of Ludwig Zinzendorf to Karl Zinzendorf, Vienna, 10 March 1767, vol. 64, DOZA; Dickson, *Finance and Government*, vol. 2, p. 74; Eichwalder, 'Starhemberg', p. 132.

arguments on the bank and the stock exchange, he came out in defence of the proposal.[78] Lines of argument, however, were not always uniform, and individuals in the circle debated ideas and implementation. Binder and Zinzendorf had discussions on the new institutions for state credit.[79] Starhemberg and Zinzendorf disagreed on the consolidation of the national debt. Starhemberg was sceptical about offering new bonds to creditors and rejected Zinzendorf's proposal to make existing bondholders change their holdings into new uniform government paper. These changes, he thought, were important and should not be forced on creditors. He finally came around to Zinzendorf's view when the latter argued that the new paper would prevent fraudulent activities by investors.[80] With Rosenberg, there is good evidence of sophisticated discussions on economic theory.[81] On a text on '*grande finance*' written by Zinzendorf, Rosenberg offered improvements on the structure to emphasise the ideas of Locke, Law, Melon and Dutot. He suggested a long, baroque-style title for Zinzendorf's work which would announce the main ideas. The chapters, Rosenberg thought, should be arranged according to the order in which the arguments were presented.[82] Of the circle, Zinzendorf probably produced most of the output and then circulated the texts and proposals among his friends. The emphasis was not on set arguments, but rather on 'thinking' and open debates on ideas and institutions. At the same time, towards other members in the administration who resisted liberal economic arguments, the individuals around Zinzendorf maintained a common front and largely supported each other's arguments.

A comparison with the group of writers around Gournay in France in the 1750s can help to clarify the nature of Zinzendorf's circle. The French writers pursued a radical initiative to open up the debate on political econ-

[78] Letter of Ludwig Zinzendorf to Karl Zinzendorf, Vienna, 10 March 1767. See also Pettenegg (ed.), *Selbstbiographien*, p. 112; Hock, Bidermann (eds.), *Staatsrath*, p. 85; Beer, 'Die Staatschulden und die Ordnung des Staatshaushaltes unter Maria Theresia', *AÖG* 82 (1894), pp. 1–135, at p. 58.

[79] Letter of Ludwig Zinzendorf to Karl Zinzendorf, Vienna, 17 July 1766, vol. 64, DOZA.

[80] Eichwalder, 'Starhemberg', pp. 130–31.

[81] Letter of Franz Xaver Wolf Rosenberg to Ludwig Zinzendorf, [undated], Archiv Zinzendorf, Karton 38, NÖLA.

[82] Rosenberg's suggestion was: 'Betrachtungen Uber den Reichthum eines Lands Und wie dieser darinnen vermehret werden könte Wobey von den wahren Verrichtungs Miteln, alß Von der Handlung, von dem Geld, Von dem Credit, Von dem Wechsel und Von den Banquen außführlich gehandelt werden soll.' See letter of Franz Xaver Wolf Rosenberg to Ludwig Zinzendorf, undated, ibid. Zinzendorf's original title is unknown.

omy.[83] The circle was a mix of about 20 individuals from a variety of backgrounds. The core of the circle—Jean Gabriel Montaudoin de la Touche, Dangeul, Forbonnais and Gournay himself—had a strong social and geographical connection: they came from merchant families in Brittany. The other members had a commercial background and were administrators or academics. The success of Gournay's enterprise also attracted clergymen, who contributed their writings for financial gain.

The debate on economic issues among the writers constituted an important dynamic of the circle. Gournay was concerned with the quality of the arguments and attached little importance to the seniority of contributors. He played the role of anchor for the exchange of ideas and wrote little himself. The aim of the circle was twofold: first, to make economic knowledge accessible outside the confines of the French court; and second, to introduce new ideas to the discussions in government. In these ways, they sought to influence decision-making and get their views accepted by the court. Several writers were involved in university life, and so the circle, led by Montaudoin and Louis-Paul Abeille, created an academic institution dedicated to the analysis of economic questions in Brittany in 1757 and known as the *Société d'agriculture, de commerce et des arts de Bretagne*. An important advantage of Gournay's initiative was the strong support it had from senior officials and economic administrators. They included Guillaume Chrétien de Lamoignon de Malesherbes (1721–1794), director of the royal library and responsible for censorship, and the controller general of finances, Étienne de Silhouette (1709–1767).

The French writers translated English and Spanish texts to disseminate ideas from other nations on political economy, in particular on the advantages of commerce.[84] To express their views in the national context, they

[83] For Gournay's circle, I follow the interpretation of Loïc Charles, 'Le Cercle de Gournay: usages culturels et pratiques savants' in Loïc Charles, Frédéric Lefebvre and Christine Théré (eds.), *Le Cercle de Vincent Gournay. Savoirs économiques et pratiques administratives en France au milieu du XVIIIe siècle* (Paris: Institut National D'Études Démographiques, 2011), pp. 63–87, On French censorship during the 1750s and the circle's activities, see also Antoin E. Murphy, *Richard Cantillon: Entrepreneur and Economist* (Oxford, 1986), pp. 299–321.

[84] On the use of translations of economic works in the eighteenth century, see Reinert, 'The Empire of Emulation: A Quantitative Analysis of Economic Translations in the European World, 1500–1849' in Sophus A. Reinert and Pernille Røge (eds.), *The Political Economy of Empire in the Early Modern World* (Basingstoke: Palgrave Macmillan, 2013). For the Gournay circle's discussion of French commercial policy and its impact on the creation of a public sphere, see Antonella Alimento, 'La Concurrence comme Politique Moderne. La

significantly re-wrote the original works adding chapters and peritext of commentary. They had good language skills and the ability to get hold of foreign literature. Their output was considerable, and topics covered agriculture, manufacturing, trade as well as economic and financial policy. With the help of influential administrators, the circle was able to publish detailed information and statistics on royal policies. In *Recherches et Considérations sur les Finances de la France*, Forbonnais used material from the royal archives. In *Divers mémoires, sur le commerce recueillis du même auteur*, he published official papers on industrial policy and included criticism of government documents.

Evidently, the French initiative was much more extensive and ambitious than the activities of the circle around Zinzendorf. The group around Gournay was much larger, individuals had diverse backgrounds and were eager to publish on all aspects of political economy. Zinzendorf and his friends did not follow the same systematic campaign of writing. For one thing, their work in government did not give them enough time, they were less organised, and political necessities often dictated the topics of their output. Zinzendorf achieved a larger impact in a smaller administration.[85] Unlike Gournay, Zinzendorf was the most prolific writer among his friends, and, except for Karl's German translation of Turgot, he read, commented upon and translated works himself, rather than developing a programme to encourage others in his circle to produce texts that he considered important.

However, there were also striking similarities between the two initiatives. Like Gournay, Zinzendorf acted as the anchor of his circle, and individuals debated questions of finance and the economy with him. Both circles placed the emphasis on open discussions. They took established ideas from rival nations and introduced them to the discourse in government. Both Gournay and Zinzendorf used translations to propagate their ideas and, as set out in Chap. 4, Zinzendorf's *Gedanken vom Gelde* had a similar structure to Le Blanc's translation of Hume's *Political Discourses*. Finally, within each circle, the social background of

Contribution de L'école de Gournay à la naissance d'une sphère publique dans la France des années 1750–1760' in Jesús Astigarraga and Javier Usoz (eds.), *L'économie politique et la sphère publique dans le débat des Lumières* (Madrid: Collection de la Casa de Velázquez, 2013), pp. 213–27.

[85] On the growth of the government administration under Maria Theresa, see the section 'Debates over Institutional Reform'.

members was similar. The core group around Gournay had a similar professional background and came from the same geographic area in France. For their part, the individuals around Zinzendorf were all career politicians who were trained by or had close relationships with Kaunitz. They were of aristocratic background, and very involved or interested in economic affairs. Zinzendorf and Starhemberg both owned landed estates in Lower Austria, and Rosenberg's family had manufacturing facilities in Carinthia.

Projectors

The government's struggle to come to terms with the economic demands of the military confrontations with Prussia opened the door to projectors. They offered their 'projects' as new sources of revenue to the ruler. Projectors were often interlopers who used their practical knowledge of the economy and finance to gain entry to the court. Once in established positions, they would turn these economic projects to their own advantage and strive to create a privileged position of wealth and influence. In his writings, Justi warned about *Plusmacher*, the label he gave to projectors.[86] The latter, he argued, completely disregarded the well-being of the population and were only interested in maximising revenues for the ruler and themselves.[87] Projectors could be distinguished through their different ambitions. Some, whom Justi called *Universal Plusmacher*, wanted to manage the revenues for the state, which included its financial instruments as well as taxes from salt, tobacco and the new coinage mint. Others, the *Particular Plusmacher*, had more limited aspirations. They were only interested in gaining a dominant economic position in a province or town. Typically, this would be done by weakening local competing merchants and manufacturers through taxes and tolls.[88] Justi strongly criticised the

[86] Johann Heinrich Gottlob von Justi, *System des Finanzwesens, nach dem vernünftigen, aus dem Endzweck der bürgerlichen Gesellschaften, und aus der Natur aller Quellen der Einkünfte des Staates hergeleiteten Grundsätzen und Regeln* (Halle, 1766), pp. 28–44, 83–94; 'Gedanken von Projecten und Plusmachern' in *Gesammelte politische und Finanzschriften* (3 vols; vols 1 and 2, Copenhagen and Leipzig, 1761; vol. 3, idem., 1764), vol. 1, pp. 256–81; 'Abhandlung von dem so genannten Plusmachen, oder der schädlichen Art, die Einkünfte des Staates zu vermehren' in ibid., vol. 3, pp. 409–38.

[87] Justi, *System des Finanzwesens*, pp. 84–5.

[88] Ibid., pp. 90–4.

system of tax farming and rejected the projectors' relentless drive to increase taxes without concern for the financial situation of ordinary people.[89]

Under Charles VI, Jews were heavily involved in state finance.[90] Maria Theresa, led by strong anti-Jewish sentiments, reduced the influence of Jewish financiers and increasingly used Christians. For alternative sources of finance, she turned to the Warehousers and Wholesalers in Vienna, the majority of whom were Germans.[91] In addition, part of Maria Theresa's governing style was to solicit advice from individuals outside the established circle to get new perspectives for dealing with particular issues. In this respect, she would readily consider ideas from projectors. The latter were numerous and circled the court in Vienna to find an opening. They were also resourceful. They sold the same idea to various rulers and sometimes decided to join forces in order to increase their chances of success. The most direct entry was to offer the government proficiency in tax farming. The more ambitious schemes included extensive agricultural development plans, a variety of smaller and larger trade companies, and the creation of financial instruments and institutions to manage state credit.

Projectors had various backgrounds. Some were outsiders willing to take large risks to quickly find fortune. Because of financial bankruptcy, Jacques Accarias de Serionne (1706–1792) fled France and offered his services to the monarchy.[92] He began his work in the Austrian Netherlands by publishing the economic periodical *Journal de Commerce*.[93] Thereafter, in 1769, he joined forces with another French projector, Chevalier de Canneau de Beauregard, who had previously failed in implementing large-

[89] Ibid., p. 88. However, in practice, Justi acted like a projector. While living in Vienna, he acquired an economic interest in a silver mine in Lower Austria. As the mine was less profitable than Justi had expected, he sold his shares back to the government: Ulrich Adam, 'Justi and the Post-Montesquieu French Debate on Commercial Nobility in 1756' in Jürgen Georg Backhaus (ed.), *The Beginnings of Political Economy: Johann Heinrich Gottlob von Justi* (New York: Springer, 2009), pp. 75–99, at p. 38. Subsequently, Justi mismanaged the iron industry of Frederick II for personal gain and was imprisoned: Andre Wakefield, *The Disordered Police State: German Cameralism as Science and Practice* (Chicago, IL and London: University of Chicago Press, 2009), pp. 81–110.

[90] Dickson, *Finance and Government*, vol. 1, pp. 140–44.

[91] Ibid., pp. 153–57.

[92] Hervé Hasquin, 'Jacques Accarias de Serionne et le *Journal de Commerce*. Un publiciste français au service de l'Autriche' in Hervé Hasquin, *Population, commerce et religion au siècle des Lumières* (Éditions de L'Université de Brussel, 2008), pp. 155–67, at p. 156.

[93] See also the section 'The Public Sphere'.

scale population resettlements along the Volga in Russia. Together, they offered Vienna a few thousand stranded colonists from Canneau's Russian enterprise for settlement in Hungary, thereby promising to increase the economic output of the Kingdom. Serionne and Canneau also hoped to raise Dutch finance for a new trading company based in Amsterdam which would facilitate the transfer of settlers and support exports from Hungary to the West. In 1769, following inconclusive debates between the *Staatsrat*, the *Hofkammer* and the *Staatswirtschaftsdeputation* about the merit of this scheme, the empress decided to end the discussions with Canneau and Serionne.[94] A similar 'recycled' enterprise was the trading company of the Dutch merchant Willem Bolts (1740–1808). After having failed with an Indian commerce company in England, he sold the same idea to the monarchy. Again, it proved unsuccessful and ended in bankruptcy in 1785.[95]

In finance, the Hamburg banker Johann Gottlieb Gerhard (1719–1789) promoted debt schemes, and the Tuscan Ranieri de Calzabigi (1714–1795) planned to set up state lotteries. In 1762, Gerhard, who was business minded and risk loving, offered the government a tontine loan in return for a success fee of 2 per cent, payable to him in advance. Not only did Gerhard refuse to disclose the details of the operation in advance of receiving the go-ahead from the state, he also sought to extend the fee arrangement to his heirs. Maria Theresa rejected his demands. Gerhard's second proposal, which he set up with a similar success fee, involved the repayment of 100 million *florins* of government debt by issuing notes with high interest.[96] This time, to examine the plan, Maria Theresa decided to set up a government commission. The discussions began in early 1766 and lasted for four months. Zinzendorf, who was a member of the commission, which also included Heinrich Blümegen and Hatzfeld, warned of the dangers of disclosing details of the monarchy's state credit position to outsiders with vested interests. At the same time, he recognised that the credibility of any plan to issue new debt could only be tested if it was based on actual

[94] Konrad Schünemann, *Österreichs Bevölkerungspolitik unter Maria Theresia* (Berlin, 1935), vol. 1, pp. 299–302. No second volume has been published. For notes on Serionne's views on agriculture in Hungary, see [Anonymous], 'Anmerkungen zu Serionne', [undated], vol. 27, Nachlaß Zinzendorf, fols 28r–32v, HHStA.

[95] Szabo, *Kaunitz*, pp. 144–45.

[96] Lorenz Mikoletzky, 'Der Hamburger Bankier Johann Gottlieb Gerhard und der Versuch der Staatsschuldentilgung in Österreich (1762–1766)' *Mitteilungen des österreichischen Staatsarchivs*, 25 (1972), pp. 277–288, at pp. 278, 281–83.

data. The commission concluded that the bonds would not be favourably received by the market and would eventually trade at discounts to par values. On 29 April 1766, Gerhard's proposal was dismissed.[97]

Calzabigi was persuaded by Serionne to set up a lottery in Brussels. They had met in Paris where Calzabigi was the secretary to the marquis de L'Hôpital, the former ambassador to Naples. Serionne forcefully promoted Calzabigi's ideas with Cobenzl.[98] In his proposal to Cobenzl, Calzabigi, together with his brother, demanded complete control over the lottery's management as well as attractive financial remunerations and pensions. Initially, the local government in Brussels as well as Kaunitz hesitated about the lottery. Eventually, Calzabigi succeeded in persuading Cobenzl of the merits of the new enterprise and was subsequently sent to Vienna to make his case directly to Kaunitz. Calzabigi's presentation must have made a strong impression on the Chancellor. Kaunitz changed his mind, and on 20 May 1760, he promoted the idea in a memorandum to Maria Theresa praising the Calzabigi brothers' abilities and honesty.[99] The lottery began in March 1761, but was unpopular with the public. Its revenues were disappointing and by the end of the year, Cobenzl decided to remove the Calzabigi brothers from their posts. They resigned in January 1762, but succeeded in obtaining good pensions.[100] Other projectors, including Caratto, a military man by profession, and Pasquale Ricci (1721–1791), a commercial counsellor in Trieste, had larger ambitions. They drafted grand plans to improve commerce and finance in the monarchy.[101]

The second type of projector had an established position in the monarchy and acted more opportunistically. These projectors were typically government officials or Warehousers and industrialists who seized on

[97] Ibid., pp. 287–88. During the discussions with Gerhard, another projector, Paul Beck, intervened and claimed that the ideas on debt restructuring had been stolen from him. Beck was a merchant from Strasburg who had fallen into disrepute in France: ibid., pp. 284–86.

[98] Georges Bigwood, 'La Loterie aux Pays Bas Autrichiens', *Annales de la Societé Royale d'Archéologie de Bruxelles*, 26 (1917), pp. 53–134, at p. 75.

[99] Ibid., pp. 76–85. In 1760, Calzabigi also wrote a long memorandum on the commerce and the economy of the monarchy. For a summary, see Dickson, *Finance and Government*, vol. 2, pp. 45–6. Karl read Calzabigi's works at his brother's house: Diary of Karl Zinzendorf, 7 October 1761 and 29 July 1763, HHStA.

[100] Bigwood, 'La Loterie', pp. 90–4.

[101] On Ricci's plan for a note issuing bank, see Dickson, *Finance and Government*, vol. 2, p. 45; for Ricci's biographical details, see Klingenstein et al. (eds.) *Europäische Aufklärung*, vol. 4, p. 476. On Caratto, see below.

opportunities to make money from government operations.[102] Count Antal Grassalkovich (1694–1771) was the President of the Hungarian Chamber. Coming from the lower nobility, he was astute in using his position to maximise personal gain. Grassalkovich competed directly with the colonisation initiatives of the state and succeeded in diverting German settlers who had been recruited by the government to his own lands in Hungary.[103] In Bohemia, Count Josef Kinsky (1705–1780), the head of the royal trade council, decided in 1767 to set up a company to promote the trade in Bohemian cloth with Spain and through this venture attempted to increase his personal wealth. At the outset, the empress considered a financial investment. However, the company swiftly became a victim of fraud. Its management, based in Prague, proved to be incompetent and negligent. It had no understanding of commerce and refused to leave the city to visit customers and industries in the province. Eventually, the treasurer took control of the business. He defrauded the company, and it had to be liquidated. This was a surprising outcome, especially since Kinsky's

[102] Some Warehousers devised plans to reorganise domestic production hoping thereby to defend their interests and win new business from competitors. In 1770, Joseph Paul Weinbrenner, who farmed Austrian customs revenues, proposed a 'system' which would favour large industrial enterprises over smaller ones, introduced barriers to new manufacturing units and grouped together trade activities while curtailing the expansion of industry in Hungary. See Karl Pribram, *Geschichte der österreichischen Gewerbepolitik von 1740 bis 1860: aufgrund der Akten vol. 1: 1740 bis 1798* (Leipzig, 1907), pp. 204–5 and Dickson, *Finance and Government*, vol. 1, p. 436. Weinbrenner probably also published articles on the importance of a public bank for commerce and industry: Herbert Matis, *Die Schwarzenberg-Bank. Kapitalbildung und Industriefinanzierung in den habsburgischen Erblanden 1787–1830* (Vienna: Verlag der österreichischen Akademie der Wissenschaften, 2005) pp. 68–9. In 1783, he was the first to ship eight boxes of produce from the monarchy to North America: Beer, 'Die österreichische Handelspolitik unter Maria Theresia und Joseph II', *AÖG* 86 (1898), pp. 1–204, at p. 112. On Weinbrenner's business activities, see Ingrid Mittenzwei, *Zwischen Gestern und Morgen. Wiens frühe Bourgeoisie an der Wende vom 18. zum 19. Jahrhundert* (Vienna, 1998), p. 108.

[103] William O'Reilly, 'Alluding to Alternatives. Sourcing and Securing Colonists in Eighteenth-Century Germany' in Claudia Schnurmann and Hartmut Lehmann (eds.), *Atlantic Understandings: Essays on European and American History in Honour of Werner Wellenreuther* (Hamburg, 2006), pp. 159–83, at pp. 170–75. On the short-lived government-supported initiative to set up a trading company to promote Hungarian produce, see Eckhart Ferenc, *A becsi udvargazdazagpolitikaja Magyarorszagon Mária Terézia korában* (Budapest, 1922), pp. 367–68.

enterprise was supported by two local bankers, including the respected Joseph Anton Zehendner von Reisdorf.[104]

Johann Fries (1719–1785) and Johann von Thys (1715–1773) were examples of prolific and successful projectors in the monarchy. Fries' family from Mulhouse was Calvinist and he became a Warehouser in 1751. Subsequently, he set up numerous manufacturing activities and began commerce with Turkey. Fries' direct operations with the state were extensive: he bought bonds of the Estate Credit Deputation for the government to support their prices, and paid himself a handsome commission of 0.5 per cent for each purchased obligation.[105] He was instrumental in trading silver *thalers* in the Levant, negotiating and administering foreign subsidies and loans, and managing the tobacco monopoly. Fries not only made a fortune for himself, but his services were also officially recognised by the government. He was made a baron in 1783.[106]

Thys was a wealthy manufacturer of cloth who was also very much involved with initiatives of the state. In 1762, he received the privileged status of a wholesale trader and benefitted from special tax concessions.[107] He was held in high regard by the rulers, and in 1765, on their way to Innsbruck, the empress and Francis Stephen made a personal visit to his manufacturing facility in Klagenfurt.[108] Thys received important state subsidies and astutely expanded his operations.[109] His involvement in the domestic economy was significant and extended beyond cloth manufac-

[104] Joseph Schreyer, *Kommerz, Fabriken und Manufakturen des Königreichs Böhmen* (Prague and Leipzig, 1790), pp. 86–90. Schreyer's account is summarised by Amand Paudler, 'Graf Josef Kinsky, Herr auf Bürgstein und Schwoyka', in *Jahresbericht des kaiserlich königlichen Staatsobergymnasium in Böhmisch-Leipa* (Böhmisch Leipa, 1885), pp. 1–47, at pp. 32–3. On Zehendner's financial company, see Dickson, *Finance and Government*, vol. 1, pp. 161–62.

[105] Gross, 'Die ständische Kredit-Deputation und der Plan eines erbländischen Nationalkredites (Ein Beitrag zur Finanzpolitik unter Maria Theresia)' (unpublished Ph.D. dissertation, University of Vienna, 1935), pp. 50–1; on Fries' role, see also Dickson, *Finance and Government*, vol. 2, p. 136.

[106] Dickson, *Finance and Government*, vol. 1, pp. 172–77. On Fries' career and relationship with Kaunitz, see Christian Steeb, 'Johann Fries (1719–1785). Vom Einwanderer zum Staatsbankier und Vertrauten des Staatskanzler' in Grete Klingenstein and Franz A.J. Szabo (eds.), *Staatskanzler Wenzel Anton von Kaunitz-Rietberg 1711–1794. Neue Perspektiven zu Politik und Kultur der europäischen Aufklärung* (Graz, 1996), pp. 305–23.

[107] Dickson, *Finance and Government*, vol. 1, pp. 154, 433–34.

[108] Klingenstein et al. (eds.), *Europäische Aufklärung*, vol. 4, p. 571.

[109] Beer, 'Die österreichische Industriepolitik', pp. 104–5.

turing. He suggested reforms to agricultural ownership.[110] In 1765, he drafted the by-laws of the first agricultural society (*Ackerbaugesellschaft*) located in Carinthia. This was a special measure designed by the empress to revive agriculture after the Seven Years War, and it became the model for other agricultural companies.[111] Thys also supported the efforts of Maria Theresa to introduce spinning schools for children between the ages of seven to fifteen and, given his expertise in dairy production was encouraged to propose enhancements to the manufacture of cheese.[112] On 20 April 1765, in recognition of his services, Thys was ennobled.[113]

The government, not knowing what was most likely to achieve results, showed a great readiness to review, sometimes at length, a multitude of projects. As the fulcrum for economic arguments, Zinzendorf invariably engaged with the projectors. With some, he worked on financial issues unrelated to their proposals. Zinzendorf corresponded with Grassalkovich on the bond issue of the Estates Credit Deputation and on 24 August 1761 learned from him about its failure in Hungary.[114] With most other projectors, however, the core of the exchange centred on their economic plans presented to the government. Zinzendorf was often asked by Kaunitz and the empress to evaluate the arguments.[115] If a committee was set up by the government to review them, Zinzendorf would be part of it. He was receptive to new ideas which could address the monarchy's economic shortcomings, but, at the same time, wanted to carefully manage the dialogue with projectors to protect the interests of the state.

Zinzendorf's interactions in the 1750s and 1760s with Caratto and Thys, in particular, are illuminating. As an outsider, heavily in debt and with a large family to support, Caratto was very active in sending proposals on the economy and finance to Vienna. He was determined to make headway and secure good careers for himself and his children in the monarchy. He had previously been offered a minor position, but was hoping to have

[110] Szabo, *Kaunitz*, p. 162.

[111] Karl Dinklage, 'Gründung und Aufbau der theresianischen Ackerbaugesellschaften', *Zeitschrift für Agrargeschichte und Agrarsoziologie*, 1:13 (1965), pp. 200–11, at pp. 201–3. On the rise of agricultural societies in eighteenth-century Europe, see Koen Stapelbroek and Jani Marjanen (eds.). *The Rise of Economic Societies in the Eighteenth Century* (Basingstoke and New York: Palgrave Macmillan, 2012).

[112] Karl Dinklage, *Geschichte der Kärtner Landwirtschaft* (Klagenfurt, 1966), pp. 150–51.

[113] Karl Dinklage, 'Gründung und Aufbau', p. 201.

[114] Gross, 'Die ständische Kredit-Deputation', p. 58.

[115] Beer, 'Die Staatsschulden', p. 9.

a larger role in war finance by becoming a *conseiller aulique de guerre* in Haugwitz's *Directorium*.[116] Caratto argued that his writings had shown that he had a good grasp of the interactions between the military and economic aspects of warfare, and that he was well qualified to help the monarchy. He marketed himself to Zinzendorf as a 'lucid thinker whose ideas had guided others'.[117] In 1757, Caratto sent his proposals directly to Zinzendorf for review and asked him to intervene on his behalf with the empress.[118] He also announced to Zinzendorf the completion of his work on finance, 'General Abbildung des zu errichtenden Creditwesens', which was purposefully concise so that it made easy reading for a government commission.[119] Zinzendorf valued Caratto's ideas and, in turn, sent him his own writings for comment.[120] Their debate on economic ideas also gave rise to disagreements and their views differed on the most appropriate credit system to finance the war. Caratto, however, urged Zinzendorf to narrow their differences. Desperate for income, Caratto was hoping that the government would accept his proposal, and he pushed Zinzendorf to arrange for the commission to meet to review the arguments.[121]

In the early 1760s, in several documents, Caratto proposed the creation of a large trading company in the monarchy which would support industry and conduct business with the Levant. The company should also manage several state monopolies, particularly the supplies to the military as well as the tobacco and coin commerce. Support would be provided by a public bank based in Vienna, with branches in the provinces, to enable a good supply and a circulation of money. The bank, Caratto argued, would be

[116] Letter of Hermann von Caratto to Ludwig Zinzendorf, 17 April 1757, Archiv Zinzendorf, Karton 39, NÖLA. Caratto did not sign with his first name, and 'Hermann' is questionable: see Klueting, *Die Lehre von der Macht der Staaten: Das aussenpolitische Machtproblem in der 'politischen Wissenschaft' und in der praktischen Politik im 18. Jahrhundert* (Berlin, 1986), p. 204, footnote 243.

[117] Letter of Hermann von Caratto to Ludwig Zinzendorf, 17 April 1757, Archiv Zinzendorf, Karton 39, NÖLA.

[118] Letters of Hermann von Caratto to Ludwig Zinzendorf, 16 March 1757, 17 April 1757 and 16 May 1757, Archiv Zinzendorf, Karton 39, NÖLA.

[119] Letter of Caratto to Ludwig Zinzendorf, 16 May 1757, Archiv Zinzendorf, Karton 39, NÖLA.

[120] Letter of Hermann von Caratto to Ludwig Zinzendorf, 20 March 1757, Archiv Zinzendorf, Karton 39, NÖLA.

[121] Letter of Hermann von Caratto to Ludwig Zinzendorf, 25 June 1757, Archiv Zinzendorf, Karton 39, NÖLA.

guaranteed by the Estates of the hereditary lands.[122] His 'Plan général pour arranger aux pais héréditaires la double industrie, le commerce, les finances', built on 16 major principles, was one version of this scheme.[123] Caratto's ideas were debated at length in Vienna, but in 1767 finally rejected.[124] Zinzendorf thought that 'the principles were sound, but the application gigantic, impractical'.[125] His assessment was shared by Kaunitz.[126] One member of the *Staatsrat* described Caratto disparagingly as having been a projector for more than 40 years, propagating ideas which were common knowledge in schools and which did not deserve any attention.[127] The empress, however, felt that his contribution in trying to reform state finances should be honoured. She agreed to reward him a financial compensation which included a higher pension and payment of his debts.[128]

With Thys, who was held in high regard by the rulers, Zinzendorf developed an interesting working relationship. He used Thys' expertise in industry and commerce to add a large state-backed trading company to his peacetime financial proposals. The idea of a trading company was not new in the monarchy, but Zinzendorf's aim was to replicate the structure of

[122] Beer, 'Die Staatsschulden', p. 35.

[123] Hermann von Caratto, 1763, 'Plan général pour arranger aux pais héréditaires la double industrie, le commerce, les finances', Vorträge, Staatskanzlei, Karton 92, HHStA.

[124] Beer, 'Die Staatsschulden', pp. 37–8. For the minutes of the government commission of 22 December 1764, 18 and 23 May 1765 which considered Caratto's plan, see Zinzendorf, 'Allergnädigst, abgeforderter Vorschlag, die Einrichtung einer Börse zur Verhandlung der öffentlichen Papiere und eines Banco di Credito betreffend, Februar 1767', vol. 20, fol. 219r–227r, Nachlaß Zinzendorf, HHStA.

[125] Letter of Ludwig Zinzendorf to Karl Zinzendorf, Vienna, 17 January 1766, vol. 64, DOZA. Maria Theresa shared Zinzendorf's view: letter of Maria Theresa to Count Hatzfeld, 1766 in *Briefe der Kaiserin Maria Theresia*, Arneth (ed.), vol. 4, p. 295. For Zinzendorf, Caratto's ideas about the bank were more radical than his own. Caratto, Zinzendorf argued, wanted to issue bonds for 25m. fl., create bank branches in more cities, and use the bank's paper for all private transactions over 1000 fl. as well for parts of the cameral- and Vienna City Bank-related expenses: Zinzendorf, 'Schluß', in 'Allergnädigst, abgeforderter Vorschlag', fol. 174r.

[126] Beer, 'Die Staatsschulden', p. 36. For a discussion of the influence of Caratto's ideas on Kaunitz's writings, see Klueting, *Die Lehre von der Macht der Staaten*, pp. 204–8.

[127] Remark by Anton Stupan von Ehrenstein, 25 January 1765 in Beer, 'Die Staatsschulden', footnote 2, pp. 37–8.

[128] Karl Freiherrn Hock and Ignaz Bidermann, *Der österreichische Staatsrath (1760–1848): Eine geschichtliche Studie* (Vienna, 1879; reprint, 1972), p. 82.

Law's system with a trading company and a political bank.[129] The latter, Zinzendorf argued, had a defining role in increasing commerce and was the necessary requirement in preparation for a significant trading company. Ultimately, the bank should be joined to the trading company or even become part of it.[130] The strength of the trading company's operations, he thought, would significantly increase the confidence in the bank's paper. At the same time, commerce was a good source of income for warfare. By contrast with Law, Zinzendorf wanted to establish a political bank first and subsequently create a company for trade. His approach was probably driven by pragmatic considerations, given that a basic banking structure existed already in the hereditary provinces whereas a trading company was a challenging undertaking. Howsoever it was ultimately organised, the important principle was that it should replicate Law's structure was what counted. In a first step, the commercial activities would support the circulation of the bank's bonds. Eventually, the bank would become an instrument to facilitate the growth of the trading company, providing liquidity for the purchase of its shares.

In 1766, the empress invited Thys to take part in the deliberations on Caratto's financial plans.[131] During the discussions, Thys came out strongly in support of Zinzendorf's ideas to create a stock exchange together with a political bank.[132] On Zinzendorf's request, he wrote a proposal for a trading company. In February 1767, it was presented to ministers as the third element of Zinzendorf's financial scheme.[133] In 78 articles, Thys set

[129] Votum des Hofrechenkammer Präsidenten Zinzendorfs, 5 June 1765, vol. 87, fols 272v–273r, Nachlaß Zinzendorf, HHStA.

[130] In Law's scheme, the Royal Bank first became a 6 per cent shareholder in the Mississippi Trading Company before eventually merging with it: Antoin E. Murphy, *The Genesis of Macroeconomics: New Ideas from Sir William Petty to Henry Thornton* (Oxford, 2009), pp. 63, 68.

[131] Pettenegg (ed.), *Selbstbiographien*, pp. 103, 106; Beer, 'Die Staatsschulden', p. 37.

[132] Johann van Thys, [undated], 'Très humbles Réflexions de J. Thys sur le Projet d'une Bourse et d'une Banque fait par son Excellence le Comte de Zinzendorff, Président de la Chambre de Compte', vol. 83, fols 150r–158r, Nachlaß Zinzendorf, HHStA. Repeating Zinzendorf's arguments in the main, Thys also wrote his own proposal for a stock exchange and '*Banque de Giro et de Deposito*'. In it, he set out the operations of the bourse and the bank. Both institutions together, Thys argued, were necessary to support the prices of public paper and keep the rate of interest low: Johann van Thys, [no title], [undated], ibid., fols 160r–176v.

[133] Johann van Thys, [undated], 'Vorschläge des Kommerzienrates von Thys zur großen Handlungs Compagnie betreffend', vol. 83, fols 60r–78v, Nachlaß Zinzendorf, HHStA. In the 1760s, the government was preoccupied with protecting the existing navigation between

out the administration, the operations and the principles on which the trading company should conduct its business. The company should be set up for a period of 25 years and receive the monopoly right to import spices and drugs to the monarchy.[134] In addition, without exclusive rights, it could import raw materials, including cotton, linen and silk. These it could only sell wholesale, and not retail. Other activities would involve the trade of tobacco, exports of agricultural and manufactured produce, including woollen and silk cloth, and commerce with the Levant. Thys also proposed that the company should receive preference for supplying provisions to the military, be granted the right to trade coins and to discount bills of exchange. Individuals would not be allowed to compete with the company in those areas in which it had been given the monopoly. In case of violation, they would lose their business assets to the company.[135]

Like the Mississippi Trading Company in Law's scheme, the company would be set up with shares. Thys proposed an initial share capital of 6 million *florins*, divided into 12,000 shares with a nominal value of 500 *florins* each. The management of the company or the general assembly of shareholders could decide on increasing the share capital and extending the scope of operations.[136] Thys suggested a mechanism for the subscription of the shares as well as procedures to appoint five directors nominated by the ruler and the general assembly.[137] The directors had to own equity in the company and had to have had professional experience in commerce or banking.[138] As an additional element of control, every three years, five representatives should be elected to help with compiling the accounts and review the company's share register.[139] The operations should also be pru-

Trieste, Ostend and Fiume. Thus, Zinzendorf and Thys had decided to delay the proposal, letter of Ludwig Zinzendorf to Karl Zinzendorf, Vienna, 13 September 1766, vol. 64, DOZA. On the piracy attacks of the Barbary States of North Africa and the Habsburg navy, see Szabo, *Kaunitz*, pp. 295–300 and Beer, 'Die österreichische Handelspolitik', pp. 89–90.

134 The period was 1 June 1767 to 1 June 1792: Thys, 'Vorschläge', fol. 60r. As a recognition for this privilege, the company should offer produce as a gift to the ruler: Article 78, ibid., fol. 78v.

135 Articles 1–3, ibid., fols 60r–64v.

136 Article 14, ibid., fols 66v–67r.

137 Articles 15–28, ibid., fols 67r–68v. The ruler would nominate three directors and the general assembly could appoint additional two: ibid., article 26, fol. 68v.

138 Articles 28 and 30, ibid., fols 68v; fol. 69r.

139 The assembly would nominate four representatives, and the state would nominate one. Copies of the financial documentation would be sent to the Archives de Commerce for storage: Article 32, ibid., fol. 69v.

dent and controlled. The most promising and lucrative commercial opportunities should be prioritised, and costs ought to be controlled by renting rather than purchasing new vessels. Before taking a decision on building new manufacturing facilities, the company should ensure that its produce was of sufficiently good quality to successfully compete internationally.[140]

Thys, Zinzendorf noted, played an 'enormous and admirable role' in presenting the plans to the government. Nevertheless, Thys was excluded from most of the deliberations of the government commission and was not consulted when ministers finally rejected the proposal.[141] The outcome put an end to Zinzendorf's ambition to create an economic system like Law's. Thys' vested business interests may have played a significant role in the adverse decision-making.[142] Also, in contrast to France, the monarchy did not have a system of state concessions for trading activities which could be administered by private entities. For Thys, the decision of the commission was surely a setback, but probably not too damaging. The trading company was just one of several business ideas he followed. He returned to his manufacturing activities in Carinthia and remained a friend and steadfast supporter of Zinzendorf.[143]

Zinzendorf was the main sounding board on finance for ministers and the rulers. He assessed most of the 'projects' for the economy which the government received. The schemes of Gerhard and Caratto were good examples. The ideas of projectors were debated by government commissions set up for that purpose. Sometimes, the ruler invited other projectors to participate in the discussions: in the case of Caratto's plans, Thys took part in their assessments. Zinzendorf was open to arguments of projectors and thought that they could potentially offer new ways to

[140] Articles 56–58, ibid., fol. 73v.

[141] Letter of Ludwig Zinzendorf to Karl Zinzendorf, Vienna, 28 March 1767, vol. 64, DOZA.

[142] The government commission chaired by Starhemberg met on several days between the end of March 1767 and mid-April 1767 to discuss the plans. The concerns of ministers were written in the margin of the first page of Thys' proposal: 'Vorschläge', fols 60r–61v. They included the threat of a monopoly right to the business of domestic merchants and industry, and the loss to a private company of the strategically important, and already established, spice trade. Thys submitted his defence in two separate documents: Johann von Thys, [no title], [undated], appendix A, vol. 87, fols 124r–127v; appendix B, vol. 87, fols 130r–132. For other plans by projectors to set up Austrian trading companies, see Beer, 'Die österreichische Handelspolitik', pp. 101–13, and Szabo, *Kaunitz*, pp. 144–46.

[143] Letter of Johann van Thys to Ludwig Zinzendorf, Klagenfurt, 18 January 1771, ArchivZinzendorf, Karton 9, NÖLA.

improve the economy of the monarchy. He looked for direct intellectual engagement with them and debated ideas. Caratto's plan, in its main line of arguments, followed Zinzendorf's. With Thys, Zinzendorf had found a kindred spirit who would not only reinforce his ideas, but who also had complementary skills through which the arguments could be expanded. With his good applied knowledge of commerce and industry, Thys helped Zinzendorf to develop a fuller economic proposal to mirror Law's scheme.

Zinzendorf's approach to projectors was pragmatic. As much as he was willing to review and discuss new ideas, he was generally sceptical about the feasibility of most of the projectors' economic projects and doubted their successful implementation. By withholding some of the sensitive financial information and avoiding plans with imprudent risks, Zinzendorf sought to protect the state's financial operations. An important exception was tax farming, where Zinzendorf recognised a role for projectors.[144] Outsiders, he argued, were generally more effective and diligent in administrating taxes. In the case of tobacco farming, Zinzendorf pointed out that receipts were much higher when they were managed by private individuals than when collected by the government.[145] Although this did not reflect the government's general policy of strengthening its power, it showed Zinzendorf's preference for measures which were proven and worked.

Debates Within Government

Debates over Institutional Reform

In Maria Theresa's government, 'change, rather than continuity, was the norm'.[146] In 1749, on the advice of Count Friedrich Wilhelm von Haugwitz, the empress embarked on an ambitious reform programme to strengthen the central administration and reassert its financial authority over the provincial Estates which collected the taxes, in particular the contribution for the military. The principal aim was to have a better control of

[144] Dickson, *Finance and Government*, vol. 2, pp. 50–1.

[145] Zinzendorf, 'Geschichte und Beschreibung der Wiener Stadt Banco', pp. [142–43]. On the farming of tobacco revenues, see Dickson, *Finance and Government*, vol. 1, 'Appendix B: The farm of Austrian tobacco revenues', pp. 397–98 and vol. 2, p. 50. Zinzendorf's biography mentions the bankruptcy of one tobacco-farming Jewish syndicate in 1764: Pettenegg (ed.), *Selbstbiographien*, p. 98.

[146] Dickson, *Finance and Government*, vol. 1, p. 207.

cash flows to adequately support the growing army in the wars against Prussia. The newly created *Directorium in publicis et cameralibus*, with Haugwitz as its president, was a state-directed administrative structure for all Austrian and Bohemian lands. It greatly increased the control of the ruler at the expense of the Estates. However, Hungary as well as the Italian and Belgian provinces were not affected. The *Directorium* replaced the Bohemian and Austrian chancelleries and took on the financial and general administration of the hereditary lands. It also separated the judicial functions from the political activities and transferred them to a Supreme Court.[147] In the *Directorium*, Haugwitz wanted maximum financial control and pursued administrative expansion. He unsuccessfully urged Maria Theresa to abolish the Treasury and pushed for supervision of the Vienna City Bank. Other financial departments, including mines and coinage, were integrated in the *Directorium*, sometimes only for a short while. The resistance in government to Haugwitz's programme of change was limited, partly because foreign and army affairs as well as Hungary remained outside the remit of the new ministry.[148]

By 1754, in order to assume the growing responsibilities of central government, the number of councillors in the *Directorium* was increased threefold to 21.[149] It was indicative of the extraordinary growth of administrators under Maria Theresa and the corresponding increase in production of state documents. Between 1740 and 1763, the number of officials in the hereditary lands almost doubled to 10,000 and, over the same period, the average number of orders issued by the government tripled.[150]

However, the new system was not robust enough to withstand the financial pressures of the Seven Years War. It could not generate the funds required. Kaunitz was an early critic. He highlighted the quarrels and the lack of co-operation among administrative units and concluded that without radical change the war might bring down the country.[151] Unlike

[147] Ibid., pp. 222–25. On the significance of the separation between political and judicial functions in Haugwitz's reforms, see Henry E. Strakosch, *State Absolutism and the Rule of Law. The Struggle for the Codification of Civil Law in Austria 1753–1811* (Sydney: Sydney University Press, 1967), pp. 29–49.

[148] Dickson, *Finance and Government*, vol. 1, pp. 227–28.

[149] Ibid., p. 229.

[150] Ibid., pp. 306–9, 318.

[151] Memorandum of Kaunitz to Maria Theresa, 9 December 1760, in Derek Beales, *Joseph II*, Vol. 1: *In the shadow of Maria Theresa, 1741–1780* (Cambridge, 1987), p. 91. For other government critics of Haugwitz's system, see Szabo, *Kaunitz*, pp. 80–1.

Haugwitz who had followed a narrow fiscal programme, Kaunitz proposed a more radical and far-reaching system. An advisory council for internal affairs, which he called Council of State (*Staatsrat*), would discuss policies for the hereditary lands and Hungary. Rather than implement simple narrow-revenue maximising measures, Kaunitz wanted to develop broad initiatives to grow the economy. Initially, the *Staatsrat*, like the *Directorium*, only dealt with the domestic affairs of Austria and Bohemia. But when Hungary and Transylvania were added, it debated the affairs of nearly the whole monarchy.[152] Unlike the *Directorium*, the creation of the *Staatsrat* was not the result of impromptu decision-making. It was first proposed by Kaunitz in 1758, but its first meeting with both Maria Theresa and the emperor present was only held on 21 January 1761.[153] Originally, the *Staatsrat* had six members and one secretary. Four members, Ministers of State, were titled nobles (*Herrenstand*), and two members, State Councillors, came from the *Ritterstand*. With the exception of Kaunitz, the other members did not have administrative responsibilities so that they might be seen to give impartial advice to the ruler.[154] This was a significant change. Zinzendorf's membership of the *Staatsrat*, though supported by Kaunitz, was refused.[155] Maria Theresa attended meetings when she wanted and occasionally decided matters immediately during meetings.[156] From 1776, it seemed, she lost interest and kept away from the Council.[157]

Kaunitz's key recommendation was to separate, once again, political from financial power. However, in keeping with Haugwitz's reforms, he advocated a stronger role for the Supreme Court and sought to unify the Austrian and Bohemian chancelleries into the 'Bohemian and Austrian Court Chancellery' and to limit the influence of the Estates. From the outset, Kaunitz manoeuvred to reduce the influence of dissenters and thereby soften opposition to his institutional changes. To this end, Haugwitz was taken out of his executive role at the *Directorium* and became a member

[152] Beales, *Joseph II*, vol. 1, p. 94. Since the beginning of the Seven Years War, Kaunitz, through the *Staatskanzlei*, also administered directly the internal affairs and hence the economy of the Austrian Netherlands and Italian provinces: Szabo, *Kaunitz*, pp. 50–1.

[153] Dickson, *Finance and Government*, vol. 1, pp. 233–34.

[154] Beales, *Joseph II*, vol. 1, p. 92. Kaunitz, Haugwitz, Daun and Blümegen were from the *Herrenstand*; Borié and Stupan from the *Ritterstand*.

[155] Dickson, *Finance and Government*, vol. 1, p. 348.

[156] Beales, *Joseph II*, vol. 1, p. 94.

[157] Dickson, *Finance and Government*, vol. 1, p. 251.

of the *Staatsrat*.[158] The finances, Kaunitz argued, should be administered within the Treasury by an enlarged *caisse générale* which would unite the funds of the country's various *caisses*, the Vienna City Bank and the Estates Credit Deputation, and by an independent court of audit.[159] These ideas came directly from Zinzendorf and will be examined below. The resistance in government to Kaunitz's proposals was strong. After much deliberation, the administrative changes of 1762 were a compromise between the traditionalist and the more progressive advocates in government around Kaunitz. The recreation of separate chancelleries for Bohemia and Austria was rejected, but a combined Bohemian-Austrian Chancellery was created, with Count Rudolf Chotek as its head. The new body, which replaced the *Directorium*, reflected the separation of financial from political activities and was intended to maintain good relations with the Estates. The split between administrative and judicial functions through the Supreme Court was upheld. The competences of the financial institutions were reshuffled again. The role of the Treasury was revived, but the creation of a united *caisse* was rejected. The Chancellery kept control of the contribution, and the independence of the Vienna City Bank was reinforced. Two new entities were created: first, an ill-defined *caisse générale* to receive the funds of the *caisses* in the hereditary lands and of the Estates Deputation; and second, a court of audit to control the revenues and the expenses of the ruler.[160]

Despite the compromise, the arguments on institutional change persisted with the same intensity. They were fuelled by the rivalries of institutions, in particular in financial matters. Institutions were unable to work together, and there was no mechanism to give them direction. It led members of the *Staatsrat* opposed to Kaunitz to look back and demand the

[158] Ibid., pp. 235–37.

[159] *Votum* of Wenzel Kaunitz, 20 November 1761, pp. 112–16, in Friedrich Walter (ed.), *Vom Sturz des Directoriums in Publicis et Cameralibus (1760/61) bis zum Ausgang der Regierung Maria Theresias: Aktenstücke*, II. Abteilung, vol. 3 (Vienna: ÖZV, 1934), pp. 101–21. Kaunitz saw the *caisse générale* evolving into a 'united hereditary bank and universal institution of credit' and eventually into a 'true giro and deposit bank' with branches in the Austrian Netherlands, Trieste and in some of the larger provinces. The aim of the new institution was not only to facilitate state credit but also to support the growth of commerce and domestic industry: ibid., pp. 114–15. For a summary of Kaunitz's *votum*, see Szabo, *Kaunitz*, pp. 89–90 and Dickson, *Finance and Government*, vol. 1, p. 241.

[160] Dickson, *Finance and Government*, vol. 1, p. 243. On the creation of the two new institutions, see Friedrich Walter, *Die Geschichte der österreichischen Zentralverwaltung in der Zeit Maria Theresias (1740–1780)*, vol. 32 (Vienna: ÖZV, 1938), pp. 335–38.

recreation of a ministry similar to the *Directorium*. Kaunitz, on the other hand, looked for ways to improve the existing set-up, again with the intellectual support of Zinzendorf. In 1765, after a three-day conference, it was decided to enlarge the Treasury with added responsibility for credit funds and the levying of the contribution. It now had oversight of the Vienna City Bank, which remained a separate unit.[161] Nevertheless, the power games in government did not go away, and the institutional restructuring continued. Three years later, the Treasury was divided into five divisions with one councillor each and in 1771 remodelled again when it was unified with the chancellery under one president.[162] Finally, in 1773, Zinzendorf's court of audit lost its independence and was demoted to a subsidiary of the Treasury.[163]

The Institutions for Commercial Affairs

The administration of commercial affairs was a particularly pertinent example of the clashes of interests in government.[164] The frequent changes reflected political disagreements, departments meddling in each other's businesses and tensions with provincial authorities. The central institution for commerce was moved back and forth between ministries, had its business cut down and was finally abolished. At the beginning of her reign, the empress had big ambitions for commercial policy. In 1746, she created the *Commercien-Directorium* to formulate uniform trade policies for the whole monarchy. It was designed as a consultative body only.[165]

[161] Dickson, *Finance and Government*, vol. 1, pp. 244–45.

[162] Ibid., pp. 247–48.

[163] Ibid., p. 250.

[164] On the institutions for commerce in the eighteenth-century monarchy, see Grete Klingenstein, 'Die Wiener Kommerzienhofkommission, 1719–1776. Einige Überlegungen zu Wirtschaftsverflechtung und staatlicher Durchdringing in einem "zusammengesetzten" Staatswesen' in Ulfried Burz, Michael Derndarsky, Werner Drobesch, *Brennpunkt Mitteleuropa. Festschrift für Helmut Rumpler zum 65. Geburtstag* (Klagenfurt, 2000), pp. 195–206. Also useful and recent, Grete Klingenstein and Eva Faber, 'Kommerzbehörden und Staatswirtschaftsdeputation' in Michael Hochedlinger, Petr Mat'a and Thomas Winkelbauer (eds.), *Verwaltungsgeschichte der Habsburgermonarchie in der frühen Neuzeit.* Band 1: *Hof und Dynastie, Kaiser und Reich, Zentralverwaltungen, Kriegswesen und landesfürstliches Finanzwesen*, *MIÖG* 62 (2 vols, Vienna: Böhlau, 2019), vol. 2, pp. 985–90. I am very grateful to Grete Klingenstein for having sent me a typescript of the article prior to publication.

[165] Klingenstein, 'Die Wiener Kommerzienhofkommission', p. 202.

Representatives of the Italian territories and Austrian Netherlands as well as Hungary took part in the deliberations. Rudolf Chotek was its president. In 1753, when Zinzendorf began to work in the *Commercien-Directorium*, it was part of Haugwitz's expanding *Directorium*. In 1757, the Chancellery of State also became involved in commercial affairs with the administration of the Italian duchies and the Austrian Netherlands.

In 1762, as part of Kaunitz's reorganisation of the *Directorium*, the *Commercien-Directorium* became an independent Board of Trade (*Commerzien-Hofrat*) with its own president, Franz Reinhold Andler-Witten (1698–1771). It also had only an advisory function. In addition to eight privy councillors (*Hofräte*), the Board would also have two merchants to help decide economic policies.[166] However, the traders were never appointed.[167] Thus, the *Commerzien-Hofrat*, which according to Kaunitz was lacking sound commercial knowledge, was unable to provide competent advice to the empress.[168] Rivalries with other departments and between heads of departments hindered its work. For example, the toll bureaus, answerable to the Bank Deputation, repudiated information requests from the *Commerzien-Hofrat*, and the Chancellery refused to relinquish its direct relationship with the provincial trade committees (*Kommerzkonsesse*).[169] Other provincial institutions also attempted to obstruct the Board's policies as much as possible. In 1763, following a request by merchants in Prague to improve trade between Austria and Bohemia, Maria Theresa instructed the Board to identify possible improvements in the navigable waterways of the Vltava. Bohemian authorities were asked to provide an assessment of the waterways. However, for more than a year, they ignored several requests to produce the documents of investigation. As they would have lost income, the owners of the waterway tolls, the city of Budweis and the archbishop of Prague, opposed the initiative.[170]

[166] Beer, 'Finanzverwaltung', pp. 274–75.

[167] Walter, *Die Geschichte der österreichischen Zentralverwaltung* (1938), p. 339. Also, Klingenstein and Faber, 'Kommerzbehörden', p. 987. The Hungarian and Transylvanian councillors only participated in discussions on Hungarian and Transylvanian matters respectively.

[168] Beer, 'Finanzverwaltung', pp. 275–76. Kaunitz criticised the *Commercien-Directorium* for only having 'cavaliers' and 'academics' as members who, lacking in practical experience, had very different mindsets to merchants and manufacturers: *Votum* of Wenzel Kaunitz, 20 November 1761; Walter, *Vom Sturz des Directoriums* (1934), vol. 3, p. 119.

[169] Beer, 'Finanzverwaltung', p. 275; Walter, *Die Geschichte der österreichischen Zentralverwaltung* (1938), vol. 1, p. 340.

[170] Beer, 'Die österreichische Handelspolitik', pp. 5–6.

In May 1765, given the poor performance of the *Commerzien-Hofrat*, the empress decided to subordinate it again to the Chancellery, headed by Chotek. Andler was forced to retire.[171] Chotek, in turn, now as president, vehemently defended the work of the Board. Its output, he pointed out to the empress, fell short because it was understaffed. Moreover, as members of the Bohemian–Austrian Chancellery participated in its discussions, political and commercial issues became muddled. In a desperate effort to save the institution and keep commercial business separate, Chotek argued for a clearer division of work between departments. In October 1768, he suggested the formation of a *Staatswirtschaftsdeputation* with responsibility for matters of economic interest for all the hereditary provinces and Hungary. It was intended as an advisory body which would monitor economic statistics and follow the development of agriculture, industry, population and tariff policies. Members from the various government departments, including the Board of Trade and the Hungarian Chancellery, were invited to attend its weekly meetings. In December, the empress accepted the plan and Chotek was named president of the new entity. The first session of the *Staatswirtschaftsdeputation* was on 19 January 1769.[172] The Board of Trade remained subordinate to the Chancellery and was given a narrower scope. Its responsibilities covered the administration of manufacturing, private commerce and shipping, which included the ports of Trieste and Fiume, as well as of the territories of the Littoral.

On 7 January 1769, Zinzendorf received the information about the creation of the new body from Maria Theresa.[173] Chotek asked him for his support and sent him the documents setting out the remit of the new institution. Conscious of the inefficient and slow pattern of administration, he reassured Zinzendorf that debates could be conducted efficiently by keeping to weekly deadlines for the review and circulation of documents. The *Staatswirtschaftsdeputation*, he made clear, had an advisory function. The execution of measures was the responsibility of the government departments.[174] The *Staatswirtschaftsdeputation* should collect eco-

[171] Walter, *Die Geschichte der österreichischen Zentralverwaltung* (1938), pp. 416–19.

[172] Beer, 'Finanzverwaltung', pp. 276–81. Also on the *Staatswirtschaftsdeputation*, see Klingenstein and Faber, 'Kommerzbehörden', pp. 988–89; Klingenstein, 'Die Wiener Kommerzienhofkommission', pp. 204–6, and Dickson, *Finance and Government*, vol. 1, p. 247.

[173] Pettenegg (ed.), *Selbstbiographien*, p. 128.

[174] Letter of Rudolf Chotek to Ludwig Zinzendorf, Vienna, 9 January 1769, vol. 127, fols 1r–5v, Nachlaß Zinzendorf, HHStA.

nomic data on the monarchy's population, agriculture and commerce to support the decision-making.[175] However, as early as the end of the year, Chotek had complained about the lack of support and the delaying tactics from other government departments. It became another ineffective government institution. Even though not formally dissolved, it probably ended in 1776.[176] At the same time, on Joseph's insistence, the *Commerzien-Hofrat* lost its semi-independence and was absorbed within the Bohemian–Austrian Chancellery. In fact, five years before, the *Commerzien-Hofrat* had already lost most of its significance when it had then been moved to the Treasury and had lost Chotek, its most vociferous supporter, to ill health. Furthermore, in 1772, as evidence of the transfer of power, the Bohemian–Austrian Chancellery had taken administrative control of the trade of the provincial commerce commissions (*Commerzkonzesse*) when merging these with the government of the provinces (*Grubernium*).[177]

Zinzendorf's Role in Institutional Change

Kaunitz followed Zinzendorf's line in the government debates. By developing the ideas on institutional reform which Kaunitz subsequently presented in the *Staatsrat*, he reinforced his role as key adviser to the empress. In this way, Zinzendorf contributed decisively to the abolition of Haugwitz's system. Ministers looked repeatedly for his analytical abilities and practical experience to help break decision deadlock over administrative issues. Kaunitz's views on the best administration for the monarchy's finances were directly taken from Zinzendorf's proposal of 7 October 1761.[178] Zinzendorf's aim was to establish a stable and transparent financial structure which would operate with three institutions: the Treasury (*Hofkammer*), a central fund for the state revenues (*General-Caße*) and a court of audit (*Rechenkammer*). State finances, Zinzendorf

[175] Klingenstein, 'Die Wiener Kommerzienhofkommission', p. 206.

[176] Walter, *Die Geschichte der österreichischen Zentralverwaltung* (1938), p. 468.

[177] Ibid., pp. 470–71; Dickson, *Finance and Government*, vol. 1, p. 251.

[178] Ludwig Zinzendorf, 'Vorschlag des Grafen Ludwig von Zinzendorf über die Einrichtung der Finanzen de dato Wien, den 7. October 1761', vol. 2b, fols 90r–103r, Nachlaß Zinzendorf, HHStA. Part of the text is printed in Walter, *Vom Sturz des Directoriums* (1934), pp. 167–68. For concise summaries, see Johann Schasching, *Staatsbildung und Finanzentwicklung: Ein Beitrag zur Geschichte des österreichischen Staatskredites in der 2. Hälfte des 18. Jahrhunderts* (Innsbruck, 1954), pp. 28–31, and Szabo, *Kaunitz*, p. 88.

argued, had to take care of two issues: first, and most important, the administration and improvement of the various sources of state income; and second, the 'simple mechanical exercise' of appropriately recording income and expenses as well as implementing a system for invoicing. It was clear, Zinzendorf continued, that state revenues ought to be centrally administered by one single government department. Then, the total income could be accounted for and appropriate decisions could be made on how best to spend the money. If, conversely, the revenues were overseen by various departments, it would create rivalry, and each department would only concentrate on maximising its own profit. Unless the revenues were collected into a single *caisse*, a state could not have a good grasp of its total income nor be in a position to use the funds wisely to cover expenses. An independent body, not involved with income and expenses, should verify figures to ensure that everything was accurately recorded. The most harmful administrative practice consisted of various government departments collecting revenues independently while also undertaking their own financial management and audit process. This, Zinzendorf argued, was the current arrangement in the monarchy.[179]

It was to address these failings in financial administration that he proposed the three institutions. Zinzendorf's plan enhanced the importance of the Treasury (*Hofkammer*). It would administer the entire central state revenues, including the contribution. As a markedly enlarged ministry, it would be structured as five independent departments managing the ordinary revenues from the Estates, the salt and mining monopolies, the international sales of mining produce, and the mint. To operate successfully, the Treasury had to attract the most talented individuals in the country. Zinzendorf also identified improvements to increase the exploitation and revenues of the mines.[180]

The *General-Caße* would receive all the revenues of the state and organise the payments. The revenues would have to combine those which were free of any charges and those which had been pledged to creditors, including the Vienna City Bank and the Estates. As important creditors to the state, the Estates opposed a system where the ruler would collect the funds first before paying them out. In case of financial need, the central government, they feared, would choose to issue paper and refuse to pay back specie. Therefore, Zinzendorf argued, in order to keep the confidence of

[179] Zinzendorf, 'Vorschlag', fols 90r–90v.
[180] Ibid., fols 91r–93r.

the creditors and especially of the Estates, it was critical that the united credit fund should be independent of the ruler. Most of the existing institutions did not qualify to manage such a fund. The Vienna City Bank, for example, even though intentionally created to be independent of the state's finances, had an opaque administration system. The bank's creditors would not agree to combine its funds with those of the state. The individual Estates of the provinces, too, were not suitable given that the size of fund was large and had to cover the state. Only the recently created combined credit of the Austrian and Bohemian lands, the *Ständische Kredit-Deputation*, Zinzendorf thought, was appropriate, and other *caisses* could be attached to it.[181]

For a transparent set-up, deputies of each province should agree for the funds to be paid to the *General-Caße*. Both the empress as well as the combined Estates Deputation should undertake that the funds which had been pledged would be paid back to the creditors. In particular, in order to reassure the creditors of the bank, the mayor of Vienna should be included in the management of the fund. As a key official of the bank who authorised the issue of its bonds, Zinzendorf explained, the mayor would make sure that he represented the bank's interests well.

The *General-Caße* would be a suitable institutional preparation for unifying the credit facilities of the Estates and the *Ministerial-Banco-Deputation*. Since the latter received customs and toll payments from various provinces, the Estates could take on their proportional share of these revenues as well as their corresponding share of the debt due to the *Ministerial-Banco-Deputation*. To the creditors, the entire debt would be guaranteed by the Estates of the provinces. In addition, the cameral credit which was under the direct control of the *Hofkammer* would be integrated into the *General-Caße*.[182] The benefit of a unified credit, Zinzendorf argued, by far outweighed the challenges which would be encountered during its implementation.[183]

For Zinzendorf, a good system of accounting was an important part of a transparent set-up. The various *caisses* directed by the government of a province were expected to send their records of revenues and expenses to the province's *Haupt-Caße*, which had four days to aggregate the num-

[181] Ibid., fols 93r–94v.

[182] Revenues from Hungary were the exception as they had to remain with the Hungarian *Hof Cammer*: ibid., fol. 102v.

[183] Ibid., fols 102r–102v.

bers and forward them to the *General-Caße*. This system, Zinzendorf argued, allowed the united credit fund to follow the development of revenues of all hereditary provinces on a monthly basis and compare them to the expenses. An annual expense forecast, to be undertaken jointly by the three institutions, Zinzendorf thought, should help money management. For extraordinary expenses, including funds for military campaigns and commercial expansion, the *General-Caße* had to inform the ruler who, as a safeguard, would ask the expert opinion of an independent specialist when evaluating the request. Financial records should be filed so that the government could track the amounts of liquid funds available, and to reduce transport costs, the movement of money between *caisses* in geographic proximity should be allowed.[184]

The third institution of Zinzendorf's financial administration was an independent court of audit. This would be a new institution of financial control for the monarchy. It should verify the government accounts. The existing system of accounting, in Zinzendorf's view, was flawed. It was unable to keep chronological records of movements of funds and hence was unable to establish a daily cash balance. Under Zinzendorf's new system, the *caisses* would enter revenues and expenses into a *Journal* and, as verification, include the original documentations of the transactions. *Journale*, compiled by the various *Haupt-Caßen*, would be collected by the *General-Caße* and sent to the court of audit which would create a dedicated *Rubriken Buch* for each *Journal*. Since the records would be verified on a monthly basis, any discrepancies in numbers could be rectified swiftly, thus removing the need to continue with the laborious annual accounting exercise. Finally, officials of the audit court would compile at the end of the year a balance sheet for all hereditary provinces which would record not only the amount of liquid funds, but also the levels of agricultural produce (*Naturalien*).[185]

The appropriate accounting system would be the double-entry bookkeeping.[186] The various types of state revenues would be recorded in *Haupt-Bücher* and these would be combined to create the general *Haupt-Buch* for all the hereditary provinces. The new method, Zinzendorf argued, would allow all government departments to have their finances reviewed by an independent institution rather than by its own officials. It

[184] Ibid., fols 94v–96r.
[185] Ibid., fols 96v–98r.
[186] For Zinzendorf's publication on accounting, see section 'The Public Sphere'.

would provide the empress with continuous and reliable information on the state of the monarchy's finances. Implementing this new system, Zinzendorf thought, would take one year. First, talented officials had to be selected who would be taught, for two hours a day, the principles of the new accounting method. Zinzendorf was confident that within six months a large enough number of financial controllers could be recruited and trained. Over the remaining six months, they could then collect and compile the financial data directly from the provinces. A good alternative, he thought, provided that the government was prepared to offer favourable remuneration, was to recruit foreign experts from Amsterdam and major German cities with good knowledge of double-entry bookkeeping.[187]

Information sharing was essential for the success of the new court of audit. To be able to work efficiently, the three ministries had to coordinate their activities. Zinzendorf suggested weekly meetings with one representative from each ministry. Policies, in particular those impacting the other ministries, should be discussed, but decisions on extraordinary expenses had to be excluded out of fear that they could jeopardise payments to existing creditors. Furthermore, the central institutions in Vienna should rely on newly created *Finanz-Cammern*, each with their own president, which would administer the revenues and payments in each province. To reduce any room for error, the *Finanz-Cammern* would only be allowed to cover two types of payments: first, capital and interest payments in relation to the national debt and, second, expenses which already had been agreed in the budget.[188]

Zinzendorf concluded his proposal with replies to two arguments put forward by critics of his proposal. The first was the contention that the power and the influence of the Estates would increase too much if they were given control of all the provinces' revenues. The idea of a *General-Caße*, Zinzendorf countered, was nothing radically new. It was merely an extension of the Estates Credit Deputation which, he argued, was the only suitable public fund for this purpose. According to the second concern, the Estates would not agree to the new system as the inclusion of their financial function into the *General-Caße* would make the work of their regional officials redundant. Mindful to tread carefully and build new

[187] Zinzendorf, 'Vorschlag', fols 98r–99r.

[188] Ibid., fols 99r–101r. Hungary was a special case. Zinzendorf proposed the creation of a German-speaking *Finanz-Collegium* to differentiate from the Hungarian diet: ibid., fol. 100v.

structures without completely abolishing existing ones, Zinzendorf gave assurances that the Estates' officials would remain part of the administration and that payments would continue to be authorised by the *caisses* of the provinces. The only significant change, in case of money shortfalls, was the possibility to transfer funds between *caisses*. However, as a safeguard against abuse, the funds could only be taken if eventually they would be returned to the *caisse* which had previously been in surplus.[189]

Between 1762 and 1764, the government remained locked in discussions over institutions, and Kaunitz again turned to Zinzendorf to find solutions.[190] On 11 September 1764, Zinzendorf presented further ideas for necessary reforms. He wrote the proposal together with Hatzfeld.[191] On 1 January 1762, Hatzfeld replaced Zinzendorf as president of the Estates Credit Deputation. Subsequently, he became a very powerful figure in government. He was also president of the Bank Deputation and, in May 1765, became head of the *Hofkammer*. In June 1771, he was named *Oberster Kanzler* and president of the Council of Trade by the empress, replacing Chotek.[192] In the methodical 'Vortrag', the two authors defended the plans of 1761 and, rather than proposing radically new measures, suggested improvements to the existing systems. After summarising the monarchy's early institutional set-up and the arrangements of 1762, the two ministers set out the shortcomings of existing operations and recommended ways of restructuring of the organisation. To ensure that their plans could be made to work, they described the mechanisms by which departments could work efficiently and enabled to take decisions without delay. The final section of their report was dedicated to improvements in the working processes of the *Staatsrat*.

On Zinzendorf and Hatzfeld's diagnosis, the monarchy's financial administration had three shortcomings which caused the difficulties in central government. First, the implementation of the new system was incomplete. The taxes were not administered by one department, but were still split between the Bohemian–Austrian Chancellery, the Treasury and the *Ministerial-Banco-Deputation*. Second, the financial administration had been too heavily modified. The *caisse générale* had lost the mili-

[189] Ibid., fols 101r–102r.

[190] Dickson, *Finance and Government*, vol. 1, p. 244 and Szabo, *Kaunitz*, pp. 97–8.

[191] Vortrag von Ludwig Zinzendorf und Karl Friedrich Hatzfeld, 11 September 1764, printed in Walter, *Vom Sturz des Directoriums* (1934), pp. 223–33.

[192] Dickson, *Finance and Government*, vol. 1, pp. 237, 249, 354.

tary *caisses* and had no control of state credit, which remained the remit of the emperor. The third factor, the defective operation of the existing arrangements, was notably important. In particular, Zinzendorf and Hatzfeld criticised the Bohemian–Austrian Chancellery for its growing influence in financial affairs.[193] It was not only responsible for the contribution, but also for an array of partially newly levied taxes, including inheritance and interest taxes, as well as provincial levies and claims by provinces for war supplies (*Supererogaten*).[194] As a result, the Bohemian–Austrian Chancellery maintained such a strong relationship with the Estates of the Bohemian–Austrian provinces that, by extension, other departments were unable to successfully deal with the Estates without the Bohemian–Austrian Chancellery being involved. Additional problems included the Treasury's lack of control over the *Ministerial-Banco-Deputation*, which refused to provide reports of its activities, and the administrative burden on the court of audit, which was inundated with requests about petty matters from various government departments. The consequences, the authors concluded, were severe. The monarchy's four financial departments—Bohemian–Austrian Chancellery, Treasury, *Ministerial-Banco-Deputation* and court of audit—blocked each other's work. The result was a 'painfully slow' business practice riddled with delays. Institutions produced much redundant writing and duplicated work.[195]

The necessary changes, they argued, involved a simplified set-up with a concentration of power. The improved system should only have two independent financial institutions: the Treasury and the court of audit, each with its own president. To oversee all taxes, the Treasury would administer the *Ministerial-Banco-Deputation* and the *caisse générale*. The *Banco*, however, would remain an autonomous unit. Importantly, the Treasury would also be responsible for the contribution and for the Bohemian–Austrian Chancellery's other taxes. The latter was the most controversial change. Once the contribution was authorised after negotiations between the Chancellery and the Estates, the authors explained, its collection and administration became the remit of the Treasury and thus should be moved from the Chancellery.[196]

[193] Walter, *Vom Sturz des Directoriums* (1934), p. 224.
[194] Ibid., p. 226.
[195] Ibid., pp. 225–26.
[196] Ibid., pp. 227–29.

In the second section of their 'Vortrag', Zinzendorf and Hatzfeld set out the daily operations of the two institutions. For the Treasury, their main concern was to ensure that it stayed operational despite its size and that its president, while being well informed, would not delay decision-making. Their proposal involved the nomination of four vice presidents for each of the Treasury's department who would discuss and agree relevant business. The plenary session, a weekly meeting run by the president, would be limited to the discussion of matters which involved more than one department, or which were the subject of contention between units.[197] The work of the court of audit would become more efficient if only accountants of the government departments would be allowed to provide information. Also, to overcome the Estates' reluctance to share financial information with Vienna and to prevent further bankruptcies of Estates' accountants, the Estates' bookkeeping offices, and those of the main cities, should become subordinate to the court of audit. Based on the use of double-entry bookkeeping methods in all government departments and by the Estates, it was a plan for state control and central accounts to provide the ruler with a consistent and accurate financial picture of the hereditary provinces.[198]

Zinzendorf and Hatzfeld's final suggestion for improvement concerned the *Staatsrat*. This advisory body could not fulfil its pivotal role of overseeing the government affairs of the monarchy because it could not cope with processing the vast amount of business which it received. Therefore, less significant matters should no longer be referred for discussion, freeing up members to concentrate on the important policy questions of the country.

In April 1765, in two documents, Zinzendorf reinforced his views of the 'Vortrag' on the new financial administrative system and on the enlarged Treasury. He also wrote a detailed reply to Kaunitz's questions about the Bohemian–Austrian Chancellery's influence on financial affairs, its relationship with the Estates and on the role of the court of audit in

[197] Ibid., pp. 229–30.

[198] Ibid., pp. 230–33. The accountants initiated themselves small and larger credit operations with the *caisses* which they were given to administer. In a *Denkschrift* of 13 April 1765, Zinzendorf provided evidence of the defective accounting standards in the provinces. Moravia, he noted, had 380,000 fl. more *Domesticalschulden* than it had previously reported. In Ob der Enns (Upper Austria), however, the debts were more than 1.8m. fl. lower than previously stated. See Walter, *Geschichte der österreichischen Zentralverwaltung* (1938), p. 390, footnote 1.

controlling bookkeeping bureaus in the provinces.[199] The emperor, consulted by Maria Theresa on the changes, supported the proposal of Zinzendorf and Hatzfeld.[200] On 14 May 1765, after more intense debates in government, it received the approval of the empress.[201]

Zinzendorf's Wider Role in Debates Within Central Government

In the debates on institutional change, Zinzendorf sought to add clear and practical ideas. In addition, as participant in the numerous debates within government, he was instrumental in creating a space where the most advanced European ideas on political economy could be discussed. Zinzendorf was interested in good arguments for re-establishing public credit and was best placed to demonstrate to ministers how new methods could be applied in the monarchy. But, as in the discussions on administrative change, he encountered firm resistance.

The debate on war finance of the late 1750s was a good indication of the pressure which Zinzendorf was under to adapt his thinking to conservative views. In the 'Projet de Finance pour la continuation de la Guerre', Zinzendorf dedicated a substantial section to his critics.[202] He listed 24 objections and gave his replies. Chotek, Anton Stupan von Ehrenstein, Franz Anton Saffran, Baron Johann Christoph Bartenstein (1689–1767)

[199] Ludwig Zinzendorf, 11 April 1765, 'Vergleichung des alten und neuen Finanzsistems', pp. 85–108; 12 April 1765, 'Promemoria betreffend die Vereinigung der Hofkammer, der General-Cassae-Direction und des Banco unter einem Praesidio', pp. 169–89; 13 April 1765, 'Eine Beantwortung der ihm vom Staatskanzler vorgelegten drey Fragen', pp. 109–45, all in vol. 2c, Nachlaß Zinzendorf, HHStA. The three documents are quoted in Walter, *Vom Sturz des Directoriums* (1934), p. 246, footnote 1.

[200] Walter, *Geschichte der österreichischen Zentralverwaltung* (1938), p. 396. The opinion of the emperor is printed in Walter, *Vom Sturz des Directoriums* (1934), pp. 246–47.

[201] Walter, *Geschichte der österreichischen Zentralverwaltung* (1938), pp. 403–4. The decision of the empress is printed in Walter, *Vom Sturz des Directoriums* (1934), pp. 253–55.

[202] Other outright rejections of Zinzendorf's war finance ideas included Karl Ferdinand Königsegg-Erps, 18 March 1758, 'Grafens Königsegg ohnmaßgebliche Anmerkungen und Meinung gegen den Plan des Grafen Zinzendorf Papiergeld zu drucken', Alte Kabinettsakten, Karton 17, HHStA. On 19 April 1758, he submitted the document to the empress. In the introduction, Königsegg-Erps argued that Zinzendorf's bond proposal would destroy the Vienna City Bank and expressed his hope that the empress would agree with him in rejecting Zinzendorf's ideas. Königsegg-Erps (1696–1759) was president of the College of Mines and subsequently became, for a short period, president of the *Hofkammer*.

and Haugwitz together made 16 objections. Zinzendorf did not provide the names of the other objectors.[203]

With five objections, Chotek was the most vociferous critic.[204] He was the president of the *Ministerial-Banco-Deputation* and thus in control of the Vienna City Bank. In general, three types of arguments were made against Zinzendorf's plan. Their first line of attack was that the scheme was incompatible with the existing financial institutions and systems of the monarchy. The new system, they argued, ran counter to the Vienna City Bank's operations and would adversely affect its credit.[205] The second set of arguments took issue with the design of Zinzendorf's scheme. The mechanics of the operation, ministers maintained, were defective. Further, the scope was insufficient and, in general, too similar to Law's failed financial scheme.[206] The third, and more ingenious type of criticism, was the acceptance in principle of Zinzendorf's ideas, but with the reservation that the conditions in the monarchy were not right to implement the plan. In peacetime, ministers argued, when the political situation was more predictable, it could be executed. However, during uncertain times of war, the public was not ready for it. The Vienna City Bank was perfectly adequate and capable of stepping in and raising the amount required within one year.

To counter the criticism of bad timing, Zinzendorf argued that his plan was transparent and that the introduction of public paper followed proven financial operations in France and England. The use of government paper in daily transactions and its acceptance in public *caisses* would convince the public of the advantages. Also, the plan was much more prudent than Law's system, which had seen the French economy flooded with paper. The argument that the implementation of a credit system was not feasible during a military conflict ignored the history of finance. Zinzendorf

[203] The section is also included in the printed document of 'Projet de Finance' without names of ministers: Zinzendorf, *Finanz-Vorschläge zur Fortsetzung des gegenwärtigen Krieges. Allerhöchst Ihro Röm- Kais.-König. Apostolischen M.M.. Alleruntertänigst übergeben von Ludwig Grafen und Herrn von Zinzendorf und Pottendorf; dero wirklichen geheimen Rathe, Cämmerern und Assessore in denen Directoriis in publicis et cameralibus. Im Monat Jul.1759.*

[204] See Chap. 5.

[205] Objections 1 and 2, both by Chotek: pp. [65–73]; objection 15, by Saffran, pp. [109–15], in Zinzendorf, 'Projet de Finance'.

[206] Objection 8, by Chotek, pp. [86–8]; objection 11, anonymous, pp. [99–105]; objection 20, by Bartenstein, p. [122], in ibid.

pointed out that the Bank of England and the Vienna City Bank, as well as the public paper scheme in Turin, had been set up during wartime. The public, he continued would welcome the new system once it recognised that it removed the threat of new taxes and forced loans. It would be an injustice to the public to assume that they were incapable of understanding the arguments. The monarchy could not progress in re-establishing its credit if it refused to follow the latest financial developments. The more appropriate argument, Zinzendorf thought, was to consider that the same ideas, which before had also been completely new to other countries, had been successfully adopted by them. Preventing their introduction, he concluded, would not be prudent. It would show a lack of courage.[207]

The institutional reforms under Maria Theresa gave a most confused picture. The debates within government were the result of a rapidly expanding administrative structure and the strong disagreements among ministers on the appropriate institutional set-up for the monarchy. The changes, according to Dickson, were unsuccessful in creating effective central power and in breaking down the 'collegiate structure of civil government'.[208] Existing institutions had important vested interests and relationships which they defended. The Bohemian–Austrian Chancellery's refusal to relinquish the contribution and its relationship with the Estates provoked intensive debate, as did its attempts to stay involved in commercial matters through dialogue with provincial trade committees. Change was often blocked by the refusal of existing central and regional departments to cooperate, and such a large organisation, with its myriad of committees, made it very difficult to establish new working methods. The government proceeded by trial and error, creating new institutions, often on an ad hoc basis.[209] The *Staatswirtschaftsdeputation* is an example of a desperate measure to overcome an impasse. The intensity of debates increased as the central government sought to expand its power to address urgent domestic and foreign matters. The result, as Zinzendorf and Hatzfeld indicated in their 'Vortrag', was very slow decision-making and cumbersome administrative procedures where arguments were presented on paper and then circulated among individuals or departments.[210]

[207] Objection 28, by Chotek, pp. [130–34]; objection 19, by Bartenstein, pp. [119–22], ibid.

[208] Dickson, *Finance and Government*, vol. 1, p. 327.

[209] Ibid.

[210] On the practice of 'much writing' (*Vielschreiberei*), see ibid., pp. 320–22. Joseph II remarked that ministers 'have worked like supermen, especially in using up paper': Beales, *Joseph II*, vol. 1, p. 165.

Zinzendorf added intellectual substance to the government debates by offering practical solutions and by introducing new economic arguments from other European countries. Kaunitz, in particular, relied on his ideas, and during key moments in the discussions, he asked Zinzendorf to intervene. The empress, often through Kaunitz's influence, generally followed Zinzendorf's line of arguments. He thus played an important part in the attempt to separate financial from political power as well as in the creation of the monarchy's first independent institution of central financial control.

Comparison with the Bureau du Commerce

It is instructive to place the system of debates within the Austrian government in a wider context. Here again, it is useful to look at France, where the *Bureau du Commerce* was evidence of a very different administrative set-up: it provided structure and offered a functioning framework for discussions of commercial policy. The French Council of Commerce was created in 1700 to consolidate economic policy-making and enforce royal decrees. In 1722, it was reorganised as the *Bureau du Commerce*. It was set up to advise the government on domestic manufacturing as well as internal and external commerce. It had an important role as a forum of debate between the government and the domestic mercantile community. The *Bureau* was the place where the merchants and manufacturers could test new ideas on existing legislation and where state officials could consult with them on intended changes of policy.[211] The *commissaires*, who were royal officials, administered the daily affairs of the *Bureau*. They were subsequently replaced by *Intendants*.

Each *Intendant* was responsible for certain provinces and types of industry in the country and oversaw the commerce with foreign nations. The merchants, in turn, elected 13 *députés* from 12 French cities or provinces.[212] The *députés* had only consultative power, without right to vote, and met separately. However, their advice, which they sent in writing to the *Intendants*, carried significant weight. They also ensured that a variety

[211] David Kammerling Smith, 'Le discours économique du Bureau du commerce, 1700–1750' in Charles, Loïc, Frédéric Lefebvre and Christine Théré (eds.). *Le Cercle de Vincent Gournay. Savoirs économiques et pratiques administratives en France au milieu du XVIIIe siècle* (Paris: Institut National D'Études Démographiques, 2011), pp. 31–61, at pp. 31–3.

[212] Paris could nominate two *députés*: ibid. p. 35.

of issues was brought to the attention of the *Intendants*. It was designed as an orderly process with standard administrative procedures in which the *Intendants* chose the topics and coordinated the debate. The information exchange was two-way: the *Intendants* consulted the local mercantile community in advance of new legislation, and merchants were able to present their concerns to the *Bureau* with a view to achieving favourable policy outcomes. Thus, the government was able to follow developments in the provinces closely and use the detailed knowledge of their representatives to address local economic problems.[213]

Despite the established procedures, the *Bureau*'s workings were not so straightforward and seamless. In the 'Mémoire sur les richesses, le commerce et les finances de la France', Zinzendorf himself pointed out how the rivalries among the *Intendants* prevented the implementation of efficient agricultural policies. Moreover, the power of the *Bureau* had limitations. From the beginning, it could only examine policies authorised by ministers, and it only acted in an advisory role. Sensitive commercial issues were rarely discussed. The trading companies were kept under close control by the government, as was the administration of the colonies.[214] From 1744, the *Bureau* met less frequently, which may have been related to its rigid and laborious consultative process.[215] Gournay, who joined the *Bureau* in 1751 as *Intendant*, complained about it. When he recognised that his work at the *Bureau* was limited to managing local commercial issues, he proposed to reform the institution into a more general commercial council which could set the kingdom's main economic policies.[216]

In terms of their emphasis on form and their slow progress, the economic debates within the government in France and the Habsburg monarchy were similar. However, France had a dedicated forum where government officials could engage with local market participants and readily discuss economic policy. The power and the administrative processes of the *Bureau* had their limitations, but the institution helped to flush out

[213] Ibid., pp. 35–7.

[214] Thomas J. Schaeper, *The French Council of Commerce 1700–1715. A Study of Mercantilism After Colbert* (Columbus, OH: Ohio State University Press, 1983), pp. 36–7.

[215] Ibid., p. 274. The discussion of individual commercial matters, which involved extensive written correspondence between the government, the *Bureau* and the local commerce, would take many months and sometimes years, Kammerling Smith, 'Le discours économique', p. 34.

[216] Simone Meyssonnier, *La Balance et l'Horloge: La Genèse de la pensée libérale en France au XVIIIe siècle* pp. 175–77.

differences and identify solutions to local economic issues. It provided a model for the *Commerzien-Hofrat* and the *Staatswirtschaftsdeputation*. However, the latter had little structure and poor information on population, domestic commerce and manufacturing. They were unable to provide useful policy advice for decision-making. With the central administration in constant flux, they had no time to develop their operations, and needed to defend their portfolio against other departments. The power-broking of ministers and departments, both regional and central, contributed to their downfall. Unlike France, the monarchy failed to create a successful institution which, through the regular exchange of information between government and merchants in Vienna, Graz, Prague, Bolzano and Trieste, could help make informed policy decisions.

The Public Sphere

An analysis of Zinzendorf's involvement in debates within government should extend to a discussion of his engagement with the public. At the outset, however, one would have to ask to what extent a public sphere emerged in the monarchy during Zinzendorf's time. In 1962, the German philosopher Jürgen Habermas developed the concept of a 'public sphere'.[217] He depicted it as a place where private individuals, independent of the constraints of the state, could engage in open discussions and exchange of ideas. At the core of Habermas' argument was the relationship between the private and the public. In the Middle Ages, he argued, there was no clear distinction between the two. Gradually, with capitalist forces, a bourgeois public sphere was created which allowed private individuals to debate their arguments in public. It was a development which took shape during the eighteenth century, as new voluntary institutions of sociability outside of government were created. The evidence Habermas used was from early eighteenth-century England. Direct government measures, including reforms in education and a stronger bureaucracy, rather than economic factors alone, enabled the growth of the public sphere.

[217] I follow the interpretation of T.C.W. Blanning, *The Culture of Power and the Power of Culture. Old Regime Europe 1660–1789* (Oxford, 2002), pp. 5–14. See also Andreas Gestrich, 'The public sphere and the Habermas-Debate', *German History*, 24 (2006), pp. 413–31.

For the monarchy, historians have made the argument that Joseph II recognised the importance of the public sphere, that in his practical, direct and simpler style of rule, Joseph took account of the public. He did away with formal practices at court and opened up buildings to the public.[218] Also, the narrative went, his censorship reform enabled a 'flood of pamphlets' and a decrease in the number of prohibited books. This, together with the growing appeal of Masonic lodges, created a 'burgeoning public sphere'.[219] Even though these were important changes, it is difficult to gauge the extent to which they were sufficient to establish a free sphere, with some width and depth, in the monarchy. Joseph did not follow a consistent censorship policy. Although he was more permissive of writings which would appeal to educated citizens, he continued to set strict censorship criteria for texts destined for ordinary people. Public performances of opera and theatre were also subject to tight control.[220]

The Masonic Lodge was an institution sometimes associated with the eighteenth-century public sphere, and Zinzendorf became a member of Vienna's first Masonic lodge. Despite Maria Theresa's apprehension about the lodges, Freemasons expanded their activities. They reached a high point during Joseph's reign.[221] It is not obvious, however, how Freemasonry was able to contribute to the public sphere. First, it was a mysterious organisation with members sworn to secrecy. Second, it seemed that the activities of most lodges in Austria did not involve intellectual exchange. They consisted of dabbling in alchemy and gambling, with a good share of dining in like-minded company.[222] Joseph eventually decided to limit their growth.

Certainly, during Zinzendorf's time, it is too early to speak of a public sphere in the monarchy. Maria Theresa was a conservative ruler despite her sweeping reforms in government and measures to loosen the Jesuits' grip on education and censorship.[223] Unlike Joseph, she was formal, and her ideas were firmly rooted in traditional Christianity.[224] She was not receptive to liberal thinking and not in favour of having an independent public opinion emerge. The government kept a close lid on the press, which was

[218] Blanning, *The Culture of Power*, pp. 430–31.
[219] T.C.W. Blanning, *Joseph II. Profiles in Power* (London, 1994), pp. 164–65.
[220] Beales, *Joseph II*, vol. 2, p. 93.
[221] For an account of Freemasonry under Joseph, see Beales, *Joseph II*, vol. 2, pp. 526–43.
[222] Ibid., pp. 531–33.
[223] Beales, *Joseph II*, vol. 1, pp. 441–45, 455–60.
[224] Charles Ingrao, *The Habsburg Monarchy, 1618–1815* (Cambridge, 1994), p. 170.

barred from critical reporting on important domestic issues. Curiously, newspapers were allowed to keep readers well informed about political developments abroad. The *Wienerische Diarium*, which changed its name in 1780 to *Wiener Zeitung*, reported in the late 1760s about the debates in the English parliament on the affairs of the outspoken journalist and politician John Wilkes.

The *Journal de Commerce*, printed in Brussels between 1759 and 1762, published advanced economic thinking from France. It was the idea of Serionne, who succeeded in convincing Johann Karl Philipp Count Cobenzl, the Governor of the Austrian Netherlands, of its merit.[225] Kaunitz was very close to Cobenzl and was free to approve the newspaper since the territory was under his direct administration. Written in French, the monthly journal was published between 1759 and 1762 and circulated in the main cities of the Austrian Netherlands, as well as in Vienna, Liège, Amsterdam and Paris. Cobenzl regularly sent copies to Kaunitz.[226] The empress added her support for the publication, noting the journal's 'usefulness to the public'.[227] In essence, the newspaper disseminated the ideas of Gournay's circle. In 1761, it printed an obituary followed by a eulogy of Gournay.[228] Serionne, who rejected the physiocratic idea of the primacy of agriculture, developed arguments for a more balanced economic policy. In addition to agriculture, good policy had to be based on the growth of commerce and the development of industry.[229] The *Journal de Commerce* made an impact in Vienna, and in 1762, Sonnenfels was instructed to use it as a model for a similar publication in German.[230]

In the interest of the state, Maria Theresa would deviate from conservative principles to get results. In the 1740s and 1750s, she created new

[225] Hasquin, 'Jacques Accarias de Serionne', pp. 157–60.

[226] Ibid., p. 160.

[227] Ibid., pp. 161–62.

[228] Marco Cavarzere, '"The New Science of Commerce" in the Holy Roman Empire: Véron de Forbonnais *Elémens du commerce* and its German Readers', *History of European Ideas*, 40:8 (2014), pp. 1130–50, at p. 1139.

[229] Hasquin, 'Jacques Accarias de Serionne', pp. 163–65.

[230] Klingenstein, 'Between Mercantilism and Physiocracy', pp. 196–97. Sonnenfels' project of a journal, 'Beyträge zur österreichischen Handlung', was never realised: Karl-Heinz Osterloh, *Joseph von Sonnenfels und die österreichische Reformbewegung im Zeitalter des aufgeklärten Absolutismus. Eine Studie zum Zusammenhang von Kameralwissenschaft und Verwaltungspraxis* (Lübeck and Hamburg: Matthiesen, 1970), p. 32. See also Simon Karstens, *Lehrer, Schriftsteller, Staatsreformer: die Karriere des Joseph von Sonnenfels (1733–1817)* (Vienna: Böhlau Verlag, 2011), p. 70, note 319.

academies for the education of her officials.[231] She also allowed select officials to have exposure to enlightened ideas from abroad.[232] Zinzendorf was one of them. In line with her political agenda, the empress made use of Zinzendorf's financial knowledge to educate the government's administrators in finance and accountancy. Between 1762 and 1774, Zinzendorf anonymously wrote or coordinated the publication of four textbooks on the use of new accounting methods. They contained practical examples and were intended for teaching. The introduction of the fourth book, *Grundsätze der Rechnungswissenschaft auf das Privatvermögen angewendet, zum Gebrauche der öffentlichen Vorlesungen bei den k.k. Ritterakademien und der Realschule*,[233] gave a clear explanation of the development the work had undergone.[234] The first textbook, printed in 1762, was based on the accounting techniques which Zinzendorf used for his own estate in Lower Austria.[235] The second, published in the same year, aimed to make mercantile accounting accessible to a wider readership and included, in two separate sections, translations of the French works of Matthieu de La Porte and Pierre Giraudeau.[236] A third textbook, eight years later, substantially revised the old bookkeeping methods used by merchants and offered the reader a greater variety of applications in different economic activities.[237] Finally, in *Grundsätze der Rechnungswissenschaft*, Zinzendorf con-

[231] Ingrao, *The Habsburg Monarchy*, p. 167.

[232] Derek Beales, *Enlightenment and Reform in Eighteenth Century Europe* (London: I.B. Tauris, 2005), p. 70.

[233] Ludwig Zinzendorf, *Grundsätze der Rechnungswissenschaft auf das Privatvermögen angewendet, zum Gebrauche der öffentlichen Vorlesungen bei den k.k. Ritterakademien und der Realschule. Erster Theil* (Vienna, Johann Thomas von Trattnern: 1774) *48.B.3, ÖNB.

[234] Ibid., 'Vorbericht', fols 3v–5v.

[235] Ludwig Zinzendorf, *Einleitung zu einem verbesserten Cameral-Rechnungs-Fuße auf die Verwaltung einer Herrschaft angewandt* (Vienna, 1762), *48.G.42, ÖNB. Zinzendorf was noticeably impressed when an army officer applied double-entry bookkeeping to his personal finances after merely three months of study: Diary of Karl Zinzendorf, 17 October 1761, HHStA.

[236] Ludwig Zinzendorf, *Einleitung zur doppelten Buchhaltung. 1. Theil: Wissenschaft der Kaufleute und Buchhalter, aus dem Französischen des Herrn de la Porte übersetzt. Zweyter Teil. Enthaltend eine Erbschaftsabtheilung, eine Wirtschaftsrechnung und eine Finanzoperation. Anwendung der Doppelten Buchhaltung auf die Finanz-Operation so von denen gewährleistenden Herren Ständen der Böhmischen und Oesterreichischen Erblande vermöge k.k. Rezeß vom 25. Junii und Ständischen Patenten vom 30. Junii 1761 übernommen worden* (Vienna, Prague and Trieste, 1762), 48.E.13, ÖNB.

[237] Ludwig Zinzendorf, *Praktischer Unterricht zu der verbeßerten doppelten Buchhaltung* (Vienna: Johann Thomas Trattner, 1770), 308458-D, ÖNB.

solidated the information and attempted to present a general system for good accounting. The aim was to offer technical tools with which individuals could understand the financial fluctuations of their wealth and avoid bankruptcies. To cover the spectrum of activities in the economy, Zinzendorf provided two general sets of examples. In the first part of the book, he applied the accounting practices to more straightforward undertakings. These included commerce and the management of debt, as well as the administration of an estate and of a private household. In the second part, he examined more complex business operations, including manufacturing, agriculture, private mining operations and commercial activities, which used bills of exchange.[238] The empress agreed to have 300 copies printed.[239] The low print run is good evidence that the intended readership was limited to the administrators. Under Maria Theresa, the public sphere had hardly any significance.

Zinzendorf's Different Kind of Economic Discussion

The distinctiveness of Zinzendorf's conception of economic discourse emerges by comparing it with the arguments of Justi and Sonnenfels on finance and banking. The two leading cameralist writers could not and did not develop their arguments on banks to the same level of sophistication and detail.

Justi published most of his important economic texts during his stay in Vienna. These include his two-volume work on cameralism, *Staatswirthschaft*,[240] which was based on his lectures and experiences in

[238] Zinzendorf, *Grundsätze der Rechnungswissenschaft*, Vorbericht, fols 3r–3v, 6r–7v. The second part was published after Zinzendorf's death by Johann Gottfried Brand, a lecturer of the *Realhandlungsakademie*: Johann Gottfried Brand, *Grundsätze der Staatsrechnungswissenschaft. Zweiter Band.entält Rechnungsentwürfe sowie die Anwendung der Grundsätze auf das Grundvermögen zeigen* (Vienna: Johann Thomas Trattner, 1785), 17.L.14., ÖNB. Subsequently, Brand also published a third volume, *Grundsätze der Staatsrechnungswissenschaft. Dritter Band, entält Rechnungsentwürfe, welche die Anwendung der allgemeinen Grundsätze auf oekonomische und Finanzgegenstände des Staatsvermögens zeigen* (Vienna: Johann Thomas Trattner, 1786), ÖNB.

[239] Pettenegg (ed.), *Selbstbiographien*, p. 143.

[240] Johann Heinrich Gottlob von Justi, *Staatswirthschaft oder systematische Abhandlung aller oekonomischen und Cameralwissenschaften, die zur Regierung eines Landes erfordert werden*, 2nd enlarged edition (Leipzig, 1758).

Vienna.[241] Justi's theoretical approach to finance was comparable to Zinzendorf's. He also wrote about the importance of a good supply and circulation of money for the economy.[242] Justi distinguished three types of credit: the credit of the ruler, of the country and third, domestic credit. The latter, he argued, had the biggest influence on the circulation of money. If, out of fear of losing money and assets, the wealthy classes would withhold credit to domestic commerce and industry, economic activity would suffer. Thus, to support domestic credit, it was important that investors had a counterpart which could ensure that large sums of money would be lent swiftly and securely. This, he thought, was the role of the bank. For Justi, two types of bank existed: *Giro* and lending banks. He proposed to combine both of them.[243] In a *Giro* institution, depositors would be able to record credits and debits in the books of the bank. As a lending bank, it would receive the guarantee of the ruler, the Estates or a national trading company that income would be made available for the payment of interest on deposits. Reliable and timely interest payments, Justi argued, would determine whether or not a bank could keep the confidence of the public. If credit was assured, a bank could issue public paper and this would add to the supply and circulation of money in the economy.[244]

The other important writer of cameralistic textbooks was Sonnenfels. He also held an academic post and was appointed in 1763 to the chair of 'Polizey and Cameralistic Sciences' at the University of Vienna. Sonnenfels taught Justi's *Staatswirthschaft*, and his own three-volume textbook, *Grundsätze der Polizey, Handlung und Finanzwissenschaft*,[245] was a standard work until the nineteenth century with nine editions published.[246] Like Justi, Sonnenfels argued that a good supply of money was necessary to support the real economy. Moreover, an increase in the circulation of money, together with low rates of interest, would help industry and com-

[241] Keith Tribe, *Governing Economy: The Reformation of German Economic Discourse 1750–1840* (Cambridge, 1988), pp. 57, 61.

[242] Johann Heinrich Gottlob von Justi, *Die Grundfeste zu der Macht und Glückseligkeit der Staaten oder ausführliche Vorstellung der gesamten Policeywissenschaft* (2 vols, Königsberg and Leipzig, 1760), vol. 1, pp. 615–19; Johann Heinrich Gottlob von Justi, *Abhandlung von der Macht, Glückseligkeit und Credit eines Staats* (Ulm, Frankfurt and Leipzig, 1760), pp. 58–9.

[243] Justi, *Abhandlung*, pp. 59–65.

[244] Ibid., pp. 66–70.

[245] Joseph von Sonnenfels, *Grundsätze der Polizey, Handlung und Finanzwissenschaft* (3 vols, Vienna, 1787).

[246] Tribe, *Governing Economy*, p. 55.

merce.[247] Sonnenfels also distinguished between *Giro* and lending banks. As a third category, he added 'political banks'. The latter were lending banks which were engaged in business with the state.[248] Sonnenfels provided a detailed description of the three types of banks using, to a large extent, similar arguments to Zinzendorf.[249] His examples of political banks included the banks of England, Venice and Stockholm.[250] The Bank of France, associated with Law's scheme, represented a warning of the abuse of credit by the state.[251]

Both Justi and Sonnenfels discussed ideas of state finance and set out different types of banks. But their arguments were not as developed and detailed as the analyses presented by Zinzendorf. Their writings were intended primarily for an academic audience, and their arguments remained theoretical. Neither writer could or did offer policy prescriptions for reforming the financial institutions of the monarchy.

Sonnenfels was aware that his teaching lacked practical comparative evidence. In 1765, he asked Maria Theresa for permission to travel in the monarchy to gain a first-hand understanding of the economic realities in the provinces. His request, however, was turned down by the *Hofkammer* and *Kommerzienhofkommission*, and the empress supported the decision of her ministers.[252] Also, Sonnenfels' subsequent demands to consult economic data in Viennese archives were not granted.[253] He very clearly had been given a narrow teaching remit. The books and the material for his lectures were prescribed to him by others in government and, in this respect, Sonnenfels followed some of Zinzendorf's arguments.[254] This deficit was compounded by his background. He was a novice in the field of economic theory and did not have the knowledge to appreciate the economic debates in Europe. Sonnenfels had originally planned to become

[247] Louise Sommer, *Die österreichischen Kameralisten in dogmengeschichtlicher Darstellung* (Vienna, 1920; reprint, Scientia Verlag Aalen, 1967), pp. 379, 380, 383.

[248] Sonnenfels, *Grundsätze*, vol. 3, p. 466.

[249] Ibid., pp. 466–75.

[250] Ibid., pp. 475–76.

[251] Ibid., pp. 477–78.

[252] Grete Klingenstein, 'Professor Sonnenfels darf nicht reisen. Beobachtungen zu den Anfängen der Wirtschafts-, Sozial- und Politikwissenschaften in Österreich' in Hedwig Kopetz, Joseph Marko and Klaus Poier (eds.), *Soziokultureller Wandel im Verfassungsstaat. Phänomene politischer Transformation* (Band 90/II, 2004), pp. 829–42, at pp. 830–31.

[253] Karstens, *Die Karriere*, pp. 97–8.

[254] Klingenstein, 'Between Mercantilism and Physiocracy', pp. 198–99; Klingenstein, 'Professor Sonnenfels', p. 835.

a university professor of German eloquence.[255] When he began his work on *Grundsätze*, he did not intend to write about cameralist theory. The first volume of *Grundsätze*, which was published in 1765, covered matters of domestic security and social order. It did not examine economic or financial questions. Only in 1769 and 1776 was the first part supplemented with two additional volumes on commerce and subsequently finance.[256]

Zinzendorf was able to comment on credit and banks in a way which no other writer in the monarchy could. He had collected relevant and detailed information on European banks, and in the mid-eighteenth century, he was the most proficient finance specialist in the country. With an exceptionally wide base of knowledge behind his arguments, Zinzendorf was more than a practical reformer. He had a different way of discussing the economy, and with privileged access to confidential information, was able to shape economic policy-making.

More generally, the distinctiveness of Zinzendorf's approach is apparent in his conception of the contribution of political economy. More than simply solving the monarchy's most pressing financial difficulties, he regarded political economy as an activity of important intellectual significance which offered a new way to understand the progress of society.[257] Economic activities, he thought, became a key determinant for political decision-making. Zinzendorf recognised that a country's political power was restrained by its economic capability, and that to compete successfully in international trade, it needed a well-developed economy and efficient financial institutions. The public should be encouraged to develop their productive activities and engage gainfully in commerce. This, Zinzendorf thought, could also be achieved by countries which were absolute monarchies like Austria, if they used their resources and social structures to their advantage. His inspiration came from Montesquieu's study of the different forms of government in *De l'Esprit des Lois*. There, the French thinker argued that success in trade was not dependent on the

[255] Tribe, *Governing Economy*, p. 78.

[256] Klingenstein, 'Between Mercantilism and Physiocracy', p. 199; Karstens, *Die Karriere*, pp. 83–4. For a discussion of the three volumes of *Grundsätze*, see Tribe, *Governing*, pp. 85–90.

[257] For the argument of political economy as a new and important intellectual discipline in the eighteenth century, see John Robertson, 'Enlightenment, Public Sphere and Political Economy' in Jesús Astigarraga and Javier Usoz (eds.), *L'économie politique et la sphère publique dans le débat des Lumières* (Madrid: Casa de Velázquez, 2013), pp. 9–32.

form of government, but rather reflected the geography and specific make up of a country.[258] For Zinzendorf, political economy was key for an understanding of the functions of government. Central to his thinking were Melon's *Essai politique*, which offered a coherent set of principles for an understanding of the economy, and Law's *Money and Trade*, which provided a general framework for the role of money in the economy. Also, important for Zinzendorf were the translations of economic writings produced by the writers around Gournay, which demonstrated that good ideas could be adapted to different political circumstances.

Zinzendorf, who in the early 1750s was living in France, was able to follow the beginnings of Gournay's radical enterprise closely. Thereafter, in particular through his brother's travels, he continued to engage with members of the circle. The way the French writers and administrators changed the discussion on economic policy made a strong impact on Zinzendorf' intellectual development. As a result, he wanted a more open debate on economic arguments within the monarchy, and to this end, Zinzendorf attempted to emulate the work of Gournay's circle in France, albeit on a smaller scale. The circle around Zinzendorf had striking similarities with that of the French writers. There were even striking parallels in the backgrounds and writings of the two men. Zinzendorf decided to apply the work of Gournay and recreate the French style of debate in the monarchy.

Zinzendorf formed a small circle of individuals to generate good arguments about the most advanced European economic ideas. Like the French, he used his specialist knowledge to open the government up to new ways of thinking about the economy. However, in terms of engaging directly with the public, Zinzendorf could not hope to match Gournay's initiative. The closed political system of the monarchy did not allow for the circulation of state documents outside the confines of the ruling elite or the use of public opinion to make ministers reconsider or adopt specific policies. Moreover, Zinzendorf could not draw on a public sphere, and of his numerous translations, only *Gedanken vom Gelde* was printed. Nevertheless, as a minister, he kept pushing to extend economic discussions and appealed forcefully to senior government officials to engage directly with the public on questions of war finance and state credit.

Clearly then, Zinzendorf attempted to do much more than cameralist writers could achieve in their academic setting. He had a very different

[258] Ibid., p. 21.

way of discussing the economy. Using his in-depth knowledge and position as the leading financial expert in government, Zinzendorf sought to introduce not only foreign ideas but also a radical foreign style of debate into the monarchy. Years later, Napoleon quipped that the Habsburg monarchy was always trailing the rest of Europe by one army and one idea. Albert Sorel, the French historian who related this anecdote, remarked that at least the Austrians, unlike the French, always had an army and an idea.[259] For new ideas in relation to political economy in the eighteenth century, Zinzendorf made sure that the monarchy had access to the most advanced thought in Europe.

[259] T.C.W. Blanning, *The French Revolutionary Wars 1787–1802* (London, 1996), p. 273.

CHAPTER 7

Conclusion

Ludwig Zinzendorf was a sophisticated economic thinker in the mid-eighteenth-century Habsburg monarchy, part of the wider intellectual movement in Europe dedicated to understanding political economy and presenting it as an independent and important activity. Self-educated, polyglot and hard-working, Zinzendorf was formidably well-read and impressively numerate. His output was detailed and analytical. Zinzendorf sought to provide a different kind of economic advice and attempted to open government up to new concepts on the economy. He was a reformer resolute in his determination to propagate the most advanced European ideas and practices. Foreign thinkers, in particular French, provided Zinzendorf with the arguments with which he developed a new system of political economy for the monarchy.[1] For Zinzendorf, who was a pragmatist, tried and tested ideas were preferable to new ones. They could be adapted to a different political environment. In this, and in his desire to generate a more open debate on economic arguments, Zinzendorf attempted to apply a moderate format of Gournay's French initiative in the monarchy.

Zinzendorf's political economy was based on Melon's neo-Colbertian competitive strategy of manufacturing-driven economic development which promoted both internal and external commerce. Like Melon,

[1] On the wider French cultural influence on the monarchy, see R.J.W. Evans, *Austria, Hungary and the Habsburgs. Central Europe c.1683–1867* (Oxford, 2006), pp. 58–61.

S. Adler, *Political Economy in the Habsburg Monarchy 1750–1774*,
Palgrave Studies in the History of Finance,
https://doi.org/10.1007/978-3-030-31007-3_7

Zinzendorf followed Law's ideas of paper money and banks as instruments of such development.[2] Zinzendorf greatly admired the programme of Gournay's circle in establishing political economy as a coherent science for France and sought to play a similar role in the monarchy.[3] Zinzendorf's adaptations of the ideas of Law, Melon and others, as well as his use of foreign financial models, were always bent towards the needs of the monarchy as he perceived them. Cameralist theories were not part of his formal education at the University of Leipzig, and they did not play any significant role in his intellectual formation. In his economic thinking, Zinzendorf clearly opted for a wider European perspective. Recent scholarly debates have sought to extend the analysis of cameralism from the theory taught in universities to its applications in administrative practice.[4] However, in the mid-eighteenth-century monarchy, cameralist thought failed to exert a decisive influence on economic policy-making. It is well known that cameralism was expounded in the works of Justi and Sonnenfels and that it was taught by them to the monarchy's future administrators. But what has been under-appreciated is the extent to which the economic theories which shaped the debates in government at that time were those propagated by Zinzendorf. No other writer or government official in the monarchy had a comparably sophisticated knowledge of finance and grasp of foreign economic systems.

In this enterprise, Zinzendorf depended on the help of others. Most importantly, he relied on the support of Kaunitz who was keen to create a

[2] On the French model and its responses, including the interventions of the Scots Hume and Smith, see Istvan Hont, *Jealousy of Trade: International Competition and the Nation-State in Historical Perspective* (Cambridge, MA, 2005).

[3] On the circulation of economic ideas and the diffusion of the works of the Gournay circle, see Sophus A. Reinert, 'The Empire of Emulation: A Quantitative Analysis of Economic Translations in the European World, 1500–1849' in Sophus A. Reinert and Pernille Røge (eds), *The Political Economy of Empire in the Early Modern World* (Basingstoke: Palgrave Macmillan, 2013), pp. 105–28; on translations of Melon, see Jesús Astigarraga, 'La dérangeante découverte de l'autre: traductions et adaptations espagnoles de *l'Essai politique sur le commerce* (1734) de Jean-François Melon', *Revue d'histoire moderne et contemporaine*, 57:1 (2010), pp. 91–118.

[4] See Marten Seppel and Keith Tribe (eds), *Cameralism in Practice: State Administration and Economy in Early Modern Europe* (Suffolk: Boydell and Brewer, 2017). Previous research had noted the impact of cameralism beyond German-speaking countries: see Ernest Lluch, 'Cameralism Beyond the Germanic World: A Note on Tribe', *History of Economic Ideas*, 5:2 (1997), pp. 85–99 and Ernest Lluch, 'Der Kameralismus, ein vieldimensionales Lehrgebäude: Seine Rezeption bei Adam Smith und im Spanien des 18. Jahrhunderts, *Jahrbuch für Wirtschaftsgeschichte*, 41:2 (2000), pp. 133–54.

pool of talent around him. Since his foreign postings in the 1740s, Kaunitz had directed his attention to finance and had recognised the importance of sound financial management for the encouragement of economic activity and the increase of available resources. He recruited Zinzendorf as his dedicated economic expert and ensured that his protégé had ready access to foreign writings and could travel in Europe.[5] Kaunitz intervened with the empress to give Zinzendorf an accelerated career track in government with good pay. He also made sure that Zinzendorf had access to the rulers and could present his ideas to them. For Zinzendorf, the years in France with Kaunitz were formative. Zinzendorf had direct exposure to French thinkers. He also developed an excellent grasp of French commercial, financial, political and military institutions which in 1752 culminated in the 'Mémoire sur les richesses, le commerce et les finances de la France'. Written for Kaunitz, it was Zinzendorf's exceptional account of the French economy and his attempt to understand why France was unable to continue to rise in Europe and how England had succeeded in overtaking her. Most of Zinzendorf's subsequent output, including his proposals on war finance, state credit and the reorganisation of the financial administration, was produced at Kaunitz's request. The second key person who was instrumental for Zinzendorf's achievements was his brother, Karl. Once established as a senior official in government and having to master an increasingly heavy workload, Zinzendorf relied on Karl to him keep up-to-date with economic thinking and practices abroad. Zinzendorf was Karl's mentor. He was closely involved in the planning of his brother's extensive travels and used Karl as his eyes and ears in Europe. Through Karl, Zinzendorf continued his dialogue with economic thinkers. The discussions with Hume showed the intellectual significance of Zinzendorf's thinking and the willingness of writers to exchange information.

Zinzendorf's approach was deductive and observational. His proposals were based on established systems and practices of foreign nations which he adapted ingeniously to the constraints of the monarchy's econ-

[5] 'Dix années de lectures et de méditations, une connoissance asséz étendue des principaux états de l'Europe, trois années de conseils qui embrassent tout l'interieur, tous ces hazards heureux dont j'ai l'obligation à Votre Excellence, m'ont peut être mis en état de render à Sa Majesté des services importans et uniques dans la partie des finances et du commerce mais pour y parvenir, il faut oser se mettre sur les rangs': letter of Ludwig Zinzendorf to Kaunitz, 21 October 1756, in Eduard Gaston von Pettenegg (ed.), *Ludwig und Karl Grafen und Herren von Zinzendorf. Ihre Selbstbiographien nebst einer kurzen Geschichte des Hauses Zinzendorf* (Vienna, 1879), p. 70.

omy.[6] European thinkers shaped the way Zinzendorf understood the economy of the monarchy. He translated a variety of foreign economic texts, including Law's *Money and Trade* and Melon's *Essai politique*. Both publications had a significant influence on Zinzendorf's thinking. For one, Melon gave a defence of Law's ideas, and Zinzendorf subsequently attempted something similar with *Gedanken vom Gelde*, his German version of *Money and Trade*. But more than that, in the *Essai politique*, Melon presented an analytical concept of the economy which appealed to Zinzendorf and had a significant impact on his writings: land and agriculture were the prime sources of wealth. A rising population and the development of manufacturing facilitated commerce, which was, in turn, the driver for economic progress, stimulating agricultural production. And, finally, good supply and good circulation of money in the economy were the engines for commercial expansion. Zinzendorf recognised that the circulation of money, in particular, was of great importance for the monarchy's economy, where commercial activity was weak and agriculture was predominant. However, money on its own was not sufficient. The monetary side had to be a support for the real economy. Like Law and Melon, Zinzendorf thought that public debt was beneficial for economic development, provided that the ruler could ensure good use of credit and was able to establish public confidence. The supply of money could be increased through the creation of liquid government paper and should be guided by the productive activity in the economy. A significant benefit of the increase in the supply of money was a lower rate of interest. Law's system, and on this point Zinzendorf agreed with Melon, had failed because it was too ambitious and had provided too much liquidity to the French economy. In the 'Mémoire sur les richesses, le commerce et les finances de la France', Zinzendorf directly applied the arguments of the *Essai politique* to the French policies of the early 1750s. He agreed with Melon on the importance of a successful national trade company, on creating an advantage to national shipping through targeted protective policies like the English Navigation Act and on the considerable economic benefits of having financial credit instruments which circulated in the market.

[6] 'Je fais gloire de ne rien proposer qui soit nouveau et qui ne soit confirmé ailleurs par une experience de plus de trente années': letter of Ludwig Zinzendorf to Kaunitz, 24 July 1756, in ibid., p. 67.

Zinzendorf's important disagreement with Melon was on currency devaluation. In *Gedanken vom Gelde*, Zinzendorf expounded on the harmful effects of a currency debasement. In the light of Prussia's efforts to finance a significant part of its war expenses through currency manipulation, Zinzendorf updated Law's analysis with more recent German debates which, he thought, ought to be useful to German readers. He also provided new French arguments against currency variations from Gournay's circle. *Gedanken vom Gelde* throws light on the importance of translations for political economy in the eighteenth century. Through his work and travels in France, Zinzendorf was well placed to follow the translations and the output of the writers around Gournay. In fact, Zinzendorf's arguments have a remarkable similarity to Gournay's. Just as Gournay had in the case of France, Zinzendorf clearly recognised that monarchy's economic policies were not working and that new measures to improve state finance and commerce were required. Like Gournay, too, Zinzendorf thought that a lower rate of interest together with an expansion of credit through easily tradeable government paper would drive commerce. Both men analysed commercial rivals to see what could usefully be imitated whilst maintaining the political structure and coherence of their country. This again was a point of symmetry between the two men's work: Zinzendorf produced very detailed accounts on France and European banks, and Gournay commissioned economic reports on European countries, including the monarchy.[7] Like Gournay for the Habsburg monarchy, Zinzendorf attempted to gain an understanding of France's permanent sources of wealth and its credit. A clear goal for both men was to identify areas for the growth of commerce.

Zinzendorf's first major application of his knowledge to the monarchy's economy was in relation to war finance. In 1757, in *Pro Memoria an eine ständische Deputation einen Vorschlag zur Erleichterung des ständischen Credites betreffend*, he first set out in a comprehensive manner the idea of increasing the supply of money and issuing new public paper to provide financing for the state. Zinzendorf used financial practices and ideas from European countries and adapted them to the monarchy. The

[7] For a list of memoirs on individual countries, see Simone Meyssonnier, 'Annexe 1. Inventaire analytique du fonds Gournay de la Bibliothèque municipale de Saint-Brieuc', in Loïc Charles, Frédéric Lefebvre and Christine Théré (eds), *Le Cercle de Vincent Gournay. Savoirs économiques et pratiques administratives en France au milieu du XVIIIe siècle* (Paris: Institut National D'Études Démographiques, 2011), pp. 307–30.

new funds, Zinzendorf proposed, would be raised by the Estates of Lower Austria which had a solid credit record and which would act prudently in issuing money. As the monarchy had no large concentrated pool of wealth, it was important to broaden the investor base. Bonds in smaller denominations, Zinzendorf thought, could be purchased by the public living in smaller towns and in villages. The operation, which would be targeted at a larger number of potential investors in the country, would create publicity and increase the supply of money. Also, with bonds issued as bearer documents, transactions could become simpler and more transparent. Some of the bonds should have cash-like qualities so that money could be swiftly made available to the state to cover urgent military expenses. Zinzendorf did not want to create a new indefinite debt burden and thus proposed the creation of a redemption fund, together with a detailed repayment schedule. State credit required financial discipline.

Zinzendorf argued that in peacetime, too, radical new financial measures were necessary because the Vienna City Bank was not operating any longer as it should. It had lost its independence from the government. It kept the interest rate high and thus diverted domestic funds away from productive use in the economy. Also, the large number of small domestic investors could not do business with the bank because Vienna was the only place where money could be deposited and the minimum amount required was too high. The bank, which was only accountable to the ruler, operated in secrecy. It no longer had the confidence of the public, and people feared the collapse of its credit. The monarchy, Zinzendorf concluded, needed a solid and transparent banking system, and European countries provided good models. In 1763, he presented to the ruling elite an exceptionally detailed and well-informed survey of European banks which took five years to complete. In individual chapters, he set out the operations of 12 European banks and classified them into three groups: the first and most basic type was the bank which operated in support of commerce. The second type of bank also kept specie for trade, but additionally issued paper to increase the supply of money in the economy. The third group finally was the most developed and consisted of political banks. It operated like the second group, but provided direct support to the state by offering short-term finance. For Zinzendorf, the Bank of England was the most sophisticated and successful example of the third group and represented the model for a political bank in the monarchy. The attraction of the English bank was the support it provided to the real economy and its ability to end the government's dependence on expensive credit. It had delivered low rates of interest on government debt, a more competitive financial system for commercial transactions, and liquidity in the economy through freely circulating *billets* and shares of the bank. It had robust operations, including an accurate system of record taking, and it had played a decisive role in supporting the financial operations of the state. Also, good financial and political controls were in place to ensure that the Bank of England would not become a threat to the economy.

Zinzendorf wanted to create a financial system in the monarchy which, like England's, was built on public confidence and a low rate of interest on public debt. These were key if the monarchy wanted to engage successfully in international trade and cover future war expenses. The new political bank would support commerce, issue new uniform bonds to increase the supply of money in the economy and should operate with transparent administrative systems. The circulation of money would be facilitated by several bank branches in different cities where bonds would be accepted. During peacetime, the bank would support state credit by ensuring good liquidity of its paper and thereby keeping the market price of bonds at or above par. It could advance emergency funding to the state at a lower rate of interest. However, to avoid abuse by and dependence on the government, new credit could only be made from cash reserves and had to be a short-term measure. A solid financial system that actively strengthened the economy was necessary to cope with the additional challenges of war finance. During military conflicts, the bank would be expected to raise additional funds to cover the government's extraordinary outlays. The money would be raised from the public so that the bank should not become a new *Schulden Caße* of the state.

The realities of the monarchy's economy forced Zinzendorf to adapt the English banking model. Unlike in England, the public in the monarchy had no confidence in the state and its financial policies. Also, there was no large pool of private capital available. Given such important weaknesses, Zinzendorf chose the Estates of the Austrian and Bohemian lands as joint guarantors of the new bank. They could show a certain independence from the state, had a better credit record and enjoyed public support. However, he did concede that the initial issue of paper by the bank had to be a forced measure since the new institution would not have gained the trust of the public. Zinzendorf also recognised that the state would have to keep using forced credit and forced taxes to finance new wars. They would remain critical elements of financial policy during military conflicts and the burden should be spread over a larger number of citizens. The other important institution was the stock exchange, which Zinzendorf modelled on the Parisian bourse. Again, he placed it under the direction of the Estates of the Austrian and Bohemian lands. The exchange would provide an orderly trading framework for the bonds and replace the right of debt redemption. With sufficient demand, the exchange should give liquidity and ensure a good circulation of public paper. To prevent a collapse of bond prices, he allowed for state intervention and lending by the new bank to prevent a drop in prices. In time, Zinzendorf hoped, as public confidence in the economy rose and the political bank became more established, voluntary credit would replace these forced measures.

Zinzendorf valued discussion and debate. His extraordinary knowledge of economic theory and financial practices attracted a circle of like-minded individuals where ideas and policies were discussed. The debates in the administration suggest that the mid-eighteenth-century Austrian government consisted more of influential groups of well-placed individuals, and less of governing institutions, although these have traditionally received most of the attention from scholars.[8] In central government, Zinzendorf led the discussions on finance and supplied the key ideas for the reorganisation of the monarchy's financial administration. His political appointments were a recognition of this. In central government, with Kaunitz as chief advocate, he strove to generate more open and sophisticated arguments on the economy. The communication channels were short, and personal connections mattered as much as ideas. Zinzendorf used his position to act as the fulcrum for economic questions in order to debate with and learn from the projectors. Their specialist knowledge, Zinzendorf thought, could be useful in implementing his plans. For example, by making use of the commercial expertise of Thys, he hoped to recreate in the monarchy the structure of Law's French scheme of a bank combined with a trading company. Within the tight confines of the political system, Zinzendorf encountered fierce resistance in government, and the absence of a public sphere did not allow him to widen the debates beyond the ruling elite, as he would have liked. Nevertheless, Zinzendorf, like the members of Gournay's circle in France, made every effort to open

[8] For a recent major publication on institutions, see Michael Hochedlinger, Petr Mat'a and Thomas Winkelbauer (eds), *Verwaltungsgeschichte der Habsburgermonarchie in der frühen Neuzeit.* Band 1: *Hof und Dynastie, Kaiser und Reich, Zentralverwaltungen, Kriegswesen und landesfürstliches Finanzwesen*, *MIÖG* 62 (2 vols, Vienna: Böhlau, 2019).

up the government to new economic concepts. He gave the debates a new direction. The monarchy, Zinzendorf thought, should not rely on its own intellectual resources when discussing the economy. Thus, he ensured that a space was created where the most advanced ideas and financial practices from other European countries were available to the rulers and senior government officials. There was a common dialogue over economic questions in eighteenth-century Europe, and thanks to the efforts of Zinzendorf, it extended to the monarchy.

Bibliography

Manuscripts

Saint-Brieuc

Bibliothèque municipale de Saint-Brieuc
[Anonymous]. 'Mémoire d'information pour les pays héréditaires de la Maison d'Autriche en Allemagne', 10 August 1752, vol. 82, number 2, fonds Gournay.

St. Pölten

Niederösterreichisches Landesarchiv, St. Pölten (NÖLA)
Archiv Zinzendorf: Kartons 9, 38, 39, 40.

Vienna

1. Haus-, Hof- und Staatsarchiv (HHStA)

Handschriften
Zinzendorf, Karl. 'Mémoires rassemblés par le Comte Charles de Zinzendorf pendant ses voyages par la France 1764, 1767 et 1769': vol. 1, Hs. Suppl. 954–W918, and vol. 2, Hs Suppl. 960–§922.
Zinzendorf, Ludwig. 'über die französische Marine und die ostindische Compagnie', Paris, 24 December 1751, HS Suppl.961–W923.
Staatenabteilung
England Berichte, 1752–1753, Kartons 102, 103.

S. Adler, *Political Economy in the Habsburg Monarchy 1750–1774*,
Palgrave Studies in the History of Finance,
https://doi.org/10.1007/978-3-030-31007-3

Frankreich Varia, 1750–1752, Karton 22.
Staatsakte Frankreich Berichte, 1750–1754, Kartons 84, 92.
Staatskanzlei
Vorträge, Kartons 81, 84, 92.
Alte Kabinettsakten
Königsegg-Erps, Karl Ferdinand, 18 March 1758, 'Grafens Königsegg ohnmaßgebliche Anmerkungen und Meinung gegen den Plan des Grafen Zinzendorf Papiergeld zu drucken', Karton 17.
Nachlaß Zinzendorf, Handschriften
Vols 2b, 2c, 4, 18, 19, 21, 22, 27, 83, 87, 100, 101, 127.
Zinzendorf, Karl
Diaries: 1759–1763, 1768.
Zinzendorf, Ludwig
'Vorschlag des Grafen Ludwig von Zinzendorf über die Einrichtung der Finanzen de dato Wien, den 7. October 1761', vol. 2b.
'Sur l'utilité de la Chambre des Comptes et la nécessité de la conserver', October 1771, vol. 4.
'Projet de Finance pour la continuation de la Guerre', vol. 18.
'Finanzvorschläge', 1 June 1763, vol. 19.
'Allergnädigst, abgeforderter Vorschlag, die Einrichtung einer Börse zur Verhandlung der öffentlichen Papiere und eines Banco di Credito betreffend, Februar 1767', vol. 20.
'Vorschlag um die Unzulänglichkeit der bisherigen Finanzmittel auf einen künftigen Krieg zu ersetzen', 18 January 1769, vol. 21.
'Système de Law. Sentiments de quelques auteurs célèbres en faveur du papier', vol. 25 (this volume is missing from the files).
Pro Memoria an eine ständische Deputation einen Vorschlag zur Erleichterung des ständischen Credites betreffend, Im September 1757, vol. 33.
'Übersetzung aus dem Englischen des Locke Geld und dessen Ausmünzung und Erhöhung der Münzen, auch die diesfällige Meinung des Herren Lowndes betr', Nachlaß Zinzendorf', vol. 93 (this volume is missing from the files).
'Geschichte und Beschreibung der Wiener Stadt Banco', vol. 101.
'Beschreibung der vornehmsten Europäischen Bancken von Ludwig Friedrich Julius Grafen und Herrn von Zinzendorf und Pottendorf, Ihrer kaiserl. König. Apostol. Majestät wirklichen geheimen Rat, Kämmerern und Assesore des Directoriums in publicis et cameralibus, Wien 1758', vols 103 and 104.
'Essai sur l'Établissement d'une Banque générale des États', 26 Septembre 1750, vol. 105.
'4 Memoiren über Banken und das System des Law', vol. 106 (this volume is missing from the files).

2. Österreichische Nationabibliothek (ÖNB)

Zinzendorf, Ludwig. 'Mémoire sur les richesses, le commerce et les finances de la France', Cod. 14302.

[Anonymous], [undated]. 'Mémoire général des recueils des pièces de finance faites par Messieurs Fougerolles, Le Bret, de Vauban, du Guerin de Rademont, de la Jonchère, de M. Le Regent, d'un anonyme, de Boulainvilliers, de M. Chevalier Renaut, de M. le Marquis de Silly, de M. l'Abbé de St.Pierre, Tome premier', Cod. 14194.

3. Deutschordenszentralarchiv (DOZA)
Handschriften
Vols 52, 53, 63, 64, 65, 66, 67, 68, 187–189.

Published Primary Works

[Anonymous]. *Herrn Laws, Controlleur general der Financen in Franckreich Gedancken vom Waaren und Geld Handel, nebst dem erst in Schottland, hernach in Frankreich vorgestellten und angenommenen neuen project und Systemate der Financen, wobey einige curieuse Fata des Autoris zu lesen. Nach dem französischen und Englischen Exemplar* (Leipzig: bey Jacob Schustern, 1720).

Beer, Adolf. 'Denkschriften des Fürsten Wenzel Kaunitz-Rittberg', *AÖG* 48 (1872), pp. 3–161.

Brand, Johann Gottfried. *Grundsätze der Staatsrechnungswissenschaft. Dritter Band, enthält Rechnungsentwürfe, welche die Anwendung der allgemeinen Grundsätze auf oekonomische und Finanzgegenstände des Staatsvermögens zeigen* (Vienna: Johann Thomas Trattner, 1786).

——— *Grundsätze der Staatsrechnungswissenschaft. Zweiter Band.enthält Rechnungsentwürfe sowie die Anwendung der Grundsätze auf das Grundvermögen zeigen* (Vienna: Johann Thomas Trattner, 1785).

Briefe der Kaiserin Maria Theresia an Ihre Kinder und Freunde, ed. Alfred Ritter von Arneth (4 vols, Vienna, 1881).

Brûlons, Jacques Savary des. *Dictionnaire Universel de Commerce* (3 vols, Geneva, 1742).

Correspondance Secrète entre le Comte A.W. Kaunitz-Rietberg, ambassadeur imperial à Paris, et le Baron Ignaz de Koch, secrétaire de l'Impératrice Marie-Thérèse, 1750–1752, ed. Hans Schlitter (Paris, 1899).

Dangeul, Louis-Joseph Plumard de. *Remarques sur les avantages et désavantages de la France et de la Grande Bretagne par rapport au Commerce et aux autres sources de la puissances des États*, 3rd edn (Leiden, 1754).

Deparcieux, Antoine. *Essai sur les probabilités de la durée de la vie humaine* (1746). *Addition à l'Essai (1760). Réédition en fac-similé avec une introduction et des notes de C. Behar, accompagnée de contributions de G. Gallais-Hamonno, C. Tietsch, J. Berthon* (Institut National D'Études Demographiques, Paris, 2003).

Die Jüngeren Matrikel der Universität Leipzig 1559–1809, ed. Georg Erler (3 vols, Leipzig: Giesecke and Devrient, 1909).

Dutot, Charles de Ferrare. *Réflexions politiques sur les finances et le commerce* (2 vols, Paris, 1738).

——— *Réflexions politiques sur les finances et le commerce*, ed. Paul Harsin (2 vols, Paris, 1754; reprint, 2 vols, Liège, 1935).

Dupré de Saint Maur, Nicholas-François. *Essai sur les monnoyes, ou rapport entre l'argent et les denrées* (Paris, 1746).

Fleetwood, William. *Chronicon Preciosum: or An Account of English Money, the Price of Corn and Other Commodities, for the Last 600 Years* (London, 1707).

Forbonnais, Francois Véron de. *Principes et observations économiques* (Paris, 1767).

——— *Recherches et Considérations sur les Finances de France depuis l'année 1595 jusqu'à l'année 1721* (2 vols, Basel, 1758).

——— *Elémens du Commerce*, 2nd edn (2 vols, Leiden, 1754).

——— *Le Négociant Anglois, ou Traduction libre du livre intitulé: The British Merchant, Contenant divers Mémoires sur le Commerce de l'Angleterre avec la France, le Portugal et l'Espagne. Publié pour la premiere fois en 1713* (2 vols, Paris and Dresden, 1753).

Gournay, Vincent de. 'Pièce détachée sur l'intérêt de l'argent' (undated), ed. Takumi Tsuda, *Mémoires et lettres de Vincent de Gournay*, Economic research series, no. 31, The Institute of Economic Research, Hitotsubashi University (Tokyo: Kinokuniya Co., 1993a).

——— 'Mémoire (sans titre)' (1753), ed. Takumi Tsuda, *Mémoires et lettres de Vincent de Gournay*, Economic research series, no. 31, The Institute of Economic Research, Hitotsubashi University (Tokyo: Kinokuniya Co., 1993b).

——— 'Estimation des richesses de L'Angleterre dans quatre époques servant à en faire voir les progrès jusqu'à aujourd'hui tirée d'une brochure intitulé: *Essai sur la dette de la nation*, 2e édition' (1752–53), ed. Takumi Tsuda, *Mémoires et lettres de Vincent de Gournay*, Economic research series, no. 31, The Institute of Economic Research, Hitotsubashi University (Tokyo: Kinokuniya Co., 1993c).

Graumann, Johann Philipp. *Vernünftige Vertheidigung des Schreibens die Teutsche und anderer Völker Münz-Verfassung betreffend, der sogenannten gründlichen Prüfung desselben entgegengesetzt. Nebst einem Anhange worin die in der Erfahrung gegründete Ursachen von dem Steigen und Fallen des Gold und Silberpreises, und dem darauf sich gründenden Steigen und Fallen des Wechsel Courses angehandelt werden* (Berlin, 1751).

——— *Abdruck von einem Schreiben, die deutsche und anderer Völker Münzverfassung und insonderheit die Höch-Fürstl. Braunschweigische Münze betreffend* (Braunschweig, 1749).

Hume, David. *Of the Balance of Trade (1752)* in ed. Eugene F. Miller, *David Hume: Essays Moral, Political, Literary* (Indianapolis: Liberty Classics, 1987).

J.K.C.H. Comte de Zinzendorf. Journal: Chronique belgo-bruxelloise 1766–1770, ed. Georges Englebert (Brussels, 1991).

John Law: Oeuvres complètes, ed. Paul Harsin (3 vols, Paris, 1934).

Justi, Johann Heinrich Gottlob von. *System des Finanzwesens, nach dem vernünftigen, aus dem Endzweck der bürgerlichen Gesellschaften, und aus der Natur aller Quellen der Einkünfte des Staates hergeleiteten Grundsätzen und Regeln* (Halle, 1766).

——— *Gesammelte politische und Finanzschriften* (3 vols; vols 1 and 2, Copenhagen and Leipzig, 1761; vol. 3, idem., 1764).

——— *Die Grundfeste zu der Macht und Glückseligkeit der Staaten oder ausführliche Vorstellung der gesamten Policeywissenschaft* (2 vols, Königsberg and Leipzig, 1760a).

——— *Abhandlung von der Macht, Glückseligkeit und Credit eines Staats* (Ulm, Frankfurt and Leipzig, 1760b).

——— *Staatswirthschaft oder systematische Abhandlung aller oekonomischen und Cameralwissenschaften, die zur Regierung eines Landes erfordert werden*, 2nd enlarged edition (Leipzig, 1758).

Kaunitz, Wenzel Anton von. 'Mémoire sur la cour de France 1752' in ed. Vicomte du Dresnay, *La revue de Paris*, 11 (1904), pp. 441–54.

Law, John. *Money and Trade, Considered with a Proposal for Supplying the Nation with Money* (1705), ed. Antoin E. Murphy, *Monetary Theory: 1601–1758* (6 vols, London, 1997), vol. 5, pp. 3–70.

Le Blanc, Abbé Jean-Bernard. *Discours politiques de Monsieur Hume traduits de l'anglois* (2 vols, Amsterdam, 1754).

Locke, John. *Some Considerations of the Consequences of the Lowering of Interest and Raising the Value of Money* (London, 1692).

Lowndes, William. *A Report Containing an Essay for the Amendment of the Silver Coins* (London, 1695).

Mann, Fritz Karl (ed.). 'Justification du Système de Law par son Auteur', *Revue D'Histoire Économique et Sociale*, 6:1 (1913), pp. 49–103.

Maria Theresia. Briefe und Aktenstücke in Auswahl, ed. Friedrich Walter (Darmstadt, 1968).

Maria Theresia und Joseph II. Ihre Correspondenz sammt Briefen Josephs an seinen Bruder Leopold, ed. Alfred Ritter von Arneth (3 vols, Vienna, 1867).

Melon, Jean-François. *Essai politique sur le commerce* (2nd edn, 1736), ed. Eugène Daire, *Économistes-Financiers du XVIIIe siècle* (Paris, 1843), pp. 707–836.

Montesquieu, Charles-Louis de Secondat, Baron de. *De l'Esprit des Lois* (1748), ed. Victor Goldschmidt (2 vols, Paris: Garnier-Flammarion, 1979).

Nemours, Dupont de. *Analyse historique de la législation des grains depuis 1692* (Paris, 1789).

Neugebauer, Wilhelm Ehrenfried. *Des Herrn von Fourbonnais Sätze und Beobachtungen aus der Oekonomie, aus dem französischen übersetzt von Wilhelm Ehrenfried Neugebauer* (Vienna, 1767).

Niehbur, Markus von. *Geschichte der Königlichen Bank in Berlin. Von der Gründung derselben (1765) bis zum Ende des Jahres 1845. Aus amtlichen Quellen* (Berlin, 1854).

Oudermeulen, Cornelius. *Recherches sur le Commerce ou Idées relatives aux intérets des différents peoples de l'Europe* (2 vols, Amsterdam, 1778).
Schreyer, Joseph. *Kommerz, Fabriken und Manufakturen des Königreichs Böhmen* (Prague and Leipzig, 1790).
Sonnenfels, Joseph von. *Grundsätze der Polizey, Handlung und Finanzwissenschaft* (3 vols, Vienna, 1787).
Strube, Julius Melchior. *Untersuchung der Frage: Ob das Silbergeld zu erhöhen sey? Worin die sogenannte Vernünftige Vertheidigung des Schreibens: die Teutsche und anderer Völker Münz-Verfassung betreffend beantwortet wird* (Hannover, 1752).
——— *Gründliche Prüfung des Schreibens, die Teutsche und anderer Völker Münzverfassung und insonderheit die Höchfürstl. Braunschweigische Münze betreffend* (Hannover, 1751).
Unger, Johann Friedrich. *Von der Ordnung der Fruchtpreise, und deren Einflusse in die wichtigsten Angelegenheiten des menschlichen Lebens* (Göttingen, 1752).
Vaterländische Blätter für den österreichischen Kaiserstaat (Vienna, 1813).
Zinzendorf, Ludwig. *Grundsätze der Rechnungswissenschaft auf das Privatvermögen angewendet, zum Gebrauche der öffentlichen Vorlesungen bei den k.k. Ritterakademien und der Realschule. Erster Theil* (Vienna: Johann Thomas von Trattnern, 1774). *48.B.3, ÖNB.
——— *Praktischer Unterricht zu der verbeßerten doppelten Buchhaltung* (Vienna: Johann Thomas Trattner, 1770). 308458-D, ÖNB.
——— *Einleitung zu einem verbesserten Cameral-Rechnungs-Fuße auf die Verwaltung einer Herrschaft angewandt* (Vienna, 1762a). *48.G.42, ÖNB.
——— *Einleitung zur doppelten Buchhaltung. 1. Theil: Wissenschaft der Kaufleute und Buchhalter, aus dem Französischen des Herrn de la Porte übersetzt. Zweyter Teil. Enthaltend eine Erbschaftsabtheilung, eine Wirtschaftsrechnung und eine Finanzoperation. Anwendung der Doppelten Buchhaltung auf die Finanz-Operation so von denen gewährleistenden Herren Ständen der Böhmischen und Oesterreichischen Erblande vermöge k.k. Rezeß vom 25. Junii und Ständischen Patenten vom 30. Junii 1761 übernommen worden* (Vienna, Prague and Trieste, 1762b). 48.E.13, ÖNB.
——— *Finanz-Vorschläge zur Fortsetzung des gegenwärtigen Krieges. Allerhöchst Ihro Röm- Kais.-König. Apostolischen M.M.. Alleruntertänigst übergeben von Ludwig Grafen und Herrn von Zinzendorf und Pottendorf; dero wirklichen geheimen Rathe, Cämmerern und Assessore in denen Directoriis in publicis et cameralibus. Im Monat Jul.1759.*
——— *Gedanken vom Gelde und von der Handlung, nebst einem Vorschlage dem Geldmangel in Schottland abzuhelfen. Aus dem Englischen übersetzt. Gedruckt von Johann Thomas Trattern* (Vienna, Prague and Trieste, 1758).

Published Secondary Works

Adam, Ulrich. *The Political Economy of J.H.G. Justi* (Berne, 2006).

——— 'Justi and the Post-Montesquieu French Debate on Commercial Nobility in 1756' in Jürgen Georg Backhaus (ed.), *The Beginnings of Political Economy: Johann Heinrich Gottlob von Justi* (New York: Springer, 2009), pp. 75–99.

Alimento, Antonella. *Réformes fiscales et crises politiques dans la France de Louis XV* (Brussels, 2008).

——— 'Between Mercantilism and Physiocracy: Forbonnais's "Est Modus in Rebus" Vision' in Steven L. Kaplan and Sophus A. Reinert (eds.), *The Economic Turn. Recasting Political Economy in Enlightenment Europe* (London and New York: Anthem Press, 2019), pp. 169–92.

——— 'La Concurrence comme Politique Moderne. La Contribution de L'école de Gournay à la naissance d'une sphère publique dans la France des années 1750–1760' in Jesús Astigarraga and Javier Usoz (eds.), *L'économie politique et la sphère publique dans le débat des Lumières* (Madrid: Collection de la Casa de Velázquez, 2013), pp. 213–27.

——— 'Entre animosité nationale et rivalité d'émulation: la position de Véron de Forbonnais face à la compétition anglaise' in Manuela Albertone (ed.), *Governare il mondo. L'economia come linguaggio della politica nell'Europa del Settecento* (Milan: Fondazione Giangiacomo Feltrinelli, 2009), pp. 125–48.

——— 'Beyond the Treaty of Utrecht: Véron de Forbonnais's French Translation of the *British Merchant* (1753)', *History of European Ideas*, 40:8 (2014), pp. 1044–66.

Arneth, Alfred Ritter von (ed.). 'Graf Philipp Cobenzl und seine Memoiren', *AÖG* 67 (1885), pp. 1–181.

——— 'Friedrich Binder von Krieglstein' in *Allgemeine Deutsche Biographie*, vol. 2 (1875), pp. 648–49.

Asbach, Olaf (ed.). *Der moderne Staat und 'le doux commerce': Politik, Ökonomie und internationale Beziehungen im politischen Denken der Aufklärung* (Baden-Baden: Nomos, 2014).

Astigarraga, Jesús. 'La dérangeante découverte de l'autre: traductions et adaptations espagnoles de *l'Essai politique sur le commerce* (1734) de Jean-François Melon', *Revue d'histoire moderne et contemporaine*, 57:1 (2010), pp. 91–118.

Balazs, Eva. *Hungary and the Habsburgs 1765–1800. An Experiment in Enlightened Absolutism* (Budapest, 1997).

Beales, Derek. *Joseph II.* Vol 2: *Against the World, 1780–1790* (Cambridge, 2009).

——— *Enlightenment and Reform in Eighteenth-Century Europe* (London: I.B. Tauris, 2005).

——— *Joseph II.* Vol. 1: *In the shadow of Maria Theresa, 1741–1780* (Cambridge, 1987).

——— 'Francis Stephen of Lorraine (Emperor Francis I, 1745–65), Consort of Maria Theresa, Ruler of the Austrian Monarchy from 1740' in Charles Beem and Miles Taylor (eds.), *The Man behind the Queen: Male Consorts in History* (New York: Palgrave Macmillan, 2014), pp. 125–43.

Beer, Adolf. 'Die österreichische Handelspolitik unter Maria Theresia und Joseph II.', *AÖG* 86 (1898), pp. 1–204.

——— 'Studien zur Geschichte der österreichischen Volkswirtschaft unter Maria Theresia. Die österreichische Industriepolitik', *AÖG* 81 (1895), pp. 1–133.

——— 'Die Staatschulden und die Ordnung des Staatshaushaltes unter Maria Theresia', *AÖG* 82 (1894a), pp. 1–135.

——— 'Die Finanzverwaltung Österreichs 1749–1816', *MIÖG* 15 (1894b), pp. 237–366.

——— 'Handelspolitische Beziehungen Österreichs zu den deutschen Staaten', *AÖG* 79 (1893a) pp. 401–669.

——— 'Die Zollpolitik und die Schaffung eines einheitlichen Zollgebietes unter Maria Theresia', *MIÖG* 14 (1893b), pp. 237–326.

Bidermann, Ignaz. 'Die Wiener Stadt-Bank, ihre Entstehung, ihre Einteilung und Wirksamkeit, ihre Schicksale', *AÖG* 20 (1858), pp. 341–445.

Bigwood, Georges. 'La Loterie aux Pays Bas Autrichiens', *Annales de la Societé Royale d'Archéologie de Bruxelles*, 26 (1917), pp. 53–134.

Blanning, T.C.W. *Frederick the Great. King of Prussia* (London: Allen Lane, 2015).

——— *The Pursuit of Glory. The Five Revolutions that Made Modern Europe: 1648–1815* (London: Penguin, 2007).

——— *The Culture of Power and the Power of Culture. Old Regime Europe 1660–1789* (Oxford, 2002).

——— *The French Revolutionary Wars 1787–1802* (London, 1996).

——— *Joseph II. Profiles in Power* (London, 1987).

Bond, Niall. 'La monnaie en Allemagne et en Autriche aux dix-huitième siècle: réflexions et recompositions' in Jérôme Blanc and Ludovic Desmedt (eds.), *Les Pensées monétaires dans l'histoire. L'Europe, 1517–1776* (Paris: Classiques Garnier, 2014), pp. 861–96.

Bonney, Richard (ed.). *The Rise of the Fiscal State in Europe, c. 1200–1815* (Oxford, 1999).

Bosher, J.F. *French Finances 1770–1795: From Business to Bureaucracy* (Cambridge, 1970).

Breunlich, Maria and Marieluise Mader (eds.). *Karl Graf von Zinzendorf, Aus den Jugendtagebüchern 1747, 1752–1763. Nach Vorarbeiten von Hans Wagner*, Veröffentlichung der Kommission für Neuere Geschichte Österreichs 84 (Vienna, 1997).

Brewer, John. *The Sinews of Power: War, Money and the English State, 1688–1783* (London, 1989).

Carpenter, Kenneth E. *Dialogue in Political Economy. Translations from and into German in the 18th Century* (Boston, MA: Kress Library Publications No. 23, 1977).

Cavarzere, Marco. '"The New Science of Commerce" in the Holy Roman Empire: Véron de Forbonnais *Elémens du commerce* and its German Readers', *History of European Ideas*, 40:8 (2014), pp. 1130–50.

Charles, Loïc and Arnaud Orain. 'François Véron de Forbonnais and the invention of Antiphysiocracy' in Steven L. Kaplan and Sophus A. Reinert (eds.), *The Economic Turn. Recasting Political Economy in Enlightenment Europe* (London and New York: Anthem Press, 2019), pp. 139–68.

Charles, Loïc, Frédéric Lefebvre and Christine Théré (eds.). *Le Cercle de Vincent Gournay. Savoirs économiques et pratiques administratives en France au milieu du XVIIIe siècle* (Paris: Institut National D'Études Démographiques, 2011).

——— 'French "New Politics" and the Dissemination of David Hume's Political Discourses on the Continent, 1750–70' in Carl Wennerlind and Margaret Schabas (eds.), *David Hume's Political Economy* (London: Routledge, 2008), pp. 181–202.

——— 'Le Moment "Vincent de Gournay": Réflexions à propos des Remarques sur les Traités sur le commerce de Josiah Child editées et préfacées par Simone de Meyssonnier', Cahiers d'économie politique, 56:1 (2009), pp. 205–11.

Charles, Loïc and Philippe Steiner, 'Entre Montesquieu et Rousseau. La Physiocratie parmi les origines intellectuelles de la Révolution française', Études Jean-Jacques Rousseau, 11 (1999/2000), pp. 83–159.

Cheney, Paul. *Revolutionary Commerce: Globalization and the French Monarchy* (Cambridge, MA: Harvard University Press, 2010).

——— 'Commerce' in Daniel Brewer (ed.), *The Cambridge Companion to the French Enlightenment* (Cambridge, 2014), pp. 44–59.

Cheynet de Beaupré, Marc. *Joseph Pâris-Duverney, Financier D'État, (1684–1770). Les sentiers du pouvoir (1684–1770)* (Paris, 2012).

Clapham, Sir John. *The Bank of England. A History, 1694–1914* (2 vols, Cambridge, 1970).

Clark, Henry C. *Compass of Society: Commerce and Absolutism in Old-Regime France* (Lanham, MD: Rowman & Littlefield/Lexington Books, 2007).

——— (ed.). *Commerce, Culture and Liberty: Readings on Capitalism Before Adam Smith* (Indianapolis: Liberty Classics, 2003).

Cunha, Alexandre Mendes. 'Administrative Centralisation, Police Regulations and Mining Sciences as Channels for the Dissemination of Cameralist Ideas in the Iberian World' in Marten Seppel and Keith Tribe (eds.), *Cameralism in Practice: State Administration and Economy in Early Modern Europe* (Suffolk: Boydell and Brewer, 2017), pp. 155–78.

Dickson, P.G.M. *Finance and Government under Maria Theresia 1740–1780* (2 vols, Oxford, 1987).

——— *The Financial Revolution in England: A Study in the Development of Public Credit, 1688–1756* (London: Macmillan, 1967).

——— 'English Commercial Negotiations with Austria, 1737–1752' in A. Whiteman, J.S. Bromley and P.G.M. Dickson (eds.), *Statesmen, Scholars and Merchants: Essays in Eighteenth-Century History Presented to Dame Lucy Sutherland* (Oxford, 1973), pp. 81–112.

——— 'Count Karl von Zinzendorf on Joseph II's New Taxation', *English Historical Review*, 133:561 (2018), pp. 323–50.

——— 'Count Karl von Zinzendorf's "New Accountancy": The Structure of Austrian Government Finance in Peace and War, 1781–1791', *International History Review*, 19 (2007), pp. 22–56.

Dinklage, Karl. *Geschichte der Kärtner Landwirtschaft* (Klagenfurt, 1966).

——— 'Gründung und Aufbau der theresianischen Ackerbaugesellschaften', *Zeitschrift für Agrargeschichte und Agrarsoziologie*, 1:13 (1965), pp. 200–11.

Drobesch, Werner. 'Typical Careers of Industrialists in the Era of Enlightenment' in Harald Heppner, Peter Urbanitsch and Renate Zedinger (eds.), *Social Change in the Habsburg Monarchy. Les transformations de la société dans la monarchie des Habsbourg: l'époque des Lumières* (Bochum: Winkler, 2011), pp. 229–47.

Dull, Jonathan. *The French Navy and the Seven Years War* (Lincoln, NB: University of Nebraska Press, 2005).

Duffy, Christopher. *The Army of Frederick the Great* (Vancouver, 1974).

Englebert, Georges (ed.). 'Deux voyages du Comte Charles de Zinzendorf, 1769–1770', *Bulletin de la Société des Bibliophiles Liegois*, 22 (1976), pp. 125–27.

Erag, Ivan. 'Übersicht der wirtschaftlichen Entwicklungen der Stadt Rijeka/Fiume' in Jürgen Schneider (ed.), *Wirtschaftskräfte und Wirtschaftswege: auf dem Weg zur Industrialisierung. Festschrift für Hermann Kellenbenz* (5 vols, Stuttgart, 1978), vol. 3, pp. 135–54.

Evans, R.J.W. *Austria, Hungary and the Habsburgs. Central Europe c.1683–1867* (Oxford, 2006).

——— *The making of the Habsburg Monarchy 1550–1700* (Oxford, 1979).

Faccarello, Gilbert and Philippe Steiner. '"Philosophie économique" and Money in France, 1750–1776: The Stakes of a Transformation', *European Journal of Economic Thought*, 19:3 (2012), pp. 325–53.

Fattinger, Elisabeth. 'Gestaltung und Gewinn einer Auftragsreise: Karl Graf Zinzendorf in Großbritannien (1768)' in Joachim Rees, Winfried Siebers and Hilmar Tilgner (eds.), *Europareisen politisch-sozialer Eliten im 18. Jahrhundert. Theoretische Neuorientierung-kommunikative Praxis- Kultur- und Wissenschaftstransfer* (Berlin, 2002), pp. 112–29.

Faure, Edgar. *La banqueroute de Law, 17 juillet 1720* (Paris, 1977).

Ferenc, Eckhart. *A becsi udvargazdazagpolitikaja Magyarorszagon Mária Terézia korában* (Budapest, 1922).

Félix, Joël. *Finances et politique au siècle des Lumières. Le ministère L'Averdy* (Paris, 1999).

——— 'The Financial Origins of the French Revolution' in Peter R. Campbell (ed.), *The Origins of the French Revolution* (London and New York: Palgrave Macmillan, 2006), pp. 35–62.

Freudenberger, Herman. *Lost Momentum: Austrian Economic Development 1750s–1830s* (Vienna: Böhlau Verlag, 2003).

Fuchs, Rudolf. *Die Wiener Stadtbank: ein Beitrag zur österreichischen Finanzgeschichte des 18. Jahrhunderts* (Frankfurt-am-Main: Peter Lang, 1997).

Gestrich, Andreas. 'The public sphere and the Habermas-Debate', *German History*, 24 (2006), pp. 413–31.

Giese, Ursula. 'Johann Thomas Edler von Trattner. Seine Bedeutung als Buchdrucker, Buchhändler und Herausgeber', *Archiv für Geschichte des Buchwesens* (Frankfurt-am-Main, 1961), vol. 3, col. 1013–1454.

Gillard, Lucien. *La Banque d'Amsterdam et le Florin Européen au temps de la République néerlandaise (1610–1820)* (Paris, 2004).

Glete, Jan. *War and the State in Early Modern Europe: Spain, the Dutch Republic and Sweden as Fiscal-Military States, 1500–1660* (London: Routledge, 2002).

Graham, Aaron and Patrick Walsh (eds.). *The British Fiscal Military States, 1660–c.1783* (London, 2016).

Godsey, William D. *The Sinews of Habsburg Power: Lower Austria in a Fiscal-Military State, 1650–1820* (Oxford, 2018).

——— 'A Habsburg financial revolution? War and public debt in the eighteenth century' in William D. Godsey, Petr Mat'a and Thomas Winkelbauer (eds.), *The Habsburg Monarchy as a Fiscal-Military State c. 1648–1815: Contours and Perspectives* (Proceedings of the British Academy/Oxford University Press, forthcoming).

Good, David F. *The Economic Rise of the Habsburg Empire 1750–1914* (Berkeley, CA, 1984).

Hasquin, Hervé. 'Jacques Accarias de Serionne et le *Journal de Commerce*. Un publiciste français au service de l'Autriche' in Hervé Hasquin, *Population, commerce et religion au siècle des Lumières* (Editions de L'Université de Brussel, 2008), pp. 155–67.

Heilingsetzer, Georg. 'Aristokratie, Aufklärung und Architektur. Fürst Georg Adam Starhemberg und die Neugestaltung des Schlosses Eferding durch Andreas Zach', *Mitteilungen des oberösterreichischen Landesarchivs*, 13 (1981), pp. 249–87.

Hochedlinger, Michael. *Austria's Wars of Emergence. War, State and Society in the Habsburg Monarchy 1683–1797* (London: Pearson, 2003).

Hochedlinger, Michael, Petr Mat'a and Thomas Winkelbauer (eds.). *Verwaltungsgeschichte der Habsburgermonarchie in der frühen Neuzeit.* Band 1: *Hof und Dynastie, Kaiser und Reich, Zentralverwaltungen, Kriegswesen und landesfürstliches Finanzwesen, MIÖG* 62 (2 vols, Vienna: Böhlau, 2019).

Hock, Karl Freiherrn and Ignaz Bidermann. *Der österreichische Staatsrath (1760–1848): Eine geschichtliche Studie* (Vienna, 1879; reprint, 1972).

Hoffman, Philip, Gille Postel-Vinay and Jean-Laurent Rosenthal, *Priceless Markets: The Political Economy of Credit in Paris, 1660–1870* (Chicago, 2000).

Hont, Istvan. *Jealousy of Trade: International Competition and the Nation-State in Historical Perspective* (Cambridge, MA, 2005).

——— 'The "Rich Country–Poor Country" Debate revisited. The Origins and French Reception of the Hume Paradox' in Carl Wennerlind and Schabas Margaret (eds.), *David Hume's Political Economy* (London: Routledge, 2008), pp. 243–323.

Hutchinson, Terence. *Before Adam Smith. The Emergence of Political Economy, 1662–1776* (Oxford, 1988).

Ingrao, Charles W. *The Habsburg Monarchy, 1618–1815* (Cambridge, 1994).

Ives, Robin J. 'Political Publicity and Political Economy in Eighteenth-Century France', *French History*, 17:1 (2003), pp. 1–18.

Kaiser, Thomas E. 'Money, Despotism and Public Opinion in Early Eighteenth-Century France: John Law and the Debate on Royal Credit', *Journal of Modern History*, 63 (1991), pp. 1–29.

Kallbrunner, Josef (ed.). *Kaiserin Maria Theresias politisches Testament* (Vienna, 1952).

Kaltenstadler, Wilhelm. 'Der österreichische Seehandel über Triest im 18. Jahrhundert', *Vierteljahresschrift für Sozial- und Wirtschaftsgeschichte*, 55 (1968), pp. 481–500; 56 (1969), pp. 1–104.

Kaplan, Steven L. *The Stakes of Regulation. Perspectives on Bread, Politics and Political Economy Forty Years Later* (London: Anthem Press, 2015).

Kaplan, Steven L. and Sophus A. Reinert (eds.). *The Economic Turn: Recasting Political Economy in Enlightenment Europe* (London and New York: Anthem Press, 2019).

Kapossy, Béla, Isaac Nakhimovsky, Sophus A. Reinert and Richard Whatmore (eds.), *Markets, Morals, Politics: Jealousy of Trade and the History of Political Thought* (Cambridge, MA and London: Harvard University Press, 2018).

Kapossy, Béla, Isaac Nakhimovsky and Richard Whatmore (eds.). *Commerce and Peace in the Enlightenment* (Cambridge, 2017).

Karstens, Simon. *Lehrer, Schriftsteller, Staatsreformer: die Karriere des Joseph von Sonnenfels (1733–1817)* (Vienna: Böhlau Verlag, 2011).

Khevenhüller-Metsch, Rudolf Graf and Hans Schlitter (eds.). *Aus der Zeit Maria Theresias. Tagebuch des Fürsten Johann Josef Khevenhüller-Metsch, Kaiserlichen Obersthofmeisters, 1742–1746* (8 vols, Vienna, 1910).

Klingenstein, Grete. *Der Aufstieg des Hauses Kaunitz, Studien zur Herkunft und Bildung des Staatskanzlers Wenzel Anton* (Göttingen, 1975).

——— 'Professor Sonnenfels darf nicht reisen. Beobachtungen zu den Anfängen der Wirtschafts-, Sozial- und Politikwissenschaften in Österreich' in Hedwig Kopetz, Joseph Marko and Klaus Poier (eds.), *Soziokultureller Wandel im Verfassungsstaat. Phänomene politischer Transformation* (Band 90/II, 2004), pp. 829–42.

——— 'Die Wiener Kommerzienhofkommission, 1719–1776. Einige Überlegungen zu Wirtschaftsverflechtung und staatlicher Durchdringing in einem "zusammengesetzten" Staatswesen' in Ulfried Burz, Michael Derndarsky and Werner Drobesch (eds.), *Brennpunkt Mitteleuropa. Festschrift für Helmut Rumpler zum 65. Geburtstag* (Klagenfurt, 2000), pp. 195–206.

——— 'Between Mercantilism and Physiocracy. Stages, Modes and Functions of Economic Theory in the Habsburg Monarchy, 1748–63' in Charles W. Ingrao (ed.), *State and Society in Early Modern Austria* (West Lafayette, IN: Purdue University Press, 1994), pp. 181–214.

——— 'Kommerz und Aussenpolitik. Habsburgische Kommerzialreisen im Vorfeld der diplomatischen Revolution, 1756' in Othmar Pickl (ed.), *Wirtschaftsbeziehungen zwischen den österreichischen Niederlanden und den österreichischen Erblanden im 18. Jahrhundert* (Graz, 1991), pp. 55–70.

——— 'Spanien im Horizont der österreichischen Aufklärung. Zinzendorfs Kommerzialreise nach Spanien im Jahre 1767' in Herwig Ebner, Horst Haselsteiner and Ingeborg Wiesflecker-Friedhuber (eds.), *Geschichtsforschung in Graz. Festschrift zum 125-Jahr-Jubiläum des Instituts für Geschichte der Karl-Franzens-Universität Graz* (Graz, 1990), pp. 115–26.

——— Die Lehre von der Macht der Staaten: Das aussenpolitische Machtproblem in der 'politischen Wissenschaft' und in der praktischen Politik im 18. Jahrhundert by Harm Klueting, *English Historical Review*, 103:406 (1988), pp. 134–38.

Klingenstein, Grete and Eva Faber. 'Kommerzbehörden und Staatswirtschaftsdeputation' in Michael Hochedlinger, Petr Mat'a and Thomas Winkelbauer (eds.), *Verwaltungsgeschichte der Habsburgermonarchie in der frühen Neuzeit.* Band 1: *Hof und Dynastie, Kaiser und Reich, Zentralverwaltungen, Kriegswesen und landesfürstliches Finanzwesen, MIÖG* 62 (2 vols, Vienna, 2019), vol. 2, pp. 985–90.

Klingenstein, Grete, Eva Faber and Antonio Trampus (eds.). *Europäische Aufklärung zwischen Wien und Triest: die Tagebücher des Gouverneurs Karl Graf von Zinzendorf, 1776–1782*, Veröffentlichung der Kommission für Neuere Geschichte Österreichs, 103 (4 vols, Vienna, 2009).

Klueting, Harm. *Die Lehre von der Macht der Staaten: Das aussenpolitische Machtproblem in der 'politischen Wissenschaft' und in der praktischen Politik im 18. Jahrhundert* (Berlin, 1986).

Khull-Kholwald, Martin. *Der Adel auf dem Lande und sein Kredit. Der Schuldschein als zentrales Finanzinstrument in der Steiermark (1515–1635)*, Forschungen zur geschichtlichen Landeskunde der Steiermark, Band 57 (Vienna and Berlin: LIT, 2013).

Lebeau, Christine. *Aristocrates et grands commis à la Cour de Vienne, 1748–1791. Le modèle français* (Paris, 1996).

——— 'Des aristocrates à la croisée des mondes. Politique aristocratique et pouvoir administratif en Europe dans la deuxième moitié du XVIIIe siècle' in Gabriele Haug-Moritz, Hans Peter Hye and Marlies Raffler (eds.), *Adel im 'langen' 18.* Jahrhundert (Vienna: Verlag der österreichischen Akademie der Wissenschaften, 2009), pp. 187–204.

——— 'Die Tagebücher des Grafen Karl von Zinzendorf' in Josef Pauser, Martin Scheutz and Thomas Winkelbauer (eds.), *Quellenkunde der Habsburgermonarchie (16.–18. Jahrhundert): Ein exemplarisches Handbuch, MIÖG* (2004), pp. 796–800.

——— 'La conversion de Karl von Zinzendorf: Affaire d'état ou affaire de famille?', Revue de sythèse, 114 (1993), pp. 473–95.

Lehmstedt, Mark. 'Über den Anteil des Leipziger Buchhandels am literarischen Austausch zwischen Frankreich und Deutschland. Das Beispiel der Peter Philipp Wolfschen Buchhandlung in Leipzig (1795–1803)' in Hans-Jürgen Lüsebrink, Rolf Reichhardt, Annette Keilhauer and René Lohr (eds.), *Kulturtransfer im Epochenbruch. Frankreich-Deutschland 1770 bis 1815* (2 vols., Leipzig, 1997), vol. 1, pp. 403–43.

Lluch, Ernest. 'Der Kameralismus, ein vieldimensionales Lehrgebäude: Seine Rezeption bei Adam Smith und im Spanien des 18. Jahrhunderts', *Jahrbuch für Wirtschaftsgeschichte*, 41:2 (2000), pp. 133–54.

——— 'Cameralism Beyond the Germanic World: A Note on Tribe', *History of Economic Ideas*, 5:2 (1997), pp. 85–99.

Loehr, August Octavian Ritter von. 'Die Finanzierung des Siebenjährigen Krieges' in *Numismatische Zeitschrift*, 18 (1925), pp. 95–110.

Lüthy, Herbert. *La Banque Protestante en France de la Révocation de l'Edit de Nantes à la Révolution* (2 vols, Paris: S.E.V.P.E.N., 1959).

McGill, William J. 'The Roots of Policy: Kaunitz in Vienna and Versailles, 1749–1753', *Journal of Modern History*, 43:2 (1971), pp. 228–44.

——— 'The Roots of Policy: Kaunitz in Italy and the Netherlands, 1742–1746', *Central European History*, 1:2 (1968), pp. 131–149.

Mann, Fritz Karl. *Finanztheorie und Finanzsoziologie* (Göttingen, 1959).

——— 'Dutot und sein Werk', *Zeitschrift für Nationalökonomie*, 7 (1936), pp. 98–103.

——— 'Der politische Ideengehalt von John Laws Finanzsystem', *Jahrbuch für Nationalökonomie und Statistik*, 113 (1919), pp. 97–122.

——— 'Die Vorgeschichte des Finanzsystems von John Law' in *Schmollers Jahrbuch für Gesetzgebung, Verwaltung und Volkswirtschaft im deutschen Reiche*, 37 (1913), pp. 81–145.

Marion, Marcel. *Machault d'Arnouville: Étude sur l'histoire du contrôle général des finances de 1749 à 1754* (Paris, 1891).

Matis, Herbert. *Die Schwarzenberg-Bank. Kapitalbildung und Industriefinanzierung in den habsburgischen Erblanden 1787–1830* (Vienna: Verlag der österreichischen Akademie der Wissenschaften, 2005).

Mensi, Franz Freiherr von. *Die Finanzen Oesterreichs 1701 bis 1740* (Vienna, 1890).

Meyssonnier, Simone. *La Balance et l'Horloge: La Genèse de la pensée libérale en France au XVIIIe siècle* (Paris, 1989).

——— (ed.). *Traités sur le commerce de Josiah Child suivis des Remarques de Jacques Vincent de Gournay* (Paris, 2008).

——— 'Vincent de Gournay, un intendant du commerce au travail. L'apport du fonds de Saint-Brieuc a l'intelligence de ses textes' in Loïc Charles, Frédéric Lefebvre and Christine Théré (eds.). *Le Cercle de Vincent Gournay. Savoirs économiques et pratiques administratives en France au milieu du XVIIIe siècle* (Paris: Institut National D'Études Démographiques, 2011a), pp. 89–110.

——— 'Annexe 1, Inventaire analytique du fonds Gournay de la Bibliothèque municipale de Saint-Brieuc' in Loïc Charles, Frédéric Lefebvre and Christine Théré (eds.), *Le Cercle de Vincent Gournay. Savoirs économiques et pratiques administratives en France au milieu du XVIIIe siècle* (Paris: Institut National D'Études Démographiques, 2011b), pp. 303–43.

Mikoletzky, Hanns Leo. 'Der Hamburger Bankier Johann Gottlieb Gerhard und der Versuch der Staatsschuldentilgung in Österreich (1762–1766)', *MÖStA* 25 (1972), pp. 277–88.

——— 'Franz Stephan von Lothringen als Wirtschaftspolitiker', *MÖStA* 13 (1960), pp. 231–57.

Mittenzwei, Ingrid. *Zwischen Gestern und Morgen. Wiens frühe Bourgeoisie an der Wende vom 18. zum 19. Jahrhundert* (Vienna, 1998).

Murphy, Antoin E. *The Genesis of Macroeconomics: New Ideas from Sir William Petty to Henry Thornton* (Oxford, 2009).

——— *John Law: Economic Theorist and Policy-Maker* (Oxford, 1997).

——— *Richard Cantillon: Entrepreneur and Economist* (Oxford, 1986).

——— (ed.). *Du Tot: Histoire du Systême de John Law (1716–1720)* (Paris: Institut National d'Études Démographiques, 2000).

——— 'The Enigmatic Monsieur Du Tot' in Gilbert Faccarello (ed.), *Studies in the History of French Political Economy. From Bodin to Walras* (London, 1998), pp. 57–77.

Museumsverein Schloß Rosenau. *Österreichische Freimaurerlogen. Humanität und Toleranz im 18. Jahrhundert* (Vienna, 1976).

Novotny, Alexander. *Staatskanzler Kaunitz als geistige Persönlichkeit. Ein österreichisches Kulturbild aus der Zeit der Aufklärung und des Josephinismus* (Vienna, 1947).

O'Reilly, William. 'Alluding to Alternatives: Sourcing and Securing Colonists in Eighteenth-Century Germany' in Claudia Schnurmann and Hartmut Lehmann (eds.), *Atlantic Understandings: Essays on European and American History in Honour of Werner Wellenreuther* (Hamburg, 2006), pp. 159–83.

Ogilvie, Sheilagh C. and Markus Cerman (eds.). *European Proto-Industrialization* (Cambridge, 1996).

Osterloh, Karl-Heinz. *Joseph von Sonnenfels und die österreichische Reformbewegung im Zeitalter des aufgeklärten Absolutismus. Eine Studie zum Zusammenhang von Kameralwissenschaft und Verwaltungspraxis* (Lübeck and Hamburg: Matthiesen, 1970).

Otruba, Gustav. *Die Wirtschaftspolitik Maria Theresias*, Österreich Reihe 192/194 (Vienna: Bergland Verlag, 1963).

——— 'Schlesien im System des österreichischen Merkantilismus' in Peter Baumgart and Ulrich Schmilewski (eds.), *Kontinuität und Wandel: Schlesien zwischen Österreich und Preußen. Ergebnisse eines Symposions in Würzburg vom 29. bis 31. Oktober 1987* (Sigmaringen: J. Thorbecke, 1990), pp. 120–34.

——— 'Staatshaushalt und Staatsschuld unter Maria Theresia und Joseph II.' in Richard Georg Plaschka and Grete Klingenstein (eds.), *Österreich im Europa der Aufklärung* (2 vols, Vienna, 1985), vol.1, pp. 197–249.

——— 'Die Wirtschaftspolitik Maria Theresias und Josephs II.' in Herbert Matis (ed.), *Von der Glückseligkeit des Staates. Staat, Wirtschaft und Gesellschaft in Österreich im Zeitalter des aufgeklärten Absolutismus* (Berlin, 1981).

——— 'Von den "Fabriksprivilegien" des 17. und 18. Jahrhunderts zum "Österreichischen Fabriksrecht" 1838', *Scripta Mercaturae*, 10:2 (1976), pp. 76–108.

Paudler, Amand. 'Graf Josef Kinsky, Herr auf Bürgstein und Schwoyka' in *Jahresbericht des kaiserlich königlichen Staatsobergymnasium in Böhmisch-Leipa* (Böhmisch Leipa, 1885), pp. 1–47.

Pettenegg, Eduard Gaston von (ed.). *Ludwig und Karl Grafen und Herren von Zinzendorf. Ihre Selbstbiographien nebst einer kurzen Geschichte des Hauses Zinzendorf* (Vienna, 1879).

Potter, Mark and Jean-Laurent Rosenthal. 'Politics and Public Finance in France: The Estates of Burgundy, 1660–1790', *Journal of Interdisciplinary History*, 27:4 (1997), pp. 577–612.

Pribram, Karl. *Geschichte der österreichischen Gewerbepolitik von 1740 bis 1860: aufgrund der Akten Vol. 1: 1740 bis 1798* (Leipzig, 1907).

Probszt, Günther. *Österreichische Münz- und Geldgeschichte* (2 vols, Vienna, 1994).

Rathery, E.J.B. (ed.). *Journal et Mémoires du Marquis D'Argenson* (9 vols, Paris, 1859).

Reiner, Elisabeth. 'Karl von Zinzendorf und das Eisenwesen in Innerösterreich. Ein Beitrag zur mariatheresianischen Wirtschaftspolitik', *Mitteilungen des österreichischen Staatsarchivs*, 13 (1960), pp. 258–330.

Reinert, Sophus A. *Translating Empire: Emulation and the Origins of Political Economy* (Cambridge, MA: Harvard University Press, 2011).

——— 'The Empire of Emulation: A Quantitative Analysis of Economic Translations in the European World, 1500–1849' in Sophus A. Reinert and Pernille Røge (eds.), *The Political Economy of Empire in the Early Modern World* (Basingstoke: Palgrave Macmillan, 2013), pp. 105–128.

Riley, James C. *The Seven Years War and the Old Regime in France: The Economic and Financial Toll* (Princeton, NJ, 1986).

——— *International Government Finance and the Amsterdam Capital Market 1740–1815* (Cambridge, 1980).

Robertson, John. *The Enlightenment. A Very Short Introduction* (Oxford, 2015).

——— *The Case for the Enlightenment: Scotland and Naples 1680–1760* (Cambridge, 2005).

——— 'Enlightenment, Public Sphere and Political Economy' in Jesús Astigarraga and Javier Usoz (eds.), *L'économie politique et la sphère publique dans le débat des Lumières* (Madrid: Casa de Velázquez, 2013), pp. 9–32.

Ross, Ian Simpson, 'The Emergence of David Hume as a Political Economist: A Biographical Sketch' in Carl Wennerlind and Margaret Schabas (eds.), *David Hume's Political Economy* (Abingdon and New York: Routledge, 2008), pp. 31–48.

Sanchez, Rafael Torres. *Constructing a Fiscal-Military State in Eighteenth-Century Spain* (Basingstoke: Palgrave Macmillan, 2015).

Schaeper, Thomas J. *The French Council of Commerce 1700–1715. A Study of Mercantilism After Colbert* (Columbus, OH: Ohio State University Press, 1983).

Schasching, Johann. *Staatsbildung und Finanzentwicklung: Ein Beitrag zur Geschichte des österreichischen Staatskredites in der 2. Hälfte des 18. Jahrhunderts* (Innsbruck, 1954).

Schieder, Theodor (ed.). *Handbuch der europäischen Geschichte*, Vol. 4 (7 vols, Stuttgart 1968).

Schilling, Lothar. *Kaunitz und das Renversement des alliances. Studien zur außenpolitischen Konzeption Wenzel Antons von Kaunitz* (Berlin: Duncker and Humblot Gmbh, 1994).

Schlitter, Hans. 'Starhemberg, Georg Adam Fürst von/seit 1765' in *Allgemeine Deutsche Biographie*, vol. 35 (1893), pp. 471–73.

Schmitt, Günther. 'Johann Friedrich Unger (1714–1781). Arithmetiker und erster bedeutender landwirtschaftlicher Marktforscher deutscher Sprache', *Agrarwirtschaft*, 16 (1967), pp. 201–6.

Schrötter, Friedrich Freiherr von. 'Die Münzverwaltung Friedrichs des Großen' in Paul Seidel (ed.), *Hohenzollern Jahrbuch*, vol. 15 (Berlin and Leipzig, 1911), pp. 91–99.

——— 'Das preußische Münzwesen im 18. Jahrhundert', *Acta Borussica, Münzgeschichtlicher Theil. Die Begründung des preußischen Münzsystems durch Friedrich d.Gr. und Graumann*, vol. 2 (Berlin, 1908), pp. 74–90.

Schui, Florian. 'Prussia's "Trans-Oceanic" Moment: The Creation of the Prussian Asiatic Trade Company in 1750', *The Historical Journal*, 49:1 (2006), pp. 143–60.

Schünemann, Konrad. *Österreichs Bevölkerungspolitik unter Maria Theresia* (Berlin, 1935).

Scott, Hamish M. 'The Habsburg "Fiscal Military State" in International Perspective' in William D. Godsey, Petr Mat'a and Thomas Winkelbauer (eds.), *The Habsburg Monarchy as a Fiscal-Military State c. 1648–1815: Contours and Perspectives* (Proceedings of the British Academy/Oxford University Press, forthcoming).

——— 'The Seven Years War and Europe's Ancien Régime', *War in History*, 18:4 (2011), pp. 419–55.

——— 'The Fiscal Military State and International Rivalry During the Long Eighteenth Century', in Christopher Storrs (ed.), *The Fiscal-Military State in Eighteenth-Century Europe: Essays in Honour of P.G.M. Dickson* (Farnham: Ashgate, 2009), pp. 23–53.

Seppel, Marten and Keith Tribe (eds.). *Cameralism in Practice: State Administration and Economy in Early Modern Europe* (Suffolk: Boydell and Brewer, 2017).

Shovlin, John. *The Political Economy of Virtue: Luxury, Patriotism, and the Origins of the French Revolution* (Ithaca, NY, and London: Cornell University Press, 2006).

——— 'Rethinking Enlightened Reform in a French Context' in Gabriel Paquette (ed.), *Enlightened Reform in Southern Europe and its Atlantic Colonies c.1750–1830* (Farnham, Ashgate, 2009), pp. 47–62.

——— 'Emulation in Eighteenth-Century French Economic Thought', Eighteenth Century Studies, 36 (2003), pp. 224–30.

Skornicki, Arnault. *L'économiste, la cour et la patrie. L'économie politique dans la France des Lumières* (Paris, 2011).

——— 'La France des Lumières et l'humanisme commercial. Bilan et perspectives historiographiques', *Histoire, Économie et Société*, 32:4 (2013), pp. 75–89.

Small, Albion W. *The Cameralists: The Pioneers of German Social Polity* (Chicago: University of Chicago Press, 1909).

Smout, T.C. 'The Road to Union' in Geoffrey Holmes (ed.), *Britain after the Glorious Revolution, 1689–1714* (London: Macmillan, 1969), pp. 176–96.

Sommer, Louise. *Die österreichischen Kameralisten in dogmengeschichtlicher Darstellung* (Vienna, 1920; reprint, Scientia Verlag Aalen, 1967).

Sonenscher, Michael. *Before the Deluge: Public Debt, Inequality, and the Intellectual Origins of the French Revolution* (Oxford, 2007).

——— 'The Nation's Debt and the Birth of the Modern Republic: The French Fiscal Deficit and the Politics of the Revolution of 1789', *History of Political Thought*, 18:1 (1997), pp. 64–103; 18:2 (1997), pp. 266–325.

Stapelbroek, Koen and Jani Marjanen (eds.). *The Rise of Economic Societies in the Eighteenth Century* (Basingstoke and New York: Palgrave Macmillan, 2012).

Steeb, Christian. 'Johann Fries (1719–1785). Vom Einwanderer zum Staatsbankier und Vertrauten des Staatskanzler' in Grete Klingenstein and Franz A.J. Szabo (eds.), *Staatskanzler Wenzel Anton von Kaunitz-Rietberg 1711–1794. Neue Perspektiven zu Politik und Kultur der europäischen Aufklärung* (Graz, 1996), pp. 305–23.

Stollberg-Rilinger, Barbara. *Maria Theresia: Die Kaiserin in Ihrer Zeit. Eine Biographie* (Munich: C.H. Beck, 2017).

Storrs, Christopher (ed.). *The Fiscal-Military State in Eighteenth-Century Europe: Essays in Honour of P.G.M. Dickson* (Farnham: Ashgate, 2009).

Strakosch, Henry E. *State Absolutism and the Rule of Law. The Struggle for the Codification of Civil Law in Austria 1753–1811* (Sydney: Sydney University Press, 1967).

Strimitzer, Birgit. *Die Freiherrn Binder von Krieglstein. Studien zur Genealogie und Besitzgeschichte einer elsäßisch-österreichischen Adelsfamilie unter besonderer Berücksichtigung der Bedeutung einzelner Familienmitglieder in der Zeit Maria Theresias und der Ära Metternich* (Graz, 1998).

Szabo, Franz A.J. *The Seven Years War in Europe, 1756–1763* (Harlow and New York: Pearson/Longman, 2008).

——— *Kaunitz and enlightened absolutism 1753–1780* (Cambridge, 1994).

Théré, Christine. 'Economic Publishing and Authors, 1566–1789' in Gilbert Faccarello (ed.), *Studies in the History of French Political Economy: From Bodin to Walras* (London, 1998), pp. 1–56.

Tribe, Keith. *Governing Economy: The Reformation of German Economic Discourse 1750–1840* (Cambridge, 1988).

——— 'Cameralism and the sciences of the state' in Mark Goldie and Robert Wokler (eds.), *The Cambridge History of Eighteenth-Century Political Thought* (Cambridge, 2006), pp. 525–46.

Velde, François R. *The Life and Times of Nicolas Dutot*, Working Paper No. 2009–10, Federal Reserve Bank of Chicago (November, 2009).

Vogl, Joseph. *Kalkül und Leidenschaft. Poetik des ökonomischen Menschen* (Zurich: Diaphanes, 2008).

Wandruszka, Adam. *Leopold II. Erzherzog von Österreich, Grossherzog von Toskana, König von Ungarn und Böhmen, Römischer Kaiser* (2 vols, Vienna, 1965).

——— 'Pietro Leopoldo e le sue riforme in Toscana (dal diario edito del conte Carlo Zinzendorf)', *Archivio storico italiano*, 117 (1960), pp. 286–87.

Wakefield, Andre. *The Disordered Police State: German Cameralism as Science and Practice* (Chicago, IL and London: University of Chicago Press, 2009).
Walter, Friedrich (ed.). *Die Geschichte der österreichischen Zentralverwaltung in der Zeit Maria Theresias (1740–1780)*, vol. 32 (Vienna: ÖZV, 1938).
——— (ed.). *Vom Sturz des Directoriums in Publicis et Cameralibus (1760/61) bis zum Ausgang der Regierung Maria Theresias: Aktenstücke*, II. Abteilung, vol. 3 (Vienna: ÖZV, 1934).
——— 'Die Wiener Stadtbank und das Staatsbankprojekt von Grafen Kaunitz aus dem Jahre 1761', *Zeitschrift für Nationalökonomie*, 8 (1937), pp. 444–60.
——— 'Kaunitz Eintritt in die innere Politik. Ein Beitrag zur Geschichte der österreichischen Innenpolitik in den Jahren 1760/61', *MIÖG* 46 (1932), pp. 37–79.
Wennerlind, Carl. *Casualties of Credit: The English Financial Revolution, 1620–1720* (Cambridge, MA: Harvard University Press, 2011).
Winkelbauer, Thomas. 'Nervus Rerum Austriacarum. Zur Finanzierungsgeschichte der Habsburgermonarchie um 1700' in Petr Mat'a and Thomas Winkelbauer (eds.), *Die Habsburgermonarchie 1620–1740. Leistungen und Grenzen des Absolutismusparadigmas* (Stuttgart, 2006), pp. 179–215.

Dissertations

Eichwalder, Reinhard. 'Georg Adam Fürst Starhemberg (1724–1807): Diplomat, Staatsmann und Grundherr' (unpublished Ph.D. dissertation, University of Vienna, 1969).
Gross, Hans. 'Die ständische Kredit-Deputation und der Plan eines erbländischen Nationalkredites (Ein Beitrag zur Finanzpolitik unter Maria Theresia)' (unpublished Ph.D. dissertation, University of Vienna, 1935).
Janetschek, Kurt. 'Die Finanzierung des Siebenjährigen Krieges' (unpublished PhD dissertation, University of Vienna, 1959).
Lebeau, Christine. 'Ludwig et Karl von Zinzendorf, administrateurs des finances. Aristocratie et pouvoir dans la Monarchie des Habsbourg, 1748–1791' (unpublished PhD dissertation, 2 vols, Université de Paris IV – Sorbonne, 1991).
Rill, Robert. 'Die Reise des Grafen Karl von Zinzendorf und Pottendorf über die britischen Inseln im Jahre 1768 an Hand seiner Tagebuchaufzeichnungen – Kommentare und Auswahledition' (unpublished PhD dissertation, University of Vienna, 1983).

Index[1]

[1] Note: Page numbers followed by 'n' refer to notes.

S. Adler, *Political Economy in the Habsburg Monarchy 1750–1774*, Palgrave Studies in the History of Finance,
https://doi.org/10.1007/978-3-030-31007-3

The manufacturer's authorised representative in the EU is Springer Nature Customer Service Centre GmbH, Europaplatz 3, 69115 Heidelberg, Germany. If you have any concerns regarding our products, please contact ProductSafety@springernature.com

Printed and bound by CPI Group (UK) Ltd, Croydon, CR0 4YY
30/09/2026
02225459-0009